Exploring Poetry

SECOND EDITION

M. L. Rosenthal   New York University

A. J. M. Smith   Michigan State University

1973

The Macmillan Company, New York

The Macmillan Company
866 Third Avenue, New York, New York 10022
Collier-Macmillan Canada, Ltd., Toronto, Ontario

Library of Congress catalog card number: 72-81660

Printing: 1 2 3 4 5 6 7 8   Year: 3 4 5 6 7 8 9

ACKNOWLEDGMENTS

Grateful acknowledgment is made to the following authors, publishers, and agents,
listed in alphabetical order, for permission to reprint the copyrighted material included
in this text.

Appleton-Century-Crofts for "The Flower-Fed Buffaloes" by Vachel Lindsay. From: A
ST. NICHOLAS ANTHOLOGY: THE EARLY YEARS. Edited by Burton Frye.
Copyright © 1969 by Meredith Corporation. By courtesy of Appleton-Century-Crofts,
Educational Division, Meredith Corporation.

Atheneum Publishers, Inc. for "The Elementary Scene" from THE WOMAN AT
THE WASHINGTON ZOO by Randall Jarrell. Copyright © 1960 by Randall Jarrell.
Reprinted by permission of Atheneum Publishers.

Jonathan Cape, Ltd. for "Lessons of the War": "I, Naming of Parts" from A MAP
OF VERONA by Henry Reed. By permission of Jonathan Cape, Ltd.

Chatto and Windus, Ltd. for "The Groundhog" and "The Fury of Aerial Bombardment" by Richard Eberhart from COLLECTED POEMS 1930–1960. Reprinted by
permission of Chatto and Windus, Ltd.

Chatto and Windus, Ltd. for "Legal Fiction" and "This Last Pain" from COL-
LECTED POEMS by William Empson. Reprinted by permission of Chatto and
Windus, Ltd.

Chatto and Windus, Ltd. for "Strange Meeting" and "Insensibility" from COL-
LECTED POEMS by Wilfred Owen, edited by C. Day Lewis. Reprinted by permission
of the Executors of the Estate of Harold Owen and Chatto and Windus, Ltd.

City Lights Books for "America" and seven lines from "Howl" from HOWL & OTHER
POEMS by Allen Ginsberg. Copyright © 1956, 1959, by Allen Ginsberg. Reprinted
by permission of City Lights Books.

City Lights Books for "Kaddish—Poem I" from KADDISH AND OTHER POEMS by Allen Ginsberg. Copyright © 1961 by Allen Ginsberg. Reprinted by permission of City Lights Books.

The Clarendon Press, Oxford for "The hill pines were sighing," "Eros," and from "Screaming tarn" from THE POETICAL WORKS OF ROBERT BRIDGES by Robert Bridges. By permission of the Clarendon Press, Oxford.

Collins-Knowlton-Wing, Inc. for "Sick Love," "The Traveller's Curse After Misdirection," and "The Persian Version" from COLLECTED POEMS by Robert Graves. Reprinted by permission of Collins-Knowlton-Wing, Inc. Copyright © 1958, 1961 by Robert Graves.

Collins-Knowlton-Wing, Inc. for "The Thieves" from COLLECTED POEMS by Robert Graves. Reprinted by permission of Collins-Knowlton-Wing, Inc. Copyright © 1955 by Robert Graves.

Corinth Books Inc. for "Way Out West" by LeRoi Jones from PREFACE TO A TWENTY-VOLUME SUICIDE NOTE. Copyright © 1961 by LeRoi Jones. Reprinted by permission of Corinth Books.

Corinth Books Inc. for "Maximus to Himself" and "The Songs of Maximus" from SELECTED WRITINGS by Charles Olson. Copyright © 1960 by Charles Olson. Reprinted by permission of Corinth Books, Inc.

Curtis Brown Ltd. for "A Dream of Fair Women" from A CASE OF SAMPLES by Kingsley Amis. Reprinted by permission of Curtis Brown Ltd.

J. M. Dent and Sons, Ltd. for "And death shall have no dominion," "The force that through the green fuse," and "Ceremony after a Fire Raid" from COLLECTED POEMS of Dylan Thomas. Reprinted by permission of J. M. Dent and Sons, Ltd. and the Trustees for the Copyrights of the late Dylan Thomas.

Doubleday & Co., Inc. for "Nothing in Heaven Functions as It Ought" from GROWING INTO LOVE by X. J. Kennedy. Copyright © 1962 by the Yeoman Committee for an Oberlin Quarterly, from the book GROWING INTO LOVE by X. J. Kennedy. Reprinted by permission of Doubleday & Co., Inc.

Doubleday & Co., Inc. for "Magic Words for Hunting Seal," Anonymous, from SONGS AND STORIES OF THE NETSILIK ESKIMOS by Edward Field, Education Development Center, Inc. Copyright © 1967 and 1968 by Education Development Center, Cambridge, 1968.

Doubleday & Company, Inc. for "Orchids" by Theodore Roethke, copyright © 1948 by Theodore Roethke. "The Meadow Mouse" by Theodore Roethke, copyright © 1963 by Beatrice Roethke, administratrix of the estate of Theodore Roethke. From the book THE COLLECTED POEMS OF THEODORE ROETHKE by Theodore Roethke. Reprinted by permission of Doubleday & Company, Inc.

The Edinburgh "Evening News" for permission to reprint "Old Wife in High Spirits" from COLLECTED POEMS of Hugh MacDiarmid.

Faber and Faber Ltd. for "O what is that sound which so thrills the ear," "On this island," "Lullaby," "Musée des Beaux Arts," and "So an age ended" from COLLECTED SHORTER POEMS, 1927–1957, by W. H. Auden. Reprinted by permission of Faber and Faber Ltd. from COLLECTED SHORTER POEMS.

Faber and Faber Ltd. for "Whispers of Immortality" by T. S. Eliot. Reprinted by permission of Faber and Faber Ltd. from COLLECTED POEMS 1909–1962.

Faber and Faber Ltd. for "The Love Song of J. Alfred Prufrock," "Preludes I," "Rhapsody on a Windy Night," "Gerontion," and an excerpt from "The Waste Land" from THE COMPLETE POEMS AND PLAYS OF T. S. ELIOT. Reprinted by permission of Faber and Faber Ltd.

Faber and Faber Ltd. for "Hawk Roosting" and "Pike" from LUPERCAL by Ted Hughes. Copyright © 1959 by Ted Hughes. Reprinted by permission of Faber and Faber Ltd.

Faber and Faber Ltd. for "Two Eskimo Songs: I. Fleeing from Eternity, II. How

Water Began to Play" from CROW by Ted Hughes. Copyright © 1971 by Ted Hughes. Reprinted by permission of Faber and Faber Ltd.

Faber and Faber Ltd. for "In Santa Maria del Popolo" from MY SAD CAPTAIN AND OTHER POEMS by Thom Gunn. Reprinted by permission of Faber and Faber Ltd.

Faber and Faber Ltd. for "Snow" and "Bagpipe Music" from THE COLLECTED POEMS OF LOUIS MACNEICE by Louis MacNeice. Reprinted by permission of Faber and Faber Ltd.

Faber and Faber Ltd. for "The Horses" from COLLECTED POEMS 1921–1958 by Edwin Muir. Reprinted by permission of Faber and Faber Ltd.

Farrar, Straus & Giroux, Inc. for "Dream Song # 29" in 77 DREAM SONGS by John Berryman. Reprinted with the permission of Farrar, Straus & Giroux, Inc. from 77 DREAM SONGS by John Berryman, copyright © 1959, 1962, 1963, 1964 by John Berryman.

Farrar, Straus & Giroux, Inc. for "Polar Bear" from MAXIMUM SECURITY WARD 1964–1970 by Ramon Guthrie. Copyright © 1968, 1969, 1970 by Ramon Guthrie. Reprinted by permission of Farrar, Straus & Giroux, Inc.

Farrar, Straus & Giroux, Inc. for "The Black Swan" by Randall Jarrell. Reprinted with the permission of Farrar, Straus & Giroux, Inc. from THE COMPLETE POEMS by Randall Jarrell. Copyright © 1951 by Randall Jarrell. Copyright © 1945, 1969 by Mrs. Randall Jarrell.

Farrar, Straus & Giroux, Inc. for "The Death of the Ball Turret Gunner" from THE COMPLETE POEMS by Randall Jarrell. Copyright © 1969 by Randall Jarrell. Reprinted with the permission of Farrar, Straus & Giroux, Inc..

Farrar, Straus & Giroux, Inc. for "Fall 1961," "Water," and "For the Union Dead" from FOR THE UNION DEAD by Robert Lowell. Copyright © 1960, 1962 by Robert Lowell. Reprinted with the permission of Farrar, Straus & Giroux, Inc.

Grove Press, Inc. for "Oread" and "The Pool" from COLLECTED POEMS OF H. D. by H. D. Copyright © 1925, 1953 by Norman Holmes Pearson. Reprinted by permission of Grove Press, Inc.

Harcourt Brace Jovanovich, Inc. for "who's most afraid of death." Copyright © 1925, 1953 by E. E. Cummings. Reprinted from his volume POEMS 1923–1954 by permission of Harcourt Brace Jovanovich, Inc.

Harcourt Brace Jovanovich, Inc. for "ponder, darling these busted statues" and "next to of course god america i." Copyright 1926 by Horace Liveright; copyright 1954, by E. E. Cummings. Reprinted from POEMS 1923–1954 by E. E. Cummings by permission of Harcourt Brace Jovanovich, Inc.

Harcourt Brace Jovanovich, Inc. for "plato told." Copyright 1944 by E. E. Cummings. Reprinted from his volume POEMS 1923–1954 by permission of Harcourt Brace Jovanovich, Inc.

Harcourt Brace Jovanovich, Inc. for "The Love Song of J. Alfred Prufrock," "Preludes I," "Rhapsody on a Windy Night," "Gerontion" and excerpt from "The Waste Land." From COLLECTED POEMS 1909–1962 by T. S. Eliot, copyright 1936, by Harcourt Brace Jovanovich, Inc., copyright © 1963, 1964, by T. S. Eliot. Reprinted by permission of the publisher.

Harcourt Brace Jovanovich, Inc., for "Whispers of Immortality" from COLLECTED POEMS 1909–1962 by T. S. Eliot, copyright 1936, by Harcourt Brace Jovanovich, Inc., copyright © 1963, 1964, by T. S. Eliot. Reprinted by permission of the publishers.

Harcourt Brace Jovanovich, Inc. for "Legal Fiction" and "This Last Pain" from COLLECTED POEMS OF WILLIAM EMPSON, copyright, 1949, by William Empson. Reprinted by permission of Harcourt Brace Jovanovich, Inc.

Harcourt Brace Jovanovich, Inc. for "Thirteen O'Clock" from AFTERNOON OF A PAWNBROKER AND OTHER POEMS by Kenneth Fearing, copyright 1943, by

Kenneth Fearing; copyright © 1970 by Bruce Fearing. Reprinted by permission of Harcourt Brace Jovanovich, Inc.

Harcourt Brace Jovanovich, Inc. for "Love Calls Us to the Things of This World" from THINGS OF THIS WORLD by Richard Wilbur. Copyright © 1956 by Richard Wilbur. Reprinted by permission of Harcourt Brace Jovanovich, Inc.

Harcourt Brace Jovanovich, Inc. for "Advice to a Prophet" by Richard Wilbur. Copyright © 1959 by Richard Wilbur. Reprinted from his volume ADVICE TO A PROPHET AND OTHER POEMS by permission of Harcourt Brace Jovanovich, Inc. First published in *The New Yorker.*

Harper & Row, Publishers, Inc. for "The Blackstone Rangers," Pt. I "As Seen by Disciplines," Pt. II "The Leaders," Pt. III "Gang Girls" from THE WORLD OF GWENDOLYN BROOKS (1971). Copyright © 1968 by Gwendolyn Brooks Blakely.

Harper & Row, Publishers, Inc. for "Hawk Roosting" and "Pike" from LUPERCAL by Ted Hughes. Copyright © 1959 by Ted Hughes. Reprinted by permission of Harper & Row, Publishers, Inc.

Harper & Row, Publishers, Inc. for "Two Eskimo Songs: I. Fleeing from Eternity. II. How Water Began to Play" from CROW by Ted Hughes. Copyright © 1971 by Ted Hughes. Reprinted by permission of Harper & Row, Publishers, Inc.

Harper & Row, Publishers, Inc. for "Ariel" and "Daddy" from ARIEL by Sylvia Plath. "Ariel" copyright © 1965 by Ted Hughes and "Daddy" copyright © 1963 by Ted Hughes. Reprinted by permission of Harper & Row, Publishers, Inc.

Harvard University Press for "There's a certain slant of light," "Twas like a Maelstrom," "A light exists in spring," "Drowning is not so pitiful," "Because I could not stop for Death," and "A narrow fellow in the grass" by Emily Dickinson. Reprinted by permission of the publishers and the Trustees of Amherst College from Thomas H. Johnson, Editor, THE POEMS OF EMILY DICKINSON, Cambridge, Mass.: The Belknap Press of Harvard University Press, Copyright 1951, 1955 by The President and Fellows of Harvard College.

Holt, Rinehart and Winston, Inc. for "Mending Wall," "The Witch of Coos," "A Hillside Thaw," "Design," and "The Silken Tent." From THE POETRY OF ROBERT FROST edited by Edward Connery Lathem. Copyright 1923, 1930, 1939 © 1969 by Holt, Rinehart and Winston, Inc. Copyright 1936, 1942, 1951, © 1958 by Robert Frost. Copyright © 1964, 1967, 1970 by Lesley Frost Ballantine. Reprinted by permission of Holt, Rinehart and Winston, Inc.

Holt, Rinehart and Winston, Inc. for "Longface Mahoney Discusses Heaven." From COLLECTED POEMS by Horace Gregory. Copyright © 1964 by Horace Gregory. Reprinted by permission of Holt, Rinehart and Winston, Inc.

Horizon Press for "To a Conscript of 1940" from COLLECTED POEMS by Sir Herbert Read. Copyright © 1966, by permission of the publisher, Horizon Press, New York.

Houghton Mifflin Company for Section 4 of "The Dead Shall Be Raised Incorruptible" from THE BOOK OF NIGHTMARES. Copyright © 1971 by Galway Kinnell. Reprinted by permission of the publisher, Houghton Mifflin Company.

Houghton Mifflin Company for "The Starry Night" from ALL MY PRETTY ONES by Anne Sexton. Copyright © 1961, 1962 by Anne Sexton. Reprinted by permission of the publisher, Houghton Mifflin Company.

Miss Olwyn Hughes for "Ariel" and "Daddy" from ARIEL, by Sylvia Plath. From ARIEL published by Faber & Faber Ltd., Copyright © 1965 by Ted Hughes.

Indiana University Press for "Green Light" by Kenneth Fearing from COLLECTED POETRY OF KENNETH FEARING. Reprinted by permission of Indiana University Press.

Alfred A. Knopf, Inc. for "Down and Out" from SELECTED POEMS by Langston Hughes. Copyright © 1959 by Langston Hughes. Reprinted by permission of Alfred A. Knopf, Inc.

Alfred A. Knopf, Inc. for "First Light" by Thomas Kinsella, copyright © 1968 by Thomas Kinsella. Reprinted from NIGHT-WALKER AND OTHER POEMS, by Thomas Kinsella, by permission of Alfred A. Knopf, Inc.

Alfred A. Knopf, Inc. for "Janet Waking" from SELECTED POEMS by John Crowe Ransom. Copyright 1927 by Alfred A. Knopf, Inc. Copyright © 1955 by John Crowe Ransom. Reprinted from SELECTED POEMS, Third Edition, revised and enlarged by John Crowe Ransom by permission of Alfred A. Knopf, Inc.

Alfred A. Knopf, Inc. for "Sunday Morning," "Anecdote of the Jar," and "Peter Quince at the Clavier" from THE COLLECTED POEMS OF WALLACE STEVENS. Copyright 1923 and renewed 1951 by Wallace Stevens. Reprinted from THE COLLECTED POEMS OF WALLACE STEVENS by permission of Alfred A. Knopf, Inc.

Alfred A. Knopf, Inc. for an excerpt from "Three Academic Pieces" in THE NECESSARY ANGEL by Wallace Stevens. Copyright 1951. Reprinted by permission of Alfred A. Knopf, Inc.

Liveright Publishing Corporation for "Proem: To Brooklyn Bridge" from THE COMPLETE POEMS AND SELECTED LETTERS AND PROSE OF HART CRANE by Hart Crane. Permission of Liveright Publishers, N.Y. Copyright © 1933, 1958, 1966 by Liveright Publishing Corporation.

Liveright Publishing Corporation for "Repose of Rivers," "Passage," and "Voyages II" from THE COMPLETE POEMS AND SELECTED LETTERS AND PROSE OF HART CRANE by Hart Crane. Permission of Liveright Publishers, N.Y. Copyright © 1933, 1958, 1966 by Liveright Publishing Corporation.

Longman's Greene & Co., Ltd. for "Not Waving, but Drowning" from SELECTED POEMS by Stevie Smith. Reprinted by permission of Longman's Greene & Co., Ltd.

Maclen Music, Inc. for "Eleanor Rigby" by John Lennon and Paul McCartney. Copyright © 1966 NORTHERN SONGS, LTD. Used by Permission. All Rights Reserved.

The Macmillan Company for "The Lordly Hudson" from THE LORDLY HUDSON by Paul Goodman. Reprinted with permission of The Macmillan Company from THE LORDLY HUDSON by Paul Goodman © by Paul Goodman, 1941, renewed 1969 by Paul Goodman.

The Macmillan Company for "After a Journey" by Thomas Hardy. Reprinted with permission of The Macmillan Company from COLLECTED POEMS by Thomas Hardy. Copyright 1925 by The Macmillan Company.

The Macmillan Company for "The Comet at Yell'ham," "Channel Firing," "The Five Students," "During Wind and Rain" from COLLECTED POEMS by Thomas Hardy. Reprinted with permission of The Macmillan Company from COLLECTED POEMS by Thomas Hardy. Copyright 1925 by The Macmillan Company.

The Macmillan Company for "The Old and the New Masters" from THE LOST WORLD by Randall Jarrell. Reprinted with permission of The Macmillan Company from THE LOST WORLD by Randall Jarrell. Copyright © by Randall Jarrell, 1965.

The Macmillan Company for "The Congo" from COLLECTED POEMS by Vachel Lindsay. Reprinted with permission of The Macmillan Company from COLLECTED POEMS by Vachel Lindsay. Copyright 1914 by The Macmillan Company, renewed 1942 by Elizabeth C. Lindsay.

The Macmillan Company for "O Wha's the Bride?" from COLLECTED POEMS by Hugh MacDiarmid. Reprinted with permission of The Macmillan Company from COLLECTED POEMS by Hugh MacDiarmid. Copyright by Christopher Murray Grieve, 1948, 1962.

The Macmillan Company for "Poetry" from COLLECTED POEMS by Marianne Moore. Reprinted with permission of The Macmillan Company from COLLECTED POEMS by Marianne Moore. Copyright 1935 by Marianne Moore, renewed 1963 by Marianne Moore and T. S. Eliot.

The Macmillan Company for "A Grave" and "Snakes, Mongooses, Snake-Charmers and the Like" from COLLECTED POEMS by Marianne Moore. Reprinted with permission of The Macmillan Company from COLLECTED POEMS by Marianne Moore. Copyright 1935 by Marianne Moore, renewed 1963 by Marianne Moore.

The Macmillan Company for "Cassandra" from COLLECTED POEMS by Edward Arlington Robinson. Reprinted with permission of The Macmillan Company from COLLECTED POEMS by Edward Arlington Robinson. Copyright 1916 by Edward Arlington Robinson, renewed 1944 by Ruth Nivison.

The Macmillan Company for "The Sheaves" from COLLECTED POEMS by Edward Arlington Robinson. Reprinted with permission of The Macmillan Company from COLLECTED POEMS by Edward Arlington Robinson. Copyright 1925 by Edwin Arlington Robinson, renewed 1953 by Ruth Nivison and Barbara R. Holt.

The Macmillan Company for "The U. S. Sailor With a Japanese Skull" from COLLECTED POEMS by Winfield Townley Scott. Reprinted with permission of The Macmillan Company from COLLECTED POEMS by Winfield Townely Scott. Copyright 1945 by Winfield Townley Scott.

The Macmillan Company for "A Glass of Beer" from COLLECTED POEMS by James Stephens. Reprinted with permission of The Macmillan Company from COLLECTED POEMS by James Stephens. Copyright 1918 by The Macmillan Company, renewed 1946 by James Stephens.

The Macmillan Company for "Nineteen Hundred Nineteen" Section I and Section V from COLLECTED POEMS by William Butler Yeats. Reprinted with permission of The Macmillan Company from COLLECTED POEMS by William Butler Yeats. Copyright 1928 by The Macmillan Company, renewed 1956 by Bertha Georgie Yeats.

The Macmillan Company for "The Mother of God" by William Butler Yeats. Reprinted with permission of The Macmillan Company from COLLECTED POEMS by William Butler Yeats. Copyright 1933 by The Macmillan Company, renewed 1961 by Bertha Georgie Yeats.

The Macmillan Company for "Purgatory" from THE COLLECTED PLAYS OF WILLIAM BUTLER YEATS by William Butler Yeats. Reprinted with permission of The Macmillan Company from THE COLLECTED PLAYS OF WILLIAM BUTLER YEATS by William Butler Yeats. Copyright 1934, 1952 by The Macmillan Company.

The Macmillan Company for "Sailing to Byzantium," "Two Songs from a Play," "Leda and the Swan," and "All Souls' Night" from COLLECTED POEMS by William Butler Yeats. Reprinted with permission of The Macmillan Company from COLLECTED POEMS by William Butler Yeats. Copyright 1928 by The Macmillan Company, renewed 1956 by Bertha Georgie Yeats.

The Macmillan Company for "For Anne Gregory," "Crazy Jane Talks with the Bishop," and "A Dialogue of Self and Soul" from COLLECTED POEMS by William Butler Yeats. Reprinted with permission of The Macmillan Company from COLLECTED POEMS by William Butler Yeats. Copyright 1933 by The Macmillan Company, renewed 1961 by Bertha Georgie Yeats.

The Macmillan Company for "Who Goes with Fergus?" from COLLECTED POEMS by William Butler Yeats. Reprinted with permission from The Macmillan Company from COLLECTED POEMS by William Butler Yeats. Copyright 1906 by The Macmillan Company, renewed 1934 by William Butler Yeats.

The Macmillan Company for "The Cold Heaven" from COLLECTED POEMS by William Butler Yeats. Reprinted with permission from The Macmillan Company from COLLECTED POEMS by William Butler Yeats. Copyright 1912 by The Macmillan Company, renewed 1940 by Bertha Georgie Yeats.

The Macmillan Company for excerpts from ESSAYS by William Butler Yeats. Reprinted with permission from The Macmillan Company from ESSAYS by William Butler Yeats. Copyright 1924 by The Macmillan Company, renewed 1952 by Bertha Georgie Yeats.

The Macmillan Company for "The Cat and the Moon," and "A Deep-Sworn Vow" from COLLECTED POEMS by William Butler Yeats. Reprinted with permission of The Macmillan Company from COLLECTED POEMS by William Butler Yeats. Copyright 1919 by The Macmillan Company, renewed 1947 by Bertha Georgie Yeats.

The Macmillan Company for "Adam's Curse" from COLLECTED POEMS by William Butler Yeats. Reprinted with permission of The Macmillan Company from COLLECTED POEMS by William Butler Yeats. Copyright 1903 by The Macmillan Company, renewed 1931 by William Butler Yeats.

The Macmillan Company for "The Second Coming" from COLLECTED POEMS by William Butler Yeats. Reprinted with permission of The Macmillan Company from COLLECTED POEMS by William Butler Yeats. Copyright 1924 by The Macmillan Company, renewed 1952 by Bertha Georgie Yeats.

The Macmillan Company of Canada, Ltd. for "The Comet at Yell'ham," "Channel Firing," "The Five Students," and "During Wind and Rain" from COLLECTED POEMS by Thomas Hardy by permission of Macmillan London & Basingstoke; and The Macmillan Company of Canada Limited.

The Macmillan Company of Canada, Ltd. for "After a Journey" from COLLECTED POEMS by Thomas Hardy, by permission of the Trustees of the Hardy Estate; Macmillan London & Basingstoke; and The Macmillan Company of Canada Limited.

The Macmillan Company of Canada, Ltd. for "A Glass of Beer" from COLLECTED POEMS by James Stephens. By permission of Mrs. Iris Wise, Macmillan London & Basingstoke; and The Macmillan Company of Canada Limited.

MacGibbon and Kee, Ltd. for "The First Invasion of Ireland" from POISONED LANDS AND OTHER POEMS by John Montague. By permission of MacGibbon and Kee, Ltd.

Margot Johnson Agency for "The Goose Fish" by Howard Nemerov. From NEW AND SELECTED POEMS by Howard Nemerov, copyright by the University of Chicago, 1960.

The Marvell Press for "Toads" from THE LESS DECEIVED by Philip Larkin. Copyright © The Marvell Press 1955, 1973 by permission of The Marvell Press, England.

Harold Matson Company, Inc. for "Not Palaces, an Era's Crown" from SELECTED POEMS by Stephen Spender, edited by C. Day Lewis. Copyright by Stephen Spender, reprinted by permission of the Harold Matson Company, Inc.

McClelland & Stewart Limited for "El Greco: Espolio" from SELECTED POEMS 1940–1966 by Earle Birney. Reprinted by permission of The Canadian Publishers, McClelland & Stewart, Limited, Toronto.

John Murray, Ltd. for "In Westminster Abbey" from COLLECTED POEMS by John Betjeman. Reprinted by permission of John Murray, Ltd. and Houghton Mifflin Company.

New Directions Publishing Corporation for "After a Passage in Baudelaire" and "Strains of Sight" Robert Duncan, ROOTS AND BRANCHES. Copyright © 1964 by Robert Duncan. Reprinted by permission of New Directions Publishing Corporation.

New Directions Publishing Corporation for "Losing Track," Denise Levertov, O TASTE AND SEE. Copyright © 1963 by Denise Levertov Goodman. "Losing Track" was first published in *Poetry*. Reprinted by permission of New Directions Publishing Corporation.

New Directions Publishing Corporation for "Strange Meeting" and "Insensibility," Wilfred Owen, COLLECTED POEMS. Copyright Chatto & Windus, Ltd. 1946, © 1963. Reprinted by permission of New Directions Publishing Corporation.

New Directions Publishing Corporation for "Greater Love," Wilfred Owen, COLLECTED POEMS. Copyright Chatto & Windus, Ltd., 1946, © 1963. Reprinted by permission of New Directions Publishing Corporation.

New Directions Publishing Corporation for "The Seafarer," "The Study in Aesthetics," "In a Station of the Metro," "Fish and the Shadow," "Homage to Sextus Propertius, I," and "Envoi (1919)," Ezra Pound, PERSONAE. Copyright 1926 by Ezra Pound. Reprinted by permission of New Directions Publishing Corporation.

New Directions Publishing Corporation for "Canto I," "Canto XVII," "Canto XVI," Ezra Pound, THE CANTOS. Copyright 1934 by Ezra Pound. Reprinted by permission of New Directions Publishing Corporation.

New Directions Publishing Corporation for "The Seeing Eye," "Villanelle: The Psychological Hour," and "The Return," Ezra Pound, PERSONAE. Copyright 1926 by Ezra Pound. Reprinted by permission of New Directions Publishing Corporation.

New Directions Publishing Corporation for "Doubled Mirrors," Kenneth Rexroth, COLLECTED SHORTER POEMS. Copyright 1952 by Kenneth Rexroth. Reprinted by permission of New Directions Publishing Corporation.

New Directions Publishing Corporation for "In the Naked Bed, in Plato's Cave," Delmore Schwartz, SELECTED POEMS: SUMMER KNOWLEDGE. Copyright 1938 by New Directions, © 1966 by Delmore Schwartz. Reprinted by permission of New Directions Publishing Corporation.

New Directions Publishing Corporation for "Not Waving, but Drowning," Stevie Smith, SELECTED POEMS. Copyright © 1964 by Stevie Smith. Reprinted by permission of New Directions Publishing Corporation.

New Directions Publishing Corporation for "Floating World Picture: Spring in the Kitagami Mountains," Gary Snyder, THE BACK COUNTRY. Copyright © 1968 by Gary Snyder. Reprinted by permission of New Directions Publishing Corporation.

New Directions Publishing Corporation for "And death shall have no dominion," "The force that through the green fuse," and "Ceremony After a Fire Raid," THE POEMS OF DYLAN THOMAS. Copyright 1939, 1943, 1946 by New Directions Publishing Corporation. Reprinted by permission of New Directions Publishing Corporation.

New Directions Publishing Corporation for "Flowers by the Sea," "Spring and All," "At the Ball Game," William Carlos Williams, COLLECTED EARLIER POEMS. Copyright 1938 by William Carlos Williams. Reprinted by permission of New Directions Publishing Corporation.

New Directions Publishing Corporation for "The Dance," William Carlos Williams, COLLECTED LATER POEMS. Copyright 1944 by William Carlos Williams. Reprinted by permission of New Directions Publishing Corporation.

New Directions Publishing Corporation for "Asphodel, that Greeny Flower," William Carlos Williams, PICTURES FROM BRUEGHEL AND OTHER POEMS. Copyright 1954 by William Carlos Williams. Reprinted by permission of New Directions Publishing Corporation.

New Directions Publishing Corporation for "Book III," (eight lines only) William Carlos Williams, PATERSON. Copyright 1949 by William Carlos Williams. Reprinted by permission of New Directions Publishing Corporation.

W. W. Norton & Company, Inc. for "A Nameless One." Reprinted from THE DUMBFOUNDING, Poems by Margaret Avison. By permission of W. W. Norton & Company, Inc. Copyright © 1966 by Margaret Avison.

Oxford University Press for "The Groundhog" and "The Fury of Aerial Bombardment" from COLLECTED POEMS 1930–1960 by Richard Eberhart. Copyright © 1960 by Richard Eberhart. Reprinted by permission of Oxford University Press, Inc.

Oxford University Press for "Winter with the Gulf Stream" and "God's Grandeur" by Gerard Manley Hopkins from THE POEMS OF GERARD MANLEY HOPKINS, 4th ed. Reprinted by permission of Oxford University Press, Inc.

Oxford University Press for "The Starlight Night" by Gerard Manley Hopkins from THE POEMS OF GERARD MANLEY HOPKINS. Reprinted by permission of Oxford University Press, Inc.

Oxford University Press for "Snow" and "Bagpipe Music" from THE COLLECTED POEMS OF LOUIS MACNEICE, edited by E. R. Dodds. Copyright © the Estate of Louis MacNeice 1966. Reprinted by permission of Oxford University Press, Inc.

Oxford University Press for "The Horses" from COLLECTED POEMS by Edwin

Muir, Copyright © 1960 by Willa Muir. Reprinted by permission of Oxford University Press, Inc.

Oxford University Press for "Jim Dandy" from BLUE BOY ON SKATES by M. L. Rosenthal. Copyright © 1964 by Oxford University Press, Inc. Reprinted by permission of Oxford University Press, Inc.

Oxford University Press, Canadian Branch for "News of the Phoenix" from COLLECTED POEMS by A. J. M. Smith. Reprinted by permission of Oxford University Press, Canadian Branch.

A. D. Peters & Co. Literary Agents for "The First Invasion of Ireland" from POISONED LANDS AND OTHER POEMS by John Montague. Reprinted by permission of A. D. Peters and Company.

Random House, Inc. for "In Praise of Limestone" by W. H. Auden. Reprinted from COLLECTED SHORTER POEMS 1927–1957 by W. H. Auden, by permission of Random House, Inc.

Random House, Inc. for "O what is that sound which so thrills the ear" and "Look, stranger, on this island now" ("On This Island") from COLLECTED SHORTER POEMS, 1927–1957 by W. H. Auden. Copyright 1937 and renewed 1965 by W. H. Auden. Reprinted from COLLECTED SHORTER POEMS, 1927–1957 by W. H. Auden, by permission of Random House, Inc.

Random House, Inc. for "Lullaby" and "Musée des Beaux Arts" from COLLECTED SHORTER POEMS, 1927–1957 by W. H. Auden. Copyright 1940 and renewed 1968 by W. H. Auden. Reprinted from COLLECTED SHORTER POEMS, 1927–1957 by W. H. Auden, by permission of Random House, Inc.

Random House, Inc. for "And the age ended" ("So an age ended") from COLLECTED SHORTER POEMS, 1927–1957 by W. H. Auden, by permission of Random House, Inc.

Random House, Inc. for "The Shield of Achilles" from COLLECTED SHORTER POEMS, 1927–1957 by W. H. Auden. Copyright 1952 by W. H. Auden. Reprinted from COLLECTED SHORTER POEMS, 1927–1957 by W. H. Auden, by permission of Random House, Inc.

Random House, Inc. for "Shine, Perishing Republic" from SELECTED POETRY OF ROBINSON JEFFERS. Copyright 1925 and 1953 by Robinson Jeffers. Reprinted from SELECTED POETRY OF ROBINSON JEFFERS, by permission of Random House, Inc.

Random House, Inc. for "Not palaces, an era's crown" from SELECTED POEMS by Stephen Spender. Copyright 1934 by The Modern Library, Inc. and renewed 1962 by Stephen Spender. Reprinted from SELECTED POEMS by Stephen Spender, by permission of Random House, Inc.

Routledge & Kegan Paul for "July 1964" from ESSEX POEMS 1963–1967 by Donald Davie. Reprinted with permission of Routledge & Kegan Paul, Ltd.

Charles Scribner's Sons for "I keep to myself such measures" from WORDS by Robert Creeley. "I keep to myself such measures" is reprinted by permission of Charles Scribner's Sons from WORDS by Robert Creeley. Copyright © 1962, 1963, 1964, 1967 Robert Creeley.

The Society of Authors for "To an Athlete Dying Young" and "Eight O'clock" from COLLECTED POEMS by A. E. Housman. Reprinted by permission of the Society of Authors as the literary representative of the Estate of A. E. Housman and Jonathan Cape, Ltd., publishers of A. E. Housman's COLLECTED POEMS.

The Sterling Lord Agency, Inc., for "An Agony as Now" by LeRoi Jones from THE DEAD LECTURER. Copyright © 1964 by LeRoi Jones. Reprinted by permission of The Sterling Lord Agency, Inc.

The Swallow Press, Inc. for "An Ode on the Despoilers of Learning in an American University." Reprinted from COLLECTED POEMS by Yvor Winters. Copyright © 1960 by permission of The Swallow Press, Inc., Chicago.

Edward and Helen Thomas Estate for "The Manor Farm" and "As the team's head-brass" from COLLECTED POEMS by Edward Thomas. Reprinted with permission by Mrs. Myfanwy Thomas.

The University of Chicago Press for "In Santa Maria del Popolo" from MY SAD CAPTAIN AND OTHER POEMS by Thom Gunn. Reprinted by permission of The University of Chicago Press. Copyright 1961.

The Viking Press, Inc. for Poem XXXVI from "Chamber Music" from COLLECTED POEMS by James Joyce. Copyright 1918 by B. W. Huebsch, Inc., 1946 by Nora Joyce. Reprinted by permission of The Viking Press, Inc.

The Viking Press, Inc. for "Hymn to Priapus" from THE COMPLETE POEMS OF D. H. LAWRENCE, ed. by Vivian de Sola Pinto and F. Warren Roberts. Copyright © 1964, 1971 by Angelo Ravagli and C. M. Weekley. All rights reserved. Reprinted by permission of The Viking Press, Inc.

The Viking Press, Inc. for "Tortoise Shell" and "The Ship of Death" from THE COMPLETE POEMS OF D. H. LAWRENCE, ed. by Vivian de Sola Pinto and F. Warren Roberts. Copyright © 1964, 1971 by Angelo Ravagli and C. M. Weekley. All rights reserved. Reprinted by permission of The Viking Press, Inc.

The Viking Press, Inc. for "Whales Weep Not" from THE COMPLETE POEMS OF D. H. LAWRENCE, ed. by Vivian de Sola Pinto and F. Warren Roberts. Copyright © 1964, 1971 by Angelo Ravagli and C. M. Weekley, Executors of The Estate of Frieda Lawrence Ravagli. Reprinted by permission of The Viking Press, Inc.

The Viking Press, Inc. for "The Song of a Man Who Has Come Through" from THE COMPLETE POEMS OF D. H. LAWRENCE, ed. by Vivian de Sola Pinto and F. Warren Roberts. Copyright © 1964, 1971 by Angelo Ravagli and C. M. Weekley. All rights reserved. Reprinted by permission of The Viking Press, Inc.

A. P. Watt & Son, Ltd. for "Nineteen Hundred and Nineteen" Section I and Section V and "The Mother of God" from THE COLLECTED POEMS OF W. B. YEATS, by permission of Mr. M. B. Yeats and The Macmillan Company of Canada Limited.

A. P. Watt & Son, Ltd. for "Purgatory" from THE COLLECTED PLAYS OF WILLIAM BUTLER YEATS. Reprinted by permission of Mr. M. B. Yeats and The Macmillan Company of Canada Limited.

A. P. Watt & Son, Ltd. for "The Cat and the Moon," "Adam's Curse," "The Second Coming," "Sailing to Byzantium," "Two Songs from a Play," "Leda and the Swan," "For Anne Gregory," "Crazy Jane Talks with the Bishop," "A Dialogue of Self and Soul," from "Who Goes with Fergus," from "The Cold Heaven," from "A Deep-Sworn Vow," and from "All Souls' Night" from THE COLLECTED POEMS OF W. B. YEATS. By permission of Mr. M. B. Yeats and The Macmillan Company of Canada Limited.

A. P. Watt & Son, Ltd. for approximately one hundred words from "The Symbolism of Poetry" from ESSAYS AND INTRODUCTIONS by W. B. Yeats. By permission of Mr. M. B. Yeats and The Macmillan Company of Canada Limited.

Wesleyan University Press for "The Performance" by James Dickey. Copyright © 1960 by James Dickey. Reprinted from POEMS 1957–1967, by James Dickey, by permission of Wesleyan University Press.

Wesleyan University Press for "Cherrylog Road" from POEMS 1957–1967 by James Dickey. Copyright © 1963 by James Dickey. Reprinted from HELMETS, by James Dickey, by permission of Wesleyan University Press. This poem first appeared in *The New Yorker*.

Preface to the Second Edition

We learn what poetry is from poems—from what poets actually write. Several poets, among them William Carlos Williams, have spoken of a poem as a "machine" for creating certain effects, making certain discoveries, completing certain constructs of insight and awareness through the medium of language. There is no standard product; each poet builds his own machines, each of which has its own elusive and individual character. Indeed, a successful poem seems to take on its own organic life from psychic sources in the poet. It is the result of human skill, and hence a kind of "machine." At the same time it is something more; it germinates, grows, and develops as if it were indeed a living thing.

If the reader will glance at the main headings in our table of contents, he will see that the first three chapters go directly to questions it is natural to ask about poems. Who is speaking? Is it the poet himself or a fictional character in the dramatic situation the poem presents? In either case, what sort of person is he? What are his feelings and ideas? What circumstance or problem leads him to speak? And from another standpoint, why is *form*—rhyme, rhythm, repetition of all kinds, and all the possible devices of technique including figures of speech—so essential to poetry? Finally, how does a poem move between its beginning and its end and what does the whole process ultimately "mean"?

These three opening chapters are an introduction to the essentials of poetry. Chapter One points out that the reader needs to listen to the voice that speaks in a poem. He must learn to let himself be guided by that voice in order to get the tone and idiom and full meaning of the poem. The opening chapter lays special emphasis on the fact that every poem projects one or more human voices. Obstacles to understanding a poem often disappear when one reads it aloud, trying to catch the intonations intended, *hearing* what is on the printed page: the pitch and rhythm, the pauses and hesitations and all the variations in speed that modify the emphasis and thus affect the meaning as the speaker's voice moves from phrase to phrase and cadence to cadence. A most useful exercise is for several people in succession to read the same poem aloud. Each reading is a clarification of what is being said and how it is being felt, and therefore helps us re-create the way the poet himself conceived and heard the poem in his own mind.

Chapter Two takes up some points of craftsmanship. These are presented as untechnically as possible, but they provide the student with basic descriptive or critical terms having to do with figurative language, imagery, and metrics. Together with the first chapter, which considered the speaking voice as the controlling element in the poem's movement, Chapter Two prepares us for the considerations in Chapter Three. The third chapter deals with the way in which the elements of a poem combine to make it a living whole.

If there is one unifying purpose to the opening chapters, it is to show concretely what is meant by sympathetic attention to a poem in itself, without preconceptions on the reader's part. The later chapters go on to explore the wide range of the possible modes of poetry and the amazing involvement of even a simple poem with the whole of life—the symbolism and the kinds of meaning, social, political, historical, philosophical, and moral, implicit in its language and structure. Chapters Four and Five deal with narrative, dramatic, and descriptive poetry. Chapter Six, devoted to the intellectual element in poetry, gives much attention to the uses of wit, ambiguity, and irony, with some special attention to satire and metaphysical verse. The ensuing discussion, in Chapter Seven, of allegory and symbolism follows naturally from the concerns of Chapter Six. Chapter Eight then presents an account of certain less consciously purposeful motifs of poetry: the relation of continuing poetic traditions to the poet's sense of his own time and place as reflected in his work. This chapter places poetry in its historical frame of reference, discusses the distinction between classical and romantic art, and shows how two of the great universal subjects—love and war—have been treated by poets through the centuries. The book concludes, in Chapter Nine, with an analysis of some major poems that deal with the great philosophical and religious themes of quest and reconciliation. A close reading of such poems as Whitman's *Out of the Cradle Endlessly Rocking* and Yeat's *A Dialogue of Self and Soul* will, it is hoped, leave the student with an aroused awareness of the strong connection between the imaginative and the moral aspects of poetry.

The main chapters are divided into shorter sections, each a single teaching unit. The copious anthology following each division of the book provides ample material, with plenty of room to allow the reader to pick and choose, to illustrate in many different ways the value and universality of poetry. The depth of this anthology, which includes many contemporary and, indeed, recent poems as well as a fresh culling from the past, will be evident at once from the table of contents. The starred poems, some of them imbedded in the explanatory text, are discussed for their own sake and for their pertinence to the subjects of the sections in which they appear. These discussions afford examples of various kinds of poetic analysis, some quite brief and some relatively extended.

Headnotes precede each group of poems in the anthology. These headnotes are short commentaries suggesting why particular poems are placed where they are and what points of comparison and contrast might be considered within a grouping of poems. Usually, too, the headnotes give simple critical tips about individual poems. They can readily be used, by students as well as teachers, as the basis of questions and classroom discussions. We have found it useful to encourage the formulation of questions about meaning, about the function of certain images, about the focal points in a change of feeling or attitude, and about similarities and differences in poems with the same subject.

Such questions help open up a poem in the context of the reader's own level of awareness. The "answer" to any question lies in the poem itself; and the question, which begins in the mind of the reader, is an important step in learning to respond to the literal language of the poem.

Footnotes are included where necessary, but in general we have avoided giving definitions found in any dictionary and information readily available in encyclopedias or handbooks of mythology. We believe that "looking it up" is part of every student's training and every good reader's experience. The pleasures of discovery and illumination are doubly sweet when earned. But we do provide glossaries for the Scottish (Lallans) poems of Hugh MacDiarmid, the Middle English poems of Chaucer, and some others. In addition, we have added explanatory footnotes for some particularly demanding passages, and here and there have incorporated a critical question in the notes as well.

Among the many poems analyzed in detail in the text are a number of complex or difficult poems, such as John Donne's *Good Friday. 1613. Riding Westward*; Hart Crane's *Passage*; T. S. Eliot's *Gerontion*; W. B. Yeats's *Sailing to Byzantium*; and Dylan Thomas's *The force that through the green fuse drives the flower*. We have left other equally subtle poems for the student (at the discretion of the instructor or on his own initiative) to try his growing skills on for himself.

While the book's overall plan is simple, proceeding from the elements of poetry to its various types and functions and then to its broader and more profound implications, the sections of explanatory text and the range of illustrative poems make it usable at many levels from the introductory to the advanced and sophisticated. The relevant questions, after all, are the same for both the untrained reader and the specialist, despite the differences in what they already know and in the scope of their developed interests. In general we recommend an open attitude toward the ability of most students to grasp and enjoy most poems—which were written by human beings and can therefore be appreciated by other human beings.

One further point: We hope the student will wander far and wide among the poems here included. Though chosen for their aptness in light of the topics being discussed in the sections, they are usually equally representative of principles developed elsewhere in the book. Our basic criterion has been the quality of the poetry, together with a desire to present the masters of various periods and to suggest modern and contemporary tendencies. Such names as Robert Lowell, Ted Hughes, Sylvia Plath, Imamu Amiri Baraka (LeRoi Jones), Charles Olson, Allen Ginsberg, and Denise Levertov—to name but a few— have come into the foreground of our poetry during the last ten or fifteen years especially. Others—for instance Ramon Guthrie—have come into belated recognition only quite recently. Their work stands side by side here with that of the most famous older moderns and with established figures of earlier eras. We would maintain that there is no *essential* difference between poetry of the past and that of our own time. Each epoch has unique features that must be appreciated, and yet each contributes to the overall continuity of the art. One can learn a great deal by looking for "modern" notes in past literature and for traditional aspects of modern poems.

In the preface to the first edition of *Exploring Poetry* we expressed our thanks to the friends and scholars to whom we were indebted for their careful reading and criticism. We need not repeat those grateful acknowledgments here. The only exception must be our naming of Oscar Cargill and J. G. Case, the beloved colleague and the cherished editor who encouraged us to write this book and then cheered and whipped us on until it was completed. To their memory this new edition is dedicated.

We are grateful also for the editorial assistance of Sally M. Gall. Our greatest indebtedness, finally, is to the ungrudging help of our wisest guides and severest critics, Victoria Rosenthal and Jeannie Smith.

M. L. R.
A. J. M. S.

Contents

* Poems indicated by asterisks in each section are discussed in that section's explanatory text, unless a footnote after the poem indicates discussion elsewhere in the book.

III   Rhythm and Music   81

Chapter Three   Structure: The Poem as a Whole   111

Chapter Five *Poetry as Description and Vision* 209

POEMS IN TEXT

ANTHOLOGY: DESCRIPTIVE AND VISIONARY POETRY

Chapter Six   *Poetry as Intellect and Wit*   257

I   *Poetic Exposition*   257

POEMS IN TEXT

ANTHOLOGY: POETIC EXPOSITION

II   *Metaphysical Poetry*   280

POEMS IN TEXT

ANTHOLOGY: METAPHYSICAL POETRY

III Irony, Invective, and Satire 305

POEMS IN TEXT

ANTHOLOGY: IRONY, INVECTIVE, AND SATIRE

IV Ambiguity and Implication 330

POEMS IN TEXT

Chapter Seven *Poetry as Symbol and Evocation* 347

I *Varieties of Symbolism* 347

POEMS IN TEXT

II *The Symbol as a Directive Force* 385

POEMS IN TEXT

II   *Two Abiding Themes: Love and War*   430

ANTHOLOGY: TWO ABIDING THEMES: LOVE AND WAR

Headnote   434

III   *The Poem's Reflection of Its Time and Place*   457

POEMS IN TEXT

Chapter Nine   Poetic Integrity: Quest and Reconciliation   481

Chapter One

The Voices of Poetry

I

THE PERSONAL AND THE UNIVERSAL

Every true poem has its voice. Sometimes it is the poet's own voice. More often, it is the voice of someone in a dramatic or fictional situation. And though we usually think of a voice as speaking, it may also sing, whisper, shout, plead, or cry. In some poems it is a traditional rather than a purely personal voice—a voice of rhetoric, incantation, prayer, or praise. In a complex poem *several* voices, or many, may join in and compete for our attention. In lyrical and reflective poetry the voice may even seem like the inner voice of our own thoughts.

When we open a volume of John Donne and find a poem beginning

For Godsake hold your tongue, and let me love,

we are thrown back violently by the voice of a proud, self-assured, magnificently impatient lover. It comes to us as fresh and clear as if we ourselves were the tedious, moralizing busybodies he is upbraiding, and as if the time were now and not three-and-a-half centuries or so ago when the poem was written.

We are not often addressed so directly as here. In many poems we listen to a voice that seems hardly aware of us at all. It creates its own ideal listener within the dramatic framework of the poem. We are privileged to *overhear*, as in Matthew Arnold's *Dover Beach* we overhear the bitter consolatory words with which the lover turns to his beloved as a refuge from the emptiness of a world without God:

Ah, love, let us be true
To one another! for the world, which seems
To lie before us, like a land of dreams,
So various, so beautiful, so new,
Hath really neither joy, nor love, nor light,
Nor certitude, nor peace, nor help for pain. . . .

The speaking voice of a poem varies infinitely, as human personality varies, as human moods vary, and as the writer's purpose varies. Poetry catches the idiom of the speaking voice, in all centuries and in all social circumstances.

> I cannot eat but little meat,
>   My stomach is not good. . . .
>   ANONYMOUS, 14th century

> Throw away thy rod,
> Throw away thy wrath:
>   O my God,
> Take the gentle path.
>   GEORGE HERBERT, 17th century

> Yes, I am proud; I must be proud to see
> Men not afraid of God, afraid of me.
>   ALEXANDER POPE, 18th century

> Had I but plenty of money, money enough and to spare,
> The house for me, no doubt, were a house in the city-square;
> Ah, such a life, such a life, as one leads at the window there!
>   ARTHUR HUGH CLOUGH, 19th century

> And the guys from Paterson
>   beat up
> the guys from Newark and told
> them to stay the hell out
> of their territory and then
> socked you one
>   across the nose
> Beautiful Thing. . . .
>   WILLIAM CARLOS WILLIAMS, 20th century

What we have called the speaking voice is sometimes called the *persona*—the character assumed to be talking. To find out who that character is, his personality and role and mood, his seriousness or frivolity or irony, the simplicity or complexity of his thought, one must try to visualize him through the kind of language he uses. The speaker in the line by Donne is very different in his imperious passion from the disillusioned man who seeks reassurance in the lines by Arnold. Both are lovers, but there the similarity ends.

In the following two passages, the first by the twentieth-century American poet Charles Olson and the second by the seventeenth-century English poet Andrew Marvell, we have another instance of great differences despite something in common. Each speaker is telling us about himself, and both passages, it is true, are made of direct statements; but the language and the tone are quite different, and for reasons it is not hard to discern.

> I have had to learn the simplest things
> last. Which made for difficulties.
> Even at sea I was slow, to get the hand out, or to cross
> a wet deck.
> > The sea was not, finally, my trade.
> But even my trade, at it, I stood estranged
> from that which was most familiar. . . .
> > CHARLES OLSON, *Maximus, to Himself*

> What wond'rous life is this I lead!
> Ripe apples drop about my head;
> The luscious clusters of the vine
> Upon my mouth do crush their wine;
> The nectarine and curious peach,
> Into my hands themselves do reach;
> Stumbling on melons, as I pass,
> Insnar'd with flow'rs, I fall on grass.
> > ANDREW MARVELL, *The Garden*

The first passage is an admission of awkwardness and unsuccess. The speech rhythms are slow and seem intentionally clumsy. They convey in their halting movement—poetically, that is—the sense of the statements being made. The speaker feels himself unsuited to, and therefore rejected from, his trade as seaman or fisherman. This idea is expressed also in his language and syntax. He almost stammers with the difficulty of getting his thoughts into focus. This is certainly not the language of a New England sailor. The "finally" in the sentence "The sea was not, finally, my trade" is sensitively intellectual in its qualifying break-up of the thought. The language as a whole is modern and commonplace enough, but is nevertheless the language of a thoughtful, honest, and educated man, who finds himself by his nature and background isolated and confused. Everything in this passage, and in the poem in which it occurs, gives an impression of a careful and awkward inward-looking truthfulness.

Marvell, on the other hand, if he stumbles and falls, falls into an excess of happiness. It is all a rapturous game, the return to the Edenlike earthly paradise and state of innocence before the Fall had made Nature the enemy of man. The language and varied but formal rhythms bespeak the seventeenth-century gentleman, scholar, and wit, privileged and lucky, at home and certain of his place both in the world of action and the world of relaxation.

Let us listen now to the development of a single voice in all its varied tones through a complete poem. Robert Frost's *Mending Wall* is excellent for this purpose. It is short, modern, and conversational; and though it appears simple, it has overtones and implications' for any reflective reader.

The poem is idiomatic, easygoing. The turns of phrase and modulations of voice are intimate and direct and local. It is the voice of a Yankee farmer we hear, shrewd, pungent, and reflective, making its point by understatement and suggestion and presenting firmly, almost obstinately, the opposing points of view of the two north-of-Boston neighbors. Their "debate" begins at once:

> Something there is that doesn't love a wall

says the one from whose standpoint the poem is presented and whose voice dominates the whole poem. His is the voice of reason and nature alike—of logic and progress, the poem seems to hint. Opposed to it is the rival voice, atavistic and insistent, stubbornly repeating,

> Good fences make good neighbors.

But here is the poem itself:

ROBERT FROST *Mending Wall*

Something there is that doesn't love a wall,
That sends the frozen-ground-swell under it,
And spills the upper boulders in the sun;
And makes gaps even two can pass abreast.
The work of hunters is another thing:
I have come after them and made repair
Where they have left not one stone on a stone,
But they would have the rabbit out of hiding,
To please the yelping dogs. The gaps I mean,
No one has seen them made or heard them made,   10
But at spring mending-time we find them there.
I let my neighbor know beyond the hill;
And on a day we meet to walk the line
And set the wall between us once again.
We keep the wall between us as we go.
To each the boulders that have fallen to each.
And some are loaves and some so nearly balls
We have to use a spell to make them balance:
"Stay where you are until our backs are turned!"
We wear our fingers rough with handling them.   20
Oh, just another kind of out-door game,

One on a side. It comes to little more:
There where it is we do not need the wall:
He is all pine and I am apple orchard.
My apple trees will never get across
And eat the cones under his pines, I tell him.
He only says, "Good fences make good neighbors."
Spring is the mischief in me, and I wonder
If I could put a notion in his head:
"*Why* do they make good neighbors? Isn't it   30
Where there are cows? But here there are no cows.
Before I built a wall I'd ask to know
What I was walling in or walling out,
And to whom I was like to give offence.
Something there is that doesn't love a wall,
That wants it down." I could say "Elves" to him,
But it's not elves exactly, and I'd rather
He said it for himself. I see him there
Bringing a stone grasped firmly by the top
In each hand, like an old-stone savage armed.   40
He moves in darkness as it seems to me,
Not of woods only and the shade of trees.
He will not go behind his father's saying,
And he likes having thought of it so well
He says again, "Good fences make good neighbors."

It is one of Robert Frost's triumphs to catch, in poetry that is reflective and dramatic, the voice of a locality or region, and at the same time to differentiate within it the individual voices of his characters. In this poem the New England countryman's manner of seeming to stray from the point as he gossips along, and yet of always coming back to it or just never leaving it, is a source of both pleasure and instruction to the reader who notices it. For the most part this poem, like so many others by Frost, is colloquial and unhurried, the tone of good talk; but in one or two places, strategically chosen for emphasis or climax, the tone changes. The lines become rhythmically more regular, cease to be talk, and approach music. The sound of

> He moves in darkness as it seems to me,
> Not of woods only and the shade of trees

is heightened and intensified. Description, narrative, and exposition have come to an end. Now is the time for reflection and criticism—for implication and judgment. The point of view of the speaker is given weight and dignity, though he modestly and characteristically adds the saving phrase "as it seems to me"—the Yankee has learned it is never safe to commit himself inescapably!

Yet the weight and dignity of these lines would seem to suggest that the poet himself is sympathetic to the speaker's dislike of walls and critical of the other man's refusal to "go behind his father's saying." The climactic and critical force of the two heightened lines quoted is not due solely to the abandonment of the informal colloquial tone. It comes also from the richness of suggestion in the word *darkness,* with its associations of superstition and ignorance—already perhaps prepared for by the earlier description of the spell to make the stones balance; and from the word *shade,* with its suggestion of death and of ghosts—ideas from the past that still haunt the present like the persistent survival of the one farmer's belief in the necessity of walls.

Two points of view—indeed two attitudes toward life—and two temperaments have been placed before us with the greatest brevity and clarity: the traditionalist and the liberal. The conflict between them dramatizes the irrationally firm hold that inherited, half-forgotten beliefs have over the minds of men. This poem is not therefore as impartial or objective as its balanced contrasts may suggest. But this is only to say that the poem is a dramatic one, with fictional elements and characterization, and not a piece of philosophical or political analysis. If the voice we hear in it is not directly the voice of the author, it is nevertheless an authentic, personal, identifiable voice. Its local idioms and personal turns are used to develop both character and plot, and are dropped or heightened at moments of climax or for reflection, criticism, or implication.

The voice the poet uses, then, is essential to the structure and meaning of his poem. It may be primarily personal expression, as though he were writing a letter to the world, but ordinarily this is not the case. The reader must learn to hear the voice and tone in relation first of all to what goes on—what is being said and thought and worked out—in the poem. From this point of view, let us now examine a deceptively light piece by another contemporary American poet, John Crowe Ransom.

JOHN CROWE RANSOM *Janet Waking*

> Beautifully Janet slept
> Till it was deeply morning. She woke then
> And thought about her dainty-feathered hen,
> To see how it had kept.
>
> One kiss she gave her mother,
> Only a small one gave she to her daddy
> Who would have kissed each curl of his shining baby;
> No kiss at all for her brother.

"Old Chucky, Old Chucky!" she cried,
Running on little pink feet upon the grass   10
To Chucky's house, and listening. But alas,
Her Chucky had died.

It was a transmogrifying bee
Came droning down on Chucky's old bald head
And sat and put the poison. It scarcely bled,
But how exceedingly

And purply did the knot
Swell with the venom and communicate
Its rigor! Now the poor comb stood up straight
But Chucky did not.   20

So there was Janet
Kneeling on the wet grass, crying her brown hen
(Translated far beyond the daughters of men)
To rise and walk upon it.

And weeping fast as she had breath
Janet implored us, "Wake her from her sleep!"
And would not be instructed in how deep
Was the forgetful kingdom of death.

The rather special effect of this poem derives from the originality of the diction and the skilful variations in tone. It may require a second reading before the inexperienced reader realizes that the voice we hear is that of the little girl's father, though as early as the third line of the second stanza we are given information that no one but he could possess. The whole stanza conveys delightfully the bemused, doting, humorously tender attitude of Janet's daddy.

This mixture of grave and gay, which is the concentrated essence of the speaker's attitude toward the child and toward the child's first bewildering contact with the mystery of life and death, is most strikingly communicated in the curiously subtle uses and seeming misuses of word and idiom in several key lines. Consider, for example, the way certain words have been pressed into the service of the poem. In the first stanza, "beautifully," "deeply," and, especially, "kept" are worked into original and slightly unidiomatic phrases that suggest in a rather subtle way the naïveté and innocence of the little girl. She is faced with something outside her experience. In the fourth stanza too there are "transmogrifying"—the horrendous big word, that might amuse and startle a child—the surprising and accurate "Chucky's old bald head," the unexpected and again accurate "sat and put," and the contrastingly sophisticated "But how exceedingly."

In the next stanza, the scientific phrase "communicate its rigor" is in ironic contrast to the language used or understood by Janet herself, and then there is the wry joke expressed by the verbal neatness of "the poor comb stood up straight/But Chucky did not."

In the stanza before the last the language begins to take on a flavor derived from the romances of the Middle Ages and thus to prepare for the climactic effect of the last two lines. Janet herself is one of the "daughters of men," and her emotion over her pet's death ("crying her brown hen") is subtly transferred to our fears for the little girl herself in face of the uncertainty of life and the imperturbability of death.

The final stanza deepens this note. A darker and richer tone emanates from the word "forgetful" and from the romantic grandeur of the rhythm and phrasing of the last two lines. The contrast between the magnificence of this close and the intimacy and lightness of the opening stanzas may serve to point to another significant aspect of poetry. In it the unique voice of an individual touches universal chords and speaks to all mankind.

For a similar deepening of tone in which the fanciful and the grotesque are transmuted into romantic grandeur, consider Thomas Hardy's *Channel Firing* (pages 338–339). That poem begins with a single line—"That night your great guns, unawares"—which promises just such grandeur. It shifts at once, however, into a dramatic scene that is macabre and surrealistically comic, and the language becomes even more homely and familiar than that in Frost's *Mending Wall*. Then, at the very end, the phrasing and swelling force of the opening line are picked up once more and developed with a richly musical thrust of imagination:

> Again the guns disturbed the hour,
> Roaring their readiness to avenge,
> As far inland as Stourton Tower,
> And Camelot, and starlit Stonehenge.

The heightened diction—the historical, legendary, and poetic associations—here throws new light over all that has gone before. What has been seen as grotesquely satirical fantasy is suddenly given tragic dignity. From the point of view of narrative technique, this shift of tone is a kind of surprise ending. As in *Janet Waking*, the speaking voice has moved from its detailed account of events real or imagined to an entranced sense of a fatality or cosmic principle reaching far back beyond recorded history.

The tone of a poem, it is clear, varies as infinitely as human moods and experiences. In Broadway show tunes or popular songs, the words tend to be representative of a type rather than an individual. Yet even here, as everyone knows, there are exceptions, as in some of the songs of the Beatles,

Bob Dylan, Joan Baez, and other popular composers—though ordinarily the words, without the music, cannot make their full poetic effect. Much of the most convincing poetry, the oldest and the newest alike, depends for its effect on catching the inward voice of a speaker's inward thought and emotion.

Sylvia Plath's poem *Daddy*, for example, presents a most individual, and indeed unique, persona. It is that of a young woman struggling to rid herself of domination by the memory of her dead father. She has to "kill" him again, in her mind, to free herself from his obsessive image.

> You do not, you do not do
> Any more, black shoe
> In which I have lived like a foot
> For thirty years, poor and white,
> Barely daring to breathe or Achoo!
>
> Daddy, I have had to kill you.
> You died before I had time—
> Marble-heavy, a bag full of God,
> Ghastly statue with one grey toe
> Big as a Frisco seal. . . .

Here the speaker is struggling with intense, tormenting, emotionally crippling psychic tensions. There is much going on in the poem that makes it more than a simple personal statement. It is the combination of the individual voice with another sort of voice, impersonal and incantatory or singing, that makes a poem out of what would otherwise be just another bit of ordinary human speech in the vast daily babble of the human race. The mind of the poet turns the language of ordinary speech over and over, and makes designs with it, and compresses and organizes it by echoes of sound and repetitions, by movements along waves of association, by pauses like musical rests, and by speeding up and slowing down very much in the manner of musical improvisation and composition. The art of the poet is an ancient one; he arranges his words according to principles and possibilities that were first glimpsed in times before there was a written language, when men and women learned to chant and gesture and respond rhythmically to one another in ways that involved their bodies quite as much as their minds.

In listening for a human voice, personal and often dramatic, we must also bear in mind that the poet uses means that are impersonal and universal to give his voice the resonance of art. This is the paradox, or apparent self-contradiction, of the nature of poetry. It subjects the rhythms of natural speech to formal patterns, sometimes quite regular and traditional, sometimes looser and more irregular, sometimes shifting from one sort to another within the same poem. This is a matter of musical beat to some extent, of movements of breath-sweep as well, and of rhymes and half-rhymes and repetitions and variations of sound. The curious thing is that the individual voice and the general voice reinforce one another. The deep exploration of private feeling and the echoes of ancient rituals of chanting and dance-movement are intensified by one another, so that we feel that we are taken further inside ourselves and at the same time are transported to states beyond ourselves.

We have seen examples—by Frost, Ransom, Williams, Olson, and Plath—of a contemporary, colloquial, and yet clearly personal idiom in the writings of modern poets. Like these five, most modern poets are vividly and knowledgeably aware of the historical traditions of poetry in English. A curious effect, sometimes intensifying and sometimes ironic, can be gained by the artful mingling of an older poetic diction with the ordinary language of the present. The contemporary American writer Paul Goodman exploits this possibility in a brilliant little poem:

PAUL GOODMAN *The Lordly Hudson*

"Driver, what stream is it," I asked, well knowing
it was our lordly Hudson hardly flowing.
"It is our lordly Hudson hardly flowing,"
he said, "under the green-grown cliffs."

Be still, heart! no one needs your passionate
suffrage to select this glory,
this is our lordly Hudson hardly flowing
under the green-grown cliffs.

"Driver! has this a peer in Europe or the East?"
"No no!" he said. Home! home!
be quiet, heart! this is our lordly Hudson
and has no peer in Europe or the East,

this is our lordly Hudson hardly flowing
under the green-grown cliffs
and has no peer in Europe or the East.
Be quiet, heart! home! home!

Here, though the occasion is ordinary and contemporary, the language is not realistic or literal but heightened, traditional, and "poetic." Indeed, the whole structure and music of the poem recalls both the heroic atmosphere of the ballad literature of a more primitive and emotional era and the lyric formality of Elizabethan poetry like Edmund Spenser's

Prothalamion. Note that "hardly" does not only mean "scarcely" or "slowly" or "with difficulty" but has an older meaning as well—"boldly" or "nobly." The music of the poem is gained by the refrain-like repetition of the few key phrases and the chiming together of "lordly" and "hardly." At the same time, it has a bitter, modern edge. The Hudson is not valued enough; its peerless quality has to be stressed and specially realized, for it is neglected, polluted, undeveloped as a joyous human resource. Hence Goodman's heightened intensity of insistence.

Rhythm, of course, whether regular or varied, is one of the essential elements of poetry. There is a simple pleasure in doing and saying things rhythmically. It derives as much from the body's rhythms—breathing, the heartbeat, walking, running—as from any other source, such as the deep satisfaction human beings feel in doing things in unison. Children and young people respond to rhythm easily and express their emotions poetically, in terms of singing and dancing, more freely than do older and staider persons. From the very beginning the love of rhythm reveals itself. The baby is rocked to sleep, and when awake he is danced up and down to some simple tune. He becomes fascinated with the ticking of a watch, the feel of his heart's beating under his hand, and the slow deceleration of a spinning top. And like the poet, he gives names to things. He imitates sounds and repeats those he likes, and he talks in poem-words: *ma-ma, da-da, bow-wow*. From this point he moves naturally into the world of nursery rhymes, children's singing games and street-chants, and the poetry of nonsense rhymes and fantasy. All this underlies the universal appeal of poetry and its rhythmic excitement.

The more the speaker in a poem opens up his inner world of memory and imagination, the more likely he is to touch on at least some of the hidden chords persisting from his childhood. In Sylvia Plath's *Daddy*, for instance, the childlike, sometimes doggerel rhymes and reiterations clash oddly with the adult notes of loss and resentment. A strange atmosphere of emotional pain emerges. A woman screams at a grotesque image of her long-dead father; it is a nightmare in which her present world is confused with that of a little girl—her past self, who might have chanted less ferocious rhymes while skipping rope or playing at jacks with other children. Thus the personal, individual voice merges with the general voice of a social group or of a traditional form that enters into the final expression of what the poet wishes to say.

Poems: The Personal and the Universal

The arrangement of the following poems is chronological to show the idiom of poetry in relation to that of speech, both colloquial and formal, from the Middle Ages to the present. The anonymous medieval drinking song and American blues song of the Depression, and the pieces by Milton (surprisingly), Stephens, Hughes, and Larkin are "popular," rough, and even coarse in texture and tone. The seventeenth-century poems by Herrick and Herbert are in the one case courtly, elegant, and refined, yet still speech and still serious; and in the other, as befits prayer, exalted and solemn, yet also speech, and natural speech. Pound's *The Study in Aesthetics* is the speech of a cultivated and slightly ironic observer of linguistic usage, while Cummings's more sharply satirical poem turns the rhythms of common everyday American speech into a free and subtle metrical music—a music of jeering mimicry. The poems by Olson and Plath have been discussed in the text; reading them in full, one can hardly fail to feel the contrast in intensity, which is brought out by their very different rhythms as well as by the statements of their subjects.

ANONYMOUS *I cannot eat but little meat*

I cannot eat but little meat,
  My stomach is not good;
But sure I think that I can drink
  With him that wears a hood.[1]
Though I go bare, take ye no care,
  I nothing am a-cold;
I stuff my skin so full within
  Of jolly good ale and old.
    Back and side go bare, go bare;
    Both foot and hand go cold;
    But, belly, God send thee good ale enough,   10
    Whether it be new or old.

I love no roast but a nut-brown toast,
  And a crab [2] laid in the fire;
A little bread shall do me stead;
  . Much bread I not desire,

---

[1] a monk or friar   [2] crab-apple

No frost nor snow, no wind, I trow,
   Can hurt me if I wold;
I am so wrapped and thoroughly lapped
   Of jolly good ale and old.   20
      Back and side go bare, go bare, *etc.*

And Tib, my wife, that as her life
   Loveth well good ale to seek,
Full oft drinks she till ye may see
   The tears run down her cheek:
Then doth she trowl to me the bowl
   Even as a maltworm should,
And saith, "Sweetheart, I took my part
   Of this jolly good ale and old."
      Back and side go bare, go bare, *etc.*   30

Now let them drink till they nod and wink,
   Even as good fellows should do;
They shall not miss to have the bliss
   Good ale doth bring men to;
And all poor souls that have scoured bowls
   Or have them lustily trolled,
God save the lives of them and their wives,
   Whether they be young or old.
      Back and side go bare, go bare;
      Both foot and hand go cold;   40
      But, belly, God send thee good ale enough,
      Whether it be new or old.

Robert Herrick   *To Daffodils*

Fair daffodils, we weep to see
   You haste away so soon;
As yet the early-rising Sun
   Has not attain'd his noon.
      Stay, stay,
    Until the hasting day
      Has run
    But to the evensong;
And, having pray'd together, we
   Will go with you along.   10

We have short time to stay, as you,
　　We have as short a Spring;
As quick a growth to meet decay,
　　As you, or anything.
　　　　We die,
　　As your hours do, and dry
　　　　Away,
　　Like to the Summer's rain;
Or as the pearls of Morning's dew,
　　Ne'er to be found again.　　　　　　　　　20

GEORGE HERBERT　*Discipline*

Throw away thy rod,
Throw away thy wrath:
　　O my God,
Take the gentle path.

For my heart's desire
Unto thine is bent:
　　I aspire
To a full consent.

Not a word or look
I affect to own,　　　　　　　　　　　　　10
　　But by book,
And thy book alone.

Though I fail, I weep:
Though I halt in pace,
　　Yet I creep
To the throne of grace.

Then let wrath remove;
Love will do the deed:
　　For with love
Stony hearts will bleed.　　　　　　　　　20

Love is swift of foot;
Love's a man of war,
　　And can shoot,
And can hit from far.

Who can scape his bow?
That which wrought on thee,
        Brought thee low,
Needs must work on me.

Throw away thy rod;
Though man frailties hath,   30
        Thou art God:
Throw away thy wrath.

JOHN MILTON *On the Detraction Which Followed upon My Writing Certain Treatises* [1]

I did but prompt the age to quit their clogs
By the known rules of ancient liberty,
When straight a barbarous noise environs me
Of owls and cuckoos, asses, apes, and dogs;
As when those hinds that were transformed to frogs
Railed at Latona's twin-born progeny
Which after held the sun and moon in fee.
But this is got by casting pearls to hogs
That bawl for freedom in their senseless mood,
And still revolt when truth would set them free.   10
License they mean when they cry Liberty;
For who loves that must first be wise and good.
But from that mark how far they rove we see,
For all this waste of wealth and loss of blood.

JAMES STEPHENS *A Glass of Beer*

The lanky hank of a she in the inn over there
Nearly killed me for asking the loan of a glass of beer:
May the devil grip the whey-faced slut by the hair,
And beat bad manners out of her skin for a year.

---

[1] Between 1643 and 1645 Milton published his prose tracts in favor of divorce. He compares the outcry against him to the behavior of the peasants who tried to keep the goddess Latona and her twin babies—Apollo and Diana, deities of the sun and the moon respectively—from drinking at a pool. Latona turned her tormenters into frogs. (See Ovid's *Metamorphoses*, VI.) Jupiter was the twins' father; Latona was fleeing the wrath of his wife, Juno. *How does Milton's use of this legend serve both to reinforce the impression of his own wise and noble aims and to justify his indignation against his critics?*

That parboiled imp, with the hardest jaw you will see
On virtue's path, and a voice that would rasp the dead,
Came roaring and raging the minute she looked at me,
And threw me out of the house on the back of my head!

If I asked her master he'd give me a cask a day;
But she with the beer at hand, not a gill would arrange!   10
May she marry a ghost and bear him a kitten and may
The High King of Glory permit her to get the mange.

ANONYMOUS *Pay Day at Coal Creek* [1]

Pay day, pay day, oh, pay day,
Pay day at Coal Creek tomorrow,
Pay day at Coal Creek tomorrow.

Pay day, pay day, oh, pay day,
Pay day don't come at Coal Creek no more.
Pay day don't come no more.

Bye-bye, bye-bye, oh, bye-bye,
Bye-bye, my woman, I'm gone.
Bye-bye, my woman, I'm gone.

You'll miss me, you'll miss me, you'll miss me.   10
You'll miss me when I'm gone.
You'll miss me when I'm gone.

I'm a poor boy, I'm a poor boy, I'm a poor boy—
I'm a poor boy and a long ways from home.
I'm a poor boy and a long ways from home.

Easy rider, oh, easy rider, oh, easy rider—
Oh, easy rider, but you'll leave the rail some time.
Oh, easy rider, but you'll leave the rail some time.

Pay day, pay day, oh, pay day,
Pay day don't come to Coal Creek no more.   20
Pay day don't come no more.

---

[1] Coal Creek, Tennessee, was the site of an explosion that forced closing of the coal mine there. *To what extent is this song a purely personal response to the closing? Is there an impersonal element in the language?*

LANGSTON HUGHES *Down and Out* [1]

Baby, if you love me
Help me when I'm down and out.
If you love me, baby,
Help me when I'm down and out,
I'm a po' gal
Nobody gives a damn about.

The credit man's done took ma clothes
And rent time's nearly here.
I'd like to buy a straightenin' comb,
And I need a dime fo' beer.   10
I need a dime fo' beer.

PHILIP LARKIN *Toads*

Why should I let the toad *work*
    Squat on my life?
Can't I use my wit as a pitchfork
    And drive the brute off?

Six days of the week it soils
    With its sickening poison—
Just for paying a few bills!
    That's out of proportion.

Lots of folk live on their wits:
    Lecturers, lispers,   10
Losels, loblolly-men, louts—
    They don't end as paupers;

Lots of folk live up lanes
    With fires in a bucket,
Eat windfalls and tinned sardines—
    They seem to like it.

[1] This poem is modeled on blues songs like *Pay Day at Coal Creek*, though its subject belongs to another class of blues songs. *Does it differ in the character of its voice and tone from such anonymous songs?*

Their nippers have got bare feet,
    Their unspeakable wives
Are skinny as whippets—and yet
    No one actually *starves*.   20

Ah, were I courageous enough
    To shout *Stuff your pension!*
But I know, all too well, that's the stuff
    That dreams are made on:

For something sufficiently toad-like
    Squats in me, too;
Its hunkers are heavy as hard luck,
    And cold as snow,

And will never allow me to blarney
    My way to getting   30
The fame and the girl and the money
    All at one sitting.

I don't say, one bodies the other
    One's spiritual truth;
But I do say it's hard to lose either,
    When you have both.

EZRA POUND   *The Study in Aesthetics*

The very small children in patched clothing,
Being smitten with an unusual wisdom,
Stopped in their play as she passed them
And cried up from their cobbles:

        Guarda! Ahi, guarda! ch' è be'a! [1]

But three years after this
I heard the young Dante, whose last name I do not know—
For there are, in Sirmione, twenty-eight young Dantes and thirty-four
    Catulli;
And there had been a great catch of sardines,
And his elders   10

---

[1] *Look. Oh, look! How beautiful! (How does this outcry affect the tone of the whole poem, which is set by the main speaker?)*

Were packing them in the great wooden boxes
For the market in Brescia, and he
Leapt about, snatching at the bright fish
And getting in both of their ways;
And in vain they commanded him to *sta fermo!*
And when they would not let him arrange
The fish in the boxes
He stroked those which were already arranged,
Murmuring for his own satisfaction
This identical phrase: 20

   Ch' è be'a.

And at this I was mildly abashed.

E. E. CUMMINGS: *plato told*[1]

plato told

him:he couldn't
believe it(jesus

told him;he
wouldn't believe
it(lao

tsze
certainly told
him,and general
(yes   10

mam)
sherman;
and even
(believe it
or

not)you
told him:i told
him:we told him
he didn't believe it,no

---

[1] American scrap-iron sold to Japan before World War II was used to manufacture ammunition and weapons. The "Sixth Avenue El" was part of New York City's transit system until dismantled and scrapped.

sir)it took
a nipponized bit of
the old sixth

avenue
el:in the top of his head:to tell

him

CHARLES OLSON   *Maximus, to Himself*

I have had to learn the simplest things
last. Which made for difficulties.
Even at sea I was slow, to get the hand out, or to cross
a wet deck.
          The sea was not, finally, my trade.
But even my trade, at it, I stood estranged
from that which was most familiar. Was delayed,
and not content with the man's argument
that such postponement
is now the nature of   10
obedience,
          that we are all late
          in a slow time,
          that we grow up many
          And the single
          is not easily
          known

It could be, though the sharpness (the *achiote*)
I note in others,
makes more sense   20
than my own distances. The agilities

          they show daily
          who do the world's
          businesses
          And who do nature's
          as I have no sense
          I have done either

I have made dialogues,
have discussed ancient texts,
have thrown what light I could, offered   30
what pleasures
doceat allows

                    But the known?
This, I have had to be given,
a life, love, and from one man
the world.

             Tokens.
             But sitting here
             I look out as a wind
             and water man, testing   40
             And missing
             some proof

I know the quarters
of the weather, where it comes from,
where it goes. But the stem of me,
this I took from their welcome,
or their rejection, of me

             And my arrogance
             was neither diminished
             nor increased,   50
             by the communication

                    2

It is undone business
I speak of, this morning,
with the sea
stretching out
from my feet

Sylvia Plath *Daddy*

You do not do, you do not do
Any more, black shoe
In which I have lived like a foot
For thirty years, poor and white,
Barely daring to breathe or Achoo!

Daddy, I have had to kill you.
You died before I had time—
Marble-heavy, a bag full of God,
Ghastly statue with one grey toe
Big as a Frisco seal   10

And a head in the freakish Atlantic
Where it pours bean green over blue
In the waters off beautiful Nauset.
I used to pray to recover you.
Ach, du!

In the German tongue, in the Polish town
Scraped flat by the roller
Of wars, wars, wars.
But the name of the town is common.
My Polack friend   20

Says there are a dozen or two.
So I never could tell where you
Put your foot, your root,
I never could talk to you.
The tongue stuck in my jaw.

It stuck in a barb wire snare.
Ich, ich, ich, ich!
I could hardly speak.
I thought every German was you.
And the language obscene   30

An engine, an engine
Chuffing me off like a Jew.
A Jew to Dachau, Auschwitz, Belsen.
I began to talk like a Jew.
I think I may well be a Jew.

The snows of the Tyrol, the clear beer of Vienna
Are not very pure or true.
With my gypsy ancestress and my weird luck
And my Tarot pack and my Tarot pack
I may be a bit of a Jew.   40

I have always been scared of *you*,
With your Luftwaffe, your gobbledygoo.

And your neat moustache
And your Aryan eye, bright blue.
Panzer-man, panzer-man, o You!

Not God but a swastika
So black no sky could squeak through.
Every woman adores a Fascist,
The boot in the face, the brute
Brute heart of a brute like you.   50

You stand at the blackboard, daddy,
In the picture I have of you,
A cleft in your chin instead of your foot
But no less a devil for that, no not
Any less the black man who

Bit my pretty red heart in two.
I was ten when they buried you.
At twenty I tried to die
And get back, back, back to you.
I thought even the bones would do.   60

But they pulled me out of the sack,
And they stuck me together with glue.
And then I knew what to do.
I made a model of you,
A man in black with a Meinkampf look

And a love of the rack and the screw.
And I said I do, I do.
So daddy, I'm finally through.
The black telephone's off at the root,
The voices just can't worm through.   70

If I've killed one man, I've killed two—
The vampire who said he was you
And drank my blood for a year—
Seven years, if you want to know.
Daddy, you can lie back now.

There's a stake in your fat black heart
And the villagers never liked you.
They are dancing and stamping on you.
They always *knew* it was you.
Daddy, daddy, you bastard, I'm through.   80

II

RITUAL AND INCANTATION

What is it that makes a good poem seem important and valuable? Ultimately—given a right response to its voice, its imagery, its whole movement—we feel that not only have we been afforded a rare sort of pleasure but that also we have been brought keenly into touch with our own common humanity—its realities, motives, aspirations.

We can understand the satisfaction of such an insight quite easily if we remember that thought and feeling are as real as money, as fateful as war, and as full of social meaning as marriage. In poetry and the other arts our full consciousness of ourselves as individual human beings capable of the widest range of imaginative projection and emotional sympathy goes into action. We forget that the origins of art are in large part practical: Among the first poems were chants to bring rain. Heads were carved on war-clubs to attract enemy heads. Charms were performed to compel love. The poet, even in ages far removed from a literal belief in magic, has never lost touch with his ancient practical functions. Though the poems of more sophisticated times and peoples run less to rain-making than to rendering vivid and concrete the most meaningful realizations of life, they still conjure up with dramatic intensity a valued attitude or a desired state of affairs. Consider, for example, *Psalm* 137, one significant instance among many in the Old Testament of this social and psychological function of poetry.

Psalm 137

By the rivers of Babylon,
There we sat down, yea, we wept,
When we remembered Zion.
We hanged our harps
Upon the willows in the midst thereof.
For there they that carried us away captive required of us a song,
And they that wasted us required of us mirth, saying,
"Sing us one of the songs of Zion."
How shall we sing the Lord's song
In a strange land?   10
If I forget thee, O Jerusalem,
Let my right hand forget her cunning.
If I do not remember thee,
Let my tongue cleave to the roof of my mouth;
If I prefer not Jerusalem above my chief joy.
Remember, O Lord, the children of Edom in the day of Jerusalem;

Who said, "Raze it, raze it, even to the foundation thereof."
O daughter of Babylon, who art to be destroyed;
Happy shall he be that rewardeth thee as thou hast served us.
Happy shall he be that taketh and dasheth thy little ones against the
    stones.   20

This is a seventeenth-century English translation of an ancient Hebrew song about the sorrows of a people in exile and in bondage. The singer laments the fate of the Jews under Babylonian rule, and we watch his passions as they well up in four brief movements, each more intense than the one before. First there is an almost calm description of the Jews' sense of loss; then an ironic comment on the callousness of the oppressor; then a nostalgic series of lines praising Jerusalem and vowing never to forget her; and finally a bitter, shocking curse directed against the Babylonians.

In *Psalm* 137 we see strong traces of the way a passionate and practical people used (and still use) poetry. In the first place the poem is not just something to sit and read at one's leisure, and then perhaps pass a judgment on. It is something sung or chanted, and experienced as part of a more or less complicated religious ritual. It speaks for the group; or rather the poet makes no real distinction between himself and his people. Like a war-dance or a prayer or a parade it is a vital *gesture* of the group. It is a way of saying things commonly felt or understood, or at least of hinting at them, with style. The style here lies partly in the ordered way in which the emotion becomes more and more savage, until at the end it is almost beyond control. It lies, too, in the skilful parallelisms (the clauses beginning with "we," the others beginning with "they," the repetitions of "if" and "happy"), and in the alternation of the shorter and longer lines. But most of all, doubtless, it lies in the words and phrases arranged in these ways—the expressions of painful memory, such as "we sat down, yea, we wept"; and the expressions of determination, such as "Let my right hand forget her cunning"; and the hot anger of the language of destruction in the concluding lines. All these emotional turns of speech do perform a kind of magic. They make the hated past seem real again; they bring the triumphant, avenging future fiercely to life. It is easy, then, with this particular piece, to see how much the form of poetry has in common with the form of prayer. And indeed, poetry and prayer do have the same origins in sacred ritual; in fact, they are indistinguishable from one another in their earliest known forms.

This early connection with prayer and ritual tells us much about the ancient motivations still present in poetry. The most striking of these motivations, quite clearly, is a desire for the *power* to be achieved through incantation. The poet of the Psalm puts himself and others into a half-hypnotized state. In that state they act out a dream of liberation and revenge. Each individual listener becomes part of a rhythmic, ritualized group movement and gains a sense of power through his spiritual unity with the group. He is able to let himself go and purify himself by giving vent to the real emotions that ordinary life forces him to suppress. And this release of his innermost self, which gives him the feeling of power, seems to him a revelation of something divine. In his *Indians of the Americas*, John Collier has described a ceremonial dance of the Pueblos that is similar in effect, though of course much more vivid and immediate (for most people) than even the greatest poem could be:

> How in many Pueblo sacred dances the oblivion of self and the corresponding inrush of power becomes almost terrifying, is known to all who frequent the dances. . . . The occasion as a whole was a summoning by the tribe of spirits of the wild, elements or cosmic kin known from ages gone by; and a summoning from within the breast of capacities and loves which had formed the ancient life and must sustain its present and future. As the hours moved on, a displacement of human and mystical factors seemed to take place. The rejoicing was not only a human rejoicing; and that marvelous ever-renewed, ever-increasing, ever-changing leap and rush of song was not only human song. A threshold had been shifted, forces of the wild and of the universe had heard the call and had taken the proffered dominion. That is what the tribe believed; that is how it seemed—physical actuality in a thunderstorm or amid ocean breakers seems no more certain. . . . A strange release of energies took place. . . . the dynamic potentiality of ancient beliefs was realized, and. . . . there was expressed a rejoicing, passionate and yet almost coldly exalted, and the fleshly raiment appeared to fall away.

Such communal "oblivion of the self" is rarely experienced through the arts nowadays, though we have seen approaches to it in Beat-poetry audiences of the 1950's and among lovers of rock and other pop music. Yet the ritual motivation, the identification by an act of wilful imagination with something larger than oneself, remains as strong if not as obvious as ever. The importance of such an identification is one of the main themes of modern poetry, and has in fact made itself felt throughout the history of the art. A hundred years ago, Walt Whitman in his *Song of Myself* described a moment of mystical identification with the divine meaning that he believed possessed everything in the universe:

> Swiftly arose and spread around me the peace and knowledge that pass
>   all the argument of the earth,
> And I know that the hand of God is the promise of my own,
> And I know that the spirit of God is the brother of my own,
> And that all the men ever born are also my brothers, and the women
>   my sisters and lovers,

And that a kelson of the creation is love,
And limitless are leaves stiff or drooping in the fields,
And brown ants in the little wells beneath them,
And mossy scabs of the worm fence, heap'd stones, elder, mullein and
    poke-weed.

Even more than this, many poems have the form of actual prayers;
many make use of religious and mythological names and incidents; and
ritualistic literary forms have retained their appeal for both poet and
reader. This ritualism is not always solemn. Magic and religion were so
intimate a part of the life of primitive peoples that they could often be
used lightly, almost casually, with vivid and even comic irony:

ROBERT GRAVES *The Traveller's Curse After Misdirection* [1]

May they wander stage by stage
Of the same vain pilgrimage,
Stumbling on, age after age,
Night and day, mile after mile,
At each and every step, a stile;
At each and every stile, withal,
May they catch their feet and fall;
At each and every fall they take,
May a bone within them break;
And may the bones that break within   10
Not be, for variation's sake,
Now rib, now thigh, now arm, now shin,
But always, without fail, THE NECK.

All poetry, indeed, has a ritual character. It organizes its subject matter
into a ceremonious, patterned dance of sounds, rhythms, images, and
thoughts. Poets have always felt and used the power of incantation, the
hypnotic effect of chanting and of simple repetition. A clear example is
Vachel Lindsay's *The Congo*, which begins almost as if it were created
to illustrate the connection between poetry and ritual.

Fat black bucks in a wine-barrel room,
Barrel-house kings, with feet unstable,
Sagged and reeled and pounded on the table,
Pounded on the table,
Beat an empty barrel with the handle of a broom,
Hard as they were able,
Boom, boom, BOOM.
With a silk umbrella and the handle of a broom,

[1] From the Welsh.

Boomlay, boomlay, boomlay, BOOM.
THEN I had religion, THEN I had a vision.   10
I could not turn from their revel in derision.
THEN I SAW THE CONGO, CREEPING THROUGH THE
    BLACK,
CUTTING THROUGH THE FOREST WITH A GOLDEN
    TRACK.

Vachel Lindsay was an extraordinary *performer* of his poetry, as recordings of his readings will demonstrate. It is important to read the
foregoing lines aloud, setting up a syncopated beat, booming out the
"BOOMS" and the other capitalized words, and virtually singing a
good many of the lines. Apart from Lindsay's originality, a forgotten
tradition of poetry recitation, revival oratory, and popular preaching in
the countryside lies behind his enormous rhythmic range. Incantation,
the summoning up of a vision, and the creation of an atmosphere of
strangeness and awe are built into the passage. Lindsay's *chanting* quality
was characteristic of many of the most popular poet-performers of his
generation. Carl Sandburg's readings (complete with banjo, for he was
a noted collector and singer of folk-songs as well) were famous for the
rocking, steady, impressive cadences he sustained. Both Yeats and Frost,
too, read in such a way as to minimize the naturalness that was so important an aspect of their poetic mastery and to emphasize rhythmic recurrence.

When, after World War II, Dylan Thomas almost single-handedly
revived the popularity of public readings, it was the rich, deep sound of
his voice that impressed his audiences most—an insistent, defiant, swelling preacher's sort of voice that was as resonant as an organ. Many of
his poems are spells against death, or conjurings of a vision of prenatal
experience or of man as the mysterious carrier of universal, transcendent
energies. Thomas, in his poems, often took on the role of a modern secular
shaman or prophet, singing the divinity of the material universe and
asserting the unyielding will of life despite the destructive power of both
nature and society:

And death shall have no dominion.
Dead men naked they shall be one
With the man in the wind and the west moon:
When their bones are picked clean and the clean bones gone,
They shall have stars at elbow and foot;
Though they go mad they shall be sane,
Though they sink through the sea they shall rise again;
Though lovers be lost love shall not;
And death shall have no dominion. . . .

At a later point, in the mid-1950's, a group of American poets—among whom the foremost was Allen Ginsberg—won huge audiences by work that combined the cadenced rhythms of prophetic writing (the Bible, Blake, Whitman) and of inspirational revolutionary rhetoric with personal tones of anguish, outrage, mockery, and exaltation. After a period of extreme postwar conservatism, this work released a great deal of pent-up hostility against Philistine repression, whether political, moral, or simply genteel.

> America when will you be angelic?
> When will you take off your clothes?
> When will you look at yourself through the grave?
> When will you be worthy of your million Trotskyites?
> America why are your libraries full of tears?
> America when will you send your eggs to India?
> I'm sick of your insane demands.

The passage by Ginsberg just quoted is mild in comparison with some of the hilarious, manic, hysterical, or high rhetorical outbursts scattered through his poetry. It does, however, show his extreme dependence on parallel constructions that are half wry political slogans and half the language of exhortation or prayer. His basic challenge to conformist attitudes and his call for a new morality of personal liberation and frankness are couched in a series of provocatively chanted questions and underlined by the contemptuous sentence at the end. Poems like *America* released and at the same time concentrated the frustrated emotions of an intellectual generation. Whatever their purely poetic value, they served a powerful ritualistic function that created a state of ecstatic enthusiasm in many readers and hearers.

It is truly striking how pervasively the incantatory mode enters poetry. We have just seen some very obvious instances, but a great deal of poetry can be grasped only when we realize how quickly or subtly the pitch of incantation can enter and leave a poem. It is easy enough to see its workings in lines like these by Wordsworth:

> And O, ye Fountains, Meadows, Hills, and Groves,
> Forebode not any severing of our loves!

The old-fashioned diction, together with the capitalization of words that deifies the places apostrophized, makes the pitch as clear as would musical scoring. So too when Yeats introduces *A Dialogue of Self and Soul* (pages 512–514) with a speech by the Soul that reverberates out of some cavernous, unreachable depth:

> I summon to the winding ancient stair;
> Set all your mind upon the steep ascent. . . .

It is virtually a voice from Heaven, a doomsday voice. And the psychological exorcism of her father performed by Sylvia Plath in *Daddy* (pages 21–23) demands a voice at once jeering and thoroughly witchlike in its invocation of murderous black magic.

But there is a *playful* side to poetic ritual, perhaps even in the loftiest and grimmest and most primitive poems. It is a special kind of "play"— that of the mind over all the many different relationships (possibilities, similarities, differences) that exist among the varied ideas and objects that come into anyone's experience. The poet takes it for granted that to allow our minds free play among these relationships is a fine and human thing, and the words that suggest them are his raw materials and his delight. "Poetry," Wallace Stevens tells us, "is a satisfying of the desire for resemblance. . . . In the act of satisfying the desire it touches the sense of reality, heightens it, intensifies it." And he illustrates one way in which a poet's mind works in this manner:

> Take, for example, a beach extending as far as the eye can reach bordered, on the one hand, by trees and, on the other, by the sea. The sky is cloudless and the sun is red. In what sense do the objects in this scene resemble each other? There is enough green in the sea to relate it to the palms. There is enough of the sky reflected in the water to create a resemblance, in some sense, between them. The sand is yellow between the green and the blue. In short, the light alone creates a unity not only in the recedings of distance, where differences become invisible, but also in the contacts of close sight. So, too, sufficiently generalized, each man resembles all other men, each woman resembles all other women, this year resembles last year. The beginning of time will, no doubt, resemble the end of time. One world is said to resemble another.[2]

William Blake put the matter more concisely almost two centuries ago at the beginning of his *Auguries of Innocence:*

> To see a World in a Grain of Sand,
> And a Heaven in a Wild Flower,
> Hold Infinity in the palm of your hand,
> And Eternity in an hour.

Blake had an amazing ability to put himself into the half-hypnotic state of mind needed to make the projections of his imagination seem real. Primitive man, we are told, had to visualize the success of his harvest or

---

[2] Wallace Stevens, *The Necessary Angel.*

hunt or war-expedition in order to believe in the real meaning of his daily activity. He had to see the completed harvest implicit in the work of sowing. Therefore, the projections of his imagination had to be made "real" through the tribal ceremonies. These ceremonies were enactments of his prayer that his plans might be fulfilled—intense games in which it was pretended that they were coming true and finally, at the climax, that they had done so. Children's play, as we have seen, often has the same kind of intensity and function, for the child too is getting in touch with reality through giving his imaginative energies free play; and very often he is projecting himself as an adult—trying on this or that personality or occupation, seeing himself in the role of father or mother, connecting the way he is now with the way he may some day be.

All this activity of the imagination, then, is quite practical, not at all "idle dreaming," since it—alone of all human activities—is what enables people to give meaning to the routine of their lives. A life without meaning would be one without any projected purpose or value, such a life as absolutely nobody could bring himself to accept. Even the poorest human derelict has his pathetic daydreams, the last surviving remnants of the fruitful ritual projections of the fulfilled life. He visualizes, it may be—

> . . . . someplace unreal
> where everybody goes after something happens,
> set up in the air, safe, a room in a hotel.
> A brass bed, military hair brushes,
> a couple of coats, trousers, maybe a dress
> on a chair or draped on the floor.
> This room is not on earth, feel the air,
> warm like heaven and far away.[3]

But Blake's stanza about seeing "a World in a Grain of Sand" and "a Heaven in a Wild Flower" goes beyond the visions of primitive and child, let alone the pipedreams of a lost soul. He is bending our attention, prophetically, to the meaning of all life, to the moral, religious, and philosophical faiths without which existence might seem pointless. Blake's lines must not be read merely as pretty sentiments, but as a revelation of the vast interpenetrating nature of experience on the one hand (the things we see, do, and feel) and the active human imagination on the other.

---

[3] Horace Gregory, *Longface Mahoney Discusses Heaven*. Notice how, in these lines, the speaker surrounds himself longingly with the atmosphere of safety, comfort, cleanliness, and a woman's companionship. The "heaven" he creates for himself is a kind of "minimum standard" existence—yet there is emotional force in the image of these commonplace objects because they are the projections of unfulfilled need and desire, just as the images in the Hebrew psalm were.

Poems: Ritual and Incantation

The grouping of the poems that follow speaks for itself. We see how ritual and incantation have entered into the lives of adults and children in all ages. Whether we consider the lives of the ancient Hebrews, the American Indians, or the Eskimos, or observe the ceremonial rites connected with the annual spring sowing and harvest reaping—illustrated here in the seventeenth-century poem by Herrick, the earlier action song by Peele, and the timeless children's rhyme *Here we come a-piping*—we find the chantlike music of incantation to be the voice of a universal magic. The modern sophisticated poems included here show the continuing power of this voice, even when it is uttered by a highly individualistic speaker in an increasingly skeptical age. The *Two Eskimo Songs* of Ted Hughes subtly introduce modern scientific and historical consciousness and modern tragic sensibility into poems that follow primitive models created in a purely oral tradition. Allen Ginsberg's poem is modeled on the *Kaddish*, the Hebrew prayer for the dead. The poems by Shelley, Dylan Thomas, and Galway Kinnell are relatively complex incantations with varying political, social, religious, and philosophical implications. In each of these nineteenth- and twentieth-century poems, a very self-conscious artist unites a personal and a public or universal voice into one voice that speaks to his own heart and to the hearts of all men.

Torlino *Therefore I Must Tell the Truth* [1] (Navajo)

I am ashamed before the earth;
I am ashamed before the heavens;
I am ashamed before the dawn;
I am ashamed before the evening twilight;
I am ashamed before the blue sky;
I am ashamed before the darkness;
I am ashamed before the sun.
I am ashamed before that standing within me which speaks with me.
Some of these things are always looking at me.
I am never out of sight.   10
Therefore I must tell the truth.
That is why I always tell the truth.
I hold my word tight to my breast.

[1] Translated by Washington Matthews. Torlino's oath to tell the truth was sworn before he recounted the Navajo cosmogony to Matthews.

ANONYMOUS *Incantation for Rain* [1] *(Navajo)*

The corn grows up.
The waters of the dark clouds drop, drop.
The rain descends.
The waters from the corn leaves drop, drop.
The rain descends.
The waters from the plants drop, drop.
The corn grows up.
The waters of the dark mists drop, drop.

[1] Translated by Washington Matthews. Torlino's oath to tell the truth was sworn before he recounted the Navajo cosmogony to Matthews.

ANONYMOUS *Magic Words for Hunting Seal* [1]
(Netsilik Eskimo)

O sea goddess Nuliajuk,
when you were a little unwanted orphan girl
we let you drown.
You fell in the water
and when you hung onto the kayaks, crying,
we cut off your fingers.
So you sank into the sea
and your fingers turned into
the innumerable seals.

You sweet orphan Nuliajuk,   10
I beg you now
bring me a gift,
not anything from the land
but a gift from the sea,
something that will make a nice soup.
Dare I say it right out?
I want a seal!

You dear little orphan,
creep out of the water
panting on this beautiful shore,   20
puh, puh, like this, puh, puh,
O welcome gift
in the shape of a seal!

[1] English version by Edward Field.

Ted Hughes   *Two Eskimo Songs* [1]

i *Fleeing from Eternity*

Man came running faceless over earth
Eyeless and mouthless baldface he ran

He knew he trod the stone of death
He knew he trod the stone of death
He knew he was a ghost it was all he knew.

Feeling a million years under stones
He found a slug
                but the lightning struck it
It fumed to a scorched halo on his numbed palm.

Feeling a million years under stones   10
He found a trout
                but a white hot frost fell
From the exhaust of a star the fish frittered to crystals.

Feeling a million years under stones
He found a mouse
                but a sigh of time
Breathed it to crumbs of knuckles.

He got a sharp rock he gashed holes in his face
Through the blood and pain he looked at the earth.

He gashed again deeper and through the blood and pain
He screeched at the lightning, at the frost, and at time.

Then, lying among the bones on the cemetery earth,
He saw a woman singing out of her belly.   20

He gave her eyes and a mouth, in exchange for the song.
She wept blood, she cried pain.

The pain and the blood were life. But the man laughed—

---

[1] *Find as many points of comparison and contrast as you can between these songs, modeled by Hughes on genuine folk-materials, and the Eskimo and Indian incantations that precede them. Is there an ultimate difference in the kind of speaking voice you find, and in the essential effects created?*

The song was worth it.

The woman felt cheated.

II *How Water Began to Play*

Water wanted to live
It went to the sun it came weeping back
Water wanted to live
It went to the trees they burned it came weeping back
They rotted it came weeping back
Water wanted to live
It went to the flowers they crumpled it came weeping back
It wanted to live
It went to the womb it met blood
It came weeping back   10
It went to the womb it met knife
It came weeping back
It went to the womb it met maggot and rottenness
It came weeping back it wanted to die

It went to time it went through the stone door
It came weeping back
It went searching through all space for nothingness
It came weeping back it wanted to die

Till it had no weeping left

It lay at the bottom of all things   20

Utterly worn out   utterly clear

GEORGE PEELE   *The Song at the Well*

(from *The Old Wives' Tale*)

(*Enter Zantippa with a pitcher to the well. A head comes up with ears of corn, and she combs them in her lap.*)

VOICE

Gently dip, but not too deep,
For fear you make the golden beard to weep.
Fair maiden, white and red,
Comb me smooth, and stroke my head,
And thou shalt have some cockell-bread.

(A second head comes up full of gold, which she combs into her lap.)

SECOND HEAD

Gently dip, but not too deep,
For fear thou make the golden beard to weep.   10
Fair maiden, white and red,
Comb me smooth and stroke my head,
And every hair a sheaf shall be,
And every sheaf a golden tree.

ROBERT HERRICK   *Corinna's Going A-Maying*

Get up, get up for shame! The blooming morn
Upon her wings presents the god unshorn.
    See how Aurora throws her fair,
    Fresh-quilted colors through the air.
    Get up, sweet slug-a-bed, and see
    The dew bespangling herb and tree!
Each flower has wept and bowed toward the east
Above an hour since, yet you not drest;
    Nay! not so much as out of bed?
    When all the birds have matins said   10
    And sung their thankful hymns, 'tis sin,
    Nay, profanation, to keep in,
Whenas a thousand virgins on this day
Spring sooner than the lark, to fetch in May.

Rise and put on your foliage, and be seen
To come forth, like the springtime, fresh and green,
    And sweet as Flora. Take no care
    For jewels for your gown or hair.
    Fear not; the leaves will strew
    Gems in abundance upon you.   20
Besides, the childhood of the day has kept
Against you come, some orient pearls unwept.
    Come, and receive them while the light
    Hangs on the dew-locks of the night;
    And Titan on the eastern hill
    Retires himself, or else stands still
Till you come forth! Wash, dress, be brief in praying;
Few beads are best when once we go a-Maying.

Come, my Corinna, come; and coming, mark
How each field turns a street, each street a park   30
    Made green and trimmed with trees! see how
    Devotion gives each house a bough
    Or branch! each porch, each door, ere this,
    An ark, a tabernacle is,
Made up of white-thorn neatly interwove,
As if here were those cooler shades of love.
    Can such delights be in the street
    And open fields, and we not see't?
    Come, we'll abroad; and let's obey
    The proclamation made for May,   40
And sin no more, as we have done, by staying;
But, my Corinna, come, let's go a-Maying.

There's not a budding boy or girl this day
But is got up and gone to bring in May.
    A deal of youth ere this is come
    Back, and with white-thorn laden home.
    Some have dispatched their cakes and cream,
    Before that we have left to dream;
And some have wept and wooed, and plighted troth,
And chose their priest, ere we can cast off sloth.   50
    Many a green-gown has been given,
    Many a kiss, both odd and even;
    Many a glance, too, has been sent
    From out the eye, love's firmament;
Many a jest told of the keys betraying
This night, and locks picked; yet we're not a-Maying!

Come, let us go, while we are in our prime,
And take the harmless folly of the time!
    We shall grow old apace, and die
    Before we know our liberty.
    Our life is short, and our days run   60
    As fast away as does the sun.
And, as a vapor or a drop of rain,
Once lost, can ne'er be found again,
    So when or you or I are made
    A fable, song, or fleeting shade,
    All love, all liking, all delight
    Lies drowned with us in endless night.
Then, while time serves, and we are but decaying,
Come, my Corinna, come, let's go a-Maying.   70

ANONYMOUS   *Here we come a-piping*

Here we come a-piping,
In Springtime and in May;
Green fruit a-ripening,
And Winter fled away.
The Queen she sits upon the strand,
Fair as lily, white as wand;
Seven billows on the sea,
Horses riding fast and free,
And bells beyond the sand.

from THE KING JAMES BIBLE   *Psalm* 23

The Lord is my shepherd; I shall not want.
He maketh me to lie down in green pastures;
He leadeth me beside the still waters.
He restoreth my soul;
He leadeth me in the paths of righteousness for his name's sake.
Yea, though I walk through the valley of the shadow of death,
I will fear no evil: for thou art with me;
Thy rod and thy staff they comfort me,
Thou preparest a table before me in the presence of mine enemies:
Thou anointest my head with oil; my cup runneth over.   10
Surely goodness and mercy shall follow me all the days of my life,
And I will dwell in the house of the Lord for ever.

PERCY BYSSHE SHELLEY   *Ode to the West Wind*

I

O wild West Wind, thou breath of Autumn's being,
Thou, from whose unseen presence the leaves dead
Are driven, like ghosts from an enchanter fleeing,

Yellow, and black, and pale, and hectic red,
Pestilence-stricken multitudes: O thou,
Who chariotest to their dark wintry bed

The wingèd seeds, where they lie cold and low,
Each like a corpse within its grave, until
Thine azure sister of the Spring shall blow

Her clarion o'er the dreaming earth, and fill   10
(Driving sweet buds like flocks to feed in air)
With living hues and odours plain and hill:

Wild Spirit, which art moving everywhere;
Destroyer and preserver; hear, oh, hear!

II

Thou on whose stream, mid the steep sky's commotion,
Loose clouds like earth's decaying leaves are shed,
Shook from the tangled boughs of Heaven and Ocean,

Angels of rain and lightning: there are spread
On the blue surface of thine aery surge,
Like the bright hair uplifted from the head   20

Of some fierce Maenad, even from the dim verge
Of the horizon to the zenith's height,
The locks of the approaching storm. Thou dirge

Of the dying year, to which this closing night
Will be the dome of a vast sepulchre
Vaulted will all thy congregated might

Of vapours, from whose solid atmosphere
Black rain, and fire, and hail will burst: oh, hear!

III

Thou who didst waken from his summer dreams
The blue Mediterranean, where he lay,   30
Lulled by the coil of his crystalline streams,

Beside a pumice isle in Baia's bay,
And saw in sleep old palaces and towers
Quivering within the wave's intenser day,

All overgrown with azure moss and flowers
So sweet, the sense faints picturing them! Thou
For whose path the Atlantic's level powers

Cleave themselves into chasms, while far below
The sea-blooms and the oozy woods which wear
The sapless foliage of the ocean, know   40

Thy voice, and suddenly grow gray with fear,
And tremble and despoil themselves: oh, hear!

IV

If I were a dead leaf thou mightest bear;
If I were a swift cloud to fly with thee;
A wave to pant beneath thy power, and share

The impulse of thy strength, only less free
Than thou, O uncontrollable! If even
I were as in my boyhood, and could be

The comrade of thy wanderings over Heaven,
As then, when to outstrip thy skiey speed   50
Scarce seemed a vision; I would ne'er have striven

As thus with thee in prayer in my sore need.
Oh, lift me as a wave, a leaf, a cloud!
I fall upon the thorns of life! I bleed!

A heavy weight of hours has chained and bowed
One too like thee: tameless, and swift, and proud.

V

Make me thy lyre, even as the forest is:
What if my leaves are falling like its own!
The tumult of thy mighty harmonies

Will take from both a deep, autumnal tone,   60
Sweet though in sadness. Be thou, Spirit fierce,
My spirit! Be thou me, impetuous one!

Drive my dead thoughts over the universe
Like withered leaves to quicken a new birth!
And, by the incantation of this verse,

Scatter, as from an unextinguished hearth
Ashes and sparks, my words among mankind!
Be through my lips to unawakened earth

The trumpet of a prophecy! O, Wind,
If Winter comes, can Spring be far behind?

Dylan Thomas *Ceremony after a Fire Raid*

I

Myselves
The grievers
Grieve
Among the street burned to tireless death
A child of a few hours
With its kneading mouth
Charred on the black breast of the grave
The mother dug, and its arms full of fires.

Begin
With singing   10
Sing
Darkness kindled back into beginning
When the caught tongue nodded blind,
A star was broken
Into the centuries of the child
Myselves grieve now, and miracles cannot atone.

Forgive
Us forgive
Us your death that myselves the believers
May hold it in a great flood   20
Till the blood shall spurt,
And the dust shall sing like a bird
As the grains blow, as your death grows, through our heart.

Crying
Your dying
Cry,
Child beyond cockcrow, by the fire-dwarfed
Street we chant the flying sea
In the body bereft.
Love is the last light spoken. Oh   30
Seed of sons in the loin of the black husk left.

II

I know not whether
Adam or Eve, the adorned holy bullock
Or the white ewe lamb
Or the chosen virgin

Laid in her snow
On the altar of London,
Was the first to die
In the cinder of the little skull,
O bride and bride groom   40
O Adam and Eve together
Lying in the lull
Under the sad breast of the head stone
White as the skeleton
Of the garden of Eden.

I know the legend
Of Adam and Eve is never for a second
Silent in my service
Over the dead infants
Over the one   50
Child who was priest and servants,
Word, singers, and tongue
In the cinder of the little skull,
Who was the serpent's
Night fall and the fruit like a sun,
Man and woman undone,
Beginning crumbled back to darkness
Bare as the nurseries
Of the garden of wilderness.

III

Into the organpipes and steeples   60
Of the luminous cathedrals,
Into the weathercocks' molten mouths
Rippling in twelve-winded circles,
Into the dead clock burning the hour
Over the urn of sabbaths
Over the whirling ditch of daybreak
Over the sun's hovel and the slum of fire
And the golden pavements laid in requiems,
Into the bread in a wheatfield of flames,
Into the wine burning like brandy,   70
The masses of the sea
The masses of the sea under
The masses of the infant-bearing sea
Erupt, fountain, and enter to utter for ever
Glory glory glory
The sundering ultimate kingdom of genesis' thunder.

DYLAN THOMAS *And death shall have no dominion*

And death shall have no dominion.
Dead men naked they shall be one
With the man in the wind and the west moon;
When their bones are picked clean and the clean bones gone,
They shall have stars at elbow and foot;
Though they go mad they shall be sane,
Though they sink through the sea they shall rise again;
Though lovers be lost love shall not;
And death shall have no dominion.

And death shall have no dominion.   10
Under the windings of the sea
They lying long shall not die windily;
Twisting on racks when sinews give way,
Strapped to a wheel, yet they shall not break;
Faith in their hands shall snap in two,
And the unicorn evils run them through;
Split all ends up they shan't crack;
And death shall have no dominion.

And death shall have no dominion.
No more may gulls cry at their ears   20
Or waves break loud on the seashores;
Where blew a flower may a flower no more
Lift its head to the blows of the rain;
Though they be mad and dead as nails,
Heads of the characters hammer through daisies;
Break in the sun till the sun breaks down,
And death shall have no dominion.

ALLEN GINSBERG   from *Kaddish for Naomi Ginsberg 1894–1956*

Proem: I

Strange now to think of you, gone without corsets & eyes, while I walk
     on the sunny pavement of Greenwich Village.
downtown Manhattan, clear winter noon, and I've been up all night,
     talking, talking, reading the Kaddish aloud, listening to Ray
     Charles blues shout blind on the phonograph
the rhythm the rhythm—and your memory in my head three years
     after—And read Adonais' last triumphant stanzas aloud—
     wept, realizing how we suffer—

And how Death is that remedy all singers dream of, sing, remember,
    prophesy as in the Hebrew Anthem, or the Buddhist Book of
    Answers—and my own imagination of a withered leaf—at
    dawn—
Dreaming back thru life, Your time—and mine accelerating toward
    Apocalypse,
the final moment—the flower burning in the Day—and what comes
    after,
looking back on the mind itself that saw an American city
a flash away, and the great dream of Me or China, or you and a
    phantom Russia, or a crumpled bed that never existed—
like a poem in the dark—escaped back to Oblivion—
No more to say, and nothing to weep for but the Beings in the Dream,
    trapped in its disappearance,
sighing, screaming with it, buying and selling pieces of phantom, wor-
    shipping each other,
worshipping the God included in it all—longing or inevitability?—
    while it lasts, a Vision—anything more?
It leaps about me, as I go out and walk the street, look back over my
    shoulder, Seventh Avenue, the battlements of window office
    buildings shouldering each other high, under a cloud, tall as
    the sky an instant—and the sky above—an old blue place.
or down the Avenue to the South, to—as I walk toward the Lower
    East Side—where you walked 50 years ago, little girl—from
    Russia, eating the first poisonous tomatoes of America—
    frightened on the dock—
then struggling in the crowds of Orchard Street toward what?—
    toward Newark—
toward candy store, first home-made sodas of the century, hand-
    churned ice cream in backroom on musty brownfloor
    boards—
Toward education marriage nervous breakdown, operation, teaching
    school, and learning to be mad, in a dream—what is this
    life?
Toward the Key in the window—and the great Key lays its head of
    light on top of Manhattan, and over the floor, and lays down
    on the sidewalk—in a single vast beam, moving, as I walk
    down First toward the Yiddish Theater—and the place of
    poverty
you knew, and I know, but without caring now—Strange to have
    moved thru Paterson, and the West, and Europe and here
    again,   19
with the cries of Spaniards now in the doorstoops doors and dark boys
    on the street, fire escapes old as you

—Tho you're not old now, that's left here with me—

Myself, anyhow, maybe as old as the universe—and I guess that dies
    with us—enough to cancel all that comes—What came is
    gone forever every time—

That's good! That leaves it open for no regret—no fear radiators,
    lacklove, torture even toothache in the end—

Though while it comes it is a lion that eats the soul—and the lamb,
    the soul, in us, alas, offering itself in sacrifice to change's
    fierce hunger—hair and teeth—and the roar of bonepain,
    skull bare, break rib, rot-skin, braintricked Implacability.

Ai! ai! we do worse! We are in a fix! And you're out, Death let you
    out, Death had the Mercy, you're done with your century,
    done with God, done with the path thru it—Done with
    yourself at last—Pure—Back to the Babe dark before your
    Father, before us all—before the world—

There, rest. No more suffering for you. I know where you've gone, it's
    good.

No more flowers in the summer fields of New York, no joy now, no
    more fear of Louis,[1]

and no more of his sweetness and glasses, his high school decades,
    debts, loves, frightened telephone calls, conception beds,
    relatives, hands—

No more of sister Elanor,—she gone before you—we kept it secret
    —you killed her—or she killed herself to bear with you—
    an arthritic heart—But Death's killed you both—No
    matter—   29

Nor your memory of your mother, 1915 tears in silent movies weeks
    and weeks—forgetting, agrieve watching Marie Dressler
    address humanity, Chaplin dance in youth,

or Boris Godunov, Chaliapin's at the Met, halling his voice of a weep-
    ing Czar—by standing room with Elanor & Max—watch-
    ing also the Capitalists take seats in Orchestra, white furs,
    diamonds,

with the YPSL's [2] hitch-hiking thru Pennsylvania, in black baggy gym
    skirts pants, photograph of 4 girls holding each other round
    the waist, and laughing eye, too coy, virginal solitude of
    1920

all girls grown old, or dead, now, and that long hair in the grave—
    lucky to have husbands later—

You made it—I came too—Eugene my brother before (still grieving
    now and will gream on to his last stiff hand, as he goes thru
    his cancer—or kill—later perhaps—soon he will think—)

---

[1] Naomi's husband   [2] members of the Young People's Socialist League

And it's the last moment I remember, which I see them all, thru
    myself, now—tho not you
I didn't foresee what you felt—what more hideous gape of bad
    mouth came first—to you—and were you prepared?
To go where? In that Dark—that—in that God? a radiance? A Lord
    in the Void? Like an eye in the black cloud in a dream?
    Adonoi at last, with you?
Beyond my remembrance! Incapable to guess! Not merely the yellow
    skull in the grave, or a box of worm dust, and a stained
    ribbon—Deathshead with Halo? can you believe it?
Is it only the sun that shines once for the mind, only the flash of
    existence, than none ever was?   39
Nothing beyond what we have—what you had—that so pitiful—
    yet Triumph,
to have been there, and changed, like a tree, broken, or flower—fed
    to the ground—but mad, with its petals, colored, thinking
    Great Universe, shaken, cut in the head, leaf stript, hid in an
    egg crate hospital, cloth wrapped, sore—freaked in the
    moon brain, Naughtless.
No flower like that flower, which knew itself in the garden, and
    fought the knife—lost
Cut down by an idiot Snowman's icy—even in the Spring—strange
    ghost thought—some Death—Sharp icicle in his hand—
    crowned with old roses—a dog for his eyes—cock of a
    sweatshop—heart of electric irons.
All the accumulations of life, that wear us out—clocks, bodies, con-
    sciousness, shoe, breasts—begotten sons—your Commu-
    nism—'Paranoia' into hospitals.
You once kicked Elanor in the leg, she died of heart failure later. You
    of stroke. Asleep? within a year, the two of you, sisters in
    death. Is Elanor happy?
Max grieves alive in an office on Lower Broadway, lone large mustache
    over midnight Accountings, not sure. His life passes—as he
    sees—and what does he doubt now? Still dream of making
    money, or that might have made money, hired nurse, had
    children, found even your Immortality, Naomi?
I'll see him soon. Now I've got to cut through—to talk to you—as I
    didn't when you had a mouth.
Forever. And we're bound for that, Forever—like Emily Dickinson's
    horses [3]—headed to the End.
They know the way—These Steeds—run faster than we think—it's
    our own life they cross—and take with them.   49

[3] A reference to Emily Dickinson's poem *Because I could not stop for Death*.

Magnificent, mourned no more, marred of heart, mind behind, married dreamed, mortal changed—Ass and face done with
murder.

In the world, given, flower maddened, made no Utopia, shut
under pine, almed in Earth, balmed in Lone, Jehovah, accept.

Nameless, One Faced, Forever beyond me, beginningless,
endless, Father in death. Tho I am not there for this Prophecy, I am
unmarried, I'm hymnless, I'm Heavenless, headless in blisshood I
would still adore

Thee, Heaven, after Death, only One blessed in Nothingness, not light or darkness, Dayless Eternity—

Take this, this Psalm, from me, burst from my hand in a
day, some of my Time, now given to Nothing—to praise Thee—But
Death

This is the end, the redemption from Wilderness, way for
the Wonderer, House sought for All, black handkerchief washed clean
by weeping—page beyond Psalm—Last change of mine and Naomi
—to God's perfect Darkness—Death, stay thy phantoms!

GALWAY KINNELL   *The Dead Shall Be Raised Incorruptible: 4*

In the Twentieth Century of my trespass on earth,
having exterminated one billion heathens,
heretics, Jews, Moslems, witches, mystical seekers,
black men, Asians, and Christian brothers,
every one of them for his own good,

a whole continent of red men for living in unnatural community
and at the same time having relations with the land,
one billion species of animals for being sub-human,
and ready to take on the bloodthirsty creatures from the other planets,
I, Christian man, groan out this testament of my last will.   10

I give my blood fifty parts polystyrene,
twenty-five parts benzene, twenty-five parts good old gasoline,
to the last bomber pilot aloft, that there shall be one acre
in the dull world where the kissing flower may bloom,
which kisses you so long your bones explode under its lips.

My tongue goes to the Secretary of the Dead
to tell the corpses, "I'm sorry, fellows,
the killing was just one of those things
difficult to pre-visualize—like a cow,
say, getting hit by lightning."   20

My stomach, which has digested
four hundred treaties giving the Indians
eternal right to their land, I give to the Indians,
I throw in my lungs which have spent four hundred years
sucking in good faith on peace pipes.

My soul I leave to the bee
that he may sting it and die, my brain
to the fly, his back the hysterical green color of slime,
that he may suck on it and die, my flesh to the advertising man,
the anti-prostitute, who loathes human flesh for money.   30

I assign my crooked backbone
to the dice maker, to chop up into dice,
for casting lots as to who shall see his own blood
on his shirt front and who his brother's,
for the race isn't to the swift but to the crooked.

To the last man surviving on earth
I give my eyelids worn out by fear, to wear
in his long nights of radiation and silence,
so that his eyes can't close, for regret
is like tears seeping through closed eyelids.   40

I give the emptiness my hand: the pinkie picks no more noses,
slag clings to the black stick of the ring finger,
a bit of flame jets from the tip of the fuck-you finger,
the first finger accuses the heart, which has vanished,
on the thumb stump wisps of smoke ask a ride into the emptiness.

In the Twentieth Century of my nightmare
on earth, I swear on my chromium testicles
to this testament
and last will
of my iron will, my fear of love, my itch for money, and my madness.

Chapter Two

The Craftsman's Work

I

SOME ELEMENTS OF TECHNIQUE

The original meaning of the word "poet," which comes to us from the Greek, is *maker*. A poem is something made, a thing shaped and constructed by conscious craftsmanship out of the resources of language. Those resources include both the common speech of the day and everything in the past that has been said or written. When the poet tries to find phrases that appeal at once to our senses and to our intelligence, he uses *imagery*. When he arranges the sound of the poem in a patterned movement that is at once speech and song, he uses *rhythm*. When he plays with echoes and contrasts of sound, and when he suggests shifting levels of sensation and emotion through subtle reverberations of words and of whole passages, he is creating a larger verbal *"music"* that marks the full energy and achievement of his art.

Ezra Pound, in his essay "How to Read," calls the first of these processes *phanopoeia*: "a casting of images upon the visual imagination." (He might have spoken of *sensuous* imagination instead, since images can appeal to any of our senses, though the visual sense seems the dominant one in poetry.) The second he calls *melopoeia*: the way in which "words are charged, over and above their plain meaning, with some musical property, which directs the bearing or trend of that meaning." The third is *logopoeia*: the overall use of words "not only for their direct meaning" but also to "take count in a special way of habits of usage, of the context we *expect* to find with the word, . . . and of ironical play." Pound's emphasis was not quite identical with ours, but he too was calling attention to poetry as a *process* of sensing the possibilities of language and of organizing or orchestrating them.

It is therefore important that we understand something of the technical problems poets have met and solved. One of the remarkable things about a good poem is that its appeal is not diminished but increased by analysis and study of the right sort. We need to read poems in a humanly sympathetic way and at the same time to think as clearly as possible about what is going on in them. And one way of thinking clearly is to realize from the start that not everything in a poem's appeal can be *logically* accounted for. For instance, there are certain memorable lines whose magic can be recognized but never caught alive in any net of paraphrase or of explanation:

> In the gloom the gold
> Gathers the light about it.
> > EZRA POUND

> To cut across the reflex of a star. . . .
> > WILLIAM WORDSWORTH

> Breaking the silence of the seas
> Among the farthest Hebrides. . . .
> > WILLIAM WORDSWORTH

> Keep up your bright swords, for the dew will rust them.
> > WILLIAM SHAKESPEARE

> And now I
> Foam to wheat, a glitter of seas. . . .
> > SYLVIA PLATH

In such lines as these there is a fusion of music, imagery, and thought which calls forth a more than intellectual response. But the more than rational power to respond to poetry, called "sensibility," must be stimulated by contact with life and with poems, and if possible by much reading aloud and listening to others read aloud. Despite the increased number of public appearances and of recordings by poets in recent years, modern readers often miss this once common experience. Shakespeare's audiences, for instance, were accustomed to hearing poetry whenever they attended the theater. That is, they were used to hearing the whole range of language, from plain colloquial speech to racy dialogue to the most exalted and unfamiliar poetic language. Near the end of *Hamlet*, the dying hero prevents his friend Horatio from committing suicide, asking him to go on living so that he can tell the truth about what has happened. Hamlet's language is natural speech heightened into poetry:

> If thou didst ever hold me in thy heart,
> Absént thee from felicity a while
> And in this harsh world draw thy breath in pain
> To tell my story.

These lines follow a scene of great violence. Their calmer, yet sad, earnest, and affectionate music remained in the audience's ears long after most of them must have forgotten the specific words. This effect comes in part from the dramatic situation, but mainly from the arrangement of images and sounds accompanying that situation and from the way the thoughts are stated—clearly and simply, yet in each line with something in the language that goes beyond literal statement.

The passage contains hardly a single literal statement, yet each phrase, by straining the truth to just the right extent, contributes to the feeling created by the whole speech. It is curious the way a series of literal untruths leads to an insight into truth of a kind. No one can literally hold another person in his heart. To die by suicide is not automatically to achieve "felicity" or perfect happiness; indeed, since Hamlet and Horatio are assumed to be devout medieval Christians, they would be expected to think suicide sinful and punishable by damnation. Finally, no healthy person feels pain at every breath, however "harsh" the world may be. But, as most of us know instinctively, we must not take what people say absolutely literally. We listen to the tone, and we respond to the feelings and the implied meaning built into the language and into the speaker's manner. This is equally true of ordinary conversation and of poetry, save that the poet makes an art of the kind of distortion of speech that enables us to see some truth freshly. Each of Hamlet's exaggerations stresses the emotional state the two friends share—first, their loyal affection for one another; then, their reluctance to go on living after such disaster as they have experienced; finally, a sense of irreversible misery. Hamlet recognizes these states of feeling in his friend, and his appeal is a remarkable gesture of consolation by which Shakespeare brings out the speaker's own gentleness and nobility.

Meanwhile, the mood, tone, and spirit of the situation are communicated also in the music of the verse. The *sounds* are echoing and reechoing one another. Notice the *h*'s, short *e*'s, *l*'s, and *r*'s in the important words *ever*, *hold*, *absént*, *harsh*, *world*, *breath*, and *story*; the long *e*'s of the secondary syllables that provide a constant background of sound—*me*, *thee*, *felicity*, *story*; and the *th*'s and long *i*'s in *thou*, *thy*, *thee*, *while*, *this*, *my*. But the word that echoes longest is *pain*, though it is linked in sound with the other important words only through the consonant *n*, which is also found in *absént*. *Pain* therefore stands out against the flow of patterned sound like a rock against a current, and *pain* is the one word that gives the passage its deepest emotional coloration.

Observe that the third line, which ends in the word *pain*, actually sounds like what the speaker is talking about, like the speech of a man gasping out strongly felt ideas with great difficulty. Whereas the previous line was lilting and fluent, this one makes us pause over almost every one of its ten monosyllabic words—and especially the fourth, fifth, sixth, eighth, and tenth. Tremendous emphasis is gained by this damming-up effect.

All speed is gone from the line by the time we have passed *harsh world draw*, and after the added barrier of *breath* there is almost a full stop at *pain*. The halting effect continues to the very end of the sentence.

A word of caution is necessary here: Sounds do not in themselves convey a meaning. Liquid sounds are lighter and more graceful than gutturals, and there are many other differences among sound-effects, but this does not mean that every *l* or *r* carries a gay, buoyant feeling with it, or every *k* a harsher feeling. However, in a passage with an unusual number of *l*'s and *k*'s we may find an underlying pattern of pure sound effects balanced against one another—an actual music of sounds. If we want to know the connection between this pure sound-pattern and the feeling and thought of the poem, we must note where the most important words fall. In a good poem, there will be a definite relationship between the points of emphasized thought and emotion and the pattern of sound. Unless we are dealing with nonsense rhymes or pure sound-effects, it is the thought and the emotion that give the sounds their meaning. The words in the *Hamlet* passage that we must emphasize because of their meaning are also the words in which the most important sound-effects are found. The *h*'s, *l*'s, and so on become associated with these words and take their emotional effect from their meaning. Thus, since *hold* and *heart* are strongly stressed, the vowels and consonants in them, when repeated in later words, recall them again. Without these important words, the alliteration alone—the musical effect gained by the repetition of sounds, particularly in stressed syllables—could not ordinarily stir us deeply.

We see, therefore, that although its character and origin have some irrational aspects poetry can certainly be understood and analyzed. To try to *write* poems out of calculation alone would be fruitless, but that is another thing altogether from trying with all our sympathies and intelligence to gain the most accurate perception and the fullest appreciation of them after they are written. Though they may be conceived through "inspiration," they are constructed by craftsmanship. Even the simplest of poems is a gathering and compression of elements, including many assumptions normally shared by writer and reader, which are neither indefinable nor irrelevant to the poem's achievement.

Poems: Some Elements of Technique

The poems that follow are either explicitly or symbolically concerned with art and its meanings, meanings inseparable from the craft that has shaped them. Wordsworth's two poems show his experience of the permanently enriching influence of sight and sound—the field of daffodils, the song of the girl in the Scottish Highlands—when the force of perception strikes indelibly. These poems perfectly illustrate Wordsworth's famous definition of poetry as "the spontaneous overflow of powerful feelings" that "takes its origin from emotion recollected in tranquility."

Marianne Moore's *Poetry* defines poetry as made with "genuine" art out of "raw" experience of every kind. Ezra Pound's translation, a fairly free recasting, of poems by the first-century B.C. poet Propertius reveals the ancient writer's lively relevance. Pound implies that the English literary scene at the end of World War I resembles that of Augustan Rome, and that his own function as a poet is like that of Propertius—to advance his lyric art rather than to serve nationalistic or sentimental aims. Williams's and Duncan's poems suggest the artistic bearing of the way we respond to experience and to the processes in our own minds—a subtle development of Wordsworth's insight. In Williams's poem, the crowd's delight in the ball game's "beauty" is inseparable from a savage power latent in man and nature. In Duncan's poem, the poet's art (Duncan's own and the French poet Baudelaire's) is inseparable from his response to love and life considered as mysterious voyages.

We may read Stevens's *Anecdote of the Jar* as a light, but not frivolous commentary on Keats's *Ode on a Grecian Urn*. Both poets are considering the relationship of the elements of a work of art to its whole shape and character, and both consider what happens when life's realities are absorbed into and transformed by art. Auden and Jarrell, in their poems, try to see the way the whole structure of a work of art reveals the artist's attitude toward his subject. Auden stresses the Old Masters' ironic sense of the world's indifference to significant suffering. Jarrell's poem, based on Auden's but pleasantly disagreeing with it, stresses the way that historical change affects basic attitudes and, as a result, also affects artistic formal emphasis.

WILLIAM WORDSWORTH *I wandered lonely as a cloud*

I wandered lonely as a cloud
That floats on high o'er vales and hills,
When all at once I saw a crowd,
A host, of golden daffodils;
Beside the lake, beneath the trees,
Fluttering and dancing in the breeze.

Continuous as the stars that shine
And twinkle on the milky way,
They stretched in never-ending line
Along the margin of a bay: 10
Ten thousand saw I at a glance,
Tossing their heads in sprightly dance.

The waves beside them danced; but they
Out-did the sparkling waves in glee:
A poet could not but be gay,
In such a jocund company:
I gazed—and gazed—but little thought
What wealth the show to me had brought:

For oft, when on my couch I lie
In vacant or in pensive mood,   20
They flash upon that inward eye
Which is the bliss of solitude;
And then my heart with pleasure fills
And dances with the daffodils.

WILLIAM WORDSWORTH   *The Solitary Reaper*

Behold her, single in the field,
Yon solitary Highland Lass!
Reaping and singing by herself;
Stop here, or gently pass!
Alone she cuts and binds the grain,
And sings a melancholy strain;
O listen! for the Vale profound
Is overflowing with the sound.

No Nightingale did ever chaunt
More welcome notes to weary bands   10
Of travellers in some shady haunt,
Among Arabian sands:
A voice so thrilling ne'er was heard
In spring-time from the Cuckoo-bird,
Breaking the silence of the seas
Among the farthest Hebrides.

Will no one tell me what she sings?—
Perhaps the plaintive numbers flow
For old, unhappy, far-off things,
And battles long ago: 20
Or is it some more humble lay,
Familiar matter of to-day?
Some natural sorrow, loss, or pain,
That has been, and may be again?

Whate'er the theme, the Maiden sang
As if her song could have no ending;
I saw her singing at her work,
And o'er the sickle bending;—
I listened, motionless and still;
And, as I mounted up the hill,   30
The music in my heart I bore,
Long after it was heard no more.

MARIANNE MOORE   *Poetry* [1]

I, too, dislike it: there are things that are important beyond all this
       fiddle.
    Reading it, however, with a perfect contempt for it, one discovers
         in
    it after all, a place for the genuine.
         Hands that can grasp, eyes
         that can dilate, hair that can rise
             if it must, these things are important not because a

high-sounding interpretation can be put upon them but because they
       are
    useful. When they become so derivative as to become unintelligible,
    the same thing may be said for all of us, that we
         do not admire what   10
         we cannot understand: the bat
             holding on upside down or in quest of something to

eat, elephants pushing, a wild horse taking a roll, a tireless wolf
       under

---

[1] In *The Complete Poems* (1967), Miss Moore reduced this poem to the first three
lines. *What has been gained or lost by this change?*

a tree, the immovable critic twitching his skin like a horse that feels
    a flea, the base-
ball fan, the statistician—
    nor is it valid
        to discriminate against 'business documents and

school-books'; [2] all these phenomena are important. One must make
    a distinction
    however: when dragged into prominence by half poets, the result
        is not poetry,
nor till the poets among us can be   20
    'literalists of
    the imagination' [3]—above
        insolence and triviality and can present

for inspection, 'imaginary gardens with real toads in them,' [4] shall
    we have
it. In the meantime, if you demand on the one hand,
    the raw material of poetry in
        all its rawness and
        that which is on the other hand
            genuine, you are interested in poetry.

[2] Tolstoy, in his *Diary*, suggests that poetry has nothing to do with such writing.
[3] Yeats's essay "William Blake and the Imagination" calls Blake a "too literal realist of the imagination."
[4] Here Miss Moore invented a "quotation" to match and refute those by Tolstoy and Yeats.

Ezra Pound   from *Homage to Sextus Propertius* [1]

I

Shades of Callimachus, Coan ghosts of Philetas
It is in your grove I would walk,

[1] Pound does "homage" to the Latin poet Propertius by translating him very freely so that he sounds both ancient and modern. Propertius refers to earlier Greek poets as his models. Like him, they were masters of a pure and supple lyric style. It was this mastery, and not any official pomposity ("Martian generalities"), that enabled Homer and others to bring ancient myths to life. Pound boldly combines exquisite lyric passages with satirically humorous ones, sometimes using traditional and even archaic diction and sometimes American colloquialisms. *What is the sequence of varied stylistic and tonal effects as they occur? What is the relation of the deeply serious final passage to the effects that have preceded it? What does the poem as a whole show about the relationship between poetic tradition and poetic form?*

I who come first from the clear font
Bringing the Grecian orgies into Italy,
                    and the dance into Italy.
Who hath taught you so subtle a measure,
                    in what hall have you heard it;
What foot beat out your time-bar,
                    what water has mellowed your whistles?

Out-weariers of Apollo will, as we know, continue their Martian gen-
    eralities,
    We have kept our erasers in order.
A new-fangled chariot follows the flower-hung horses;
A young Muse with young loves clustered about her   10
                    ascends with me into the æther, . . .
And there is no high-road to the Muses.

Annalists will continue to record Roman reputations,
Celebrities from the Trans-Caucasus will belaud Roman celebrities
And expound the distentions of Empire,
But for something to read in normal circumstances?
For a few pages brought down from the forked hill unsullied?
I ask a wreath which will not crush my head.
                    And there is no hurry about it;
I shall have, doubtless, a boom after my funeral,
Seeing that long standing increases all things
                    regardless of quality.

And who would have known the towers   20
                    pulled down by a deal-wood horse;
Or of Achilles withstaying waters by Simois
Or of Hector spattering wheel-rims,
Or of Polydmantus, by Scamander, or Helenus and Deiphoibos?
Their door-yards would scarcely know them, or Paris.
Small talk O Ilion, and O Troad
                    twice taken by Oetian gods,
If Homer had not stated your case!

And I also among the later nephews of this city
                    shall have my dog's day,
With no stone upon my contemptible sepulchre;
My vote coming from the temple of Phoebus in Lycia, at Patara,
And in the mean time my songs will travel,   30

And the devirginated young ladies will enjoy them
            when they have got over the strangeness,
For Orpheus tamed the wild beasts—
                        and held up the Threician river;
And Citharaon shook up the rocks by Thebes
        and danced them into a bulwark at his pleasure,
And you, O Polyphemus? Did harsh Galatea almost
Turn to your dripping horses, because of a tune, under Aetna?
We must look into the matter.
Bacchus and Apollo in favour of it,
There will be a crowd of young women doing homage to my palaver,
Though my house is not propped up by Taenarian columns from
        Laconia (associated with Neptune and Cerberus),
Though it is not stretched upon gilded beams;   40
My orchards do not lie level and wide
                    as the forests of Phaecia,
                    the luxurious and Ionian,
Nor are my caverns stuffed stiff with a Marcian vintage,
My cellar does not date from Numa Pompilius,
Nor bristle with wine jars,
Nor is it equipped with a frigidaire patent;
Yet the companions of the Muses
            will keep their collective nose in my books,
And weary with historical data, they will turn to my dance tune.

Happy who are mentioned in my pamphlets,
        the songs shall be a fine tomb-stone over their beauty.
                    But against this?
Neither expensive pyramids scraping the stars in their route,
Nor houses modelled upon that of Jove in East Elis,   50
Nor the monumental effigies of Mausolus,
                    are a complete elucidation of death.

Flame burns, rain sinks into the cracks
And they all go to rack ruin beneath the thud of the years.
Stands genius a deathless adornment,
            a name not to be worn out with the years.

WILLIAM CARLOS WILLIAMS   *At the Ball Game*

    The crowd at the ball game
    is moved uniformly

by a spirit of uselessness
which delights them—

all the exciting detail
of the chase

and the escape, the error
the flash of genius—

all to no end save beauty
the eternal—   10

So in detail they, the crowd,
are beautiful

for this
to be warned against

saluted and defied—
It is alive, venomous

it smiles grimly
its words cut—

The flashy female with her
mother, gets it—   20

The Jew gets it straight—it
is deadly, terrifying—

It is the Inquisition, the
Revolution

It is beauty itself
that lives

day by day in them
idly—

This is
the power of their faces   30

It is summer, it is the solstice
the crowd is

cheering, the crowd is laughing
in detail

permanently, seriously
without thought

ROBERT DUNCAN   *After a Passage in Baudelaire* [1]

Ship, leaving or arriving, of my lover,
my soul, leaving or coming into this harbor,
among your lights and shadows   sheltered,
at home in your bulk, the cunning
regularity and symmetry thruout
of love's design, of will, of your
attractive cells and chambers

riding forward, darkest of shades
over the shadowd waters
into the light, neat, symmetrically   10
arranged above your watery reflections
disturbing your own image, moving as you are

    What passenger, what sailor,
looks out into the swirling currents round you
as if into those depths into a mirror?

What lights in what port-holes
raise in my mind again   hunger and impatience?
to make my bed down again, there, beyond me,
as if this room too, my bedroom, my lamp at my side,
were among those lights sailing out   20
           away from me.

We too, among the others, passengers
in that *charme infini et mystérieux*,
in that suitable symmetry, that precision
everywhere, the shining fittings, the fit

---

[1] The French phrases, in sequence of appearance, mean: *infinite and mysterious enchantment, the poetic idea* (or *idea of a poetry*), and *is the assumption of a vast, limitless, complex yet harmonious being.* The prose passage by Baudelaire referred to appears in his *Intimate Journals*.

of lights and polisht surfaces to the dark,
to the flickering shadows of them,
we too, unfaithful to me, sailing away,
leaving me.

L'idée poétique, the idea of a poetry,   30
that rises from the movement, from the
outswirling curves and imaginary figures
round this ship, this fate, this sure thing,

est l'hypothèse d'une être vaste, immense,

compliqué, mais eurythmique.

JOHN KEATS   *Ode on a Grecian Urn*

Thou still unravish'd bride of quietness,
   Thou foster-child of silence and slow time,
Sylvan historian, who canst thus express
   A flowery tale more sweetly than our rhyme:
What leaf-fring'd legend haunts about thy shape
   Of deities or mortals, or of both
      In Tempe or the dales of Arcady?
What men or gods are these? What maidens loth?
   What mad pursuit? What struggle to escape?
      What pipes and timbrels? What wild ecstasy?   10

Heard melodies are sweet, but those unheard
   Are sweeter; therefore, ye soft pipes, play on;
Not to the sensual ear, but, more endear'd,
   Pipe to the spirit ditties of no tone:
Fair youth, beneath the trees, thou canst not leave
   Thy song, nor ever can those trees be bare;
      Bold lover, never, never canst thou kiss,
Though winning near the goal—yet, do not grieve;
   She cannot fade, though thou hast not thy bliss,
      For ever wilt thou love, and she be fair!   20

Ah, happy, happy boughs! that cannot shed
   Your leaves, nor ever bid the Spring adieu;
And, happy melodist, unwearièd,

For ever piping songs for ever new;
More happy love! more happy, happy love!
For ever warm, and still to be enjoy'd,
    For ever panting, and for ever young;
All breathing human passion far above,
    That leaves a heart high-sorrowful and cloy'd,
        A burning forehead, and a parching tongue.   30

Who are these coming to the sacrifice?
    To what green altar, O mysterious priest,
Lead'st thou that heifer lowing at the skies,
    And all her silken flanks with garlands drest?
What little town by river or sea shore,
    Or mountain-built with peaceful citadel,
        Is emptied of this folk, this pious morn?
And, little town, thy streets for evermore
    Will silent be; and not a soul to tell
        Why thou are desolate, can e'er return.   40

O attic shape! Fair attitude! with brede
    Of marble men and maidens overwrought,
With forest branches and the trodden weed;
    Thou, silent form, dost tease us out of thought
As doth eternity: Cold Pastoral!
    When old age shall this generation waste,
        Thou shalt remain, in midst of other woe
Than ours, a friend to man, to whom thou say'st,
    "Beauty is truth, truth beauty,"—that is all
        Ye know on earth, and all ye need to know.   50

WALLACE STEVENS   *Anecdote of the Jar*

I placed a jar in Tennessee,
And round it was, upon a hill.
It made the slovenly wilderness
Surround that hill.

The wilderness rose up to it,
And sprawled around, no longer wild.
The jar was round upon the ground
And tall and of a port in air.

It took dominion everywhere.
The jar was gray and bare.   10
It did not give of bird or bush,
Like nothing else in Tennessee.

W. H. Auden   *Musée des Beaux Arts* [1]

About suffering they were never wrong,
The Old Masters: how well they understood
Its human position; how it takes place
While someone else is eating or opening a window or just walking
      dully along;
How, when the aged are reverently, passionately waiting
For the miraculous birth, there always must be
Children who did not specially want it to happen, skating
On a pond at the edge of the wood:
They never forgot
That even the dreadful martyrdom must run its course   10
Anyhow in a corner, some untidy spot
Where the dogs go on with their doggy life and the torturer's horse
Scratches its innocent behind on a tree.

In Brueghel's *Icarus*, for instance: how everything turns away
Quite leisurely from the disaster; the ploughman may
Have heard the splash, the forsaken cry,
But for him it was not an important failure; the sun shone
As it had to on the white legs disappearing into the green
Water; and the expensive delicate ship that must have seen
Something amazing, a boy falling out of the sky,   20
Had somewhere to get to and sailed calmly on.

Randall Jarrell   *The Old and the New Masters*

About suffering, about adoration, the old masters
Disagree. When someone suffers, no one else eats
Or walks or opens the window—no one breathes
As the sufferers watch the sufferer.
In *St. Sebastian Mourned by St. Irene*
The flame of one torch is the only light.
All the eyes except the maidservant's (she weeps

[1] Museum of Art, or Art Gallery

And covers them with a cloth) are fixed on the shaft
Set in his chest like a column; St. Irene's
Hands are spread in the gesture of the Madonna,   10
Revealing, accepting, what she does not understand.
Her hands say: "Lo! Behold!"
Beside her a monk's hooded head is bowed, his hands
Are put together in the work of mourning.
It is as if they were still looking at the lance
Piercing the side of Christ, nailed on his cross.
The same nails pierce all their hands and feet, the same
Thin blood, mixed with water, trickles from their sides.
The taste of vinegar is on every tongue
That gasps, "My God, my God, why hast Thou forsaken me?"   20
They watch, they are, the one thing in the world.

So, earlier, everything is pointed
In van der Goes' *Nativity*, toward the naked
Shining baby, like the needle of a compass.
The different orders and sizes of the world:
The angels like Little People, perched in the rafters
Or hovering in mid-air like hummingbirds;
The shepherds, so big and crude, so plainly adoring;
The medium-sized donor, his little family,
And their big patron saints; the Virgin who kneels   30
Before her child in worship; the Magi out in the hills
With their camels—they ask directions, and have pointed out
By a man kneeling, the true way; the ox
And the donkey, two heads in the manger
So much greater than a human head, who also adore;
Even the offerings, a sheaf of wheat,
A jar and a glass of flowers, are absolutely still
In natural concentration, as they take their part
In the salvation of the natural world.
The time of the world concentrates   40
On this one instant: far off in the rocks
You can see Mary and Joseph and their donkey
Coming to Bethlehem; on the grassy hillside
Where their flocks are grazing, the shepherds gesticulate
In wonder at the star; and so many hundreds
Of years in the future, the donor, his wife,
And their children are kneeling, looking: everything
That was or will be in the world is fixed
On its small, helpless, human center.

After a while the masters show the crucifixion   50
In one corner of the canvas: the men come to see
What is important, see that it is not important.
The new masters paint a subject as they please,
And Veronese is prosecuted by the Inquisition
For the dogs playing at the feet of Christ,
The earth is a planet among galaxies.
Later Christ disappears, the dogs disappear: in abstract
Understanding, without adoration, the last master puts
Colors on canvas, a picture of the universe
In which a bright spot somewhere in the corner   60
Is the small radioactive planet men called Earth.

II

Poetic Imagery

Together with his handling of sound, the most important element in the poet's art is the way he presents *images*—physical impressions and pictured comparisons. It is through images that the threefold nature of poetic experience and expression—accurate and intense sense-perception of objects, stimulation of feeling, and intellectual contemplation—reveals itself. Poetic imagery communicates on all three of these levels.

The first level, the sensuous, is the most immediate, and is seen most clearly in visual imagery. There is a certain delight and love, a visual thirst—

> Eye, gazelle, delicate wanderer,
> Drinker of horizon's fluid line—

as Stephen Spender has expressed it. In the finest poetry the pictures presented to our senses and imagination are not contrived merely as ornament or illustration, but they themselves generate the meaning of the poem. Over three hundred years ago the Elizabethan poet Samuel Daniel spoke of the way this creation of a meaning through the senses takes place:

> Glory is most bright and gay
> In a flash, and so away.
> Feed apace then, greedy eyes,
> On the wonder you behold.
> Take it sudden as it flies
> Though you take it not to hold:
> When your eyes have done their part,
> Thought must length it in the heart.

But thought cannot ponder fruitfully what our senses have perceived, unless the perceptions are accurate and sharply defined. Accuracy and clarity are marks both of the poet's sincerity and of his craftsmanship. Consider Browning's

> The wild tulip, at end of its tube, blows out its great red bell
> Like a thin clear bubble of blood

or Whitman's

> Earth of the vitreous pour of the full moon just tinged with blue!
> Earth of shine and dark mottling the tide of the river!

These sense-impressions appeal to the eye. The following lines by Herrick add movement, touch, and sound in their presentation of the rippling glitter and swish of a lady's silks as she walks:

ROBERT HERRICK *Upon Julia's Clothes*

> Whenas in silks my Julia goes,
> Then, then (methinks), how sweetly flows
> The liquefaction of her clothes.
>
> Next, when I cast mine eyes and see
> That brave vibration each way free,
> O how that glittering taketh me!

Marianne Moore gives us a curiously comparable sound-picture as she describes a ship's boat on the water:

> —the blades of the oars
> moving together like the feet of water-spiders. . . .
> The wrinkles progress upon themselves in a phalanx—beautiful under
> networks of foam,
> and fade breathlessly while the sea rustles in and out of the seaweed. . . .

And Milton, to suggest the beauty of a woman's singing, and the loveliness and virtue of the singer herself, actually presents one sensation in terms of another:

> At last a soft and solemn breathing sound
> Rose like a steam of rich distilled perfumes,
> And stole upon the air. . . .

The complex process that underlies a simple image is described by Ezra Pound in one of his essays. One day in a station of the Paris *metro* (subway), he

> saw suddenly a beautiful face, and then another and another, and then a beautiful child's face, and then another beautiful woman, and I tried all that day to find words for what this had meant to me, and I could not find any words that seemed to me worthy, or as lovely as that sudden emotion. And that evening, as I went home along the Rue Raynouard, I was still trying, and I found, suddenly, the expression. I do not mean that I found words, but there came an equation . . . not in speech, but in little splotches of color. It was just that—a pattern, or hardly a pattern, if by pattern you mean something with a repeat in it. But it was a word, the beginning, for me, of a language in color. . . .

Pound's essay, "Vorticism," develops this thought interestingly and at length. Let us turn, though, to the poem itself that eventually emerged from this experience after much revision and paring down.

EZRA POUND *In a Station of the Metro*

> The apparition of these faces in the crowd;
> Petals on a wet, black bough.

The first line tells us, like a theatrical program note, what the setting is—or more precisely, what the general problem of description is that the poet has set himself. The second line finds the exact image, or concrete picture-example, for what people in a Parisian subway station look like. It might be more natural to say, "These faces in the crowd look to me like petals on a wet, black bough," but it would not be as satisfying. The little dance of the introductory line followed by the sharply clear image is both attractive and amusing, and it has the effect of a sudden discovery. The pale faces in the semidarkness immediately become vivid and meaningful—quite different from the big-city dweller's usual impression of the subway as a dull, uninteresting necessity that one lives through somehow on one's way to somewhere else.

This is the sort of image that Ezra Pound has himself called "an intellectual and emotional complex in an instant of time." It opens up to us, suddenly, a world of pathetic meaning through its suggestion of petals that have been blown off flowers in a rainstorm. It implies a criticism of a way of life—the mechanized urban existence in which the individual is tragically "blacked out," and which can be made to seem bearable only by the metaphor of an "apparition," a ghost of the bright beauty of things that grew freely in the sunlight. It suggests, again pathetically, the frailty, the transience, and the mortality of all natural beauty. The faces, too, are "petals," the brevity of the vision corresponding to that of their potential blooming in actual life. The poem also becomes a poignant gesture of affection toward these other lives glimpsed in darkness and in passing.

To return to the general subject of imagery: an image is very often the direct concrete expression of vivid sense perceptions, but often—as in most of the foregoing instances—it is figurative rather than literal. Figures of speech are not, of course, confined to poetry; they are a part of all linguistic activity except the most rigorously factual, and are familiar to most of us in slang and other popular, inventive, and indeed poetic adventures with language.

In poetry itself the commonest and most useful figures of speech—*simile*, *metaphor*, *personification*, and *conceit*—involve comparison, not so much a comparison between things that are actually very much alike as between things that have one often unexpected quality in common. The function of the figure is to direct our attention with special vividness to this particular quality. There is no figure involved in comparing a rose to a carnation, but when a poet compares his girl to a rose (in order to suggest her sweetness, freshness, loveliness, and perhaps also the frailty and impermanence of that loveliness) he is not making a literal factual statement; he is appealing to the imagination. Such poetic statements as Burns's "O my luve is like a red, red rose" or Shakespeare's "My Mistress' eyes are nothing like the sun" or Campion's "Her brows like bended bows"—statements in which almost always the comparison is explicitly expressed by the use of some such words as *like, as,* and *similar to*—are called similes.

When a figure is presented not as a directly stated comparison but as an identity, then we have not a simile but a metaphor. Campion's "her diamond eyes" and Tennyson's "The black bat Night" are metaphors. One of the most frequently encountered types of metaphor is personification, well illustrated in such a characteristic image as this from Shelley's *To Night:*

> Blind with thine hair the eyes of Day;
> Kiss her until she be wearied out. . . .

or in Milton's address to the spirit of Melancholy:

> Come, pensive nun, devout and pure,
> Sober, steadfast, and demure. . . .

Sometimes personification is combined with simile, as in the exciting virtuosity of T. S. Eliot's

> . . . the evening is spread out against the sky
> Like a patient etherised upon a table. . . .

The boldness and originality of this image is characteristic of the conceit—a favorite device of the seventeenth-century Metaphysical poets and their modern followers. The principle behind the conceit is that the greater the gap between the two things compared in a simile or identified in a metaphor—the greater, that is, the imaginative leap the poet's mind achieves—the greater the satisfaction and the sharper the conviction. Many successful images, therefore, are paradoxical; they seem fanciful or out-of-kilter until the reader's own mind makes the leap.

From both the esthetic and the psychological points of view, the meta-

physical poet's aim is to achieve the *widest* possible gap between the arms
of his comparison. If the gap is too narrow, that is, if the things or qualities compared are too much alike, the result is flat and dull. If on the
other hand, the comparison is, literally, too far-fetched, the failure is of
a different sort, and the result is unconvincing or ridiculous.

Any bold far-fetched figure of comparison, whether successful or not,
is called a conceit. (The word is related to *concept*, a mental image.)
The description of the evening as an etherised patient is a conceit; so
is John Donne's famous comparison of absent lovers to a pair of compasses:

> If they be two, they are two so
>   As stiff twin compasses are two;
> Thy soul, the fix'd foot, makes no show
>   To move, but doth, if th' other do.
>
> And though it in the centre sit,
>   Yet, when the other far doth roam,
> It leans, and hearkens after it,
>   And grows erect, as that comes home.

From these brief illustrations it should be clear that an effective figure
of speech is both a perception of reality and a projection of the imagination. It is a sudden insight into a meaningful resemblance between
things not often thought to be alike.

Perhaps it would be well to examine a short modern poem in order
to see the application of some of the principles we have been discussing.
In William Carlos Williams's brief poem *Flowers by the Sea*, there is a
new and surprising, but sharply convincing vision of something we may
often have looked at but have never actually seen with the eye of imagination until the poet showed it to us.

WILLIAM CARLOS WILLIAMS *Flowers by the Sea*

> When over the flowery, sharp pasture's
> edge, unseen, the salt ocean
>
> lifts its form—chickory and daisies
> tied, released, seem hardly flowers alone
>
> but color and the movement—or the shape
> perhaps—of restlessness, whereas

the sea is circled and sways
peacefully upon its plantlike stem

Brief and clear as it is, this little poem states, or, rather, illustrates, a paradox—the paradox that the sea and the pasture suggest one another's basic natures rather than their own. But the curious thing about it is that the unexpected reversal of images that makes the point of the poem emerges suddenly, only after we have absorbed the whole dazzling picture of the sunny, windswept seaside pasture and felt the tousled, salt-laden atmosphere of the summer day. The first unexpected identification is that of the restless amalgam of color and movement in the flowers—"the shape perhaps of restlessness"—with the ebb and flow ("tied, released") of the sea waves; and parallel to it, but much richer and grander, is the sudden awareness of the vast blue round of the ocean itself, swaying like an enormous flower. The poem expresses an experience that culminates for poet and reader alike in the intuitive flash at the close: it is not so much that the flowers and the sea are *like* one another as that the flowers *are* a sea and the sea *is* a flower. The imagination leaves out all but the common elements shared by the flowers and the waves, all but color and movement, that is, or all but the circular shape and the gently swaying motion. Here is the most intense concentration upon what the imagination has isolated for the sake of emphasis. The result is a form of truth, more limited but more precious too than the truth of science and fact, since this is a truth perceived simultaneously by the heart, the imagination, and the mind.

As to the methods by which the poem achieves its effect, the most striking consists in a metaphorical perception—in a seeing of things in terms of other things, which emphasizes a hitherto unsuspected identity. Besides this metaphorical structure, we may notice first the simplicity and unaffected rightness of the diction, and then the easy, natural, exact, and colloquial structure of the clauses—virtues common to good prose and good poetry alike. Then again, if we look and listen we grow aware of the skilful but unobtrusive pattern of repeated sounds that marks the poem's movement. And finally, we notice how the unifying paradox of the poem is matched in the contrast between the short, sharp, variable rhythm of the opening half of the poem and the slow, majestic, peaceful swaying of the close.

But what, the reader may now ask, does the poem *mean?*

We would answer: Two things are involved in the poem's meaning. First, there is the evocation of all the associations of delight gathering around the sunny windswept landscape of flowers by the dancing sea. Second, there is the delight that accompanies the appreciation of a paradox. It is the paradoxical reversal of ordinary experience, when in a flash the flowers are seen as a sea and the sea as a flower, that gives the poem unity and point. The effect of the whole poem—what it does for and to us—*that* is the meaning of the poem. For this reason it is all-important to read the plain sense of the poem correctly. We must submit ourselves to the poem the author wrote, not to a vague approximation that our own intuitions, prejudices, and limitations have substituted for it. And in the poem we have been considering this depends on our recognition of its one tremendous metaphor of the flowers and the sea.

Poems: Poetic Imagery

This group begins with the Elizabethan poet Samuel Daniel's vivid statement of the sequence of events behind the creation of a poem: the eye perceives, the mind reflects, and the heart is stirred. Daniel's poem sees the process much as does Wordsworth's *I wandered lonely as a cloud*, in the preceding section. The poems that follow are first and foremost poems of the perceiving eye. They assume one of the basic premises of art, and of modern art in particular: the intrinsic significance of intensely realized sensation. The poems of H. D., one of the most rigorous of the Imagist poets of the 1920's, are almost mystical in their search for this value, and Theodore Roethke's personified orchids have an effect that is still more mystical because of its strongly primitive essence. MacNeice's *Snow*, though it deals with an abstract idea, and Frost's *The Silken Tent*, though it presents a complex symbolic description of a woman, both take off from a concrete sensuous impression.

After these poems come the highly concentrated and dramatic *The Eagle* of Tennyson and Ted Hughes's longer, more ambitious, *Hawk Roosting*. In the latter poem and the pieces that follow it, the dominant images are visual although the scope and power of the poems are extended to include character, drama, and idea. In two of them, the ones by Thom Gunn and Earle Birney, this fact is underlined by the circumstance that the speaker is contemplating a painting.

SAMUEL DANIEL   Are they shadows that we see?

> Are they shadows that we see?
> And can shadows pleasure give?
> Pleasures only shadows be
> Cast by bodies we conceive,
> And are made the things we deem,
> In those figures which they seem.
> But these pleasures vanish fast,
> Which by shadows are exprest:
> Pleasures are not, if they last,
> In their passing, is their best.
> Glory is most bright and gay
> In a flash, and so away.
> Feed apace then, greedy eyes,
> On the wonder you behold.
> Take it sudden as it flies
> Though you take it not to hold:
> When your eyes have done their part,
> Thought must length it in the heart.

10

H. D.   *The Pool*

Are you alive?
I touch you.
You quiver like a sea-fish.
I cover you with my net.
What are you—banded one?

H. D.   *Oread*

Whirl up, sea—
whirl your pointed pines,
splash your great pines
on our rocks,
hurl your green over us,
cover us with your pools of fir.

Theodore Roethke   *Orchids*

They lean over the path,
Adder-mouthed,
Swaying close to the face,
Coming out, soft and deceptive,
Limp and damp, delicate as a young bird's tongue;
Their fluttery fledgling lips
Move slowly,
Drawing in the warm air.

And at night,
The faint moon falling through whitewashed glass,   10
The heat going down
So their musky smell comes even stronger,
Drifting down from their mossy cradles:
So many devouring infants!
Soft luminescent fingers,
Lips neither dead nor alive,
Loose ghostly mouths
Breathing.

Louis MacNeice *Snow*

The room was suddenly rich and the great bay-window was
Spawning snow and pink roses against it
Soundlessly collateral and incompatible:
World is suddener than we fancy it.

World is crazier and more of it than we think,
Incorrigibly plural. I peel and portion
A tangerine and spit the pips and feel
The drunkenness of things being various.

And the fire flames with a bubbling sound for world
Is more spiteful and gay than one supposes—   10
On the tongue on the eyes on the ears in the palms of your hands—
There is more than glass between the snow and the huge roses.

Robert Frost *The Silken Tent*

She is as in a field a silken tent
At midday when a sunny summer breeze
Has dried the dew and all its ropes relent,
So that in guys it gently sways at ease,
And its supporting central cedar pole,
That is its pinnacle to heavenward
And signifies the sureness of the soul,
Seems to owe naught to any single cord,
But strictly held by none, is loosely bound
By countless silken ties of love and thought   10
To everything on earth the compass round,
And only by one's going slightly taut
In the capriciousness of summer air
Is of the slightest bondage made aware.

Alfred, Lord Tennyson *The Eagle*

He clasps the crag with crooked hands;
Close to the sun in lonely lands,
Ring'd with the azure world, he stands.

The wrinkled sea beneath him crawls;
He watches from his mountain walls,
And like a thunderbolt he falls.

TED HUGHES   *Hawk Roosting*

I sit in the top of the wood, my eyes closed.
Inaction, no falsifying dream
Between my hooked head and hooked feet:
Or in sleep rehearse perfect kills and eat.

The convenience of the high trees!
The air's buoyancy and the sun's ray
Are of advantage to me;
And the earth's face upward for my inspection.

My feet are locked upon the rough bark.
It took the whole of Creation   10
To produce my foot, my each feather:
Now I hold Creation in my foot

Or fly up, and revolve it all slowly—
I kill where I please because it is all mine.
There is no sophistry in my body:
My manners are tearing off heads—

The allotment of death.
For the one path of my flight is direct
Through the bones of the living.
No arguments assert my right: 20

The sun is behind me.
Nothing has changed since I began.
My eye has permitted no change.
I am going to keep things like this.

MARIANNE MOORE   *A Grave*

Man looking into the sea,
taking the view from those who have as much right to it as you have
      to it yourself,
it is human nature to stand in the middle of a thing,

but you cannot stand in the middle of this;
the sea has nothing to give but a well excavated grave.
The firs stand in a procession, each with an emerald turkey-foot at
    the top,
reserved as their contours, saying nothing;
repression, however, is not the most obvious characteristic of the sea;
the sea is a collector, quick to return a rapacious look.
There are others besides you who have worn that look—   10
whose expression is no longer a protest; the fish no longer investigate
    them
for their bones have not lasted:
men lower nets, unconscious of the fact that they are desecrating a
    grave,
and row quickly away—the blades of the oars
moving together like the feet of water-spiders as if there were no such
    thing as death.
The wrinkles progress among themselves in a phalanx—beautiful
    under networks of foam,
and fade breathlessly while the sea rustles in and out of the seaweed;
the birds swim through the air at top speed, emitting catcalls as
    heretofore—
the tortoise-shell scourges about the feet of the cliffs, in motion
    beneath them;
and the ocean, under the pulsation of lighthouses and noise of bell-
    buoys,   20
advances as usual, looking as if it were not that ocean in which
    dropped things are bound to sink—
in which if they turn and twist, it is neither with volition nor
    consciousness.

EZRA POUND   *Fish and the Shadow*

The salmon-trout drifts in the stream,
The soul of the salmon-trout floats over the stream
    Like a little wafer of light.

The salmon moves in the sun-shot, bright shallow sea. . . .

As light as the shadow of the fish
    that falls through the water,
She came into the large room by the stair,
Yawning a little she came with the sleep still upon her.

"I am just from bed. The sleep is still in my eyes.
"Come. I have had a long dream."   10
And I: "That wood?
"And two springs have passed us."
"Not so far, no, not so far now,
There is a place—but no one else knows it—
A field in a valley . . .
                                    Qu'ieu sui avinen,
Ieu lo sai."

She must speak of the time
Of Arnaut de Mareuil,[1] I thought, *"qu'ieu sui avinen."*

Light as the shadow of the fish   20
That falls through the pale green water.

THOM GUNN   *In Santa Maria del Popolo*

Waiting for when the sun an hour or less
Conveniently oblique makes visible
The painting on one wall of this recess
By Caravaggio, of the Roman School,
I see how shadow in the painting brims
With a real shadow, drowning all shapes out
But a dim horse's haunch and various limbs,
Until the very subject is in doubt.

But evening gives the act, beneath the horse
And one indifferent groom, I see him sprawl,   10
Foreshortened from the head, with hidden face,
Where he has fallen, Saul becoming Paul.
O wily painter, limiting the scene
From a cacophony of dusty forms
To the one convulsion, what is it you mean
In that wide gesture of the lifting arms?

No Ananias croons a mystery yet,
Casting the pain out under name of sin.
The painter saw what was, an alternate

---

[1] Twelfth-century Provençal troubadour, whose verse the woman speaks: *"That I am
pleasing/I know."*

Candor and secrecy inside the skin. 20
He painted, elsewhere, that firm insolent
Young whore in Venus' clothes, those pudgy cheats,
Those sharpers; and was strangled, as things went,
For money, by one such picked off the streets.

I turn, hardly enlightened, from the chapel
To the dim interior of the church instead,
In which there kneel already several people,
Mostly old women: each head closeted
In tiny fists holds comfort as it can.
Their poor arms are too tired for more than this 30
—For the large gesture of solitary man,
Resisting, by embracing, nothingness.

Earle Birney *El Greco:* Espolio

The carpenter is intent on the pressure of his hand

on the awl   and the trick of pinpointing his strength
through the awl to the wood   which is tough
He has no effort to spare for despoilings
or to worry if he'll be cut in on the dice
His skill is vital to the scene   and the safety of the state
Anyone can perform the indignities   It's his hard arms
and craft that hold the eyes of the convict's women
There is the problem of getting the holes exact
(in the middle of this elbowing crowd) 10
and deep enough to hold the spikes
after they've sunk through those bared feet
and inadequate wrists he knows are waiting behind him

He doesn't sense perhaps that one of the hands
is held in a curious gesture over him—
giving   or asking   forgiveness?—
but he'd scarcely take time to be puzzled by poses
Criminals come in all sorts   as anyone knows who makes crosses
are as mad or sane as those who decide on their killings
Our one at least has been quiet so far 20
though they say he talked himself into this trouble
a carpenter's son who got notions of preaching

Well here's a carpenter's son who'll have carpenter sons
God willing   and build what's wanted   temples or tables
mangers or crosses   and shape them decently
working alone in that firm and profound abstraction
which blots out the bawling of rag-snatchers
To construct with hands   knee-weight   braced thigh
keeps the back turned from death

But it's too late now for the other carpenter's boy   30
to return to this peace before the nails are hammered

KENNETH REXROTH   *Doubled Mirrors*

It is the dark of the moon.
Late at night, the end of summer,
The autumn constellations
Glow in the arid heaven.
The air smells of cattle, hay,
And dust. In the old orchard
The pears are ripe. The trees
Have sprouted from old rootstocks
And the fruit is inedible.
As I pass them I hear something   10
Rustling and grunting and turn
My light into the branches.
Two raccoons with acrid pear
Juice and saliva drooling
From their mouths stare back at me,
Their eyes deep sponges of light.
They know me and do not run
Away. Coming up the road
Through the black oak shadows, I
See ahead of me, glinting   20
Everywhere from the dusty
Gravel, tiny points of cold
Blue light, like the sparkle of
Iron snow. I suspect what it is,
And kneel to see. Under each
Pebble and oak leaf is a
Spider, her eyes shining at
Me with my reflected light
Across immeasurable distance.

III

RHYTHM AND MUSIC

Through its rhythmic movement, poetry that is alive projects its precise mood and tone. Rhythmic movement has the power to subordinate our conscious thought to the emotional pulsation of the moment. The skilful poet can evoke the beat and the dynamics of a musical performance, the running excitement of a mob, the stately monotony of an official ceremony, the suspenseful restraint and then the climactic outburst of a violent experience. "The sound must seem an echo to the sense," wrote Alexander Pope; the thought applies to much more than the imitation of the rhythm of such events. It applies as well to our sense of the inner harmony, and its interruptions, of human awareness. And it applies to the very character of that awareness: its hesitations, its complexities, and its moments of high, transcendent intensity. There is rhythmic technique in even the simplest effective poem.

Even when contemporary poetry makes use of breath and thought movements of an unconventional and improvised kind, it is useful in thinking about poetic rhythm to have some familiarity with the traditional terms of metrical analysis. For one thing, the great mass of poetry of the past, as well as a large proportion of the best modern work (by poets such as Yeats, Stevens, Frost, Lowell, and many others), has been written according to the traditional meters, though all the poetic masters from the very start have employed them with sophistication and freedom. The terms are useful in helping anyone to think about what is going on in a poem and to see the relationship between its more conventional and its more improvisational features.

Every sound, every syllable, contributes to a poem's movement. Sounds and syllables are more than the elements of particular words; they are also the elements of the basic rhythmic units called *feet*, units generally made up of two or three syllables. The point at which the main stress or accent in a foot will fall is basically controlled by the normal pronunciation of the words in a naturally spoken sentence. However, the individual foot, in relation to the line and larger structure within which it occurs, is a unit something like a bar of music as well. A poem is enough like a musical score to suggest a pattern that uses ordinary speech rhythms but intensifies and formalizes them to at least some degree. Take the beginning of Wallace Stevens's poem *Peter Quince at the Clavier*:

> Just as my fingers on these keys
> Make music, so the selfsame sounds
> On my spirit make a music too.

> Music is feeling, then, not sound;
> And thus it is that what I feel,
> Here in this room, desiring you,
>
> Thinking of your blue-shadowed silk,
> Is music. . . .

A man is sitting at the piano, musing philosophically over the two
kinds of music he is making—the sound that strikes the ear, and the
effect of that sound on his spirit. It is the latter, he decides, that is the
real music: "Music is feeling, then, not sound." And therefore, it is implied, any feeling is a kind of music. For instance, his desire for the
woman to whom he is speaking "is music." The dreamy, meditative
sentences seem to grow right out of the situation. We can see that the
language is that of a cultivated person. If we rearrange the lines as prose,
they will read as the rather direct, if elegant and romantic, statement
of a lover. And yet a great deal of art has gone into them, to make them
read as a composition far more compressed and full of design than most
prose. Each of the lines (except the eighth, which we have broken off
before the end) consists of four feet. Most of these feet, but by no
means all, consist of a single unaccented syllable followed by a single
accented one:

Júst as/ my fín/ gers on/ these keys

Make mu/ sic, so/ the self/ same sounds

On my spir/ it make/ a mu/ sic too. . . .

Except for the first foot in line one, and the first foot in line three,
all the lines just quoted are made up of feet in which an unstressed
syllable is followed by a stressed one—the iambic foot, which is the
most common in poetry written in English. Of course, the values are not
the same in every iambic foot. In the first line, the stressing of "on"
could not possibly be as heavy as that of "fin" or of "keys." Again, the
words "so" and "make" and even "too" are stressed more heavily than
"on" but probably not as heavily as the other accented syllables; and
some of them will be pronounced more gently than others, depending
on their location in the line and sentence.

Different readers will perhaps argue for a scansion varying in some
respect or other from the one we have given. Once again, the analogy
with music is useful, for we have a clearly patterned structure with a
great deal of room for individual interpretation. The important consideration is that Stevens has arranged his poem in a way that enables

him to make it sound both like human speech and like a song composed to express a mood. The lines are long enough to allow for the development of abstract ideas without their being cramped, but not too long to lose the flavor of song. In reading the poem, one must give each stressed syllable slightly more force than if one were reading matter-of-fact prose, and one should pause ever so slightly, for the tiniest split fraction of an instant, between the feet to bring out the values of the tempo, and also to allow the many sound-echoes (the *m*'s and *u*'s and *n*'s, for instance) to come into play. The stressed syllables and the words in which the key sounds are repeated coincide with the most important ideas and notes of feeling and sensation. These effects give body to the meaning of the poem; without them it would be a collection of statements with very little life.

Now for a few basic terms. The most commonly used foot, as we have observed, is the *iamb*. Since iambic feet are closest to the rhythm of natural speech, any other kind of foot seems to create a special effect. Lines that are predominantly iambic often begin with a *trochaic* foot (a stressed syllable followed by an unstressed one—just the reverse of iambic) for initial emphasis, as in the first line of Stevens's poem, already quoted and analyzed:

Júst ăs m̆y fíngĕrs ón th̆ese kéys. . . .

Often, too, one finds *anapestic* feet substituted for iambic ones to gain variety and speed, as in the opening foot of line three in the Stevens poem. It consists of two unaccented syllables followed by an accented one:

Ŏn m̆y spírĭt máke ă músĭc tóo.

In the same way, the *dactyl*—one stressed syllable followed by two unstressed ones—is often substituted for a trochaic foot, with a similar effect of heightened speed. Here is a line in which the two kinds of feet alternate in a truly "rocking" movement:

Óut ŏf th̆e crádle éndlĕssly̆ róckinğ
WHITMAN

Hovering accents, when the accented syllables that come together are in the same foot, are called *spondees*. The spondaic foot is used for unusually strong emphasis:

Bríght dáy, gréen gráss, sóft aír, wárm lóve
A. J. M. SMITH

As we have observed, not every accented syllable is as heavily stressed as every other, nor is every unstressed one as light as every other. Such shadings of stress or lightness make for a richer, more complicated sound-effect than rough scansion will indicate. Sometimes, therefore, it is convenient to speak of secondary stresses, as in the final syllable of

Séasŏn ŏf mǐsts ănd mellŏw fruitfŭlnèss

And on the other hand, it is often sufficient for descriptive purposes simply to indicate the number of heavily stressed syllables without regard to such differences. Thus, we may speak of Shakespeare's characteristic five-stress line. In general, however, we can describe a line with some degree at least of precision by referring to the type of foot predominating in it, and to the number of feet and the kind of substitute feet it contains. A one-foot line is called monometer, a two-foot line dimeter, and so on through trimeter, tetrameter, pentameter, hexameter (or Alexandrine, if predominantly iambic), and heptameter. In using this technical terminology, of course, we must remain aware of its true end: to aid our appreciation of the chiming together of the varied elements in any given poem.

If we now examine briefly a complete poem by A. E. Housman—a quite dramatic piece of writing, with a human figure firmly occupying the center of the stage—we shall see readily how metrical technique contributes to poetic meaning and effect.

A. E. Housman *Eight O'Clock*

> He stood, and heard the steeple
>   Sprinkle the quarters on the morning town.
> One, two, three, four, to market-place and people
>   It tossed them down.
>
> Strapped, noosed, nighing his hour,
>   He stood and counted them and cursed his luck;
> And then the clock collected in the tower
>   Its strength, and struck.

The impact of this poem is truly terrific. Its force is intensified by the sharpest possible contrast in rhythm between the scattered tinkling diversity of the second line and the slow forceful beat of the first half of the third line. This contrast is intensified in the second stanza and is brought to a climax in the deliberate, wavelike build-up of weight in the last two lines. The effect is redoubled by the suspenseful pause after "strength," followed by the final heavy blow at the very end.

The voice we hear speaking in *Eight O'Clock* is that of a narrator who is very closely in sympathy with the psychological state of the doomed man. He feels the pressure of time weighing on him, and is aware of the irony in the fact that the clock itself seems to the doomed man to be the agent of his death. The impact would not be so great were it not that the beat, or rhythm, of the poem goes on in two ways at once. There is the effect of the contrasts, the suspense and gathering, and the final blow built up by the individual, dramatic manner of presentation; and there is also the basic, conventional pattern of the form the poet has chosen— the four-line stanza with alternating rhymes, and with a basic iambic pattern of alternating light and heavy stresses: "He stóod, and héard the stéeple. . . ." Not all the syllables alternate so regularly, but this is the predominant pattern; and when, as in the second, third, and fifth lines, we find other variations, we can feel them pulling against this pattern to create a special emphasis. So also, each stanza begins with a line of three feet; the second and third lines have five feet, and the fourth, after this effect of expansion, contracts sharply to two. Meaningful variation within a pattern, and the use of skilfully contrived forms to suggest the sound of real speech, are signs of poetic craftsmanship.

This poem shows how important to poetic rhythm are its pauses. If a line makes a complete unit of meaning in itself, coming to a halt of some kind at its end, we say it is end-stopped. If its meaning and movement carry over to the succeeding line we call it a run-on line (*enjambment*). A good poet can control his effects to a high degree by his skill in handling longer and shorter units. He therefore knows how to manage the *caesura*, a definite pause, usually near the middle of a line, which marks a break both in meaning and metrical pattern:

He stood,//and heard the steeple. . . .

Notice how, in the first stanza of *Eight O'Clock*, Housman achieves great variety by placing the caesura early in the first line, then using a long breathsweep without another break until the end of the second line, then giving us three sharp pauses and a long fourth one in his third line, and at last sweeping on again without a pause to the end of the stanza. In the second stanza, he begins with two heavy stresses, each followed by a caesura, brings the first line up short, focuses on the doomed man's feelings in the harshly alliterative but unpausing second line, and then continues without a break until the middle of the last line. Here he pauses weightily, coming down with all the force he can in the concluding foot. Thus, the placing of the pauses has a great deal to do with the pacing and final force of the poem.

A good deal of the music, emotional subtlety, and tempo of a poem derives from such interplay between its "natural" and its "artificial" rhythms. Though the poet may seem to be concentrating all of his energies on the ideas, images, and general content of his poem, he organizes and displays them through the underlying conventional pattern of rhythm and stanza-form. The situation is analogous to the working of the human body. We act as though we were perfectly free agents, yet all the time we are profoundly disciplined by mechanical controls of innumerable physiological processes.

This point brings us to what is called free verse, or *vers libre*. Free verse, speaking very generally, is poetry written according to some other pattern than that of regularly recurring conventional feet—poetry composed, to use the words of Ezra Pound, once one of its chief exponents, "in the sequence of the musical phrase, not in the sequence of the metronome." [1] This distinction is not exact, for fine conventional verse always has its special music. But it is the kind of language often used by experimental writers who, wanting to get back to the essentials of a fresh and living poetic technique, strike out against more timid writers whose work is conservative in form. A slavish adherence to a few traditional types of versification, particularly to blank verse—that is, iambic pentameter, or a sequence of five groups of recurring light and heavy stresses in one line— was what Pound meant by the "sequence of the metronome." In the hands of such masters as Shakespeare, Milton, and Tennyson, no form would produce merely the *tock-tock-tock* of the metronome. In the hands of their imitators in the late nineteenth and the early twentieth century, blank verse became mechanical in rhythm and artificial in diction.

The same sort of difference exists between the brilliant versification of Dryden and Pope (in the later seventeenth and earlier eighteenth centuries) and the work of *their* more tepid followers. These two poets, also, were great masters of their craft. They created the most varied effects with their "heroic couplets"—rhyming pairs of iambic pentameter lines that were especially suitable for forceful intellectual statement, wit, or satire, and that in the hands of these masters became also a vehicle for the expression of sensuous richness and powerful emotion. In the late eighteenth century, the imitators of Pope, and of Milton as well, were often sentimental, pompous, or simply dull. Consequently, Wordsworth and other poets turned against the deadened verse-forms that had become predominant by the end of the 1700's and argued for greater freedom of style and rhythm and greater idiomatic freshness of diction. They were the "experimental" poets of their day, though now we think of the great Romantics as a sanctified part of the English verse tradition.

[1] Ezra Pound, *Make It New*.

Good free verse, as has often been pointed out, is *not* free in the sense of being unpatterned and uncontrolled. It always has its own formal consistency, employing certain kinds of grammatical parallelism, repeated phrasings with slight variations that do not quite fit the beat of conventional meter, images that provide balance and contrast for one another, questions and answers that reinforce one another in sound as well as in meaning, and other similar devices. All the methods just listed may be found in the following lines from Walt Whitman's *When lilacs last in the dooryard bloom'd*:

> O how shall I warble myself for the dead one there I loved?
> And how shall I deck my song for the large sweet soul that has gone?
> And what shall my perfume be for the grave of him I love?
>
> Sea-winds blown from east and west,
> Blown from the Eastern sea and blown from the Western sea, till there
> on the prairies meeting,
> These and with these and the breath of my chant,
> I'll perfume the grave of him I love.

Though Whitman wrote before Pound and the other twentieth-century experimentalists, he rediscovered, as other poets before him also had done, the value of *cadenced* rhythms, in which the poet depends on his own ear for sound and on patterns of rhythm determined by the feeling and general content of what he is writing. The translators of the Psalms and the Song of Songs in the King James Bible, the eighteenth-century experimentalists Christopher Smart and William Blake, and others had long preceded Whitman in creating such effects.

The competent free-verse poet may use rhymes if he feels it necessary— or any other combination of effects that might ordinarily be found in more conventional verse. The point is, he is *free* to use any technique, but he will use it in his own unique manner. We may observe how, when he is truly skilful, he achieves patterns of rhythm and sound quite as rich as those of the great masters of conventional forms, by examining another passage from *When lilacs last in the dooryard bloom'd*—the opening section of the poem:

> When lilacs last in the dooryard bloom'd
> And the great star early droop'd in the western sky in the night,
> I mourn'd, and yet shall mourn with ever-returning spring.
>
> Ever-returning spring, trinity sure to me you bring,
> Lilac blooming perennial and drooping star in the west,
> And thought of him I love.

These lines from the beginning of Whitman's elegy on Abraham Lincoln show how much patterned arrangement can be found in an unconventional form. We shall simply note a few of the more obvious points: the "internal" rhyming of "spring" and "bring" in the fourth line; the unstressed -*ing* sounds that, in the third, fourth, and fifth lines, give us fainter rhymes with these words, together with the sound of "in," "trinity," and "him"; the repetition of "spring" and "bring" and "ever-returning"; the many *l*'s, *d*'s, *r*'s, *t*'s, and *n*'s; the fact that in each of these three-line stanzas the second line seems to expand in space and the third line gives a sharp personal turn of feeling to the stanza. Note also how the first two lines give us two pictures that counteract each other, each presented in one-half of a compound clause. This contrast-and-balance is repeated in the two phrases of the fifth line. Only very superficially could we say that these lines are "free"; all the important phrases and effects are associated with the patterns we have just mentioned. Indeed, the *whole* pattern of repeated and related vowels (*assonance*) and consonants (*alliteration*) in any poem is more important than any "regularity" of line-length or of rhyme-scheme could be to its musical effect. If we appreciate this fact, we shall also appreciate the deliberate use poets often make of dissonances which alert the reader through a surprising disharmony of sound that makes key words and phrases stand out in reading.

Looking for deliberate design again, we can say that despite the apparently arbitrary arrangement of such lines as those by Whitman just quoted, the passage actually presents a pattern of balanced impressions typical of many prayers and free-verse poems. Let us, for instance, consider how the two closing lines picture forth the "trinity" that the poet says the spring always recalls to him:

> Lilac blooming perennial and drooping star in the west,
> And thought of him I love.

Each of these three phrases joined by "and" contains three stressed syllables, each begins emphatically, and each repeats and builds up the significance of language already used in preceding stanzas. Such effects as these, which the skilled poet employs to fix pictures and ideas and feelings in our minds, are essential in creating a sense of a meaningfully patterned work of poetic art.

Actually, the term *free verse* is rarely used today by practicing poets. For the most part, they recognize that there is no difference in the essentials of technique between good free verse and good conventional poetry. Both depend for their success on the same qualities of imaginative precision of imagery, rightness of diction, and the adaptation of rhythm to the effect the poet wishes to produce. Under the influence especially of William Carlos Williams and Ezra Pound, a renewed movement toward *open form* has developed in recent years. In part, this movement opposes the very idea of what we have called "a meaningfully patterned work of poetic art." In the work of such poets as Robert Duncan, Charles Olson, and Gary Snyder, we often find a deliberate refusal to accept the poet's traditional aim of creating a beautifully consistent, concentrated, self-contained work that moves in a pure curve from the initial situation of the poem to its resolution. These poets, highly talented from a conventional standpoint, are nevertheless more interested in reflecting the process that goes on in their minds than in giving us a finished product that conceals the process but presents a complete structure that has grown out of it. Their real triumph, when they succeed, is in the way they focus on the caught moment of consciousness—like a snapshot of the mind in action—as it flickers across the surface of the deep reverie of our private awareness. The rhythm then becomes a kind of fingerprint of the personality that is speaking. Here is an instance, a passage from Olson's *The Songs of Maximus*:

> This morning of the small snow
> I count the blessings, the leak in the faucet
> which makes of the sink time, the drop
> of the water on water as sweet
> as the Seth Thomas
> in the old kitchen
> my father stood in his drawers to wind (always
> he forgot the 30th day, as I don't want to remember
> the rent
>   a house these days   10
> so much somebody else's,
> especially,
> Congoleum's
>
>
>   Or the plumbing,
> that it doesn't work, this I like, have even used paper clips
> as well as string to hold the ball up And flush it
> with my hand
>   But that the car doesn't, that no living thing moves
> without that song I'd void my ear of, the musickracket
> of all ownership . . .   20
>   Holes
> in my shoes, that's all right, my fly
> gaping, me out
> at the elbows, the blessing
>   that difficulties are once more. . . .

Clearly a passage like this is very different from the typical chanting music of Whitman. Its ragged irregularity of movement is no more like the artful patterns of most earlier free verse than it is like the highly controlled formal movement of the poems by Wallace Stevens and A. E. Housman that we have examined. Yet the fusion of diction, rhythm, and sentence movement—that is, the poem's *music*—is inseparable from its speaker's self and communicates his sense of life and his natural posture. We can see—to take another example—a similar unification of all the tonal elements in Yeats's brief love lyric A *Deep-Sworn Vow* to communicate again a sense of the poet's own unique and unified being. As we can see from the first two lines of Yeats's poem, it is written in basically iambic tetrameter lines with much metrical variation.

> Others, because you did not keep
> That deep-sworn vow, have been friends of mine.

The poet's understatement, his subdued internal rhyme ("you did not *keep* that *deep*-sworn vow"), and his colloquial edge serve to bring out very quietly the wryness of his thought: because the woman he loved was untrue to him, he has had other "friends"—that is, other loves who were, however, really hardly more than friends compared with the "you" of the poem.

Olson's poem, too, has some subtle echoings of sound, and a powerful emotion held in check at first by a certain minimizing effect—in the word "small," in the attention to minutiae ("the leak in the faucet," the domestic detail, the water-drops). But Olson is after something entirely unlike Yeats's purpose. He is not presenting a highly romantic image of a man who cannot forget his one true love; he is presenting himself in the midst of his everyday, empirical existence. He dreams, not of an overwhelming love, but of a sufficiently simple, sufficiently laborious and physical existence. The speaker is a humorously cross-grained man, deliberately using vernacular speech, somewhat gropingly, to sustain an image of himself without romantic clichés. He is a rejecter of the new, slickly mechanical civilization that drains men of significant personality, experience, and memory all at once, bribing them with conveniences. He *likes* his old house with its old problems, where his father used to wind the thirty-day clock, and his shabby, slightly inconvenient clothing. These are emblems of his resistance to the profiteering salesmanship of modern America. It may seem odd to say that the way he breaks his rhythmic patterns, so that there is no line-length, arrangement of stresses, or parallelism of structure that lasts longer than a few lines, is crucial to his success in conveying that resistance. The broken rhythmic movement gives us an intimate sense of a man who chooses to lead the kind of trivially harassed life most of us associate with the films of old-time comedians like Chaplin or Laurel and Hardy. The closing lines of the quotation—"Holes in my shoes, etc."—show that Olson was well aware of this effect.

Olson's rhythms, to which we can apply traditional metrical analysis only in bits, represent a new approach to poetry strongly influenced by the practice and theory of Pound and Williams. In this approach, the units are breath-sweeps, large phrasal units, and blocks of language seen in relation to one another and to the overall structure. The approach may be used quite as well with traditional verse; Milton, for instance, thought out vast units of musical patterning although he worked with conventionally conceived lines. Williams tried to suggest the relationship of traditional and experimental verse through his conception of the "variable foot," a unit based on musical duration and rest as felt in natural speech. Williams argued that the traditional system of "counted syllables" has, in the best modern free verse, "become entirely divorced from the beat, that is the measure. The musical pace proceeds without them." The poet, he said, needs "to keep in mind the *tune* which the lines (not necessarily the words) make in our ears." Thus, each of the following lines is conceived as filling the same space of time as the others despite the differences in length:

> Of asphodel, that greeny flower,
>   like a buttercup
>   upon its branching stem—
> save that it's green and wooden—
>   I come, my sweet,
>   to sing to you. . . .

The conception is literally of a "space of time." Each of the line units is isolated in space, as it were, and hovers there in a sort of architectural relation to the others, while at the same time there is a temporal, sequential progression. Sometimes, in long poems, especially of the sort we now call *sequences*, this extended conception of free verse enables the poet to employ blocks of prose (quotations from documents, descriptive or narrative passages, or any other prose he thinks effective for his purposes) that cut into the more strictly poetic sections. There is something spatial, or even pictorial, about this method; actually, it gives a poem some of the structural character of the sort of "sculpture" we call a mobile when done by an artist like Alexander Calder. It is helpful for the reader to think of *any* poem as a verbal mobile, with each of its parts moving in its own way and yet related to the conception and overall character of the whole. But when the form is broken up by the mixture of different kinds of verse and the inclusion of prose and other "nonpoetic" materials (such as visual designs of individual words, lists, and diagrams), the concept of the poem as mobile is essential for understanding.

In Williams's long poem *Paterson*, for instance, the verse-form often changes, and there are many interruptions by prose passages. The poet was preoccupied with the quality of life in the region where he lived and worked as a doctor—the area around Paterson, New Jersey. He wanted to look closely at its actual population, its landscape, and its history. The poem broods over the problem of finding a "common language"— that is, a way of living and a sense of social communion that will enable a truly human culture to flourish in the cities of industrial America despite their violence, filth, and loss of touch with the meaningful past. The poet's mind goes over these themes, shifting in tone and rhythmic pattern according to the feelings and topics involved. Occasionally he quotes from old newspaper accounts and historical documents. At other times he quotes from letters sent him by a woman writer expressing a personal despair and isolation central to the poem's theme—for *Paterson* is not just about the region but about the state of America's soul, and to an important degree about how that state is manifested in the situation of women and in the relations of the sexes. The documents, letters, and other such materials are touchstones of literal reality, of the actual world within which the poet writes and speaks. His voice is defined by its relation to that world. Thus, we may see the poem as a mobile made up of the poet's own varied voices (lyrical, colloquial, argumentative, meditative, and satirical) and of various "documentary" voices out of literal reality. There are many reasons why modern poets resort to a scheme like Williams's from time to time. The primary reason is the fact that so much varied information is available to us, that so many apparently unrelated types of experience and attitude exist side by side in our world; hence, the poet cannot be sure that his readers will share his assumptions or his knowledge unless he builds them into his poem. The process creates a reciprocal rhythm between the objective or "documentary" elements and the subjective movement of the basic poetic voice.

The intrusion of visual effects related to breaks in voice and to the balancing of different types of material within a single poem should not lead us to think that poetry no longer depends heavily on its sounds and rhythms, its whole "music," for much of its character. That idea would be as naïve as the idea that contemporary music itself is not truly musical because it lacks the melodic base of classical music. From its beginnings poetry has been associated with dance and song, and though it is by no means always purely lyrical, it always makes some use of the musical effect in the sounds of words. The more skilful the artist and the deeper the excitement with which he writes, the greater will be the harmony between the sound and the sense. The complete meaning of his poem will be communicated by *how* he says what he is saying. It is this aspect of poetry that we think of as ultimately untranslatable. We can—and often must, if we are to understand it—paraphrase any poem. But a paraphrase is no substitute for a poem. You cannot say in any other way what is said by such a line as Shakespeare's

If music be the food of love, play on.

Change the words or change the order of the words and the effect is gone and something different and less memorable is substituted for it.

The part played by the music of poetry in stirring the senses and entering into the listener's awareness with tenacious power has been suggested (and illustrated) by Shelley in the little song beginning

Music, when soft voices die,
Vibrates in the memory

and by Tennyson in the famous *Choric Song of the Lotos Eaters*:

There is sweet music here that softer falls
Than petals from blown roses on the grass,
Or night-dews on still waters between walls
Of shadowy granite, in a gleaming pass;
Music that gentlier on the spirit lies,
Than tired eyelids upon tired eyes;
Music that brings sweet sleep down from the blissful skies.
Here are cool mosses deep,
And through the moss the ivies creep,
And in the stream the long-leaved flowers weep.
And from the craggy ledge the poppy hangs in sleep.

Here the sureness with which the poet as hypnotist goes to work on us commands the utmost admiration. The words are the simplest. The sounds are full, open, and resonant. Key sounds and key words are repeated, and they re-echo among themselves. The rhythm wavers, slackens, thickens, and slows up, until at the end we ourselves are under the spell of the lotos. This effect is gained by the intermingling of similar and nearly similar vowel sounds in an intricate pattern of repetition, assonance, and rhyme; by the use of a complex and subtle system of alliterations; and by a progressive slowing up of the rhythm that can be seen at its most striking in the cumulatively increasing length of the last four lines linked together by the one rhyme.

Sometimes the music of a poem, and the expression of meaning through sound, depends on even subtler effects than the very elaborate alliteration and cross-alliteration in the passage we have been considering. In Keats's *Ode to a Nightingale* we find a reference to the musk-rose, "full of dewy wine,"

> The murmurous haunt of flies on summer eves.

It is clear that the sound of the line itself helps to suggest the subdued humming of the insects, and the line is a straightforward and uncomplex example of what is called onomatopoeia—the formation of words in imitation of natural sounds.

Another line in the same poem illustrates a more subtle form of the harmonization of sense and sound, or the utilization of sound to reinforce, emphasize, and make memorable the purely logical meaning of the words. If we read aloud the line

> Through verdurous glooms and winding mossy ways

our lips and tongues must imitate muscularly the sinuous movement of the line and its suggestion of mysterious, almost secret seclusion.

Something of the same effect is to be found in a line of John Donne's fantastic theological poem *The Progress of the Soul*. The poet is telling how the largest, though not the brightest, of all beasts, the mighty elephant, was destroyed by a tiny, clever mouse, and he writes:

> His sinewy proboscis did remissly lie.

Taking advantage of this negligence, the rodent climbs the tunnel of the trunk and gnaws at the elephant's brain, bringing the mighty animal crashing to the ground. The effect of the undulating rhythm of the line is partly grotesque, partly comic, and partly realistic. Some of the comic effect no doubt is due to calling the elephant's trunk a proboscis—an elongated and exaggerated one of course it is—and to the use of the pompous word "remissly," but the total effect, that of grotesque incongruity, is due mainly to the sound and rhythm of the line. In *Paradise Lost* Milton mentions the elephant and his characteristic appendage in an equally brilliant and entertaining passage. He is describing how the still tame and obedient animals gamboled around Adam and Eve in the state of innocence. Among them

> . . . th' unwieldy Elephant
> To make them mirth us'd all his might, and wreath'd
> His lithe Proboscis. . . .

Milton, like Donne and Keats, was, of course, an accomplished virtuoso, and many illustrations might be cited of his skill. We must content ourselves with one—a line, which, like some of those already quoted, reinforces the sense by an actually muscular effect. It occurs in a passage describing how the fallen angels had tried to allay their thirst with delicious-seeming fruit that turned to ashes in their mouths.

With hatefullest disrelish writh'd their jaws,

writes the poet, and the reader finds that his own lips are forced into a nimble twisting movement that communicates the bitterness of the subject with an almost physical intensity.

Here everything is dry, harsh, and grating. Our own mouths are filled with ashes as we read. The poet can, however,—as Keats does in *The Eve of St. Agnes*—flood our senses with richness and make our mouths water with his soft vocables and luscious vowel sounds as he describes the midnight feast Prophyro prepares for his beloved Madeleine:

> And still she slept an azure-lidded sleep,
> In blanchèd linen, smooth, and lavendered,
> While he from forth the closet brought a heap
> Of candied apple, quince, and plum, and gourd;
> With jellies soother than the creamy curd,
> And lucent syrups, tinct with cinnamon;
> Manna and dates, in argosy transferred
> From Fez; and spicèd dainties, every one,
> From silken Samarcand to cedared Lebanon.

Often poetry does not attempt, as in these examples, to offer concrete perceptions or impressions, to imitate, that is, or re-create reality. Instead it may seek through the medium of the artful combinations of sounds and of meanings not very easily definable to approach the quality of pure music. A poem by James Joyce may serve as a concluding illustration.

JAMES JOYCE *I hear an army charging upon the land*

> I hear an army charging upon the land
>   And the thunder of horses plunging, foam about their knees:
> Arrogant, in black armour, behind them stand,
>   Disdaining the reins, with fluttering whips, the charioteers.
>
> They cry unto the night their battle name:
>   I moan in sleep when I hear afar their whirling laughter.
> They cleave the gloom of dreams, a blinding flame,
>   Clanging, clanging upon the heart as upon an anvil.

They come shaking in triumph their long green hair:
They come out of the sea and run shouting by the shore.   10
My heart, have you no wisdom thus to despair?
My love, my love, my love, why have you left me alone?

Such a poem eludes an exact literal interpretation—or, more precisely, derives its effects from elements having little to do with its literal meaning. It conveys, through sounds and pictures, and through an elegant and stylized use of language, something that cannot be defined in any other terms but the sounds and pictures themselves, and that can only be described as a mood, a tone, or an atmosphere: something emotional rather than rational.

This emotional, irrational element in poetic meaning is its "magic." In Joyce's poem, the magic is psychological—a nightmare imagery of terror, loss, and despair. There are many ways to "interpret" the contemptuous, cruel, green-haired sea-charioteers who threaten the moaning speaker, but their relation to his frustrated love is made apparent at the very end. The poem, like so much of music itself, is both lucid and elusive. Music, finally, is the key to the poem's magic: the actual sound of "Clanging, clanging upon the heart as upon an anvil."

The musical aspects of poetry are its earliest and most striking features. They by no means lead only into a private and somewhat rarefied world of essences, partly untranslatable as the songs we have just been considering may be. It has often been these very untranslatable aspects of poetry—its rhythm and harmony—that have made it function as one kind of social and even religious ritual by which men express their sense of kinship and emotional communion.

Poems: Rhythm and Music

This section begins with a re-creation of the alliterative four-stress line of Anglo-Saxon verse in Ezra Pound's translation of *The Seafarer*. It continues with the delicate, pure music of Elizabethan song, including an unrhymed lyric by the poet-musician Thomas Campion, and with a nineteenth-century postscript: Shelley's brief evocation of the power of music. The longer and more elaborate poems by Milton, Tennyson, and Swinburne that follow are all remarkable for their orchestration of melody and rhythm. Bridges's poem, despite its simple form and direct statement, is a remarkably subtle construct of succeeding waves of sound—each different in character from those preceding —that accelerate in power. Wallace Stevens's poem, already discussed in the text, seeks to make a different kind of musical pattern for each of the qualitatively differing situations and modes of thought it presents. The poems by Williams, Lindsay, and Rosenthal are energetic and lively in a rough and ready, thoroughly American tradition. Those by Whitman, Creeley, and Lowell discover rhythms—variously incantatory, hesitantly exploratory, and anguished —to match the inward state or consciousness of the speaker.

EZRA POUND   *The Seafarer* [1]

> May I for my own self song's truth reckon,
> Journey's jargon, how I in harsh days
> Hardship endured oft.
> Bitter breast-cares have I abided,
> Known on my keel many a care's hold,
> And dire sea-surge, and there I oft spent
> Narrow nightwatch nigh the ship's head
> While she tossed close to cliffs. Coldly afflicted,
> My feet were by frost benumbed.
> Chill its chains are; chafing sighs   10
> Hew my heart round and hunger begot
> Mere-weary mood. Lest man know not

[1] In Anglo-Saxon poetry, the typical line has two units of phrasing or statement, marked by alliteration—the repetition of a sound in stressed positions. (This means the exact repetition of a given consonant, but any vowel is considered alliterative with any other one.) The rhythm has been compared to that of rowers because of the chanting, repetitive effort. *Is Pound consistent in this technique, or does he mix it with the metrics of later English poetry? Do the alliteration, the archaic diction, and the stock metaphors (kennings) such as "whale-path" and "whale's acre" for sea make the poem too alien in tone for us to read sympathetically today? Or, on the contrary, do they create a harsh vigor that makes it more immediate for us than some of the poems that follow it?*

That he on dry land loveliest liveth,
List how I, care-wretched, on ice-cold sea,
Weathered the winter, wretched outcast
Deprived of my kinsmen;
Hung with hard ice-flakes, where hail-scur flew,
There I heard naught save the harsh sea
And ice-cold wave, at whiles the swan cries,
Did for my games the gannet's clamour,   20
Sea-fowls' loudness was for me laughter,
The mews' singing all my mead-drink.
Storms, on the stone-cliffs beaten, fell on the stern
In icy feathers; full oft the eagle screamed
With spray on his pinion.
                            Not any protector
May make merry man faring needy.
This he little believes, who aye in winsome life
Abides 'mid burghers some heavy business,
Wealthy and wine-flushed, how I weary often   30
Must bide above brine.
Neareth nightshade, snoweth from north,
Frost froze the land, hail fell on earth then,
Corn of the coldest. Nathless there knocketh now
The heart's thought that I on high streams
The salt-wavy tumult traverse alone.
Moaneth alway my mind's lust
That I fare forth, that I afar hence
Seek out a foreign fastness.
For this there's no mood-lofty man over earth's midst,   40
Not though he be given his good, but will have in his youth greed;
Nor his deed to the daring, nor his king to the faithful
But shall have his sorrow for sea-fare
Whatever his lord will.
He hath not heart for harping, nor in ring-having
Nor winsomeness to wife, nor world's delight
Nor any whit else save the wave's slash,
Yet longing comes upon him to fare forth on the water.
Bosque taketh blossom, cometh beauty of berries,
Fields to fairness, land fares brisker,   50
All this admonisheth man eager of mood,
The heart turns to travel so that he then thinks
On flood-ways to be far departing.
Cuckoo calleth with gloomy crying,
He singeth summerward, bodeth sorrow,

The bitter heart's blood. Burgher knows not—
He the prosperous man—what some perform
Where wandering them widest draweth.
So that but now my heart burst from my breast-lock,
My mood 'mid the mere-flood,   60
Over the whale's acre, would wander wide.
On earth's shelter cometh oft to me,
Eager and ready, the crying lone-flyer,
Whets for the whale-path the heart irresistibly,
O'er tracks of ocean; seeing that anyhow
My lord deems to me this dead life
On loan and on land, I believe not
That any earth-weal eternal standeth
Save there be somewhat calamitous
That, ere a man's tide go, turn it to twain.   70
Disease or oldness or sword-hate
Beats out the breath from doom-gripped body.
And for this, every earl whatever, for those speaking after—
Laud of the living, boasteth some last word,
That he will work ere he pass onward,
Frame on the fair earth 'gainst foes his malice,
Daring ado, . . .
So that all men shall honour him after
And his laud beyond them remain 'mid the English,
Aye, for ever, a lasting life's-blast,   80
Delight 'mid the doughty.
                        Days little durable,
And all arrogance of earthen riches,
There come now no kings nor Cæsars
Nor gold-giving lords like those gone.
Howe'er in mirth most magnified,
Whoe'er lived in life most lordliest,
Drear all this excellence, delights undurable!
Waneth the watch, but the world holdeth.
Tomb hideth trouble. The blade is laid low.   90
Earthly glory ageth and seareth.
No man at all going the earth's gait,
But age fares against him, his face paleth,
Grey-haired he groaneth, knows gone companions,
Lordly men, are to earth o'ergiven,
Nor may he then the flesh-cover, whose life ceaseth,
Nor eat the sweet nor feel the sorry,
Nor stir hand nor think in mid heart,

And though he strew the grave with gold,
His born brothers, their buried bodies
Be an unlikely treasure hoard.

WILLIAM SHAKESPEARE   *Full fathom five thy father lies*

(from *The Tempest*)

Full fathom five thy father lies;
  Of his bones are coral made;
Those are pearls that were his eyes:
  Nothing of him that doth fade
But doth suffer a sea-change
Into something rich and strange.
Sea-nymphs hourly ring his knell:
                     Ding-dong.
Hark! now I hear them,—Ding-dong, bell.

THOMAS CAMPION   *Rose-cheekt Laura, come*

    Rose-cheekt Laura, come
Sing thou smoothly with thy beauty's
Silent music, either other
    Sweetly gracing.

    Lovely forms do flow
From concent divinely framed;
Heav'n is music, and thy beauty's
    Birth is heavenly.

    These dull notes we sing
Discords need for helps to grace them;   10
Only beauty purely loving
    Knows no discord,

    But still moves delight,
Like clear springs renew'd by flowing,
Ever perfect, ever in them-
    selves eternal.

BEN JONSON *Slow, slow, fresh fount, keep time with*
  my salt tears

> Slow, slow, fresh fount, keep time with my salt tears;
>   Yet slower, yet; o faintly, gentle springs:
> List to the heavy part the music bears;
>   Woe weeps out her division when she sings.
>   Droop herbs and flowers;
>   Fall grief in showers;
>   Our beauties are not ours.
>   O, I could still,
> Like melting snow upon some craggy hill,
>   Drop, drop, drop, drop,
> Since Nature's pride is now a withered daffodil.

10

PERCY BYSSHE SHELLEY *To* ——

> Music, when soft voices die,
> Vibrates in the memory—
> Odours, when sweet violets sicken,
> Live within the sense they quicken.
>
> Rose leaves, when the rose is dead,
> Are heaped for the beloved's bed;
> And so thy thoughts, when thou art gone,
> Love itself shall slumber on.

JOHN MILTON *At a Solemn Music*

> Blest pair of Sirens, pledges of Heav'n's joy,
> Sphere-born harmonious sisters, Voice and Verse,
> Wed your divine sounds, and mixt power employ,
> Dead things with inbreath'd sense able to pierce;
> And to our high-rais'd phantasy present
> That undisturbèd song of pure concent,
> Aye sung before the sapphire-coloured throne
> To him that sits thereon
> With saintly shout and solemn jubilee;
> Where the bright Seraphim in burning row
> Their loud uplifted angel trumpets blow,

10

And the Cherubic host in thousand quires
Touch their immortal harps of golden wires,
With those just Spirits that wear victorious palms,
Hymns devout and holy psalms
Singing everlastingly:
That we on Earth, with undiscording voice,
May rightly answer that melodious noise;
As once we did, till disproportion'd sin
Jarr'd against nature's chime, and with harsh din   20
Broke the fair music that all creatures made
To their great Lord, whose love their motion sway'd
In perfect diapason, whilst they stood
In first obedience, and their state of good.
O may we soon again renew that song,
And keep in tune with Heaven, till God ere long
To his celestial consort us unite,
To live with him, and sing in endless morn of light.

ALFRED, LORD TENNYSON   from *The Lotos-Eaters* [1]

"Courage!" he said, and pointed toward the land,
"This mounting wave will roll us shoreward soon."
In the afternoon they came unto a land
In which it seemed always afternoon.
All round the coast the languid air did swoon,
Breathing like one that hath a weary dream.
Full-faced above the valley stood the moon;
And like a downward smoke, the slender stream
Along the cliff to fall and pause and fall did seem.

A land of streams! some, like a downward smoke,   10
Slow-dropping veils of thinnest lawn, did go;
And some through wavering lights and shadows broke,
Rolling a slumbrous sheet of foam below.
They saw the gleaming river seaward flow
From the inner land: far off, three mountain-tops,
Three silent pinnacles of aged snow,
Stood sunset-flushed: and, dewed with showery drops,
Up-clomb the shadowy pine above the woven copse.

[1] See Homer's *Odyssey*, Book IX.

The charmed sunset lingered low adown
In the red West: through mountain clefts the dale   20
Was seen far inland, and the yellow down
Bordered with palm, and many a winding vale
And meadow, set with slender galingale;
A land where all things always seemed the same!
And round about the keel with faces pale,
Dark faces pale against that rosy flame,
The mild-eyed melancholy Lotos-eaters came.

Branches they bore of that enchanted stem,
Laden with flower and fruit, whereof they gave
To each, but whoso did receive of them,   30
And taste, to him the gushing of the wave
Far far away did seem to mourn and rave
On alien shores; and if his fellow spake,
His voice was thin, as voices from the grave;
And deep-asleep he seemed, yet all awake,
And music in his ears his beating heart did make.

They sat them down upon the yellow sand,
Between the sun and moon upon the shore;
And sweet it was to dream of Fatherland,
Of child, and wife, and slave; but evermore   40
Most weary seemed the sea, weary the oar,
Weary the wandering fields of barren foam.
Then someone said, "We will return no more";
And all at once they sang, "Our island home
Is far beyond the wave; we will no longer roam."

ALGERNON CHARLES SWINBURNE   *Chorus* from *Atalanta in Calydon*

When the hounds of spring are on winter's traces,
   The mother of months in meadow or plain
Fills the shadows and windy places
   With lisp of leaves and ripple of rain;
And the brown bright nightingale amorous
Is half assuaged for Itylus,
For the Thracian ships and the foreign faces,
   The tongueless vigil, and all the pain.

Come with bows bent and with emptying of quivers,
    Maiden most perfect, lady of light,   10
With a noise of winds and many rivers,
    With a clamour of waters, and with might;
Bind on thy sandals, O thou most fleet,
Over the splendour and speed of thy feet;
For the faint east quickens, the wan west shivers,
    Round the feet of the day and the feet of the night.

Where shall we find her, how shall we sing to her,
    Fold our hands round her knees, and cling?
O that man's heart were as fire and could spring to her,
    Fire, or the strength of the streams that spring!   20
For the stars and the winds are unto her
As raiment, as songs of the harp-player;
For the risen stars and the fallen cling to her,
    And the southwest-wind and the west-wind sing.

For winter's rains and ruins are over,
    And all the season of snows and sins;
The days dividing lover and lover,
    The light that loses, the night that wins;
And time remember'd is grief forgotten,
And frosts are slain and flowers begotten,   30
And in green underwood and cover
    Blossom by blossom the spring begins.

The full streams feed on flower of rushes,
    Ripe grasses trammel a travelling foot,
The faint fresh flame of the young year flushes
    From leaf to flower and flower to fruit;
And fruit and leaf are as gold and fire,
And the oat is heard above the lyre,
And the hoofed heel of a satyr crushes
    The chestnut-husk at the chestnut-root.   40

And Pan by noon and Bacchus by night,
    Fleeter of foot than the fleet-foot kid,
Follows with dancing and fills with delight
    The Mænad and the Bassarid;
And soft as lips that laugh and hide
The laughing leaves of the trees divide,
And screen from seeing and leave in sight
    The god pursuing, the maiden hid.

The ivy falls with the Bacchanal's hair
　　Over her eyebrows hiding her eyes;   50
The wild vine slipping down leaves bare
　　Her bright breast shortening into sighs;
The wild vine slips with the weight of its leaves,
But the berried ivy catches and cleaves
To the limbs that glitter, the feet that scare
　　The wolf that follows, the fawn that flies.

ROBERT BRIDGES *The hill pines were sighing*

The hill pines were sighing,
O'ercast and chill was the day:
A mist in the valley lying
Blotted the pleasant May.

But deep in the glen's bosom
Summer slept in the fire
Of the odorous gorse-blossom
And the hot scent of the brier.

A ribald cuckoo clamoured,
And out of the copse the stroke
Of the iron axe that hammered
The iron heart of the oak.

Anon a sound appalling,
As a hundred years of pride
Crashed, in the silence falling:
And the shadowy pine-trees sighed.

WALLACE STEVENS *Peter Quince at the Clavier* [1]

I

Just as my fingers on these keys
Make music, so the self-same sounds
On my spirit make a music too.

[1] Peter Quince is one of the country bumpkins in Shakespeare's *A Midsummer Night's Dream*. (*Why does the speaker in this poem call himself Peter Quince?*) The story of Susanna and the Elders appeared in the Apocryphal version of the Book of Daniel in the *Bible*. Susanna, Joacim's beautiful and virtuous wife, refused the advances of two judges (the elders) who had watched her bathe in her garden. They thereupon claimed to have caught her in adultery with a young man. Condemned to death, she was saved by the prophet Daniel. He proved that the elders had borne false witness, and they were put to death instead.

Music is feeling, then, not sound;
And thus it is that what I feel,
Here in this room, desiring you,

Thinking of your blue-shadowed silk,
Is music. It is like the strain
Waked in the elders by Susanna:

Of a green evening, clear and warm,   10
She bathed in her still garden, while
The red-eyed elders, watching, felt

The basses of their being throb
In witching chords, and their thin blood
Pulse pizzicati of Hosanna.

                    II

In the green water, clear and warm,
Susanna lay.
She searched
The touch of springs,
And found   20
Concealed imaginings.
She sighed
For so much melody.

Upon the bank she stood
In the cool
Of spent emotions.
She felt, among the leaves,
The dew
Of old devotions.

She walked upon the grass,   30
Still quavering.
The winds were like her maids,
On timid feet,
Fetching her woven scarves,
Yet wavering.

A breath upon her hand
Muted the night.
She turned—
A cymbal crashed,
And roaring horns.   40

III

Soon, with a noise like tambourines,
Came her attendant Byzantines.

They wondered why Susanna cried
Against the elders by her side:

And as they whispered, the refrain
Was like a willow swept by rain.

Anon their lamps' uplifted flame
Revealed Susanna and her shame.

And then the simpering Byzantines
Fled, with a noise like tambourines.   50

IV

Beauty is momentary in the mind—
The fitful tracing of a portal;
But in the flesh it is immortal.

The body dies; the body's beauty lives.
So evenings die, in their green going,
A wave, interminably flowing.

So gardens die, their meek breath scenting
The cowl of Winter, done repenting.
So maidens die, to the auroral
Celebration of a maiden's choral.   60

Susanna's music touched the bawdy strings
Of those white elders; but, escaping,
Left only Death's ironic scraping.
Now, in its immortality, it plays
On the clear viol of her memory,
And makes a constant sacrament of praise.

WILLIAM CARLOS WILLIAMS   *The Dance*

In Breughel's great picture, The Kermess,
the dancers go round, they go round and
around, the squeal and the blare and the

tweedle of bagpipes, a bugle and fiddles
tipping their bellies (round as the thick-
sided glasses whose wash they impound)
their hips and their bellies off balance
to turn them. Kicking and rolling about
the Fair Grounds, swinging their butts, those
shanks must be sound to bear up under such   10
rollicking measures, prance as they dance
in Breughel's great picture, The Kermess.

VACHEL LINDSAY   *The Flower-fed Buffaloes*

The flower-fed buffaloes of the spring
In the days of long ago
Ranged where the locomotives sing
And the prairie flowers lie low:—
The tossing, blooming, perfumed grass
Is swept away by the wheat,
Wheels and wheels and wheels spin by
In the spring that still is sweet.
But the flower-fed buffaloes of the spring
Left us, long ago.   10
They gore no more, they bellow no more,
They trundle around the hills no more:—
With the Blackfeet, lying low,
With the Pawnees, lying low,
Lying low.

M. L. ROSENTHAL   *Jim Dandy*

He diddled the ivory keys.
He babbled in Chimpanzese.
   He dabbled in honey
   And made big money
And gave it all back to the bees.

He twirled a gay guitar.
He smoked the sweetest cigar.
   He lay on the grass
   With the head of the class
And left her all ajar.   10

He piped once down your lane.
He warbled a randy refrain.
  He plucked a flower
  From your mama's bower
And rode off on a golden cane.

WALT WHITMAN *I am he that walks with the tender and growing night*

(from *Song of Myself*)

I am he that walks with the tender and growing night,
I call to the earth and sea half-held by the night.

Press close bare-bosom'd night—press close magnetic nourishing
    night!
Night of south winds—night of the large few stars!
Still nodding night—mad naked summer night.

Smile O voluptuous cool-breath'd earth!
Earth of the slumbering and liquid trees!
Earth of the departed sunset—earth of the mountains misty-topt!
Earth of the vitreous pour of the full moon just tinged with blue!
Earth of shine and dark mottling the tide of the river!   10
Earth of the limpid gray of clouds brighter and clearer for my sake!
Far-swooping elbow'd earth—rich apple-blossom'd earth!
Smile, for your lover comes.

ROBERT CREELEY *"I Keep to Myself Such Measures . . ."*

I keep to myself such
measures as I care for,
daily the rocks
accumulate position.

There is nothing
but what thinking makes
it less tangible. The mind,
fast as it goes, loses

pace, puts in place of it
like rocks simple markers,   10
for a way only to
hopefully come back to

where it cannot. All
forgets. My mind sinks.
I hold in both hands such weight
it is my only description.

Robert Lowell   *Fall 1961*

Back and forth, back and forth
goes the tock, tock, tock
of the orange, bland, ambassadorial
face of the moon
on the grandfather clock.

All autumn, the chafe and jar
of nuclear war;
we have talked our extinction to death.
I swim like a minnow
behind my studio window.   10

Our end drifts nearer,
the moon lifts,
radiant with terror.
The state
is a diver under a glass bell.

A father's no shield
for his child.
We are like a lot of wild
spiders crying together,
but without tears.   20

Nature holds up a mirror.
One swallow makes a summer.
It's easy to tick
off the minutes,
but the clockhands stick.

Back and forth!
Back and forth, back and forth—
my one point of rest
is the orange and black
oriole's swinging nest!   30

Chapter Three

Structure: The Poem as a Whole

In examining *Flowers by the Sea*, we took special note of its imagery; and in examining *Eight O'Clock*, of its rhythmic movement. But we could not ignore the other qualities of these poems, since poetic accomplishment involves thought and feeling as well as sound and imagery. It is the interrelationship of many elements that counts—elements that make for a poem's sense of reality, its intellectual and moral realizations, and its level of emotional intensity. If we may here venture a summarizing definition, we might say: A poem is a form of expression in which an unusual number of the resources of language are concentrated into a patterned, organic unit of significant experience.

In the poems by Williams and Housman, the meaning at the heart of this experience is not specifically stated, but is forcefully implied through the selection of detail and the whole manner of presentation. In other poems, however, the significant meaning holds the center of the stage. As in the following example, it is the climax and culmination of the experience:

WILLIAM WORDSWORTH A *slumber did my spirit seal*

> A slumber did my spirit seal;
>   I had no human fears:
> She seemed a thing that could not feel
>   The touch of earthly years.
>
> No motion has she now, no force;
>   She neither hears nor sees;
> Rolled round in earth's diurnal course,
>   With rocks, and stones, and trees.

These two stanzas make an elementary, pathetic contrast between the speaker's past blind illusion concerning a woman who has died and his present bleak awareness of her physical death. His spirit has been asleep.

It had not occurred to him that she might, like more common humanity, be subject to death and decay. But now he is compelled to face this fact— and facing it, he experiences a new and terrible insight that is actually an expansion of his sensibility. He becomes aware as never before of the geographical and astronomical round, impersonal and monotonous, within which we exist. His final helpless vision of the dead woman within the dead globe that carries her endlessly, and meaninglessly, through its daily course is therefore an expression of surrender to the desolate truth.

A simple pattern of sound supports the directness of statement in this poem and its uncomplicated rhymes and stanza-form. The repeated *e*'s, *r*'s, and *s*'s weave a definite design into the poem's fabric. In the last two lines, the *r*'s become especially important and we find, in the words "rolled round," the only strong variation from the regular iambic sequence of light and heavy syllables. This variation corresponds with the heightened emotion—the appalled realization that the beloved woman, now passive and impervious with the rest of subhuman nature, is after all completely under "the touch of earthly years."

It is perhaps easiest to see the emergence of an organic structure in successful poems written in some conventional, simple, and familiar form such as the sonnet. A sonnet is a fourteen-line reflective poem that almost always falls into one of two fairly strictly defined patterns, one known as the English (or sometimes Shakespearean, or Elizabethan) sonnet and the other as the Italian (or Petrarchan) sonnet. The English sonnet is made up of three four-line stanzas, called quatrains, and a final couplet. In each of the quatrains, the first and third lines rhyme with one another, and the second and fourth rhyme with each other also, while the closing couplet adds yet another rhyming unit. (We describe this rhyme-scheme as *abab, cdcd, efef, gg*.) Finally, the sonnet line is ordinarily an iambic pentameter; that is, each line contains five stressed syllables, and if the meter were perfectly regular these stressed syllables would each be preceded by an unstressed syllable. However, we shall almost always find some variations from the pattern, for mere regularity makes for monotonous and slavish rhythm.

It is interesting to observe how, in the following sonnet by Shakespeare, these quite arbitrary conventional limitations are so used as to make the form of the poem seem both natural and especially suitable for its unique thought and feeling. A simple thought grows into a complex meaning intensely experienced because of the way in which all its formal elements support and affect one another.

WILLIAM SHAKESPEARE *Sonnet LXXIII*

> That time of year thou mayst in me behold
> When yellow leaves, or none, or few, do hang

> Upon those boughs which shake against the cold,
> Bare ruin'd choirs, where late the sweet birds sang.
> In me thou seest the twilight of such day
> As after sunset fadeth in the West,
> Which by and by black night doth take away,
> Death's second self that seals up all in rest.
> In me thou seest the glowing of such fire,
> That on the ashes of his youth doth lie,   10
> As the death-bed, whereon it must expire
> Consum'd with that which it was nourish'd by.
> This thou perceiv'st, which makes thy love more strong
> To love that well, which thou must leave ere long.

The logical structure of this poem is quite clear: the same thing is said three times (in a different way each time), and then a consequence of it is stated in the concluding couplet. Reduced to its essence, the argument runs as follows: I am growing old and my youth must die. You, beloved, see the signs of this, yet it makes you love me all the more.

But a poem is much more than a mere summary of its argument. Each of the three quatrains making up the main part of the sonnet presents the idea of age and the approach of an ending in terms of a different image: autumn, the ending of the year, in the first; twilight and sunset, the ending of a day, in the second; and the dying of a fire in the third. These images are not, on the surface, original. What strikes us first in them is their appropriateness, their universality, and especially the rich emotional overtones with which the poet's musical language endows them.

The line

> Bare ruin'd choirs, where late the sweet birds sang

is particularly rich in its evocations, even though some of the implications it would leave in the mind of an Elizabethan Englishman may need to be pointed out in a note. (The reference, though indirect, is clear: it is to the many cathedrals and churches which with the coming of the Protestant monarchs were stripped of their rich and often beautiful ornaments and hangings.)

The reference to "black night" as "Death's second self," though a commonplace of medieval poetry, serves to suggest, without stating it directly, that it is not only youth which will soon be gone, but life itself, and this is reinforced by the image of the dying fire and the reference to the "death-bed."

The line

> Consum'd with that which it was nourish'd by,

is a good instance of Shakespeare's concentrated accuracy. The key idea is that, as it slowly burns out, an aging man's life must feed on its own accumulated richness. This idea emerges perfectly in the image of a fire choked with ashes because of the very abundance of the fuel—a thought that gains in intensity and clarity because it is presented thus in terms of a concrete image.

The organic growth, as though it were a living thing, of this poem may be seen in this sequence of images. All suggest aging and dying, but each provides a different shade of feeling or thought. Each image, indeed, has a second image lurking within it, and it is this second image that makes each stage of the poem significantly different from the others. The speaker compares himself to trees in late autumn; but almost at once our attention is turned to a second image, of the trees as abandoned choirs where sweet music was once heard. The painful loss of a beautiful, vital youth is what age is shown to mean here, at the beginning of the poem. At the next phase of its growth, the poem gives us another image of the coming of old age—the twilight of the day—but now shifts our attention to the future rather than to the past: Death, of which night is the "second self" or twin, is not far in the offing. And in the third stage, the image of the dying fire, at first apparently so simple, is seen as the most complex of all. An aging man is a dying fire, but that fire's own ashes, once its source of nourishment, are also its deathbed. And to this paradoxical picture still another paradox is added: the ashes are actually "consuming" the fire that once fed on *them*.

The third image, it is clear, brings together the connotations of the first (the sense of lost beauty and richness) and of the second (the unavoidable coming on of death). But it also, because of its intricacy and clever suggestion of the ironic and surprising nature of life, prepares us for the speaker's own admiration and delight, at the close of the sonnet, in the character of the beloved person he is addressing.

The poem, therefore, grows into paradox as well as surprise. It has an unexpected, and therefore forceful, happy ending that is nevertheless an integral part of the body of the poem. The strangely intense love granted the poet grows, increases, and does not die. This love becomes an image of glowing life and permanence, and throws back a new, unforeseen, and cheering ray on all that has gone before—all the dark, gloomy images of change and decay. It is as if the birds, the daylight, and the fire were not to be lost forever after all. All this is embodied in the neat concluding couplet, which serves to convey the poet's sense of his own lucky uniqueness. Because of his beloved's devotion, he has been singled out by fortune to triumph over age and death.

Thus we see how a great, original poet used a conventional form for his own purposes. Yet he did have to adapt his art to the demands of that form, and his poem would have been quite different had he employed the so-called Italian rather than the English type of sonnet. Instead of following a pattern of three parallel statements and a striking conclusion, the Italian (or Petrarchan) sonnet falls into two basic movements—an octave (eight-line stanza) and a sestet (six-line stanza). The octave rhymes *abbaabba*, while in the sestet any combination of either two or three rhymes is permitted. (The sonnet below, for example, rhymes *abbaabba, cdcdcd*.) These larger units, with their more demanding rhyme-scheme, present a special problem for the poet who wishes to make them move with conviction and intensity toward an effective conclusion in something of the manner that Shakespeare's sonnet does.

GERARD MANLEY HOPKINS   *God's Grandeur*

> The world is charged with the grandeur of God.
>   It will flame out, like shining from shook foil;
>   It gathers to a greatness, like the ooze of oil
> Crushed. Why do men then now not reck his rod?
> Generations have trod, have trod, have trod;
>   And all is seared with trade; bleared, smeared with toil;
>   And wears man's smudge and shares man's smell: the soil
> Is bare now, nor can foot feel, being shod.
>
> And for all this, nature is never spent;
>   There lives the dearest freshness deep down things;   10
> And though the last lights off the black West went
>   Oh, morning, at the brown brink eastward, springs—
> Because the Holy Ghost over the bent
>   World broods with warm breast and with ah! bright wings.

The movement of this sonnet by a Jesuit priest can be described very simply. In the octave an awestruck outcry of joy at the omnipresent "grandeur of God" is countered by a depressing picture of man's insensitivity to this grandeur; but in the sestet the feeling of joy springs up again and the innate glory of all being and the loving presence of the Holy Ghost are reasserted. This second assertion of pious, joyous faith is quieter (except for the "Oh" and the "ah!" near the end) but even more insistent and powerful than the earlier one, because it is made in the face of the honest recognition that men in general have not responded to the love and beauty implicit in the universe. The octave has been used to present a dilemma, and the sestet to break out of it by the power of its statement of religious belief.

Thus, one of the most important features of the Italian sonnet is the logical and emotional relationship of its two sections. At the break between the octave and the sestet there is a pause in the continuity of the development and a change, or *turn*, in the thought and feeling. The turn may be of various sorts. Perhaps the problem stated in the first part of the poem is solved in the second; a generalization asserted in the octave receives a particular, concrete application in the sestet, or conversely a specific situation is broadened into a consideration of its universal consequences. Sometimes a question, an aspiration, or a doubt presented in the first eight lines is answered, attained to, or resolved in the final six. Along with this logical, dramatic, or narrative development there is also an emotional change: the two sections of the sonnet are contrasted in feeling and tone as well as in thought.

This, of course, is the strict ideal of formal perfection. Not all sonnets, even by the most accomplished masters, maintain the sharp division precisely at the end of the eighth line, and there is often some variation in the rhyme scheme, particularly in the sestet, where a concluding couplet, with its own special climactic effect, is sometimes introduced. The effect produced by formal perfection in the sonnet can be judged by a careful reading of Keats's *On the Sea* (page 126). Many of the most powerful of the sonnets of Milton and Wordsworth vary the position of the break, but they all have the twofold emotional and intellectual structure characteristic of the Italian sonnet.

Looking more closely at *God's Grandeur*, we can see that its twofold structure has nothing mechanical about it, but is suggested at every point along the way. That is, the sense of a glory and hope and beauty waiting to be released in all things, but needing the spur of will and faith so that they can be revealed despite the appearance of unworthiness in men and the experience of despair, is implied in various ways throughout the poem. The very first line, with its delighted picture of a world "charged" with this divine meaning, sets the tone immediately. But there must be a desire in men to discover the meaning, an effort to bring it forth. Foil must be *shook* to manifest its brilliance. (In a letter concerning this poem, Hopkins wrote, "I mean foil in its sense of leaf or tinsel. . . . Shaken goldfoil gives off broad glares like sheet lightning and also . . . a sort of fork lightning too.") The essential "oil" of things will not appear of itself; it must be *pressed* out of them. Generations of men, ignoring the miraculous quality of life, have lost touch with and become callous to it. Their efforts have all been *away* from what is most essential to them. Commerce and labor and the belief in man's self-sufficiency (not "recking" God's "rod") have led to the view of nature as meaningless in itself and to man's total immersion in an odious and filthy isolation from God. Lines four to eight make clear the immensity of the effort needed if the grandeur of God is to be rediscovered.[1] Even the sestet, though it directly proclaims that gran-

---

[1] Since this is an explicitly religious poem, we may take these lines to refer to the state of man since his fall from Eden, just as the rest of the poem refers indirectly to the possibility of grace resulting from the birth and crucifixion of Jesus.

deur again, nevertheless similarly shows that the rediscovery will not be easy. The phrase "for all this" recognizes this fact; "the dearest freshness" is said to exist, but only "deep down things"; and then the poet says that even if all light were to disappear at the sunset, even if, in fact, there seemed to be universal death in "the black West," yet morning *would* reappear (as it does in nature, in which sunset and dawn occur simultaneously in different parts of the world). And the final two lines account for this idea in an image at once comforting, devout, and glowing.

We shall not go into detail concerning the technical aspects of this unusual sonnet, which is at once conventional and unorthodox in form. Its author was one of the nineteenth century's most significant experimentalists in verse, and his sonnet vividly illustrates the way in which a good poet takes advantage of the opportunities a "set" form provides for him. In a general way, *God's Grandeur* follows the traditional iambic pentameter pattern of the sonnet, but there are so many variations from this pattern that its melodic effect is most unlike that of Shakespeare's poem. Thus, we often find two or three stressed syllables coming together; in the fourth line, indeed, almost every syllable can be stressed. Four to six stresses per line seems the special pattern here, speaking very broadly. The many monosyllables make the poem heavily emphatic, and words that would not ordinarily be stressed, such as *is* in the first line and *will* in the second, are accented as part of the assertive effort, in the face of man's failure, which the poem is making. The surprising repetition of "have trod," such forceful internal rhymes as "seared," "bleared," and "smeared," and the interjection of the "ah!" are similar devices for achieving this assertive effect, as are such alliterative pairings as "shining" and "shook," and "smudge" and "smell."

It is instructive to compare the structures of these two sonnets. Both Shakespeare and Hopkins describe a disheartening state of affairs, and both nevertheless arrive at a strong positive feeling. But Shakespeare's sonnet takes us ever farther downward in a deepening spiral movement toward the speaker's full anticipation of his own death. The praise given to the beloved person at the very end of the sonnet does not stop this movement. Rather, it intensifies it by pointing to the paradox of such a love—by its wonder that such feeling should exist for one so inexorably doomed. Hopkins's sonnet, on the other hand, keeps striving toward a vision of perfection despite the limits of human nature. From the generalized "grandeur" to the shining foil to the generalized "dearest freshness" to the protective, brooding, shining Holy Ghost, the movement is uneven and difficult, especially during the passage concerning the unworthiness of men. The effect is of an effort, through wonder and prayer and faith, that does succeed at last, though not without tragic connotations.

We have thus far considered a series of very short poems, mostly sonnets, because they suggest their structures to us in almost a single sweep of the eye. Like the two simple quatrains of Wordsworth's *A slumber did my spirit seal*, both the English and the Italian sonnet allow for an overall unity of pattern and for variety and complexity within that unity. Both demand of the poet the ability to write within a given cadence or metrical scheme and yet to create a distinctive and dramatically magnetic voice, a convincingly real speaking personality. Each has been handled successfully by poets writing within the traditional limits of the form, as Shakespeare does; and by experimental poets pushing beyond these limits, as Hopkins does. However, the important thing is not whether we can *call* a poem experimental or conventional. Many apparently experimental or "free" poems are in fact simply imitations without much originality, and many apparently conventional ones are extraordinarily original in their effects of language and rhyme. We have made a better test of a poem's success when, having read it sympathetically, we are left with a sense of rich meaning embodied in a living form.

A slightly longer poem than any thus far discussed, Ramon Guthrie's *Polar Bear*, has a structure undetermined by any set form. By looking at the poem now, and simply adapting to what is going on in it without regard to preconceived expectations, we can help ourselves see the approach to structure that is most useful in reading even a traditional sonnet.

RAMON GUTHRIE   *Polar Bear*

> That time coming out from under
> sodium pentathol my first words were,
> "I dreamt I was a polar bear
> that couldn't write poetry."
> Literally but to unhearing ears.
>
> Adrift upon that slab of floe
> under a slate sky
> his conic white
> snout swaying in unison
> with words that never came.   10
>
> The small deft nurse who held
> the glass tube to my lips
> said, "Sip slowly,
> a little at a time. Don't raise your head."
>
> I, not yet aware that words were speech,
> informed her,
> "You are quite lovely

with your copper hair.
You look like something that was turned into a flower
before it was a girl again . . . I can't explain."   20

Later she came back and asked
how I was feeling, "Not bad," I lied,
the anaesthesia now wearing thin.
She laid her hand against my face.
"Still you had better have this though."
An easy needle slipped into my shoulder.

A polar bear who could not . . .
Rocking his baffled muzzle to and fro
groping for the tempo of a world
empty of both sense and sound.   30

I wondered—whatever was in the needle
taking now effect—what had become of him
and brooded over not trying to find a way to help him,
staying at least to share
the anguish of his white bewilderment.

The speaker is remembering a hospital experience. Coming out from the anaesthetic, he had recalled his dream-state, which continued to haunt him. The coldness, remoteness, inarticulateness, and bewildered anguish of that state (created both by the drug and by his closeness to death) are all packed into the dream-image of being a man—a poet—who has somehow become the polar bear of the poem. All this is going on in his innermost consciousness. Meanwhile, we have the actual hospital scene, with the nurse who has practical things to do and say while the awakening poet struggles to get his speech and thought under control.

The scene and the situation as we have just described it opens out as the poem develops. The colloquial, half-humorous, and yet imaginative style is easily perceived; so too is the emotional sensitivity of the speaker—the poem's protagonist, who is, in this case, the poet himself. As the poem progresses, however, there are surprising movements of thought and feeling, and we can find a pleasure in observing, upon reflection and perhaps after several readings, how surely, if unexpectedly, it moves to the pathos of its end. Let us look at it a little more closely.

The first stanza is anecdotal and perhaps a little whimsical. It quickly outlines the general situation, and then introduces the symbol of the bear and identifies it with the poet. Although the stanza evokes a state of helplessness, the first and strongest impression is of the comic side of the speaker's identification of himself with "a polar bear that couldn't write poetry." The final stanza, however, presents the bear and the dreamer with a concentrated and anguished seriousness. At the end, the implications of the dream under anaesthesia are no longer whimsical or comic, but profoundly disturbing.

How was this development brought about? One way was to isolate, in the second stanza, the image of that strange polar bear who is the poet himself *in extremis*—the perhaps dying poet vainly seeking the words he needs. Not only is a whole stanza given to this image of absolute loss; the stanza is sharply separated from all the others visually by being set off to the right. Perhaps the scene still has a slightly comic grotesqueness, but even that element contributes to the effect of desolate and incommunicable isolation. At the same time, the poet uses no specifically emotion-laden words here, as he will in his closing stanza.

A poem is a sequence of effects. After the whimsical-sad opening, we have had a projection of defeat and loss. We are now taken through three stanzas that are lightly factual and conversational, with an interval of lyrical imagination, to the powerfully sad and bewildered effects with which the final two stanzas leave us. This sequence of impacts constitutes the dynamics, or succession of intensities, of the poem. The two most intensely concentrated stanzas, the second and the sixth, are made up of prolonged but grammatically incomplete sentences. While the *image* of the polar bear is fully developed in these stanzas, the *thought* is left open; the image carries its obvious associations and meanings, but also there is something in it the poem fights to get through to but cannot quite reach— that is one of the poem's compelling themes. Certain repeated words and half-rhymes and echoes reinforce the structure; this is particularly true of words that in one way or another echo the sounds of "polar" and "bear." For instance, we find "under," "first," "words," "were," "poetry," "literally," and "unhearing ears" in the first stanza alone.

The whole poem is bound together by a tissue of such sounds, a large proportion of them at the ends of lines. But the main point about structure is that it consists of the dynamics of movement between the state of thought and feeling projected at the start and that projected at the end. Everything in a good poem, whether a matter of sound or imagery or rhythm or explicit thought or emotion, plays its part by contributing to this structural dynamics. The key sounds, tones, and other effects that recur throughout a poem serve to keep it moving as a unified construct, but they must be used so that they will serve the various demands of the poem in its different phases. "Polar bear," "never," "copper hair," "flower," "shoulder," and "bewilderment" echo each other in sound and thus have a binding function, yet each is appropriate to the affect (the emotional tone) of the passage in which it appears. Similarly, as we have seen, the two stanzas that comprise grammatically incomplete sentences serve an important function; they embody the speaker's sense of a tragic meaning that at the same time eludes him.

The structure of *Polar Bear* illustrates two somewhat mysteriously related characteristics of the structure of lyrical poems generally. In one sense, a lyrical poem is an open field of sound and association, what we have called a sequence of effects. These effects build up from an initial phrasing, an opening line or image or passage, into a final, yet tentative balancing of all the elements that have been suggested in the course of the poem's movement. In this sense, a poem is very much like a musical composition or a mobile construct. One must not translate it into something else like a set of ideas or an interpretation of a speaker's emotional state of mind, but must let its effects strike one's perception of it as a design, in time, of effects of language—something very different from the way language ordinarily communicates with us at a conscious level. To think of *language* as made up of sounds, tones, and evocations, even more than of well-defined meanings, is to think of it as the poet and his best readers do.

At the same time, those meanings are present as well, and the reader who does not try to see what the sentences of a poem actually say will miss the whole point of that precision in diction which is one special mark of the accomplished poet. *Polar Bear* is a fine instance of the typical structure of meaning in a great many poems. It begins with an unhappy or depressed state of mind, explores it in detail, and then—in the light of that exploration—comes back to it with a fuller or transcendental statement of it. The poet comes out from under the anaesthetic with the feeling of coldness and inarticulateness still with him. His polar bear image projects the feeling sharply, and the account of his confusion and of his submission to the nurse's ministrations develops the notes of helplessness, sadness, and loss with subtle, sometimes humorous accuracy. When he returns once more, at the end, to the polar bear image, the effect is of a reaffirmation of the "anguish" that was only suggested at the beginning. This reaffirmation, or clarification, of a feeling after it has been investigated has the effect of a triumphant resolution, even though the feeling is a darkly depressive one. This paradoxical quality of artistic structure reveals a profound human meaning: that we take real strength from getting an insight, however painful, into sharp focus.

Poems: Varied Structures

We begin with a group of a dozen sonnets. Notice that, of the three Elizabethan sonnets that head this group, Spenser's is more tightly knit together by an unusual rhyme scheme than are the others. The next eight sonnets follow the Italian model with differing variations in the sestet, the most unconventional of them in Frost's *Design*. Cummings is, characteristically, the most experimental of the sonnet-writers. If we reassemble his poem into a conventional-appearing sonnet, we see that the rhyme is *abbacddc eeffgg*: a modification of both the Italian and the Shakespearean forms at once. But he has rearranged it on the printed page to make visible the internal dynamics of its thought and emotion as no mechanically conventional "sonnet form" could do. The way he breaks his lines and stanzas guides us through the movement from the speaker's first sense of his beloved's horror of death (because she is so thoroughly and fragilely alive) to his final passionate assertion of the way he would wish to share death with her.

The dramatic or narrative structure of the poems by Herbert, Hardy, Yeats, and Lowell is in each instance self-evident. It is essential for the reader to visualize the character, the setting, and the role of the speakers in these poems clearly. Yeats's *Adam's Curse* is particularly interesting structurally because of the relation of the two speakers to the silent "you" of the poem and, even more, because of the effect of introducing the symbol of the moon in the evening sky in the next-to-last stanza. The open-structured poems by Baraka (Jones) and Duncan that conclude the group are inward journeys of associative meditation. (See pages 89–92 for discussion of open form.)

1. Sonnets

EDMUND SPENSER   *Sonnet LXVIII*

> Most glorious Lord of Life, that on this day
> Didst make thy triumph over death and sin
> And, having harrowed hell, didst bring away
> Captivity thence captive us to win:
> This joyous day, dear Lord, with joy begin,
> And grant that we for whom thou diddest die,
> Being with thy dear blood clean washt from sin,
> May live forever in felicity;
> And that thy love we, weighing worthily,
> May likewise love thee for the same again,   10
> And for thy sake, that all like dear didst buy,
> With love may one another entertain.
> So let us love, dear love, like as we ought:
> Love is the lesson which the Lord us taught.

WILLIAM SHAKESPEARE *Sonnet XXX*

When to the sessions of sweet silent thought
I summon up remembrance of things past,
I sigh the lack of many a thing I sought,
And with old woes new wail my dear times' waste:
Then can I drown an eye, unus'd to flow,
For precious friends hid in death's dateless night,
And weep afresh love's long since cancell'd woe,
And moan th' expense of many a vanish'd sight:
Then can I grieve at grievances foregone,
And heavily from woe to woe tell o'er   10
The sad account of fore-bemoaned moan,
Which I new pay, as if not paid before.
   But if the while I think on thee, dear friend,
   All losses are restor'd, and sorrows end.

MICHAEL DRAYTON *Since there's no help, come, let us kiss and part*

Since there's no help, come, let us kiss and part;
Nay, I have done: You get no more of me,
And I am glad, yea, glad with all my heart,
That thus so cleanly I myself can free.
Shake hands for ever, cancel all our vows,
And when we meet at any time again
Be it not seen in either of our brows
That we one jot of former love retain.
Now at the last gasp of Love's latest breath,
When, his pulse failing, Passion speechless lies,   10
When Faith is kneeling by his bed of death,
And Innocence is closing up his eyes,
   Now, if thou wouldst, when all have given him over,
   From death to life thou might'st him yet recover.

JOHN MILTON *How soon hath Time, the subtle thief of youth*

How soon hath Time, the subtle thief of youth,
   Stol'n on his wing my three-and-twentieth year!
   My hasting days fly on with full career,

But my late spring no bud or blossom shew'th.
Perhaps my semblance might deceive the truth
    That I to manhood am arriv'd so near;
    And inward ripeness doth much less appear,
    That some more timely-happy spirits indu'th.
Yet be it less or more, or soon or slow,
    It shall be still in strictest measure ev'n   10
    To that same lot, however mean or high,
Toward which Time leads me, and the will of Heav'n.
    All is, if I have grace to use it so,
    As ever in my great Task-Master's eye.

JOHN MILTON   *When I consider how my light is spent*

When I consider how my light is spent,
    Ere half my days, in this dark world and wide,
    And that one Talent which is death to hide
    Lodg'd with me useless, though my Soul more bent
To serve therewith my Maker, and present
    My true account, lest he returning chide,
    "Doth God exact day-labour, light deny'd?"
    I fondly ask. But Patience, to prevent
That murmur, soon replies, "God doth not need
    Either man's work or his own gifts. Who best   10
    Bear his mild yoke, they serve him best. His state
Is kingly: thousands at his bidding speed
    And post o'er land and ocean without rest;
    They also serve who only stand and wait."

WILLIAM WORDSWORTH   *London, 1802*

Milton! thou shouldst be living at this hour:
England hath need of thee: she is a fen
Of stagnant waters: altar, sword, and pen,
Fireside, the heroic wealth of hall and bower,
Have forfeited their ancient English dower
Of inward happiness. We are selfish men;
Oh! raise us up, return to us again;
And give us manners, virtue, freedom, power.
Thy soul was like a Star, and dwelt apart;
Thou hadst a voice whose sound was like the sea: 10

Pure as the naked heavens, majestic, free,
So didst thou travel on life's common way,
In cheerful godliness; and yet thy heart
The lowliest duties on herself did lay.

WILLIAM WORDSWORTH   *The world is too much with us;
late and soon*

The world is too much with us; late and soon,
Getting and spending, we lay waste our powers:
Little we see in Nature that is ours;
We have given our hearts away, a sordid boon!
This Sea that bares her bosom to the moon;
The winds that will be howling at all hours,
And are up-gathered now like sleeping flowers;
For this, for everything, we are out of tune;
It moves us not.—Great God! I'd rather be
A Pagan suckled in a creed outworn;   10
So might I, standing on this pleasant lea,
Have glimpses that would make me less forlorn;
Have sight of Proteus rising from the sea;
Or hear old Triton blow his wreathèd horn.

JOHN KEATS   *On First Looking into Chapman's Homer* [1]

Much have I travell'd in the realms of gold,
    And many goodly states and kingdoms seen;
    Round many western islands have I been
Which bards in fealty to Apollo hold.
Oft of one wide expanse had I been told
    That deep-brow'd Homer ruled as his demesne;
    Yet did I never breathe its pure serene
Till I heard Chapman speak out loud and bold:
Then felt I like some watcher of the skies
    When a new planet swims into his ken;   10
Or like stout Cortez when with eagle eyes
    He stared at the Pacific—and all his men
Look'd at each other with a wild surmise—
    Silent, upon a peak in Darien.

[1] George Chapman, the Elizabethan poet and playwright, translated Homer's *Iliad* and *Odyssey*.

John Keats   *On the Sea*

It keeps eternal whisperings around
Desolate shores, and with its mighty swell
Gluts twice ten thousand Caverns, till the spell
Of Hecate leaves them their old shadowy sound.
Often 'tis in such gentle temper found,
That scarcely will the very smallest shell
Be moved for days from where it sometime fell,
When last the winds of Heaven were unbound.
Oh ye! who have your eye-balls vexed and tired,
Feast them upon the wideness of the Sea;   10
Oh ye! whose ears are dinned with uproar rude,
Or fed too much with cloying melody—
Sit ye near some old Cavern's Mouth, and brood
Until ye start, as if the sea-nymphs quired!

E. A. Robinson   *The Sheaves*

Where long the shadows of the wind had rolled,
Green wheat was yielding to the change assigned;
And as by some vast magic undivined
The world was turning slowly into gold.
Like nothing that was ever bought or sold
It waited there, the body and the mind;
And with a mighty meaning of a kind
That tells the more the more it is not told.

So in a land where all days are not fair,
Fair days went on till on another day   10
A thousand golden sheaves were lying there,
Shining and still, but not for long to stay—
As if a thousand girls with golden hair
Might rise from where they slept and go away.

Robert Frost   *Design*

I found a dimpled spider, fat and white,
On a white heal-all, holding up a moth
Like a white piece of rigid satin cloth—
Assorted characters of death and blight

Mixed ready to begin the morning right,
Like the ingredients of a witches' broth—
A snow-drop spider, a flower like a froth,
And dead wings carried like a paper kite.

What had that flower to do with being white,
The wayside blue and innocent heal-all?　　　　10
What brought the kindred spider to that height,
Then steered the white moth thither in the night?
What but design of darkness to appall?—
If design govern in a thing so small.

E. E. Cummings　*who's most afraid of death? thou*

who's most afraid of death? thou
　　　　　　　　　　art of him
utterly afraid, i love of thee
(beloved) this

　　　　　　and truly i would be
near when his scythe takes crisply the whim
of thy smoothness. and mark the fainting
murdered petals. with the caving stem.

But of all most would i be one of them

round the hurt heart which do so frailly cling . . . .)　　　　10
i who am but imperfect in my fear

Or with thy mind against my mind, to hear
nearing our hearts' irrevocable play—
through the mysterious high futile day

an enormous stride
　　　　　　(and drawing thy mouth toward

my mouth, steer our lost bodies carefully downward)

2. Poems in Closed and Open Form

GEORGE HERBERT   *The Collar*

I struck the board, and cry'd, No more.
        I will abroad.
What? shall I ever sigh and pine?
My lines and life are free; free as the road,
    Loose as the wind, as large as store.
        Shall I be still in suit?
Have I no harvest but a thorn
To let me blood, and not restore
What I have lost with cordial fruit?
        Sure there was wine   10
Before my sighs did dry it: there was corn
    Before my tears did drown it.
Is the year only lost to me?
    Have I no bays to crown it?
No flowers, no garlands gay? all blasted?
        All wasted?
Not so, my heart: but there is fruit,
    And thou hast hands.
Recover all thy sigh-blown age
On double pleasures: leave thy cold dispute   20
Of what is fit, and not. Forsake thy cage,
        Thy rope of sands,
Which petty thoughts have made, and made to thee
    Good cable, to enforce and draw,
        And be thy law,
While thou didst wink and wouldst not see.
        Away; take heed:
        I will abroad.
Call in thy death's head there: tie up thy fears.
        He that forbears   30
    To suit and serve his need,
        Deserves his load.
But as I rav'd and grew more fierce and wild
    At every word,
Methought I heard one calling, *Child!*
And I reply'd, *My Lord.*

THOMAS HARDY   *During Wind and Rain*

> They sing their dearest songs—
> He, she, all of them—yea,
> Treble and tenor and bass,
>   And one to play;
> With the candles mooning each face. . . .
>   Ah, no; the years O!
> How the sick leaves reel down in throngs!
>
> They clear the creeping moss—
> Elders and juniors—aye,
> Making the pathways neat   10
>   And the garden gay;
> And they build a shady seat. . . .
>   Ah, no; the years, the years;
> See, the white storm-birds wing across!
>
> They are blithely breakfasting all—
> Men and maidens—yea,
> Under the summer tree,
>   With a glimpse of the bay,
> While pet fowl come to the knee. . . .
>   Ah, no; the years O!   20
> And the rotten rose is ript from the wall.
>
> They change to a high new house,
> He, she, all of them—aye,
> Clocks and carpets and chairs
>   On the lawn all day,
> And brightest things that are theirs. . . .
>   Ah, no; the years, the years;
> Down their carved names the rain-drop ploughs.

THOMAS HARDY   *The Five Students* [1]

> The sparrow dips in his wheel-rut bath,
>   The sun grows passionate-eyed,
> And boils the dew to smoke by the paddock-path;
>   As strenuously we stride,—
> Five of us; dark He, fair He, dark She, fair She, I,
>   All beating by.

[1] See comment in chapter five (p. 213).

The air is shaken, the high-road hot,
    Shadowless swoons the day,
The greens are sobered and cattle at rest; but not
        We on our urgent way,—   10
Four of us; fair She, dark She, fair He, I are there,
        But one—elsewhere.

Autumn moulds the hard fruit mellow,
    And forward still we press
Through moors, briar-meshed plantations, clay-pits yellow,
        As in the spring hours—yes,
Three of us; fair He, fair She, I, as heretofore,
        But—fallen one more.

The leaf drops: earthworms draw it in
    At night-time noiselessly,   20
The fingers of birch and beech are skeleton-thin,
        And yet on the beat are we,—
Two of us; fair She, I. But no more left to go
        The track we know.

Icicles tag the church-aisle leads,
    The flag-rope gibbers hoarse,
The home-bound foot-folk wrap their snow-flaked heads,
        Yet I still stalk the course—
One of us. . . . Dark and fair He, dark and fair She, gone.
        The rest—anon.   30

WILLIAM BUTLER YEATS *Adam's Curse* [1]

We sat together at one summer's end,
That beautiful mild woman, your close friend,
And you and I, and talked of poetry.
I said: "A line will take us hours maybe;
Yet if it does not seem a moment's thought,
Our stitching and unstitching has been naught.
Better go down upon your marrow-bones
And scrub a kitchen pavement, or break stones
Like an old pauper, in all kinds of weather;
For to articulate sweet sounds together   10

---

[1] *How does the fourth stanza serve as a pivot for this poem? Does the introduction of the moon image affect the change of tone with which the poem ends? Does it sustain the tone and thought of stanzas 1–3?*

Is to work harder than all these, and yet
Be thought an idler by the noisy set
Of bankers, schoolmasters, and clergymen
The martyrs call the world."

                        And thereupon
That beautiful mild woman for whose sake
There's many a one shall find out all heartache
On finding that her voice is sweet and low
Replied: "To be born woman is to know—
Although they do not talk of it at school—   20
That we must labour to be beautiful."

I said: "It's certain there is no fine thing
Since Adam's fall but needs much labouring.
There have been lovers who thought love should be
So much compounded of high courtesy
That they would sigh and quote with learned **looks**
Precedents out of beautiful old books;
Yet now it seems an idle trade enough."

We sat grown quiet at the name of love;
We saw the last embers of daylight die,   30
And in the trembling blue-green of the sky
A moon, worn as if it had been a shell
Washed by time's waters as they rose and fell
About the stars and broke in days and years.

I had a thought for no one's but your ears:
That you were beautiful, and that I strove
To love you in the old high way of love;
That it had all seemed happy, and yet we'd grown
As weary-hearted as that hollow moon.

ROBERT LOWELL   *Water*

It was a Maine lobster town—
each morning boatloads of hands
pushed off for granite
quarries on the islands,

and left dozens of bleak
white frame houses stuck
like oyster shells
on a hill of rock,

and below us, the sea lapped
the raw little match-stick   10
mazes of a weir,
where the fish for bait were trapped.

Remember? We sat on a slab of rock.
From this distance in time,
it seems the color
of iris, rotting and turning purpler,

but it was only
the usual gray rock
turning the usual green
when drenched by the sea.   20

The sea drenched the rock
at our feet all day,
and kept tearing away
flake after flake.

One night you dreamed
you were a mermaid clinging to a wharf-pile,
and trying to pull
off the barnacles with your hands.

We wished our two souls
might return like gulls   30
to the rock. In the end,
the water is too cold for us.

Imamu Amiri Baraka (LeRoi Jones)   Way Out West [1]

For Gary Snyder

As simple an act
as opening the eyes. Merely
coming into things by degrees.

---

[1] This poem and the following one, Robert Duncan's "Strains of Sight," may be contrasted with any of the five poems preceding them as far more open in form. If you trace the turns of thought in them, however, you will find a real continuity in both that somewhat resembles the clear narrative structure of the five preceding poems without making these two so definitely "stories." *What is the basis of the movement, association, and structure in the poems by Baraka and Duncan?*

Morning: some tear is broken
on the wooden stairs
of my lady's eyes. Profusions
of green. The leaves. Their
constant prehensions. Like old
junkies on Sheridan Square, eyes
cold and round. There is a song
Nat Cole sings . . . This city
& the intricate disorder
of the seasons.

Unable to mention
something as abstract as time.

Even so, (bowing low in thick
smoke from cheap incense; all
kinds of questions filling the mouth,
till you suffocate & fall dead
to opulent carpet.) Even so,

shadows will creep over your flesh
& hide your disorder, your lies.

There are unattractive wild ferns
outside the window
where the cats hide. They yowl
from there at nights. In heat
& bleeding on my tulips.

Steel bells, like the evil
unwashed Sphinx, towing in the twilight.
Childless old murderers, for centuries
with musty eyes.

I am distressed. Thinking
of the seasons, how they pass,
how I pass, my very youth, the
ripe sweet of my life; drained off . . .

Like giant rhesus monkeys;
picking their skulls,
with ingenious cruelty
sucking out the brains.

No use for beauty   40
collapsed, with moldy breath
done in. Insidious weight
of cankered dreams. Tiresias'
weathered cock.

Walking into the sea, shells
caught in the hair. Coarse
waves tearing the tongue.

Closing the eyes. As
simply an act. You float

Robert Duncan   *Strains of Sight*

1

He brought a light so she could see
Adam move nakedly in the lighted room.
It was a window in the tree.
It was a shelter where there was none.

She saw his naked back and thigh
and heard the notes of a melody
where Adam out of his nature came
into four walls, roof and floor.

He turnd on the light and turnd back,
moving with grace to catch her eye.   10
She saw his naked loneliness.

Now I shall never rest, she sighd,
until he strips his heart for me.
The body flashes such thoughts of death
so that time leaps up, and a man's hand

seen naked catches upon my breath
the risk we took in Paradise.
The serpent thought before the tomb
laid naked, naked, naked before the eyes,

reflects upon itself in a bare room.   20

2

In the questioning phrase the voice
—he raises his eyes from the page—
follows towards some last
curve of the air, suspended above

its sign, that point, that
And asks, Who am I then?
Where am I going? There is no time
like now that is not like now.

Who?   turns upon some body where
the hand striving to tune
curves of the first lute whose strings are nerves   30
sees in the touch the phrase will

rise   break
as the voice does? above some moving obscurity

ripples out in the disturbd pool,
shadows and showings where we would read
—raising his eyes from the body's lure—

what the question is,
where the heart reflects.

Chapter Four

Poetry as Narrative and Drama

Many poems are narrative or dramatic in form, and even more poems have at least some such aspect. They present or suggest a story, with characters, either told in the third person or presented through what the characters say and think. They may describe incidents, show the workings of cause and effect, reveal the personalities of people who are sometimes confronting others and sometimes struggling with themselves or with circumstance, and involve action that is charged with suspense or fulfillment. A natural question about such writing is: Why should it be done as poetry? What does poetic form contribute that prose narrative and prose drama do not?

There are many possible answers. The best one is not very satisfying logically. It is like the best definition of poetry: "Poetry is what poets write." So, here, our best answer is that poetic narrative and poetic drama have always intrigued both poets and readers. Shakespeare is a great playwright, but an even greater dramatic poet, and there are strong elements of the narrative and the dramatic in most great lyric poetry. Indeed, the origins of our lyric tradition can partly be traced to classic Greek drama, in which the songs and dances of the chorus served to express the dominant mood of a play at a given point in its progress. They served also to underline the ritual formality implicit in art and in its original, primitive functions.

There is a more obvious answer as well. A story in verse should be *poetically* effective. The advantage of poetic compression for intensity, and of poetic imagery, rhythm, balance, and sound-play lies in the way they free a story from being merely a literal account. To a certain extent all storytelling and playacting have poetic elements of rhythmic pacing, evocative reverberations, and symbolic projection. The works of writers like James Joyce, Samuel Beckett, and Harold Pinter must often be read and heard as one reads and hears poetry; often they break down the ultimately arbitrary distinction between prose and poetry, which is really a matter of the degree of exploitation of the possibilities for musical echoing, suggestiveness, and patterning implicit in language. The more tightly contained the structure—what Dylan Thomas called the "moving column of words"—is, and the more every word and every small effect of sound-echoing and of speeding up and relaxing of energies count in that structure, the closer one is to poetry. Even in so "objective" a narrative poem as the one by John Clare that follows, every word and every construction counts far more than in most prose fiction. Clare presents his facts without comment. He depends on precise detail, vividly accurate verbs, and a good deal of simple parallelism both of grammatical elements and of the phrasing in his lines. What emerges is a harsh vision, created and sustained at a single pitch throughout the poem's duration, of the common life in its unconscious, relentless brutality; and this vision goes beyond its literal place and moment to something instinctual in man and in animal existence.

JOHN CLARE   *Badger*

When midnight comes a host of dogs and men
Go out and track the badger to his den,
And put a sack within the hole, and lie
Till the old grunting badger passes by.
He comes and hears—they let the strongest loose.
The old fox hears the noise and drops the goose.
The poacher shoots and hurries from the cry,
And the old hare half wounded buzzes by.
They get a forkèd stick to bear him down
And clap the dogs and take him to the town,   10
And bait him all the day with many dogs,
And laugh and shout and fright the scampering hogs.
He runs along and bites at all he meets:
They shout and hollo down the noisy streets.

He turns about to face the loud uproar
And drives the rebels to their very door.
The frequent stone is hurled where'er they go;
When badgers fight, then everyone's a foe.
The dogs are clapt and urged to join the fray;
The badger turns and drives them all away.   20
Though scarcely half as big, demure and small,
He fights with dogs for hours and beats them all.
The heavy mastiff, savage in the fray,
Lies down and licks his feet and turns away.
The bulldog knows his match and waxes cold,
The badger grins and never leaves his hold.
He drives the crowd and follows at their heels
And bites them through—the drunkard swears and reels.

The frightened women take the boys away,
The blackguard laughs and hurries on the fray.   30
He tries to reach the woods, an awkward race,
But sticks and cudgels quickly stop the chase.
He turns agen and drives the noisy crowd
And beats the dogs in noises loud.
He drives away and beats them every one,
And then they loose them all and set them on.
He falls as dead and kicked by boys and men,
Then starts and grins and drives the crowd again;
Till kicked and torn and beaten out he lies
And leaves his hold and cackles, groans, and dies.   40

This picture taken from English village life of the last century is very close to bare reporting. We may feel the cruelty of the "sport," but that is the result of the facts and not of the poet's expressed feelings. Against the savagery, and implied cowardice, of men and dogs the badger resists with strength, endurance and cunning; he is vigorous and dangerous until at last he is beaten, harassed, bitten to death. The poem reduces the meaning of physical perseverance and the struggle for existence to its unpleasant essence: a grim, torturous competition in bestiality that men share with subhuman species and in which there is no room for any compensating beauty. But as a story it relies on the establishment of the situation—the beginning of the badger-baiting expedition at midnight—and the subsequent events throughout the next day. As a criticism of the desperate boredom of the townspeople's existence and of their fundamental inhumanity, however, the account is ruthless, since the badger is much closer, after all, to being a "hero"—grotesque as the term is in this setting—than are the people.

John Clare's straightforward narrative poem is an example of the form stripped down to its essentials. The student of poetry will eventually wish to familiarize himself with at least three forms of verse-narrative that are not only sanctified by age and by the reverence that has been paid them, but that continue to have a vital influence on poets and their methods. These are the epic, the metrical romance, and the ballad.

We do not represent fully either the epic poem or the true metrical romance in this book, the first because of the length of such a poem, the second because of both its length and its inaccessibility in modern English. The great epics of the past, however—those by Homer, Vergil, and Milton especially—have provided an immense amount of subject matter for later writers, who have also studied them for training in metrics, diction, and grandeur of outlook. For the epic poem is constructed "on the grand scale." Its mythological hero is set an enormous task or given a tremendously significant moral choice to make. Gods, angels, the spirits of the dead in

Hell, all men and all women are concerned in what happens to him as he sets out to resist the hostile forces arrayed to prevent his success. In him are combined the highest social ideals of the world in which his creator lived and thought. Many elements—battle-descriptions, ringing debates, long descriptive or rhetorical or philosophical digressions—are put into meaningful relation with one another by the end of the poem. Through the hero, who is both a real person with real feelings and a superhuman performer of extraordinary deeds, we come to see the vast scope and moral significance of man's struggle, under the pressures of time and fate, to change reality in accordance with his dream-aspirations.

Metrical romances too are comparatively long poems, though seldom as long as epics, or as serious. The favorite verse-form of a special social group, the great courts of the Middle Ages in which skilled minstrels sang or chanted to the élite, they strove to create an air of gaiety, excitement, and elegance: the adventures of knights and ladies, the perfection of chivalry and pride, the torments and disasters of adulterous love. Sometimes the tragic seriousness of the love-affairs, or the seriousness of a knight's mission, will suggest the profundities of the epic. But most of all, perhaps, the metrical romance is the forerunner of the modern adventure story and also of the modern novel of high social life. The minstrel-poet was careful to show, for instance, how accomplished in table-manners, conversation, and dress his hero was, and sometimes to strive for real wit in dialogue and characterization. He was often a great virtuoso in the handling of rhyme, sound-effects, and stanza-forms, too.

Later poets have often assumed a reading-acquaintance by their audiences with the figures and events of the great epics and the most famous of the metrical romances. Thus, George Meredith's sonnet *Lucifer in Starlight* depends on our knowledge of Milton's description of Satan and his eternal exile from Heaven.

GEORGE MEREDITH *Lucifer in Starlight*

> On a starred night Prince Lucifer uprose.
>> Tired of his dark dominion swung the fiend
>> Above the rolling ball in cloud part screened,
> Where sinners hugged their specter of repose.
> Poor prey to his hot fit of pride were those.
>> And now upon his western wing he leaned,
>> Now his huge bulk o'er Afric's sands careened,
> Now the black planet shadowed Arctic snows.
> Soaring through wider zones that pricked his scars
>> With memory of the old revolt from Awe,   10
> He reached a middle height, and at the stars,
> Which are the brain of heaven, he looked, and sank.
> Around the ancient track marched, rank on rank,
>> The army of unalterable law.

The poem takes for granted our knowing how, in Milton's poem, Lucifer (or Satan) was hurled into hell and plotted to frustrate God by corrupting mankind. We are expected to understand that Meredith, in describing Lucifer's movements, is paralleling a similar journey in *Paradise Lost*, to recall the bitter futility of Lucifer's efforts in Milton's work, and to recognize the old "scars" of his memory of defeat and consignment to eternal punishment. We can understand the poem without this knowledge, but the precise emotional effect of our having it will be lost, as will the specific associations of the phrase—"hot fit of pride," "Afric's sands," "the old revolt from Awe"—that bring to mind Milton's style.

In a more general way, we may say that a good many poems, such as Keats's *The Eve of St. Agnes*, Morris's *The Haystack in the Floods*, and Rossetti's *The Blessed Damozel*, tell stories that have their setting in the Middle Ages or take their tone from the romance and religiosity of medieval literature. These are obvious examples of the continuing force of the metrical romance, with its highly sensuous descriptions and its vision of a life rich with mystical ardor, extreme peril, extreme desire—an "argent revelry," as Keats wrote, "with plume, tiara, and all rich array."

We come closer to the bare bones of narrative when we turn from these more sophisticated forms to the folk-ballads. There is no wide gap between the anonymous nursery rhymes that children learn and these songs. Both have their creative origin, like other folk-poetry, in association with music and dance—and in both the musical elements of refrain and varied repetition, as well as the pleasure of a simple rhyme and meter, are actively important in the dramatic and narrative presentation. In both, too, specific pictures and actions are presented without comment, and their meaning left to make itself felt without connective explanations.

Ballads are usually lively and direct, and charged with feeling despite the unknown author's reluctance to comment on what is happening. *The Hangman's Tree*, an American version of an old ballad known throughout Europe, well illustrates their stark, dramatic directness:

ANONYMOUS *The Hangman's Tree*

> "Slack your rope, hangs-a-man,
>   O slack it for a while.
>   I think I see my father coming,
>   Riding many a mile."
>
> "O father, have you brought me gold?
>   Or have you paid my fee?
>   Or have you come to see me hanging
>   On the gallows tree?"
> "I have not brought you gold.
>   I have not paid your fee.

10

But I have come to see you hanging
On the gallows tree."

"Slack your rope, hangs-a-man,
O slack it for a while.
I think I see my mother coming,
Riding many a mile."

"O mother have you brought me gold?
Or have you paid my fee?
Or have you come to see me hanging
On the gallows tree?"   20
"I have not brought you gold.
I have not paid your fee.
But I have come to see you hanging
On the gallows tree."

"Slack your rope, hangs-a-man,
O slack it for a while,
I think I see my true love coming,
Riding many a mile."

"O true love, have you brought me gold?
Or have you paid my fee?   30
Or have you come to see me hanging
On the gallows tree?"
"Yes, I have brought you gold.
Yes, I have paid your fee.
Nor have I come to see you hanging
On the gallows tree."

   Why the speaker has been condemned to death—and a host of other
questions—we cannot answer from this version of the song. Nor do the
questions matter. The agonized, growing suspense, and then the suddenly
relaxed tension, of the sentenced man does matter, however. We have
certainly got down to the "bare bones" of plot in this series of alternating
appeals, always in very nearly the same words, to the hangman and ex-
changes with father, mother, and sweetheart. The essence of danger,
suspense, and release is dramatized in the simple idiomatic repetitions.
The "hangs-a-man" is waiting there, silent and ready; the words "rope,"
"hangs-a-man," "hanging," "gallows tree" make it impossible for us to
forget him at any point in the story, and that unassuming little rhyme of
"while" and "mile" stresses the speaker's complete dependence on the
luck of time and space. The back-and-forth movement of appeal and
question-and-answer carries both the story and the dramatic charge of the
story, and the music of the poem lies largely in the echoing of the same
poignant colloquial phrases from beginning to end.

Many ballads come to us from the late Middle Ages, usually in several differing versions. Sometimes when we speak of ballads we think especially of a group of Scottish and English songs mostly collected since the eighteenth century, songs derived perhaps from the common folk's preliterate days, the products of anonymous authorship in a ceremonial setting, transmitted by memory until, often centuries later, interested students set them down for the first time. Their elemental simplicity, plus the fact that they deal with themes common to all folklore, doubtless accounts for their durability. A few stanzas selected at random may suggest better than a detailed explanation why they have haunted the imaginations of later writers.

> The wind doth blow today, my love
>   And a few small drops of rain;
> I never had but one true love,
>   In cold grave she was lain.
>   *The Unquiet Grave*

> I dreamed I saw a battle fought
>   Beyond the Isle o' Sky,
> When lo, a dead man won the field,
>   And I thought that man was I.
>   *The Battle of Otterburn*

> And fair Margret, and rare Margret,
>   And Margret o' veritie,
> Gin e'er ye love another man,
>   Ne'er love him as ye did me.
>   *Clerk Saunders*

And here are some stanzas from poems by modern authors who have employed the ballad form to get the same starkly suggestive effects:

> Day after day, day after day,
> We stuck, nor breath nor motion;
> As idle as a painted ship
> Upon a painted ocean.
>   COLERIDGE, *The Rime of the
>   Ancient Mariner*

> Down came the storm, and smote amain
>   The vessel in its strength;
> She shuddered and paused, like a frightened steed,
>   Then leaped her cable's length.
>   LONGFELLOW, *The Wreck of the Hesperus*

He touched not gold, it was not cold,
   It was not hard, it felt like flesh.
He drew out by the curling hair
   A young man's head, and murder'd fresh. . . .
                BRIDGES, *Screaming Tarn*

One of the more striking medieval ballads is *The Three Ravens*, which
is printed below for extended analysis since, though it is characteristic of
the type, it is unusual in the number of elements which it combines.[1]

ANONYMOUS   *The Three Ravens*

There were three ravens sat on a tree—
   Down a down, hay down, hay down
There were three ravens sat on a tree—
   With a down
There were three ravens sat on a tree—
They were as black as they might be.
   With a down, derry, derry, derry, down, down.

The one of them said to his mate,
"Where shall we our breakfast take?"

"Down in yonder green field   10
There lies a knight slain under his shield.

"His hounds they lie down at his feet;
So well they can their master keep.

"His hawks they fly so eagerly
There's no fowl dare him come nigh."

Down there comes a fallow doe
As great with young as she might go.

She lift up his bloody head
And kissed his wounds that were so red.

She got him up upon her back   20
And carried him to earthen lake.

[1] Notice that each of the stanzas follows the pattern of the first one. That is, the
first line is repeated three times and the second sung only once; also, the "down a
down" refrain arrangement is the same for each stanza. In the final three stanzas, "lake"
means pit; "prime" is the first hour of the morning and "evensong" is evening—both
terms referring to church-services as well as to times of day; and "leman" means sweetheart.

She buried him before the prime;
She was dead herself ere evensong time.

God send every gentleman
Such hawks, such hounds, and such a leman.

In this ballad, the unexplained elements excite our curiosity. But such questions as how did the knight die? and why and how did the doe move him to the burial pit? are comparatively insignificant. Because there is much here that would ordinarily demand explanation, what *is* given—and the way it is arranged—takes on an enhanced importance. It is the consequences of what has happened, not the cause, that the ballad emphasizes. This touching only on the high spots and skipping of transitional and explanatory details is typical of the ballads and, with the give and take of dialogue, is largely responsible for their dramatic power. It is a psychological strategy that keeps the reader in suspense and ready for new developments, a way of limiting the drama to its significant consequences.

The five beginning stanzas move more quickly and complexly than may at once be apparent. First we have the black ravens conversing, with that grisly understatement of a question about "breakfast." Then we stop looking at them, but through *their* eyes we turn our attention to a second point of concentration, the slain knight in the green fields.

Because these ominous scavenger birds literally live off death, there is a fierce and unsentimental logic in their use by the poet to set the mood of the song and to direct our thoughts toward the knight. (The "logic" is like that of the motion-picture camera pointing up the most important related elements of a scene.) Meanwhile, the greenness of the field is in sharp contrast with the atmosphere of death, and so is the lively refrain with its three variations in every stanza. The net result of these effects set side by side—the black ravens, the gay refrain, the grotesquely comic reference to breakfast, the picture of the dead body in the midst of growing life (a theme repeated in another way later, when the pregnant doe enters the scene)—is a clear yet many-sided view of the relatedness of all experience: of life with death, tragedy with comedy, cruelty with sympathy. After the casual but morbid beginning there has been a startling close-up of a tragic end. The ravens remain consistently frivolous, horrible, antihuman; they complain that the knight's faithful hounds and hawks are keeping them from breakfast. But the other animals, with their pure devotion, provide a counterbalancing sort of ferocity.

So we have had several movements of focus in these five stanzas. Now the poem drops the ravens altogether, moving into straight narrative. In four stages, the effect of which is precisely opposite to that of the stanzas on the ravens, we see the gentle, loving, self-sacrificing movements of the doe. The hounds and hawks, it is true, were also self-sacrificing and loving; but they, like the knight himself, are in their own ways deadly fighters too. The doe, however, swings us to the extreme of absolute gentleness and suffering.

Left this way, the ballad would be complete and suggestive enough, but the last two lines give yet one more turn. In them the storyteller himself comments, expressing his admiration of the animals' loyalty; furthermore, he suggests that by "doe" he really means the knight's sweetheart, doubtless bearing his child. He is hinting too, it may be, that by hounds and hawks are symbolized faithful friends. We do not care whether the poem deals with some actual occurrence—a murder by ambush on a dark night, occasioned perhaps by a forbidden love-affair—that took place in the locality of the ballad's origin, or whether it is a product of pure imagination. But it does affect us that the final observation, though perhaps added at a later date than the original ballad, implies a chivalric ideal of loyalty and love. The speaker even seems to consider the dead knight fortunate, as though life itself were less important than the earning of such devotion.

There are other implications, too. For instance, the ravens, in one sense at least, symbolize the brute evil, indifferent and destructive, against which man constructs his systems of value:

> God send every gentleman
> Such hawks, such hounds, and such a leman.

The values in which we believe are felt to be capable of surviving the death of individuals, whether we see them in a religious or in some other light. Serious lyric, dramatic, and narrative poetry ordinarily presents images, or pictures, which can be understood as ways of viewing the world and deriving values from it. (Remember Blake's vision of the tiger, or Arnold's picture of the lovers looking from their window at a world of darkness and deceptive beauty, or the picture in *The Hangman's Tree* of the lover arriving to change the fate of the condemned person.) To understand this fact is not necessarily to understand why a poem is or is not effective, though it does deepen our perception. There are mystical and religious associations in *The Three Ravens*: in the human speech and behavior of bird and beast, in the corpse in the living grass, and in the self-sacrifice that may bear a relation to the sacrifice of Christ or analogous sacrifices in primitive religions. But nothing is explained; all is *presented*, as in most ballads, mainly through vivid conversation and pictures that the reader himself must explore for the implied meanings. And always there is the refrain, dancing in and out among the lines of narrative and helping to make of the whole song a self-contained pattern of repeated sounds, parallel constructions, clear pictures, and ironic and tragic moments of concentration.

The importance of the refrain as a musical counterpoint and as a dividing mark between stanzas, should remind us that, while important, the *story* in a ballad or any other narrative poem is hardly what makes the poem. It is at best the skeleton underlying the living form. A time-sequence arrangement is probably the simplest method of organizing pictures, thoughts, and emotions, as well as sound-effects, into an organic whole that sings, dances, and implies a world of meaning and feeling. But it is easy to see that in *The Three Ravens* the final effect is more influenced by the shifting of attention from ravens to knight to hounds and hawks to doe to the final comment than by the order of events in time. Ballads, like other poems, consist of many elements clashing and harmonizing until a point of equilibrium and overall inclusiveness is reached.

Because of the great attraction of narrative form, there are many fine "literary ballads," imitations and variations of the folk-ballad form by professional poets. A great proportion of English verse, indeed, has some element or other of the ballad in it. Here is a fine example, by W. H. Auden, of a modern literary ballad:

W. H. Auden *O what is that sound which so thrills the ear*

> O what is that sound which so thrills the ear
>   Down in the valley drumming, drumming?
> Only the scarlet soldiers, dear,
>   The soldiers coming.
>
> O what is that light I see flashing so clear
>   Over the distance brightly, brightly?
> Only the sun on their weapons, dear,
>   As they step lightly.
>
> O what are they doing with all that gear,
>   What are they doing this morning, this morning?   10
> Only their usual manoeuvres, dear,
>   Or perhaps a warning.
>
> O why have they left the road down there,
>   Why are they suddenly wheeling, wheeling?
> Perhaps a change in their orders, dear.
>   Why are you kneeling?
>
> O haven't they stopped for the doctor's care,
>   Haven't they reined their horses, their horses?
> Why, they are none of the wounded, dear,
>   None of these forces.   20

Or is it the parson they want, with white hair,
  Is it the parson, is it, is it?
No, they are passing his gateway, dear,
  Without a visit.

O it must be the farmer who lives so near.
  It must be the farmer so cunning, so cunning?
They have passed the farmyard already, dear,
  And now they are running.

O where are you going? Stay with me here!
  Were the vows you swore deceiving, deceiving?   30
No, I promised to love you, dear,
  But I must be leaving.

O it's broken the lock and splintered the door,
  O it's the gate where they're turning, turning;
Their boots are heavy on the floor
  And their eyes are burning.

In its dramatic, colloquial phrasing and "incremental repetition" (repetition of form—such as question and answer—with the content changing in each stanza), this ballad by a contemporary writer is certainly very like a traditional ballad. Another similarity lies in its omissions. Just who the soldiers are and what the exact circumstances of the two speakers may be we cannot tell, but we do know that the coming of the troops has a terrible inevitability and will leave the destruction of the lovers' relationship in its wake.

One important difference can be observed. In a ballad like *The Three Ravens* the final situation is always fairly clear; such poetry is close enough to simple storytelling to have it important that the story *get* somewhere, as a story. In Auden's poem, though, the sense of terror is more important than the actual pictures of the narrative. Whether the soldiers are coming to conscript or arrest or murder the lover, or represent some other purpose still, would be hard to say finally. Nor do we know whether or not the poet feels completely sympathetic with the girl who is being abandoned. Auden's poem is as impersonal (that is, he hides his emotional sympathies to a certain extent) as most other ballads are, for they too present dynamic situations rather than private feelings or interpretation. But his poem ends not after a completed action or relationship but at the moment when crisis actually breaks in on his characters. He is more consciously interested in exploring the emotions associated with a moral problem or predicament than the ballad-makers were. He has sacrificed true simplicity for this conscious purpose, but at the same time has borrowed strength from the poetry of folk-tradition.

The main quality distinguishing dramatic poetry from narrative poetry is that in the former everything is presented as if directly from the minds and hearts of the personalities involved. Hence the dramatic poet is as impersonal as the anonymous ballad-maker, for he need never express himself in his own right. Of shorter dramatic poems, the most easily defined type is the dramatic monologue. This sort of poem is closely related to the soliloquy, a speech by a character in a play who appears alone on the stage and, by a sort of unspoken compact between the dramatist and his audience, is permitted to utter his thoughts and describe the impressions passing in his mind.

My Last Duchess (pages 178–180), by Robert Browning, is a brief, subtle, and almost perfect example of the type. The reader should consider the originality of the poet's method—which is a method of gradually revealing a dramatic situation by artfully presenting a series of details in such a way as to make drama out of our acquirement of information. Our curiosity is quickly aroused and with such speed and over such a wide area of material that the progressive satisfaction of our curiosity and the allaying of our suspense proceeds much more slowly, only overtaking the mystification at the very end of the poem.

One of the conventions of the dramatic monologue that helps to make this effect possible is that nothing may be presented in the way of explanation or comment from the outside. Everything must be given in the direct words of a speaker upon whom, as it were, we suddenly begin to eavesdrop in the middle of a dramatic situation. Furthermore, the speaker must be imagined as totally unaware of our listening, and while he says a great deal to intrigue he may say nothing directly to enlighten us.

The following dramatic monologue appears in Herman Melville's novel *Billy Budd*. It gives us the hero's thoughts on the eve of his execution aboard ship for the crime of killing one of the ship's officers. The crime had been an unintentional one, and it has done no discredit to the much-loved young sailor who committed it. The sympathetic quality of Billy's character can be seen in the humble way he has of putting things, in his affectionate tone when speaking of his messmates, and in his inability to visualize his own death as being of any great importance. At the same time, there is a saintly quality to his thoughts, as though he had long ago agreed that he was dying in a good cause. In itself, the poem is a little like *The Hangman's Tree*; it is more introspective, but gives no fuller explanation of the speaker's predicament. Notice how the slight touch of humor deepens the pathos of Melville's effect here, and how Billy's resignation to his destiny makes the pathos a minor aspect of his essentially heroic character—in which there is not a trace of whining or self-pitying bitterness. ("Darbies" are manacles. The Dansker and Taff are shipmates of Billy's; Taff is now dead.)

HERMAN MELVILLE *Billy in the Darbies*

> Good of the Chaplain to enter Lone Bay
> And down on his marrow-bones here and pray
> For the likes just o' me, Billy Budd.—But look:
> Through the port comes the moon-shine astray!
> It tips the guard's cutlass and silvers this nook;
> But 'twill die in the dawning of Billy's last day.
> A jewel-block they'll make of me to-morrow,
> Pendent pearl from the yard-arm-end
> Like the ear-drop I gave to Bristol Molly—
> O, 'tis me, not the sentence they'll suspend.   10
> Ay, ay, all is up; and I must up too
> Early in the morning, aloft from alow.
> On an empty stomach, now, never it would do.
> They'll give me a nibble-bit o' biscuit ere I go.
> Sure, a messmate will reach me the last parting cup;
> But, turning heads away from the hoist and the belay,
> Heaven knows who will have the running of me up!
> No pipe to those halyards—but aren't it all sham?
> A blur's in my eyes; it is dreaming that I am.
> A hatchet to my hawser? all adrift to go?   20
> The drum roll to grog, and Billy never know?
> But the Dansker he has promised to stand by the plank;
> So, I'll shake a friendly hand ere I sink.
> But—no! It is dead then I'll be, come to think.—
> I remember Taff the Welshman when he sank.
> And his cheek it was like the budding pink.
> But me they'll lash in hammock, drop me deep.
> Fathoms down, fathoms down, how I'll dream fast asleep.
> I feel it stealing now. Sentry, are you there?
> Just ease these darbies at the wrist,   30
> And roll me over fair.
> I am sleepy, and the oozy weeds about me twist.

This monologue, in addition to what it tells us of Billy's character, becomes, indirectly, something more—a humble, loving but fatalistic view of the world. Through the doomed sailor's thoughts, first of all, we receive a picture of the good life as one in which a few creature-comforts would be available and in which men would judge each other's motives genially and affectionately. Even if he has some "bad" thoughts, Billy's mind does not rest with them. It passes sadly over to details of his coming execution, halts momentarily with the all-too-answerable question "But aren't it all sham?"—but finally moves to calm acceptance of his lot. He knows, as a matter of fact, that it *is* "all sham," that the laws of society have arbitrarily made him the scapegoat in a ritual-travesty of justice that he does not quite understand. But although he could not at first imagine his own death, he at last comes to see himself as already, literally, dead: "I am sleepy, and the oozy weeds about me twist."

As so often happens, in the dramatic monologue and in other kinds of poetry as well, the "story" here involves a projection into the future: first a recognition that a change must come about and a parallel tension at the prospect (as in Billy's inability to get his imagination fastened on the precise fact of his own physical death), then the realization of its full meaning, and finally the crystallization of an attitude or insight (in this case, Billy's complete acceptance of his future condition).

We too must "accept." We must accept the truth of this projection of imagination. We shall do so if we feel that we know the speaker's essential character, if the progression of his thoughts and feelings is credible, and if the external objects he observes and the way they enter his consciousness are acutely enough conceived. In such case, the "meanings" the monologue carries along with it will be seen as having their own truth and life and will exercise a certain power over us whether we are prepared to believe in them generally or not. Artifice and realism move together in Melville's poem to bring this conviction about in us. Every reader separately will have come to his own conclusion, of course, about the degree of psychological realism present in Billy's thinking. But realism is not in any case the only consideration, for the phrasing and the balanced movements of the poem are not always of the kind one would expect in a simple, untutored person like Billy. There are humble picturings—"down on his marrow-bones," "a nibble-bit o' biscuit," and "a blur's in my eyes." And there are others with the poet's own trademark on them—"the moon-shine astray," "a jewel-block they'll make of me," "pendent pearl from the yard-arm-end," "his cheek . . . like the budding pink." There is a rough correspondence between the alternation of the two kinds of language and the swinging, up-down movements of the physical visualization in this poem. The chaplain goes *down* on his knees; the moon comes *up* and then, in forecast, *down*; Billy imagines himself *up* in the air, then *down* to the moment before he is *raised* to be hanged; and so on until the movement is quieted in his vision of himself *sinking* and, finally, rocking slowly at the *bottom* of the sea. Through much of the monologue, the sense of emotional depression grows deeper the more clearly Billy visualizes his coming death. Yet the closing lines, with their steadily downward movement until they reach a point of final rest at the ocean-bottom, actually represent a heightening of his morale as his agitation of spirit subsides and he moves into total acceptance. The poet behind the scenes—somewhat like a theatrical director—has been experimentally manipulating basic dramatic feeling toward this final impression. To do so, he has had to distort nature and add something to it. Without such distortions and additions, however, poetry and the other arts would lose their inner truthfulness to the felt meaning of experience.

In our own century, some poets have become deeply interested in the esthetic and psychological problems of creating and communicating emotional states. In their work the overall psychological effect often becomes the key to the poem's design, and thus the thread of continuous thought and story, though actually present, is less significant than the arrangement of images and dramatic moments that at first seem disconnected. A characteristic example of the dramatic monologue written in this fashion is T. S. Eliot's *The Love Song of J. Alfred Prufrock* (pages 180–184).

This poem presents the thoughts of a sensitive, genteel, middle-aged man who is paralyzed with timidity when he thinks of himself in relation to any of the more physical and passionate demands of life. There is a story "hidden" in the poem, a story of a woman whom the man has desired and wanted to marry although he has not dared to make love to her. Prufrock is secretly ashamed of his own lack of virile aggressiveness or romantic appeal; he sees himself as neurotic, indulges in daydreams of beauty, pleasure, and heroic endeavor, but wakes himself abruptly from these dreams with the whiplash of his scorn for himself.

Critics have seen in Eliot's poem a conception of modern culture as without vitality, full of echoes of a past that no longer has living significance, dying of emptiness. But the poem itself presents Prufrock (his very name suggests stuffiness and effeminacy) talking apparently without coherence. First he seems to be proposing a walk on a dreary evening through some rather sinister streets. Then he tells us that

> In the room the women come and go
> Talking of Michelangelo.

Then he talks about the fog, makes a digression on time, goes on about his self-consciousness and hesitations, discusses the voices, eyes, and arms of women, and so through a number of other moods and topics and observations until the poem ends with a vision of loveliness suddenly jolted into despair in the very last line. Three stanzas in the middle part—lines 62–74—illustrate the poem's method.

Each image in these three stanzas is a picture colored or even distorted by the feelings of Mr. Prufrock. A sense of despondency rises from the images even though there is nothing about fashionable women, about men looking out of windows, or about crabs or lobsters that would *necessarily* sadden anyone. But accompanying the pictures are words and rhythms that point up the mood. Among these are the repetition of "known" and "arms" in the first two lines of the passage under discussion, the uncertain tone of the two lines closing the first stanza, the word "lonely" in the next stanza, and the word "silent" in the third. We recognize the men in shirt-sleeves looking out of windows as a symbol of the loneliness Prufrock fears, and knows, will be his own future. In his abject sense of failure as a man, he despairingly cries out that he "should have been a pair of ragged claws"—that is, a mere instinctive organism. He suffers from an inability to make a choice or come to a decision. A regression to elemental instinct would set him free from human responsibility. The deeper irony here is that though he really ought to allow his natural human instincts to have their way he suppresses and perverts them by too scrupulous introspection.

These images throw us back to Prufrock's relationship to women, and to the one woman he has dreamed might be the loving companion he needs. He has been allured by womanly beauty, yet startled and frightened too by the sudden realization that love makes strong physical demands, calls for animal vitality; seeing women's arms in lamplight he has seen also that they are "downed with light brown hair." After these lines we understand his alienation, his sense of fear and loneliness. And as we read on through the poem, the pattern brings itself into focus. We have a man speculating on what, if he had the courage, he would say to a woman to whom he cannot even *suggest* his thoughts for fear she will think him impossibly absurd. Everything contributes to his fear of life. The streets are insidious. The women, though superficial, are confident. The city is sordid. Time and nature are indifferent or contemptuous. He dreams of what he would like to be if he dared and confesses himself no tragic hero or sainted martyr. He is only a hanger-on, a second-rate character, a ridiculous buffoon. Despising himself for all his fussy concern about appearance and dress, he sees himself at last a figure in a spoiled romantic dream:

> We have lingered in the chambers of the sea
> By sea-girls wreathed with seaweed red and brown
> Till human voices wake us, and we drown.

The dramatic monologue, because it always gives us a particular person in a particular situation, presenting aloud to himself or some other person both the physical details and the emotional character of that situation, is one of the poetic forms most rewarding for study. Through such study the reader can perfect himself in that primary requirement of critical understanding—identification of the supposed speaker in a poem: his personality, his moral and intellectual outlook, his whole manner of life. Every poem demands identification of the speaking voice, but the dramatic monologue does so most openly and directly.

In general, dramatic verse—because it presents living figures that move, converse, affect one another—is more readily available to our sympathies than most other poetry. It can set up a vivid illusion of familiar reality and then link that illusion with profoundly imaginative motifs. The great power of Shakespeare's dramatic poetry is the best possible illustration of this principle. His *Hamlet,* for instance, takes us, before we know where we are going, from a most prosaic situation to the most poetically suggestive exploration of supernatural and psychological themes. The changing of the guard at the very beginning, the idiomatic gossip and political talk, and the practical arrangements are all quite normal and commonplace. They lower our resistance to the really vital portions of the early scenes—the appearance of the Ghost, his effect on the men standing watch, and then Hamlet's conversation with and reaction to him. The opening lines of *Hamlet,* T. S. Eliot points out, are "built of the simplest words in the most homely idiom"—"short, brusque ejaculations." [2] Then, subtly, the tone and rhythm are adapted to mood-effects of a different nature. There are "solemn and sonorous" effects at the Ghost's appearance, and a lyrical, exalted expression in the description of morning. By the end of the first scene, the audience has been carried by the poet's skilful maneuvering into a realm where it no longer seems unnatural for a man to say:

> But, look, the morn, in russet mantle clad,
> Walks o'er the dew of yon high eastward hill. . . .

Another critic, Kenneth Burke, discusses the similar development in the fourth scene of the first act. Hamlet and his friends are awaiting the Ghost. It is midnight.

> It is time for the ghost. Sounds off-stage, and of course it is not the ghost. It is, rather, the sound of the king's carousal. . . . A tricky, and effective detail. We have been waiting for the ghost, and get, startlingly, a blare of trumpets. And again, once the trumpets are silent, we feel all the more just how desolate are these three men waiting for a ghost, on a bare "platform," feel it by this sudden juxtaposition of an imagined scene of lights and merriment. But the trumpets announcing a carousal have suggested a subject of conversation. In the darkness Hamlet discusses the excessive drinking of his countrymen. . . . Indeed, there in the gloom he is talking very intelligently on these matters, and Horatio answers, "Look, my Lord, it comes." All this time we had been waiting for a ghost, and it comes at the one moment which was not pointing towards it. This ghost, so assiduously prepared for, is yet a surprise. And now that the ghost has come, we are waiting for something further. . . .

2 T. S. Eliot, "Poetry and Drama" *(Selected Essays).*

Hamlet must confront the ghost. Here again Shakespeare can feed well upon the use of contrast for his effects. Hamlet has just been talking in a sober, rather argumentative manner—but now the flood-gates are unloosed:

Angels and ministers of grace defend us!
Be thou a spirit of health or goblin damn'd,
Bring with thee airs from heaven or blasts from hell. . . .

and the transition from the matter-of-fact to the grandiose, the full-throated and full-vowelled, is a second burst of trumpets, perhaps even more effective than the first, since it is the rich fulfillment of a promise.[3]

In *Hamlet*, almost without realizing it, we are drawn into the deeper reality of psychological vision. Reality has become as wide as the poet's ability to use his imaginative power can make it. Thus, the ghost becomes a more convincing spokesman for Hamlet's feelings than Hamlet himself. No words of his own could more powerfully convey Hamlet's horror at his mother's behavior than the Ghost's disgusted picture of lust "to a radiant angel link't." And nothing, again, that Hamlet himself could say would betray his secret fear of death and purgatory half so startlingly as the Ghost's reference to unspeakable "secrets of my prison-house" which he is forbidden to tell. A major function of poetry in drama, we see, is to lead us to hear the language of imaginative association as natural speech and to see pure vision as concrete experience.

[3] Reprinted from *Counter-Statement*, by Kenneth Burke; new, augmented edition, 1953; Hermes Publications, Los Altos, California. Copyright 1953 by Kenneth Burke.

Poems: Narrative and Dramatic

We begin here with an example of epic narrative: Ezra Pound's translation of Book XI of Homer's *Odyssey*. In it Odysseus describes sailing from the goddess Circe's isle to the point where, after suitable rituals, he could speak with the shades of the dead, including his own mother Anticlea. His main task is to learn from the dead prophet Tiresias what his mission is to be after he has returned home and restored order in his own land. Until the last nine lines all this is straightforward, condensed translation that catches the spirit of Homer's archaic yet beautiful and powerfully active text, partly through Pound's masterly use of Ango-Saxon diction and alliteration.

Two examples of medieval allegorical narrative follow: Dante's opening lines of the *Inferno*, and his account, later in the same work, of the tragic passion of Paolo and Francesca. Four traditional ballads of England and Scotland and a popular ballad (*Eleanor Rigby*) sung by the Beatles, together with literary ballads by Keats and the modern Scottish poet Hugh MacDiarmid and a gently satirical semiballad by the modern Irish poet John Montague, come next.

Dramatic poetry is represented by three of Browning's psychologically complex dramatic monologues, by the completely subjective monologues of T. S. Eliot's Prufrock and of Pound speaking in his own character, and by the grotesque horror-comedy in Robert Frost's poem. Two rich examples of poetic drama, both embodying the psychological and symbolic use of ghost-story materials, are found in the scenes from *Hamlet* and in Yeats's modern play *Purgatory*.

EZRA POUND   Canto I [1]

> And then went down to the ship,
> Set keel to breakers, forth on the godly sea, and

[1] Although this poem is mostly a translation, in the closing nine lines Pound begins speaking in his own right. He acknowledges that his own work is based on a Latin translation of the *Odyssey* by Andreas Divus, published in 1538 at the workshop (*officina*) of Wechel in Paris. Later, he makes reference to *Homeric Hymn VI: To Aphrodite*, translated into Latin by Georgius Dartona Cretensis ("the Cretan"). Aphrodite, goddess of sexual beauty and therefore of the earth's treasures, was divinely appointed to rule over Cyprus's defenses (*Cypri . . . est*), and is associated with men's restless search for riches (gold and *oricalchi*—yellow copper ore). Hermes, the messenger of the gods and carrier of luck and wealth, is also invoked (*Argicida*). Thus Pound presents himself as picking up an ancient tradition, taking on Odysseus's role and repeating his search "a second time," as Tiresias the prophet says, guiding himself by that tradition and yet moving into uncharted modern directions. The "So that:" at the end prepares us for the many *Cantos* to follow.—*What does the shift of emphasis in these closing lines do to the effect of* Canto I *as a whole?*

We set up mast and sail on that swart ship,
Bore sheep aboard her, and our bodies also
Heavy with weeping, and winds from sternward
Bore us out onward with bellying canvas,
Circe's this craft, the trim-coifed goddess.
Then sat we amidships, wind jamming the tiller,
Thus with stretched sail, we went over sea till day's end.
Sun to his slumber, shadows o'er all the ocean,   10
Came we then to the bounds of deepest water,
To the Kimmerian lands, and peopled cities
Covered with close-webbed mist, unpierced ever
With glitter of sun-rays
Nor with stars stretched, nor looking back from heaven
Swartest night stretched over wretched men there.
The ocean flowing backward, came we then to the place
Aforesaid by Circe.
Here did they rites, Perimedes and Eurylochus,
And drawing sword from my hip   20
I dug the ell-square pitkin;
Poured we libations unto each the dead,
First mead and then sweet wine, water mixed with white flour.
Then prayed I many a prayer to the sickly death's-heads;
As set in Ithaca, sterile bulls of the best
For sacrifice, heaping the pyre with goods,
A sheep to Tiresias only, black and a bell-sheep.
Dark blood flowed in the fosse,
Souls out of Erebus, cadaverous dead, of brides
Of youths and of the old who had borne much;   30
Souls stained with recent tears, girls tender,
Men many, mauled with bronze lance heads,
Battle spoil, bearing yet dreory arms,
These many crowded about me; with shouting,
Pallor upon me, cried to my men for more beasts;
Slaughtered the herds, sheep slain of bronze;
Poured ointment, cried to the gods,
To Pluto the strong, and praised Proserpine;
Unsheathed the narrow sword,
I sat to keep off the impetuous impotent dead,   40
Till I should hear Tiresias.
But first Elpenor came, our friend Elpenor,
Unburied, cast on the wide earth,
Limbs that we left in the house of Circe,
Unwept, unwrapped in sepulchre, since toils urged other.

Pitiful spirit. And I cried in hurried speech:
"Elpenor, how art thou come to this dark coast?
"Cam'st thou afoot, outstripping seamen?"
                    And he in heavy speech:
"Ill fate and abundant wine. I slept in Circe's ingle.   50
"Going down the long ladder unguarded,
"I fell against the buttress,
"Shattered the nape-nerve, the soul sought Avernus.
"But thou, O King, I bid remember me, unwept, unburied,
"Heap up mine arms, be tomb by sea-bord, and inscribed:
"A *man of no fortune, and with a name to come.*
"And set my oar up, that I swung mid fellows."

And Anticlea came, whom I beat off, and then Tiresias Theban,
Holding his golden wand, knew me, and spoke first:
"A second time? why? man of ill star,   60
"Facing the sunless dead and this joyless region?
"Stand from the fosse, leave me my bloody bever
"For soothsay."
                    And I stepped back,
And he strong with the blood, said then: "Odysseus
"Shalt return through spiteful Neptune, over dark seas,
"Lose all companions." And then Anticlea came.
Lie quiet Divus. I mean, that is Andreas Divus,
In officina Wecheli, 1538, out of Homer.
And he sailed, by Sirens and thence outward and away   70
And unto Circe.
                    Venerandam,
In the Cretan's phrase, with the golden crown, Aphrodite,
Cypri munimenta sortita est, mirthful, oricalchi, with golden
Girdles and breast bands, thou with dark eyelids
Bearing the golden bough of Argicida. So that:

Dante Alighieri   *Midway the Journey* [1]

(from *Inferno:* Canto I)

Midway the the journey of this life I was 'ware
   That I had strayed into a dark forest,

---

[1] Translated by Laurence Binyon. Dante gives each of the beasts described here both a moral and a political symbolism. The Leopard is worldly pleasure and the city-state of Florence The Lion is ambition and the royal house of France. The She-Wolf is avarice and the papacy.

And the right path appeared not anywhere.
Ah, tongue cannot describe how it oppressed,
    This wood, so harsh, dismal and wild, that fear
    At thought of it strikes now into my breast.
So bitter it is, death is scarce bitterer.
    But, for the good it was my hap to find,
    I speak of the other things that I saw there.
I cannot well remember in my mind   10
    How I came thither, so was I immersed
    In sleep, when the true way I left behind.
But when my footsteps had attained the first
    Slope of a hill, at the end of that drear vale
    Which with such terror had my spirit pierced,
I looked up, and beheld its shoulders pale
    Already in clothing of that planet's light
    Which guideth men on all roads without fail.
Then had my bosom a little of respite
    From what had all the lake of my heart tost   20
    While I so piteously endured the night.
As one, whom pantings of his breath exhaust,
    Escaped from the deep water to the shore,
    Turns back and gazes on the danger crost,
So my mind, fleeing still and stricken sore,
    Turned back to gaze astonished on that pass
    Which none hath ever left alive before.
When my tired body had rested a brief space
    I trod anew the slope, desert and bare,
    With the firmer foot still in the lower place.   30
And at the ascent, as 't were on the first stair,
    Behold! a Leopard light and swift of limb
    And covered with a hide of spotted hair.
And he would not depart, but still would trim
    His pace to front me, so that many a time
    I turned me to go back, because of him.
The moment was the morning's earliest prime,
    And the sun mounted up, accompanied
    With those stars chosen in his choir to climb
When divine Love first motioned and enskied   40
    Those beauteous things; so that a hope I caught
    To evade that creature with the freckled hide.
The hour of time and the sweet season wrought
    Thus on me; yet not so much, but when appeared
    A Lion, terror to my heart he brought.

He seemed coming against me with head reared
  Ravening with hunger, and so terrible
  That the very air seemed of his breath afeared;
And a She-Wolf, that in her famished fell
  Looked all infuriate craving; she hath meant   50
  To many ere now that they in misery dwell.
On me the grimness of her aspect sent
  A burden that my spirit overpowered,
  So that I lost the hope of the ascent.
As one that is with lust of gain devoured,
  When comes the time that makes him lose, will rack
  His thoughts, lamenting all his hope deflowered,
To such state brought me, in dread of his attack,
  That restless beast, who by degrees perforce
  To where the Sun is silent drove me back. . . .   60

Dante Alighieri   *Paolo and Francesca* [1]

(from *Inferno:* Canto V)

Now begin wailing notes; the flesh is thrilled
  To hear them and to feel them. I am come
  Where thronging lamentations hold me chilled.
I came into a place of all light dumb
  That bellows like a storm in the sea-deep
  When the thwart winds that strike it roar and hum.
The abysmal tempest that can never sleep
  Snatches the spirits and headlong hurries them,
  Beats and besets them with its whirling sweep.
When they arrive before the ruin, stream   10
  The cries up; there the wail is and the moan,
  There the divine perfection they blaspheme.
I learnt that in such restless violence blown
  This punishment the carnal sinners share
  Who let Desire pull Reason from her throne.
And as their beating wings the starlings bear
  At the cold season, in broad flocking flight,
  So those corrupted spirits were rapt in air
To and fro, down, up, driven in helpless flight,
  Comforted by no hope ever to lie   20
  At rest, nor even to bear a pain more light.

[1] Translated by Laurence Binyon.

And as the cranes in long line streak the sky
   And in procession chant their mournful call,
   So I saw come with sound of wailing by
The shadows fluttering in the tempest's brawl.
   Whereat, "O Master,[2] who are these," I said,
   "On whom the black winds with their scourges fall?" . . . .
After that I had heard my Teacher name
   Each lady of old, lost with her lovely knight,
   My thoughts were mazed, such pity upon me came.   30
I began: "Poet, I fain would, if I might,
   Speak with those two that hand in hand appear
   And, as they move, seem to the wind so light."
And he to me: "When they approach more near,
   Thou shalt see. By the love which is their guide
   Do thou entreat them then, and they will hear."
Soon as the wind's whirl made them nearer glide,
   I raised my voice up: "O tired spirits, come
   And speak with us, if that be not denied."
Eagerly as a pair of pigeons, whom   40
   Desire calls, and their will bears, down the sky
   On wide unfaltering wings to their sweet home,
So swerved those spirits from out the company
   Where Dido is, flying toward us underneath
   The ghast mirk; such a power had my fond cry.
"O kind and gracious creature that hast breath
   And comest journeying through the black air
   To us who made the earth bloody with our death,
Were but the world's Lord friend to us, a prayer
   Should from us both implore Him for thy peace   50
   Because thou hast taken pity on our despair.
Whether to speak or listen better please,
   We will speak with you, and hear and understand,
   Now while the lull'd wind spares a little ease.
The place where I was born sits on the strand
   Where Po descends to his peace, and with him takes
   All the other streams that follow him down the land.
Love, that in gentle heart so soon awakes,
   Took him with this fair body, which from me
   Was torn: the way and wound of it yet aches.   60

---

[2] The shade of Vergil, the great Roman poet, guides Dante in his symbolic journey through Hell. Vergil names many famous lovers (such as Tristan and Isolde, Helen of Troy, and others) whose unrepented carnality has led to eternal damnation.

Love, that to no loved one remits his fee,
     Took me with joy of him, so deep in-wrought,
     Even now it hath not left me, as thou dost see.
Love led us both to one death. He that sought
     And split our life—Cain's place awaits him now." [3]
     These words to us upon the wind were brought.
When I had heard those wounded spirits, my brow
     Sank downward, and I held it where it was,
     Until the Poet spoke: "What musest thou?"
And when I answered, I began: "Alas!   70
     How many sweet thoughts and what longings fain
     Led them into the lamentable pass!"
I turned, and I began to speak again:
     "Francesca, the tears prick into mine eyes
     For sorrow, and for pity of thy pain.
But tell me: in the time of the sweet sighs
     How did Love vouchsafe proof of what he is,
     And of the obscure yearnings make you wise?"
And she to me: "No grief surpasses this
     (And that thy Teacher also knows full well)—   80
     In the midst of misery to remember bliss.
But if thou so desire to know how fell
     The seed whose first root in our bosoms fed,
     I'll tell, as one who can but weep and tell.
One day together, for pastime, we read
     Of Launcelot, and how Love held him in thrall.
     We were alone, and without any dread.
Sometimes our eyes, at the word's secret call,
     Met, and our cheeks a changing colour wore.
     But it was one page only that did all.   90
When we read how that smile, so thirsted for,
     Was kissed by such a lover, he that may
     Never from me be separated more
All trembling kissed my mouth. The book I say
     Was a Galahalt [4] to us, and he beside
     That wrote the book. We read no more that day."
While the one spirit spoke thus, the other cried
     So lamentably, that the whole life fled
     For pity out of me, as if I died;
And I fell, like a body falling dead.

[3] Francesca's husband murdered her before she could repent. His place is to be in the lowest depths of Hell.
 [4] a go-between

Anonymous   *Sir Patrick Spens* [1]

The king sits in Dunfermline town
    Drinking the blude-red wine:
"O whar will I get guid sailor,
    To sail this ship of mine?"

Up and spake an eldern knight,
    Sat at the king's right knee;
"Sir Patrick Spens is the best sailor
    That sails upon the sea."

The King has written a braid letter,
    And sign'd it wi' his hand,
And sent it to Sir Patrick Spens,
    Was walking on the sand.   10

The first line that Sir Patrick read,
    A loud laugh laughed he;
The next line that Sir Patrick read,
    The tear blinded his e'e.

"O wha is this has done this deed,
    This ill deed done to me,
To send me out this time o' the year,
    To sail upon the sea!   20

"Make haste, make haste, my merry men all,
    Our guid ship sails the morn":
"O say na sae, my master dear,
    For I fear a deadly storm.

"Late late yestre'en I saw the new moon,
    Wi' the auld moon in her arm,
And I fear, I fear, my dear master,
    That we will come to harm."

O our Scots nobles were right laith
    To wet their cork-heel'd schoon;
But lang ere a' the play were play'd,   30
    Their hats they swam aboon.

---

[1] Glossary: *aboon* above; *kames* combs.

O lang, lang may their ladies sit,
    Wi' their fans into their hand,
Or e'er they see Sir Patrick Spens
    Come sailing to the land.

O lang, lang may the ladies stand,
    Wi' their golden kames in their hair,
Waiting for their ain dear lords
    For they'll see them na mair.   40

Ha'f o'er, ha'f o'er to Aberdour,
    It's fifty fathom deep,
And there lies guid Sir Patrick Spens,
    Wi' the Scots lords at his feet.

ANONYMOUS   *Edward, Edward* [1]

I

"Why does your brand sae drop wi' blude,
    Edward, Edward?
Why does your brand sae drop wi' blude,
    And why sae sad gang ye, O?"—
"O I hae kill'd my hawk sae gude,
    Mither, mither;
O I hae kill'd my hawk sae gude,
    And I had nae mair but he, O."

II

"Your hawk's blude was never sae red,
    Edward, Edward;   10
Your hawk's blude was never sae red,
    My dear son, I tell thee, O."—
"O I hae kill'd my red-roan steed,
    Mither, mither;
O I hae kill'd my red-roan steed,
    That erst was sae fair and free, O."

III

"Your steed was auld, and ye hae got mair,
    Edward, Edward;

---

[1] GLOSSARY: *brand* sword; *dree* suffer; *dule* grief; *gang* go; *sic* such.

Your steed was auld, and ye hae got mair;
   Some other dule ye dree, O."   20
"Oh I hae kill'd my father dear,
   Mither, mither;
O I hae kill'd my father dear,
   Alas, and wae is me, O!"

IV

"And whatten penance will ye dree for that,
   Edward, Edward?
Whatten penance will ye dree for that?
   My dear son, now tell me, O."—
"I'll set my feet in yonder boat,
   Mither, mither;   30
I'll set my feet in yonder boat,
   And I'll fare over the sea, O."

V

"And what will ye do wi' your tow'rs and your ha',
   Edward, Edward?
And what will ye do wi' your tow'rs and your ha',
   That were sae fair to see, O?"—
"I'll let them stand till they doun fa',
   Mither, mither;
I'll let them stand till they doun fa',
   For here never mair maun I be, O."   40

VI

"And what will ye leave to your bairns and your wife,
   Edward, Edward?
And what will ye leave to your bairns and your wife,
   When ye gang owre the sea, O?"—
"The warld's room: let them beg through life,
   Mither, mither;
The warld's room: let them beg through life;
   For them never mair will I see, O."

VII

"And what will ye leave to your ain mither dear,
   Edward, Edward?   50
And what will ye leave to your ain mither dear,
   My dear son, now tell me, O?"—

"The curse of hell frae me sall ye bear,
    Mither, mither;
The curse of hell frae me sall ye bear:
    Sic counsels ye gave to me, O!"

ANONYMOUS *The Twa Corbies* [1]

As I was walking all alane,
I heard twa corbies making a mane;
The tane unto the t' other say,
"Where sall we gang and dine today?"

"In behint yon auld fail dyke,
I wot there lies a new-slain knight;
And naebody kens that he lies there,
But his hawk, his hound, and lady fair.

"His hound is to the hunting gane,
His hawk to fetch the wild-fowl hame,   10
His lady's ta'en another mate,
So we may mak our dinner sweet.

"Ye'll sit on his white hause-bane,
And I'll pick out his bonny blue een;
Wi' ae lock o' his gowden hair
We'll theek our nest when it grows bare.

"Mony a one for him makes mane,
But nane sall ken where he is gane;
O'er his white banes when they are bare,
The wind sall blaw for evermair."   20

ANONYMOUS *The Unquiet Grave*

"The wind doth blow today, my love,
    And a few small drops of rain;
I never had but one true-love,
    In cold grave she was lain.

---

[1] GLOSSARY: *corbies* ravens; *een* eyes; *fail dyke* earth-wall thrown up from a ditch; *gang* go; *hause-bane* neckbone; *mane* moan, croak; *sall* shall; *theek* thatch; *twa* two.

"I'll do as much for my true-love
  As any young man may;
I'll sit and mourn all at her grave
  For a twelvemonth and a day."

The twelvemonth and a day being up,
  The dead began to speak: 10
"Oh who sits weeping on my grave,
  And will not let me sleep?"

" 'Tis I, my love, sits on your grave,
  And will not let you sleep;
For I crave one kiss of your clay-cold lips,
  And that is all I seek."

"You crave one kiss of my clay-cold lips;
  But my breath smells earthy strong;
If you have one kiss of my clay-cold lips,
  Your time will not be long.   20

" 'Tis down in yonder garden green,
  Love, where we used to walk,
The finest flower that e'er was seen
  Is withered to a stalk.

"The stalk is withered dry, my love,
  So will our hearts decay;
So make yourself content, my love,
  Till God calls you away."

JOHN LENNON AND PAUL McCARTNEY   *Eleanor Rigby* [1]

Ah look at all the lonely people! Ah look at all the lonely people!

Eleanor Rigby, picks up the rice in the church where a wedding has
  been, lives in a dream.
Waits at the window, wearing the face that she keeps in a jar by
  the door, who is it for?
All the lonely people, where do they all come from? All the lonely
  people, where do they all belong?

---

[1] *If possible, play a recording of this song and consider the difference in effect, if any, created by the presence or absence of the music.*

Father McKenzie, writing the words of a sermon that no one will
hear, no one comes near.
Look at him working, darning his socks in the night when there's
nobody there, what does he care?
All the lonely people, where do they all come from? All the lonely
people, where do they all belong?

Eleanor Rigby, died in the church and was buried along with her
name, nobody came.
Father McKenzie, wiping the dirt from his hands as he walks from
the grave, no one was saved.
All the lonely people, where do they all come from? All the lonely
people, where do they all belong?

HUGH MACDIARMID (CHRISTOPHER GRIEVE)   *O Wha's the Bride?* [1]

O wha's the bride that cairries the bunch
O' thistles blinterin' white?
Her cuckold bridegroom little dreids
What he sall ken this nicht.

For closer than gudeman can come
And closer to'r than hersel',
Wha didna need her maidenheid
Has wrocht his purpose fell.

O wha's been here afore me, lass,
And hoo did he get in?   10
—A man that deed or was I born
This evil thing has din.

And left, as it were on a corpse,
Your maidenheid to me?
—Nae lass, gudeman, sin' Time began
'S hed ony mair to gi'e.

But I can gi'e ye kindness, lad,
And a pair o' willin' hands,
And you sall ha'e my breists like stars,
My limbs like willow wands.   20

[1] GLOSSARY: *blinterin'* gleaming; *deed* died; *mair* more; *or* before; *sall* shall; *wha's* who's.

And on my lips ye'll heed nae mair,
And in my hair forget,
The seed o' a' the men that in
My virgin womb ha'e met. . . .

John Keats *La Belle Dame sans Merci*

O what can ail thee, knight-at-arms,
    Alone and palely loitering?
The sedge has wither'd from the lake,
    And no birds sing.

O what can ail thee, knight-at-arms,
    So haggard and so woe-begone?
The squirrel's granary is full,
    And the harvest's done.

I see a lilly on thy brow
    With anguish moist and fever dew,   10
And on thy cheek a fading rose
    Fast withereth too.

I met a lady in the meads,
    Full beautiful—a faery's child,
Her hair was long, her foot was light,
    And her eyes were wild.

I made a garland for her head,
    And bracelets too, and fragrant zone;
She look'd at me as she did love,
    And made sweet moan.   20

I set her on my pacing steed,
    And nothing else saw all day long,
For sidelong would she bend, and sing
    A faery's song.

She found me roots of relish sweet,
    And honey wild, and manna dew,
And sure in language strange she said—
    "I love thee true."

She took me to her elfin grot,
   And there she wept, and sigh'd full sore.   30
And there I shut her wild wild eyes
   With kisses four.

And there she lulled me asleep,
   And there I dream'd—Ah! woe betide!
The latest dream I ever dream'd
   On the cold hill side.

I saw pale kings and princes too,
   Pale warriors, death-pale were they all;
They cried—"La Belle Dame sans Merci
   Hath thee in thrall!"   40

I saw their starved lips in the gloam,
   With horrid warning gaped wide,
And I awoke and found me here,
   On the cold hill side.

And this is why I sojourn here,
   Alone and palely loitering,
Though the sedge has wither'd from the lake,
   And no birds sing.

JOHN MONTAGUE   *The First Invasion of Ireland*

for Michael Walsh

According to Leabhar Gabhàla, *the Book of Conquests, the first invasion of Ireland was by relatives of Noah, just before the Flood. Refused entry into the Ark, they consulted an idol which told them to flee to Ireland. There were three men and fifty-one women in the party and their behaviour has so little common with subsequent tradition in Ireland that one must take the story to be mythological.*

Fleeing from threatened flood, they sailed,
Seeking the fair island, without serpent or claw;
From the deck of their hasty windjammer watched
The soft edge of Ireland nearward draw.

A sweet confluence of waters, a trinity of rivers,
Was their first resting place:
They unloaded the women and the sensual idol,
Guiding image of their disgrace.

Division of damsels they did there,
The slender, the tender, the dimpled, the round,   10
It was the first just bargain in Ireland,
There was enough to go round.

Lightly they lay and pleasured
In the green grass of that guileless place:
Ladhra was the first to die;
He perished of an embrace.

Bith was buried in a stone heap,
Riot of mind, all passion spent.
Fintan fled from the ferocious women
Before he, too, by love was rent.   20

Great primitive princes of our line
They were the first, with stately freedom,
To sleep with women in Ireland:
Soft the eternal bed they lie upon.

On a lonely headland the women assembled,
Chill as worshippers in a nave,
And watched the eastern waters gather
Into a great virile flooding wave.

ROBERT BROWNING   *Childe Roland to the Dark Tower Came*

(See Edgar's song in 'Lear')

My first thought was, he lied in every word,
  That hoary cripple, with malicious eye
  Askance to watch the working of his lie
On mine, and mouth scarce able to afford
Suppression of the glee that pursed and scored
  Its edge at one more victim gained thereby.

What else should he be set for, with his staff?
  What, save to waylay with his lies, ensnare
  All travellers that might find him posted there,
And ask the road? I guessed what skull-like laugh   10
Would break, what crutch 'gin write my epitaph
  For pastime in the dusty thoroughfare,

If at his counsel I should turn aside
   Into that ominous tract which, all agree,
   Hides the Dark Tower. Yet acquiescingly
I did turn as he pointed; neither pride
Nor hope rekindling at the end descried,
   So much as gladness that some end might be.

For, what with my whole world-wide wandering,
   What with my search drawn out thro' years, my hope   20
   Dwindled into a ghost not fit to cope
With that obstreperous joy success would bring,—
I hardly tried now to rebuke the spring
   My heart made, finding failure in its scope.

As when a sick man very near to death
   Seems dead indeed, and feels begin and end
   The tears and takes the farewell of each friend,
And hears one bid the other go, draw breath
Freelier outside, ('since all is o'er,' he saith,
   'And the blow fallen no grieving can amend;')   30

While some discuss if near the other graves
   Be room enough for this, and when a day
   Suits best for carrying the corpse away,
With care about the banners, scarves and staves,—
And still the man hears all, and only craves
   He may not shame such tender love and stay.

Thus, I had so long suffered in this quest,
   Heard failure prophesied so oft, been writ
   So many times among 'The Band'—to wit,
The knights who to the Dark Tower's search addressed   40
Their steps—that just to fail as they, seemed best,
   And all the doubt was now—should I be fit.

So, quiet as despair, I turned from him,
   That hateful cripple, out of his highway
   Into the path he pointed. All the day
Had been a dreary one at best, and dim
Was settling to its close, yet shot one grim
   Red leer to see the plain catch its estray.

For mark! no sooner was I fairly found
　Pledged to the plain, after a pace or two,　　　　50
　Than, pausing to throw backward a last view
To the safe road, 'twas gone; grey plain all round:
Nothing but plain to the horizon's bound.
　I might go on; nought else remained to do.

So, on I went. I think I never saw
　Such starved ignoble nature; nothing throve:
　For flowers—as well expect a cedar grove!
But cockle, spurge, according to their law
Might propagate their kind, with none to awe,
　You'd think; a burr had been a treasure-trove.　　　60

No! penury, inertness and grimace,
　In some strange sort, were the land's portion. 'See
　Or shut your eyes,' said Nature peevishly,
'It nothing skills: I cannot help my case:
'Tis the Last Judgment's fire must cure this place,
　Calcine its clods and set my prisoners free.'

If there pushed any ragged thistle-stalk
　Above its mates, the head was chopped—the bents
　Were jealous else. What made those holes and rents
In the dock's harsh swarth leaves—bruised as to baulk　　　70
All hope of greenness? 'tis a brute must walk
　Pashing their life out, with a brute's intents.

As for the grass, it grew as scant as hair
　In leprosy; thin dry blades pricked the mud
　Which underneath looked kneaded up with blood.
One stiff blind horse, his every bone a-stare,
Stood stupefied, however he came there:
　Thrust out past service from the devil's stud!

Alive? he might be dead for aught I know,
　With that red, gaunt and colloped neck a-strain,　　　80
　And shut eyes underneath the rusty mane;
Seldom went such grotesqueness with such woe;
I never saw a brute I hated so;
　He must be wicked to deserve such pain.

I shut my eyes and turned them on my heart.
　　As a man calls for wine before he fights,
　　I asked one draught of earlier, happier sights,
Ere fitly I could hope to play my part.
Think first, fight afterwards—the soldier's art:
　　One taste of the old time sets all to rights!　　　　　90

Not it! I fancied Cuthbert's reddening face
　　Beneath its garniture of curly gold,
　　Dear fellow, till I almost felt him fold
An arm in mine to fix me to the place,
That way he used. Alas, one night's disgrace!
　　Out went my heart's new fire and left it cold.

Giles, then, the soul of honour—there he stands
　　Frank as ten years ago when knighted first.
　　What honest men should dare (he said) he durst.
Good—but the scene shifts—faugh! what hangman's hands　　100
Pin to his breast a parchment? his own bands
　　Read it. Poor traitor, spit upon and curst!

Better this Present than a Past like that;
　　Back therefore to my darkening path again.
　　No sound, no sight as far as eye could strain.
Will the night send a howlet or a bat?
I asked: when something on the dismal flat
　　Came to arrest my thoughts and change their train.

A sudden little river crossed my path
　　As unexpected as a serpent comes.　　　　　　　110
　　No sluggish tide congenial to the glooms—
This, as it frothed by, might have been a bath
For the fiend's glowing hoof—to see the wrath
　　Of its black eddy bespate with flakes and spumes.

So petty yet so spiteful! all along,
　　Low scrubby alders kneeled down over it;
　　Drenched willows flung them headlong in a fit
Of mute despair, a suicidal throng:
The river which had done them all the wrong,
　　Whate'er that was, rolled by, deterred no whit.　　　120

Which, while I forded,—good saints, how I feared
   To set my foot upon a dead man's cheek,
   Each step, or feel the spear I thrust to seek
For hollows, tangled in his hair or beard!
—It may have been a water-rat I speared,
   But, ugh! it sounded like a baby's shriek.

Glad was I when I reached the other bank.
   Now for a better country. Vain presage!
   Who were the strugglers, what war did they wage
Whose savage trample thus could pad the dank   130
Soil to a plash? toads in a poisoned tank,
   Or wild cats in a red-hot iron cage—

The fight must so have seemed in that fell cirque.
   What penned them there, with all the plain to choose?
   No foot-print leading to that horrid mews,
None out of it. Mad brewage set to work
Their brains, no doubt, like galley-slaves the Turk
   Pits for his pastime, Christians against Jews.

And more than that—a furlong on—why, there!
   What bad use was that engine for, that wheel,   140
   Or brake, not wheel—that harrow fit to reel
Men's bodies out like silk? with all the air
Of Tophet's tool, on earth left unaware,
   Or brought to sharpen its rusty teeth of steel.

Then came a bit of stubbed ground, once a wood,
   Next a marsh, it would seem, and now mere earth
   Desperate and done with; (so a fool finds mirth,
Makes a thing and then mars it, till his mood
Changes and off he goes!) within a rood—
   Bog, clay and rubble, sand and stark black dearth.   150

Now blotches rankling, coloured gay and grim,
   Now patches where some leanness of the soil's
   Broke into moss or substances like boils;
Then came some palsied oak, a cleft in him
Like a distorted mouth that splits its rim
   Gaping at death, and dies while it recoils.

And just as far as ever from the end!
   Nought in the distance but the evening, nought
   To point my footstep further! At the thought,
A great black bird, Apollyon's bosom-friend,   160
Sailed past, nor beat his wide wing dragon-penned
   That brushed my cap—perchance the guide I sought.

For, looking up, aware I somehow grew,
   'Spite of the dusk, the plain had given place
   All round to mountains—with such name to grace
Mere ugly heights and heaps now stolen in view.
How thus they had surprised me,—solve it, you!
   How to get from them was no clearer case.

Yet half I seemed to recognise some trick
   Of mischief happened to me, God knows when—   170
   In a bad dream perhaps. Here ended, then,
Progress this way. When, in the very nick
Of giving up, one time more, came a click
   As when a trap shuts—you're inside the den!

Burningly it came on me all at once,
   This was the place! those two hills on the right,
   Crouched like two bulls locked horn in horn in fight;
While to the left, a tall scalped mountain . . . Dunce,
Fool, to be dozing at the very nonce,
   After a life spent training for the sight!   180

What in the midst lay but the Tower itself?
   The round squat turret, blind as the fool's heart,
   Built of brown stone, without a counterpart
In the whole world. The tempest's mocking elf
Points to the shipman thus the unseen shelf
   He strikes on, only when the timbers start.

Not see? because of night perhaps?—Why, day
   Came back again for that! before it left,
   The dying sunset kindled through a cleft:
The hills, like giants at a hunting, lay,   190
Chin upon hand, to see the game at bay,—
   'Now stab and end the creature—to the heft!'

Not hear? when noise was everywhere! it tolled
   Increasing like a bell. Names in my ears,

Of all the lost adventurers my peers,—
How such a one was strong, and such was bold,
And such was fortunate, yet each of old
    Lost, lost! one moment knelled the woe of years.

There they stood, ranged along the hillsides, met
    To view the last of me, a living frame 200
    For one more picture! in a sheet of flame
I saw them and I knew them all. And yet
Dauntless the slug-horn to my lips I set,
    And blew. '*Childe Roland to the Dark Tower came.*'

ROBERT BROWNING   *Porphyria's Lover*

The rain set early in to-night,
    The sullen wind was soon awake,
It tore the elm-tops down for spite,
    And did its worst to vex the lake,
I listened with heart fit to break.
When glided in Porphyria; straight
    She shut the cold out and the storm,
And kneeled and made the cheerless grate
    Blaze up, and all the cottage warm;
Which done, she rose, and from her form 10
Withdrew the dripping cloak and shawl,
    And laid her soiled gloves by, untied
Her hat and let the damp hair fall,
    And, last, she sat down by my side
And called me. When no voice replied,
She put my arm about her waist,
    And made her smoooth white shoulder bare,
And all her yellow hair displaced,
    And, stooping, made my cheek lie there,
And spread o'er all her yellow hair, 20
Murmuring how she loved me—she
    Too weak, for all her heart's endeavour
To set its struggling passion free
    From pride, and vainer ties dissever,
And give herself to me for ever.
But passion sometimes would prevail,
    Nor could to-night's gay feast restrain
A sudden thought of one so pale
    For love of her, and all in vain;

So, she was come through wind and rain.   30
Be sure I looked up at her eyes
    Happy and proud; at last I knew
Porphyria worshipped me; surprise
    Made my heart swell, and still it grew
While I debated what to do.
That moment she was mine, mine, fair,
    Perfectly pure and good: I found
A thing to do, and all her hair
    In one long yellow string I wound
Three times her little throat around,   40
And strangled her. No pain felt she;
    I am quite sure she felt no pain.
As a shut bud that holds a bee,
    I warily oped her lids; again
Laughed the blue eyes without a stain.
And I untightened next the tress
    About her neck; her cheek once more
Blushed bright beneath my burning kiss:
    I propped her head up as before,
Only, this time *my* shoulder bore   50
Her head, which droops upon it still:
    The smiling rosy little head,
So glad it has its utmost will,
    That all it scorned at once is fled,
And I, its love, am gained instead!
Porphyria's love: she guessed not how
    Her darling one wish would be heard.
And thus we sit together now,
    And all night long we have not stirred,
And yet God has not said a word!   60

ROBERT BROWNING   *My Last Duchess* [1]

Ferrara

That's my last Duchess painted on the wall,
Looking as if she were alive. I call

---

[1] The Duke who speaks here is in certain respects representative of Italian Renaissance aristocracy. *Try to imagine his appearance and describe his character. Is there good as well as evil in him? To whom, and under what circumstances, does he speak? What is the unspoken purpose behind his confidences? What message is the listener expected to take back to his master?*

That piece a wonder, now: Frà Pandolf's hands
Worked busily a day, and there she stands.
Will't please you sit and look at her? I said
"Frà Pandolf" by design, for never read
Strangers like you that pictured countenance,
The depth and passion of its earnest glance,
But to myself they turned (since none puts by
The curtain I have drawn for you, but I)   10
And seemed as they would ask me, if they durst,
How such a glance came there; so, not the first
Are you to turn and ask thus. Sir, 'twas not
Her husband's presence only, called that spot
Of joy into the Duchess' cheek; perhaps
Frà Pandolf chanced to say, "Her mantle laps
Over my lady's wrist too much," or "Paint
Must never hope to reproduce the faint
Half-flush that dies along her throat": such stuff
Was courtesy, she thought, and cause enough   20
For calling up that spot of joy. She had
A heart—how shall I say?—too soon made glad,
Too easily impressed: she liked whate'er
She looked on, and her looks went everywhere.
Sir, 'twas all one! My favour at her breast,
The dropping of the daylight in the West,
The bough of cherries some officious fool
Broke in the orchard for her, the white mule
She rode with round the terrace—all and each
Would draw from her alike the approving speech,   30
Or blush, at least. She thanked men,—good! but thanked
Somehow—I know not how—as if she ranked
My gift of a nine-hundred-years-old name
With anybody's gift. Who'd stoop to blame
This sort of trifling? Even had you skill
In speech—(which I have not)—to make your will
Quite clear to such an one, and say, "Just this
Or that in you disgusts me; here you miss,
Or there exceed the mark"—and if she let
Herself be lessoned so, nor plainly set   40
Her wits to yours, forsooth, and made excuse,
—E'en then would be some stooping; and I choose
Never to stoop. Oh sir, she smiled, no doubt,
Whene'er I passed her; but who passed without
Much the same smile? This grew; I gave commands;

Then all smiles stopped together. There she stands
As if alive. Will't please you rise? We'll meet
The company below, then. I repeat,
The Count your master's known munificence
Is ample warrant that no just pretence   50
Of mine for dowry will be disallowed;
Though his fair daughter's self, as I avowed
At starting, is my object. Nay, we'll go
Together down, sir. Notice Neptune, though,
Taming a sea-horse, thought a rarity,
Which Claus of Innsbruck cast in bronze for me!

T. S. Eliot   *The Love Song of J. Alfred Prufrock*

S'io credesse che mia risposta fosse
A persona che mai tornasse al mondo,
Questa fiamma staria senza piu scosse.
Ma perciocche giammai di questo fondo
Non torno vivo alcun, s'i'odo il vero,
Senza tema d'infamia ti rispondo.[1]

Let us go then, you and I,
When the evening is spread out against the sky
Like a patient etherized upon a table;
Let us go, through certain half-deserted streets,
The muttering retreats
Of restless nights in one-night cheap hotels
And sawdust restaurants with oyster-shells:
Streets that follow like a tedious argument
Of insidious intent
To lead you to an overwhelming question. . . .   10
Oh, do not ask, "What is it?"
Let us go and make our visit.

In the room the women come and go
Talking of Michelangelo.

The yellow fog that rubs its back upon the window-panes,
The yellow smoke that rubs its muzzle on the window-panes,

[1] If I believed my answer might be heard by anyone who could return to the world, this flame would leap no more. But since no one ever returned alive from these depths, as far as I know, then I answer without fear of infamy. (Dante, *Inferno:* Canto XXVII. lines 61–66.)

Licked its tongue into the corners of the evening,
Lingered upon the pools that stand in drains,
Let fall upon its back the soot that falls from chimneys,
Slipped by the terrace, made a sudden leap,   20
And seeing that it was a soft October night,
Curled once about the house, and fell asleep.

And indeed there will be time
For the yellow smoke that slides along the street,
Rubbing its back upon the window-panes;
There will be time, there will be time
To prepare a face to meet the faces that you meet;
There will be time to murder and create,
And time for all the works and days of hands
That lift and drop a question on your plate;   30
Time for you and time for me,
And time yet for a hundred indecisions,
And for a hundred visions and revisions,
Before the taking of a toast and tea.

In the room the women come and go
Talking of Michelangelo.

And indeed there will be time
To wonder, "Do I dare?" and, "Do I dare?"
Time to turn back and descend the stair,
With a bald spot in the middle of my hair—   40
[They will say: "How his hair is growing thin!"]
My morning coat, my collar mounting firmly to the chin,
My necktie rich and modest, but asserted by a simple pin—
[They will say: "But how his arms and legs are thin!"]
Do I dare
Disturb the universe?
In a minute there is time
For decisions and revisions which a minute will reverse.

For I have known them all already, known them all:—
Have known the evenings, mornings, afternoons,   50
I have measured out my life with coffee spoons;
I know the voices dying with a dying fall
Beneath the music from a farther room.
    So how should I presume?

And I have known the eyes already, known them all—
The eyes that fix you in a formulated phrase,
And when I am formulated, sprawling on a pin,
When I am pinned and wriggling on the wall,
Then how should I begin
To spit out all the butt-ends of my days and ways?   60
          And how should I presume?

And I have known the arms already, known them all—
Arms that are braceleted and white and bare
[But in the lamplight, downed with light brown hair!]
Is it perfume from a dress
That makes me so digress?
Arms that lie along a table, or wrap about a shawl.
          And should I then presume?
          And how should I begin?

                    .   .   .

Shall I say, I have gone at dusk through narrow streets   70
And watched the smoke that rises from the pipes
Of lonely men in shirt-sleeves, leaning out of windows? . . .

I should have been a pair of ragged claws
Scuttling across the floors of silent seas.

                    .   .   .

And the afternoon, the evening, sleeps so peacefully!
Smoothed by long fingers,
Asleep . . . tired . . . or it malingers,
Stretched on the floor, here beside you and me.
Should I, after tea and cakes and ices,
Have the strength to force the moment to its crisis?   80
But though I have wept and fasted, wept and prayed,
Though I have seen my head [grown slightly bald] brought in upon a
          platter,
I am no prophet—and here's no great matter;
I have seen the moment of my greatness flicker,
And I have seen the eternal Footman hold my coat, and snicker,
And in short, I was afraid.

And would it have been worth it, after all,
After the cups, the marmalade, the tea,
Among the porcelain, among some talk of you and me,

Would it have been worth while, 90
To have bitten off the matter with a smile,
To have squeezed the universe into a ball
To roll it toward some overwhelming question,
To say: "I am Lazarus, come from the dead,
Come back to tell you all, I shall tell you all"—
If one, settling a pillow by her head,
    Should say: "That is not what I meant at all.
    That is not it, at all."

And would it have been worth it, after all,
Would it have been worth while, 100
After the sunsets and the dooryards and the sprinkled streets,
After the novels, after the teacups, after the skirts that trail along
        the floor—
And this, and so much more?—
It is impossible to say just what I mean!
But as if a magic lantern threw the nerves in patterns on a screen:
Would it have been worth while
If one, settling a pillow or throwing off a shawl,
And turning toward the window, should say:
    "That is not it at all,
    That is not what I meant, at all." 110

                    .   .   .

No! I am not Prince Hamlet, nor was meant to be;
Am an attendant lord, one that will do
To swell a progress, start a scene or two,
Advise the prince; no doubt, an easy tool,
Deferential, glad to be of use,
Politic, cautious, and meticulous;
Full of high sentence, but a bit obtuse;
At times, indeed, almost ridiculous—
Almost, at times, the Fool.

I grow old. . . . I grow old. . . . 120
I shall wear the bottoms of my trousers rolled.

Shall I part my hair behind? Do I dare to eat a peach?
I shall wear white flannel trousers, and walk upon the beach.
I have heard the mermaids singing, each to each.

I do not think that they will sing to me.

I have seen them riding seaward on the waves
Combing the white hair of the waves blown back
When the wind blows the water white and black.

We have lingered in the chambers of the sea
By sea-girls wreathed with seaweed red and brown   130
Till human voices wake us, and we drown.

Ezra Pound *Villanelle: The Psychological Hour* [1]

I had over-prepared the event,
        that much was ominous.
    With middle-ageing care
        I had laid out just the right books.
I had almost turned down the pages.

        Beauty is so rare a thing.
        So few drink of my fountain.

So much barren regret,
So many hours wasted!
And now I watch, from the window,
        the rain, the wandering busses.

"Their little cosmos is shaken"—
        the air is alive with that fact.   10
In their parts of the city
        they are played on by diverse forces.
How do I know?
        Oh, I know well enough.
For them there is something afoot.
        As for me;
I had over-prepared the event—

        Beauty is so rare a thing
        So few drink of my fountain.

Two friends: a breath of the forest . . .
Friends? Are people less friends
        because one has just, at last, found them?
Twice they promised to come.   20

[1] *In what sense does Pound present himself as a kind of Prufrock in this poem? How alike are the two poems in tone and structural methods?*

> "Between the night and morning?"

Beauty would drink of my mind.
Youth would awhile forget
      my youth is gone from me.

II

("Speak up! You have danced so stiffly?
   Someone admired your works,
   And said so frankly.

"Did you talk like a fool,
The first night?
The second evening?"

"But they promised again:
      'To-morrow at tea-time.' ")

III

Now the third day is here—
      no word from either;
No word from her nor him,
Only another man's note:
      "Dear Pound, I am leaving England."

ROBERT FROST   *The Witch of Coös*

I stayed the night for shelter at a farm
Behind the mountain, with a mother and son,
Two old-believers. They did all the talking.

MOTHER. Folks think a witch who has familiar spirits
She could call up to pass a winter evening,
But won't, should be burned at the stake or something.
Summoning spirits isn't "Button, button,
Who's got the button," I would have them know.

SON. Mother can make a common table rear
And kick with two legs like an army mule.   10

MOTHER. And when I've done it, what good have I done?
Rather than tip a table for you, let me
Tell you what Ralle the Sioux Control once told me.

He said the dead had souls, but when I asked him
How could that be—I thought the dead were souls,
He broke my trance. Don't that make you suspicious
That there's something the dead are keeping back?
Yes, there's something the dead are keeping back.

SON. You wouldn't want to tell him what we have
Up attic, mother?   20

MOTHER. Bones—a skeleton.

SON. But the headboard of mother's bed is pushed
Against the attic door: the door is nailed.
It's harmless. Mother hears it in the night
Halting perplexed behind the barrier
Of door and headboard. Where it wants to get
Is back into the cellar where it came from.

MOTHER. We'll never let them, will we, son! We'll never!

SON. It left the cellar forty years ago
And carried itself like a pile of dishes   30
Up one flight from the cellar to the kitchen,
Another from the kitchen to the bedroom,
Another from the bedroom to the attic,
Right past both father and mother, and neither stopped it.
Father had gone upstairs; mother was downstairs.
I was a baby: I don't know where I was.

MOTHER. The only fault my husband found with me—
I went to sleep before I went to bed,
Especially in winter when the bed
Might just as well be ice and the clothes snow.   40
The night the bones came up the cellar-stairs
Toffile had gone to bed alone and left me,
But left an open door to cool the room off
So as to sort of turn me out of it.
I was just coming to myself enough
To wonder where the cold was coming from,
When I heard Toffile upstairs in the bedroom
And thought I heard him downstairs in the cellar.
The board we had laid down to walk dry-shod on
When there was water in the cellar in spring   50

Struck the hard cellar bottom. And then someone
Began the stairs, two footsteps for each step,
The way a man with one leg and a crutch,
Or a little child, comes up. It wasn't Toffile:
It wasn't anyone who could be there.
The bulkhead double-doors were double-locked
And swollen tight and buried under snow.
The cellar windows were banked up with sawdust
And swollen tight and buried under snow.
It was the bones. I knew them—and good reason.   60
My first impulse was to get to the knob
And hold the door. But the bones didn't try
The door; they halted helpless on the landing,
Waiting for things to happen in their favor.
The faintest restless rustling ran all through them.
I never could have done the thing I did
If the wish hadn't been too strong in me
To see how they were mounted for this walk.
I had a vision of them put together
Not like a man, but like a chandelier.   70
So suddenly I flung the door wide on him.
A moment he stood balancing with emotion,
And all but lost himself. (A tongue of fire
Flashed out and licked along his upper teeth.
Smoke rolled inside the sockets of his eyes.)
Then he came at me with one hand outstretched,
The way he did in life once; but this time
I struck the hand off brittle on the floor,
And fell back from him on the floor myself.
The finger-pieces slid in all directions.   80
(Where did I see one of those pieces lately?
Hand me my button-box—it must be there.)
I sat up on the floor and shouted, "Toffile,
It's coming up to you." It had its choice
Of the door to the cellar or the hall.
It took the hall door for the novelty,
And set off briskly for so slow a thing,
Still going every which way in the joints, though,
So that it looked like lightning or a scribble,
From the slap I had just now given its hand.   90
I listened till it almost climbed the stairs
From the hall to the only finished bedroom,
Before I got up to do anything;

Then ran and shouted, "Shut the bedroom door,
Toffile, for my sake!" "Company?" he said,
"Don't make me get up; I'm too warm in bed."
So lying forward weakly on the handrail
I pushed myself upstairs, and in the light
(The kitchen had been dark) I had to own
I could see nothing. "Toffile, I don't see it.   100
It's with us in the room though. It's the bones."
"What bones?" "The cellar bones—out of the grave."
That made him throw his bare legs out of bed
And sit up by me and take hold of me.
I wanted to put out the light and see
If I could see it, or else mow the room,
With our arms at the level of our knees,
And bring the chalk-pile down. "I'll tell you what—
It's looking for another door to try.
The uncommonly deep snow has made him think   110
Of his old song, *The Wild Colonial Boy,*
He always used to sing along the tote-road.
He's after an open door to get out-doors.
Let's trap him with an open door up attic."
Toffile agreed to that, and sure enough,
Almost the moment he was given an opening,
The steps began to climb the attic stairs.
I heard them. Toffile didn't seem to hear them.
"Quick!" I slammed to the door and held the knob.
"Toffile, get nails." I made him nail the door shut,   120
And push the headboard of the bed against it.
Then we asked was there anything
Up attic that we'd ever want again.
The attic was less to us than the cellar.
If the bones liked the attic, let them have it.
Let them stay in the attic. When they sometimes
Come down the stairs at night and stand perplexed
Behind the door and headboard of the bed,
Brushing their chalky skull with chalky fingers,
With sounds like the dry rattling of a shutter,   130
That's what I sit up in the dark to say—
To no one any more since Toffile died.
Let them stay in the attic since they went there.
I promised Toffile to be cruel to them
For helping them be cruel once to him.

SON. We think they had a grave down in the cellar.

MOTHER. We know they had a grave down in the cellar.

SON. We never could find out whose bones they were.

MOTHER. Yes, we could too, son. Tell the truth for once
They were a man's his father killed for me.   140
I mean a man he killed instead of me.
The least I could do was to help dig their grave.
We were about it one night in the cellar.
Son knows the story: but 'twas not for him
To tell the truth, suppose the time had come.
Son looks surprised to see me end a lie
We'd kept all these years between ourselves
So as to have it ready for outsiders.
But tonight I don't care enough to lie—
I don't remember why I ever cared.   150
Toffile, if he were here, I don't believe
Could tell you why he ever cared himself . . .

She hadn't found the finger-bone she wanted
Among the buttons poured out in her lap.
I verified the name next morning: Toffile.
The rural letter-box said Toffile Lajway.

WILLIAM SHAKESPEARE   from *Hamlet* [1]

Act I, Scenes i, iv, and v.

SCENE I. ELSINORE. A *platform before the castle.*

[FRANCISCO *at his post. Enter to him* BERNARDO.]
BERNARDO. Who's there?
FRANCISCO. Nay, answer me: stand, and unfold yourself.
BERNARDO. Long live the king!
FRANCISCO. Bernardo?

[1] GLOSSARY: *buried Denmark* Prince Hamlet's dead father; *the dram . . . dout* a touch of evil often nullifies a man's essential nobility; *eager* sour; *extravagant* vagrant; *Hic et ubique* Here and everywhere; *lets* hinders; *moist star* moon; *probation* proof; *rivals* partners; *strike* exert evil influence; *tax'd* blamed; *toys* impulses; *unanel'd* without receiving last rites; *unimproved* untried; *wake* hold revels.

BERNARDO. He.

FRANCISCO. You come most carefully upon your hour.

BERNARDO. 'Tis now struck twelve; get thee to bed, Francisco.

FRANCISCO. For this relief much thanks: 'tis bitter cold,
And I am sick at heart.

BERNARDO. Have you had quiet guard?   10

FRANCISCO.   Not a mouse stirring.

BERNARDO. Well, good night.
If you do meet Horatio and Marcellus,
The rivals of my watch, bid them make haste.

FRANCISCO. I think I hear them. Stand, ho! Who is there?

[*Enter* HORATIO *and* MARCELLUS.]

HORATIO. Friends to this ground.

MARCELLUS.   And liegemen to the Dane.

FRANCISCO. Give you good night.

MARCELLUS.   O, farewell, honest soldier:
Who hath relieved you?   20

FRANCISCO.   Bernardo hath my place.
Give you good night.   [*Exit.*

MARCELLUS.   Holla! Bernardo!

BERNARDO.   Say,
What, is Horatio there?

HORATIO.   A piece of him.

BERNARDO. Welcome, Horatio; welcome, good Marcellus.

MARCELLUS. What, has this thing appear'd again to-night?

BERNARDO. I have seen nothing.

MARCELLUS. Horatio says 'tis but our fantasy,   30
And will not let belief take hold of him
Touching this dreaded sight, twice seen of us:
Therefore I have entreated him along
With us to watch the minutes of this night,
That if again this apparition come,
He may approve our eyes and speak to it.

HORATIO. Tush, tush, 'twill not appear.

BERNARDO.   Sit down a while;
And let us once again assail your ears,
That are so fortified against our story   40
What we have two nights seen.

HORATIO.   Well, sit we down,
And let us hear Bernardo speak of this.

BERNARDO. Last night of all,
When yond same star that's westward from the pole
Had made his course to illume that part of heaven

Where now it burns, Marcellus and myself,
The bell then beating one,—
Enter GHOST.]
MARCELLUS. Peace, break thee off; look, where it comes again!
BERNARDO. In the same figure, like the king that's dead.   50
MARCELLUS. Thou art a scholar; speak to it, Horatio.
BERNARDO. Looks it not like the king? mark it, Horatio.
HORATIO. Most like; it harrows me with fear and wonder.
BERNARDO. It would be spoke to.
MARCELLUS.   Question it, Horatio.
HORATIO. What art thou, that usurp'st this time of night,
    Together with that fair and warlike form
    In which the majesty of buried Denmark
    Did sometimes march? by heaven I charge thee, speak!
MARCELLUS. It is offended.   60
BERNARDO.   See, it stalks away!
HORATIO. Stay! speak, speak! I charge thee, speak!
                                                        [*Exit* GHOST.

MARCELLUS. 'Tis gone, and will not answer.
BERNARDO. How now, Horatio! you tremble and look pale:
    Is not this something more than fantasy?
    What think you on't?
HORATIO. Before my God, I might not this believe
    Without the sensible and true avouch
    Of mine own eyes.
MARCELLUS.   Is it not like the king?   70
HORATIO. As thou art to thyself:
    Such was the very armor he had on
    When he the ambitious Norway combated;
    So frown'd he once, when, in an angry parle,
    He smote the sledded Polacks on the ice.
    'Tis strange.
MARCELLUS. Thus twice before, and jump at this dead hour,
    With martial stalk hath he gone by our watch.
HORATIO. In what particular thought to work I know not;
    But, in the gross and scope of my opinion,   80
    This bodes some strange eruption to our state.
MARCELLUS. Good now, sit down, and tell me, he that knows,
    Why this same strict and most observant watch
    So nightly toils the subject of the land,
    And why such daily cast of brazen cannon,
    And foreign mart for implements of war;
    Why such impress of shipwrights, whose sore task

Does not divide the Sunday from the week;
What might be toward, that this sweaty haste
Doth make the night joint-laborer with the day: 90
Who is't that can inform me?
HORATIO.   That can I;
At least the whisper goes so. Our last king,
Whose image even but now appear'd to us,
Was, as you know, by Fortinbras of Norway,
Thereto prick'd on by a most emulate pride,
Dared to the combat; in which our valiant Hamlet—
For so this side of our known world esteem'd him—
Did slay this Fortinbras; who by a seal'd compact
Well ratified by law and heraldry,   100
Did forfeit, with his life, all those his lands
Which he stood seized of, to the conqueror:
Against the which, a moiety competent
Was gaged by our king; which had return'd
To the inheritance of Fortinbras,
Had he been vanquisher; as, by the same covenant
And carriage of the article design'd,
His fell to Hamlet. Now, sir, young Fortinbras,
Of unimproved metal hot and full,
Hath in the skirts of Norway here and there   110
Shark'd up a list of lawless resolutes,
For food and diet, to some enterprise
That hath a stomach in't: which is no other—
As it doth well appear unto our state—
But to recover of us, by strong hand
And terms compulsatory, those foresaid lands
So by his father lost: and this, I take it,
Is the main motive of our preparations,
The source of this our watch and the chief head
Of this post-haste and romage in the land.   120
BERNARDO. I think it be no other but e'en so:
Well may it sort, that this portentous figure
Comes armed through our watch, so like the king
That was and is the question of these wars.
HORATIO. A mote it is to trouble the mind's eye.
In the most high and palmy state of Rome,
A little ere the mightiest Julius fell,
The graves stood tenantless, and the sheeted dead
Did squeak and gibber in the Roman streets:
As stars with trains of fire and dews of blood,   130

Disasters in the sun; and the moist star,
Upon whose influence Neptune's empire stands,
Was sick almost to doomsday with eclipse:
And even the like precurse of fierce events,
As harbingers preceding still the fates
And prologue to the omen coming on,
Have heaven and earth together demonstrated
Unto our climatures and countrymen.
      Re-enter GHOST.]
But soft, behold! lo, where it comes again!
I'll cross it, though it blast me. Stay, illusion!   140
If thou hast any sound, or use of voice,
Speak to me:
If there be any good thing to be done,
That may to thee do ease and grace to me,
Speak to me:
If thou art privy to thy country's fate,
Which, happily, foreknowing may avoid,
O, speak!
Or if thou hast uphoarded in thy life
Extorted treasure in the womb of earth,   150
For which, they say, you spirits oft walk in death,
Speak of it: stay, and speak! [*The cock crows.*] Stop it,
    Marcellus.
MARCELLUS. Shall I strike at it with my partisan?
HORATIO. Do, if it will not stand.
BERNARDO.   'Tis here!
HORATIO.   'Tis here!
MARCELLUS. 'Tis gone!   [*Exit* GHOST.
    We do it wrong, being so majestical,
    To offer it the show of violence;
    For it is, as the air, invulnerable,
    And our vain blows malicious mockery.   160
BERNARDO. It was about to speak, when the cock crew.
HORATIO. And then it started like a guilty thing
    Upon a fearful summons. I have heard,
    The cock, that is the trumpet to the morn,
    Doth with his lofty and shrill-sounding throat
    Awake the god of day, and at his warning,
    Whether in sea or fire, in earth or air,
    The extravagant and erring spirit hies
    To his confine: and of the truth herein   170
    This present object made probation.

MARCELLUS. It faded on the crowing of the cock.
　　Some say that ever 'gainst that season comes
　　Wherein our Saviour's birth is celebrated,
　　The bird of dawning singeth all night long:
　　And then, they say, no spirit dare stir abroad,
　　The nights are wholesome, then no planets strike,
　　No fairy takes nor witch hath power to charm,
　　So hallow'd and so gracious is the time.
HORATIO. So have I heard and do in part believe it.　　　　180
　　But look, the morn, in russet mantle clad,
　　Walks o'er the dew of yon high eastward hill:
　　Break we our watch up; and by my advice,
　　Let us impart what we have seen to-night
　　Unto young Hamlet; for, upon my life,
　　This spirit, dumb to us, will speak to him:
　　Do you consent we shall acquaint him with it,
　　As needful in our loves, fitting our duty?
MARCELLUS. Let's do't, I pray; and I this morning know　　189
　　Where we shall find him most conveniently.　　　　　[*Exeunt.*

SCENE IV—*The platform.*

　　Enter HAMLET, HORATIO, *and* MARCELLUS.]
HAMLET. The air bites shrewdly; it is very cold.
HORATIO. It is a nipping and an eager air.
HAMLET. What hour now?
HORATIO.　　　　　　　　　I think it lacks of twelve.
MARCELLUS. No, it is struck.
HORATIO. Indeed? I heard it not: it then draws near the season
　　Wherein the spirit held his wont to walk.
　　　　[*A flourish of trumpets, and ordnance shot off within.*
　　What doth this mean, my lord?
HAMLET. The king doth wake to-night, and takes his rouse,
　　Keeps wassail, and the swaggering up-spring reels;　　10
　　And as he drains his draughts of Rhenish down,
　　The kettle-drum and trumpet thus bray out
　　The triumph of his pledge.
HORATIO.　　　　　　　　Is it a custom?
HAMLET. Aye, marry, is't:
　　But to my mind, though I am native here
　　And to the manner born, it is a custom
　　More honor'd in the breach than the observance.
　　This heavy-headed revel east and west

Makes us traduced and tax'd of other nations: 20
They clepe us drunkards, and with swinish phrase
Soil our addition; and indeed it takes
From our achievements, though perform'd at height,
The pith and marrow of our attribute.
So, oft it chances in particular men,
That for some vicious mole of nature in them,
As, in their birth,—wherein they are not guilty,
Since nature cannot choose his origin,—
By the o'ergrowth of some complexion,
Oft breaking down the pales and forts of reason, 30
Or by some habit that too much o'er-leavens
The form of plausive manners, that these men,—
Carrying, I say, the stamp of one defect,
Being nature's livery, or fortune's star,—
Their virtues else—be they as pure as grace,
As infinite as man may undergo—
Shall in the general censure take corruption
From that particular fault: the dram of e'il
Doth all the noble substance often dout
To his own scandal. 40
Enter GHOST.]
HORATIO.   Look, my lord it comes!
HAMLET. Angels and ministers of grace defend us!
Be thou a spirit of health or goblin damn'd,
Bring with thee airs from heaven or blasts from hell,
Be thy intents wicked or charitable,
Thou comest in such a questionable shape
That I will speak to thee: I'll call thee Hamlet,
King, father, royal Dane: O, answer me!
Let me not burst in ignorance; but tell
Why thy canonized bones, hearsed in death, 50
Have burst their cerements; why the sepulchre,
Wherein we saw thee quietly inurn'd,
Hath oped his ponderous and marble jaws,
To cast thee up again. What may this mean,
That thou, dead corse, again, in complete steel,
Revisit'st thus the glimpses of the moon,
Making night hideous; and we fools of nature
So horridly to shake our disposition
With thoughts beyond the reaches of our souls?
Say, why is this? wherefore? what should we do? 60
[GHOST *beckons* HAMLET.

HORATIO. It beckons you to go away with it,
  As if it some impartment did desire
  To you alone.
MARCELLUS. Look, with what courteous action
  It waves you to a more removed ground:
  But do not go with it.
HORATIO.   No, by no means.
HAMLET. It will not speak; then I will follow it.
HORATIO. Do not, my lord.
HAMLET.   Why, what should be the fear?   70
  I do not set my life at a pin's fee;
  And for my soul, what can it do to that,
  Being a thing immortal as itself?
  It waves me forth again: I'll follow it.
HORATIO. What if it tempt you toward the flood, my lord,
  Or to the dreadful summit of the cliff
  That beetles o'er his base into the sea,
  And there assume some other horrible form,
  Which might deprive your sovereignty of reason
  And draw you into madness? think of it: 80
  The very place puts toys of desperation,
  Without more motive, into every brain
  That looks so many fathoms to the sea
  And hears it roar beneath.
HAMLET.   It waves me still.
  Go on; I'll follow thee.
MARCELLUS. You shall not go, my lord.
HAMLET.   Hold off your hands.
HORATIO. Be ruled; you shall not go.
HAMLET.   My fate cries out,   90
  And makes each petty artery in this body
  As hardy as the Nemean lion's nerve.
  Still am I call'd, unhand me, gentlemen;
  By heaven, I'll make a ghost of him that lets me:
  I say, away! Go on; I'll follow thee.
                              [*Exeunt* GHOST *and* HAMLET.
HORATIO. He waxes desperate with imagination.
MARCELLUS. Let's follow; 'tis not fit thus to obey him.
HORATIO. Have after. To what issue will this come?
MARCELLUS. Something is rotten in the state of Denmark.
HORATIO. Heaven will direct it.   100
MARCELLUS.   Nay, let's follow him.   [*Exeunt.*

SCENE V—*Another part of the platform.*

Enter GHOST *and* HAMLET.]

HAMLET. Whither wilt thou lead me? speak; I'll go no further.

GHOST. Mark me.

HAMLET.   I will.

GHOST.   My hour is almost come,
   When I to sulphurous and tormenting flames
   Must render up myself.

HAMLET.   Alas, poor ghost!

GHOST. Pity me not, but lend thy serious hearing
   To what I shall unfold.

HAMLET.   Speak; I am bound to hear.   10

GHOST. So art thou to revenge, when thou shalt hear.

HAMLET. What?

GHOST. I am thy father's spirit;
   Doom'd for a certain term to walk the night,
   And for the day confined to fast in fires,
   Till the foul crimes done in my days of nature
   Are burnt and purged away. But that I am forbid
   To tell the secrets of my prison-house,
   I could tell a tale unfold whose lightest word
   Would harrow up thy soul, freeze thy young blood,   20
   Make thy two eyes, like stars, start from their spheres,
   Thy knotted and combined locks to part
   And each particular hair to stand on end,
   Like quills upon the fretful porpentine:
   But this eternal blazon must not be
   To ears of flesh and blood. List, list, O, list!
   If thou didst ever thy dear father love—

HAMLET. O God!

GHOST. Revenge his foul and most unnatural murder.   29

HAMLET.   Murder!

GHOST. Murder most foul, as in the best it is,
   But this most foul, strange, and unnatural.

HAMLET. Haste me to know't, that I, with wings as swift
   As meditation or the thought of love,
   May sweep to my revenge.

GHOST.   I find thee apt;
   And duller shouldst thou be than the fat weed
   That roots itself in ease on Lethe wharf,
   Wouldst thou not stir in this. Now, Hamlet, hear:

'Tis given out that, sleeping in my orchard,   40
A serpent stung me; so the whole ear of Denmark
Is by a forged process of my death
Rankly abused: but know, thou noble youth,
The serpent that did sting thy father's life
Now wears his crown.

HAMLET.   O my prophetic soul!
My uncle!

GHOST. Aye, that incestuous, that adulterate beast,
With witchcraft of his wit, with traitorous gifts,—
O wicked wit and gifts, that have the power   50
So to seduce!—won to his shameful lust
The will of my most seeming-virtuous queen:
O Hamlet, what a falling-off was there!
From me, whose love was of that dignity
That it went hand in hand even with the vow
I made to her in marriage; and to decline
Upon a wretch, whose natural gifts were poor
To those of mine!
But virtue, as it never will be moved,
Though lewdness court it in a shape of heaven,   60
So lust, though to a radiant angel link'd,
Will sate itself in a celestial bed
And prey on garbage.
But, soft! methinks I scent the morning air;
Brief let me be. Sleeping within my orchard,
My custom always of the afternoon,
Upon my secure hour thy uncle stole,
With juice of cursed hebenon in a vial,
And in the porches of my ears did pour
The leperous distilment; whose effect   70
Holds such an enmity with blood of man
That swift as quicksilver it courses through
The natural gates and alleys of the body;
And with a sudden vigor it doth posset
And curd, like eager droppings into milk,
The thin and wholesome blood: so did it mine;
And a most instant tetter bark'd about,
Most lazar-like, with vile and loathsome crust,
All my smooth body.
Thus was I, sleeping, by a brother's hand   80
Of life, of crown, of queen, at once dispatch'd:
Cut off even in the blossoms of my sin,

Unhousel'd, disappointed, unanel'd;
No reckoning made, but sent to my account
With all my imperfections on my head:
O, horrible! O, horrible! most horrible!
If thou hast nature in thee, bear it not;
Let not the royal bed of Denmark be
A couch for luxury and damned incest.
But, howsoever thou pursuest this act,   90
Taint not thy mind, nor let thy soul contrive
Against thy mother aught: leave her to heaven,
And to those thorns that in her bosom lodge,
To prick and sting her. Fare thee well at once!
The glow-worm shows the matin to be near,
And 'gins to pale his uneffectual fire:
Adieu, adieu, adieu! remember me.   [*Exit.*
HAMLET. O all you host of heaven! O earth! what else?
And shall I couple hell? O, fie! Hold, hold, my heart;
And you, my sinews, grow not instant old,   100
But bear me stiffly up. Remember thee!
Aye, thou poor ghost, while memory holds a seat
In this distracted globe. Remember thee!
Yea, from the table of my memory
I'll wipe away all trivial fond records,
All saws of books, all forms, all pressures past,
That youth and observation copied there;
And thy commandment all alone shall live
Within the book and volume of my brain,
Unmix'd with baser matter; yes, by heaven!   110
O most pernicious woman!
O villain, villain, smiling, damned villain!
My tables,—meet it is I set it down,
That one may smile, and smile, and be a villain;
At least I'm sure it may be so in Denmark.   [*Writing.*
So, uncle, there you are. Now to my word;
It is "Adieu, adieu! remember me."
I have sworn't.
MARCELLUS. ⎫
HORATIO. ⎬ [*Within*] My lord, my lord!
                    Enter HORATIO *and* MARCELLUS.]
MARCELLUS.   Lord Hamlet!   120
HORATIO.   Heaven secure him!
HAMLET. So be it!
MARCELLUS. Illo, ho, ho, my lord!

HAMLET. Hillo, ho, ho, boy! come, bird, come.

MARCELLUS. How is't, my noble lord?

HORATIO.   What news, my lord?

HAMLET. O, wonderful!

HORATIO. Good my lord, tell it.

HAMLET.   No; you will reveal it.

HORATIO. Not I, my lord, by heaven.   130

MARCELLUS.   Nor I, my lord.

HAMLET. How say you, then; would heart of man once think it?
    But you'll be secret?

HORATIO.   }
MARCELLUS. } Aye, by heaven, my lord.

HAMLET. There's ne'er a villain dwelling in all Denmark
    But he's an arrant knave.

HORATIO. There needs no ghost, my lord, come from the grave
    To tell us this.

HAMLET.   Why, right; you are i' the right;
    And so, without more circumstance at all,   140
    I hold it fit that we shake hands and part:
    You, as your business and desire shall point you;
    For every man hath business and desire,
    Such as it is; and for my own poor part,
    Look you, I'll go pray.

HORATIO. These are but wild and whirling words, my lord.

HAMLET. I'm sorry they offend you, heartily;
    Yes, faith, heartily.

HORATIO.   There's no offense, my lord.

HAMLET. Yes, by Saint Patrick, but there is, Horatio.   150
    And much offense too. Touching this vision here,
    It is an honest ghost, that let me tell you:
    For your desire to know what is between us,
    O'ermaster't as you may. And now, good friends,
    As you are friends, scholars and soldiers,
    Give me one poor request.

HORATIO.   What is't, my lord? we will.

HAMLET. Never make known what you have seen tonight.

MARCELLUS. }
HORATIO.   } My lord, we will not.

HAMLET.   Nay, but swear't.   160

HORATIO.   In faith,
    My lord, not I.

MARCELLUS.   Nor I, my lord, in faith.

HAMLET. Upon my sword.

MARCELLUS. We have sworn, my lord, already.
HAMLET. Indeed, upon my sword, indeed.
GHOST. [*Beneath*] Swear.
HAMLET. Ah, ha, boy! say'st thou so? art thou there, truepenny?
  Come on: you hear this fellow in the cellarage:
  Consent to swear. 170
HORATIO. Propose the oath, my lord.
HAMLET. Never to speak of this that you have seen,
  Swear by my sword.
GHOST. [*Beneath*] Swear.
HAMLET. *Hic et ubique?* then we'll shift our ground.
  Come hither, gentlemen,
  And lay your hands again upon my sword:
  Never to speak of this that you have heard,
  Swear by my sword.
GHOST. [*Beneath*] Swear. 180
HAMLET. Well said, old mole! canst work i' the earth so fast?
  A worthy pioneer! Once more remove, good friends.
HORATIO. O day and night, but this is wondrous strange!
HAMLET. And therefore as a stranger give it welcome.
  There are more things in heaven and earth, Horatio,
  Than are dreamt of in your philosophy.
  But come;
  Here, as before, never, so help you mercy,
  How strange or odd soe'er I bear myself,
  As I perchance hereafter shall think meet 190
  To put an antic disposition on,
  That you, at such times seeing me, never shall,
  With arms encumber'd thus, or this head-shake,
  Or by pronouncing of some doubtful phrase,
  As "Well, well, we know," or "We could, an if we would,"
  Or "If we list to speak," or "There be, an if they might,"
  Or such ambiguous giving out, to note
  That you know aught of me: this not to do,
  So grace and mercy at your most need help you,
  Swear. 200
GHOST. [*Beneath*] Swear.
HAMLET. Rest, rest, perturbed spirit! [*They swear.*]
  So, gentlemen,
  With all my love I do commend me to you:
  And what so poor a man as Hamlet is
  May do, to express his love and friending to you,
  God willing, shall not lack. Let us go in together;

And still your fingers on your lips, I pray.
The time is out of joint: O cursed spite,
That ever I was born to set it right!   210
Nay, come, let's go together.   [*Exeunt.*

WILLIAM BUTLER YEATS   *Purgatory*

Persons in the Play: A Boy   An Old Man

[*Scene: a ruined house and a bare tree in the background.*]

BOY. Half-door, hall door,
    Hither and thither, day and night,
    Hill or hollow, shouldering this pack,
    Hearing you talk.
OLD MAN.   Study that house.
    I think about its jokes and stories;
    I try to remember what the butler
    Said to a drunken gamekeeper
    In mid-October, but I cannot.
    If I cannot, none living can.
    Where are the jokes and stories of a house,   10
    Its threshold gone to patch a pig-sty?
BOY. So you have come this path before?
OLD MAN. The moonlight falls upon the path,
    The shadow of a cloud upon the house,
    And that's symbolical; study that tree,
    What is it like?
BOY.   A silly old man.
OLD MAN. It's like—no matter what it's like.
    I saw it a year ago stripped bare as now,
    So I chose a better trade.
    I saw it fifty years ago   20
    Before the thunderbolt had riven it,
    Green leaves, ripe leaves, leaves thick as butter,
    Fat, greasy life. Stand there and look,
    Because there is somebody in that house.

[*The Boy puts down pack and stands in the doorway.*]

BOY. There's nobody here.
OLD MAN.   There's somebody there.
BOY. The floor is gone, the window's gone,
    And where there should be roof there's sky,

And here's a bit of an egg-shell thrown
Out of a jackdaw's nest.
OLD MAN.   But there are some
That do not care what's gone, what's left: 30
The souls in Purgatory that come back
To habitations and familiar spots.
BOY. Your wits are out again.
OLD MAN.   Re-live
Their transgressions, and that not once
But many times; they know at last
The consequence of those transgressions
Whether upon others or upon themselves;
Upon others, others may bring help,
For when the consequence is at an end
The dream must end; if upon themselves,   40
There is no help but in themselves
And in the mercy of God.
BOY.   I have had enough!
Talk to the jackdaws, if talk you must.
OLD MAN. Stop! Sit there upon that stone.
That is the house where I was born.
BOY. The big old house that was burnt down?
OLD MAN. My mother that was your grand-dam owned it,
This scenery and this countryside,
Kennel and stable, horse and hound—
She had a horse at the Curragh, and there met   50
My father, a groom in a training stable,
Looked at him and married him.
Her mother never spoke to her again,
And she did right.
BOY.   What's right and wrong?
My grand-dad got the girl and the money.
OLD MAN. Looked at him and married him,
And he squandered everything she had.
She never knew the worst, because
She died in giving birth to me,
But now she knows it all, being dead.   60
Great people lived and died in this house;
Magistrates, colonels, members of Parliament,
Captains and Governors, and long ago
Men that had fought at Aughrim and the Boyne.
Some that had gone on Government work
To London or to India came home to die,

Or came from London every spring
To look at the may-blossom in the park.
They had loved the trees that he cut down
To pay what he had lost at cards   70
Or spent on horses, drink and women;
Had loved the house, had loved all
The intricate passages of the house,
But he killed the house; to kill a house
Where great men grew up, married, died,
I here declare a capital offence.
BOY. My God, but you had luck! Grand clothes,
And maybe a grand horse to ride.
OLD MAN. That he might keep me upon his level
He never sent me to school, but some   80
Half-loved me for my half of her:
A gamekeeper's wife taught me to read,
A Catholic curate taught me Latin.
There were old books and books made fine
By eighteenth-century French binding, books
Modern and ancient, books by the ton.
BOY. What education have you given me?
OLD MAN. I gave the education that befits
A bastard that a pedlar got
Upon a tinker's daughter in a ditch.   90
When I had come to sixteen years old
My father burned down the house when drunk.
BOY. But that is my age, sixteen years old,
At the Puck Fair.
OLD MAN.   And everything was burnt;
Books, library, all were burnt.
BOY. Is what I have heard upon the road the truth,
That you killed him in the burning house?
OLD MAN. There's nobody here but our two selves?
BOY. Nobody, Father.
OLD MAN.   I stuck him with a knife,
That knife that cuts my dinner now,   100
And after that I left him in the fire.
They dragged him out, somebody saw
The knife-wound but could not be certain
Because the body was all black and charred.
Then some that were his drunken friends
Swore they would put me upon trial,
Spoke of quarrels, a threat I had made.

The gamekeeper gave me some old clothes,
I ran away, worked here and there
Till I became a pedlar on the roads,   110
No good trade, but good enough
Because I am my father's son,
Because of what I did or may do.
Listen to the hoof-beats! Listen, listen!
BOY. I cannot hear a sound.
OLD MAN.   Beat! Beat!
This night is the anniversary
Of my mother's wedding night,
Or of the night wherein I was begotten.
My father is riding from the public-house,
A whiskey-bottle under his arm.   120

[A *window is lit showing a young girl.*]

Look at the window; she stands there
Listening, the servants are all in bed,
She is alone, he has stayed late
Bragging and drinking in the public-house.
BOY. There's nothing but an empty gap in the wall.
You have made it up. No, you are mad!
You are getting madder every day.
OLD MAN. It's louder now because he rides
Upon a gravelled avenue
All grass to-day. The hoof-beat stops,   130
He has gone to the other side of the house,
Gone to the stable, put the horse up.
She has gone down to open the door.
This night she is no better than her man
And does not mind that he is half drunk,
She is mad about him. They mount the stairs,
She brings him into her own chamber.
And that is the marriage-chamber now.
The window is dimly lit again.   140

Do not let him touch you! It is not true
That drunken men cannot beget,
And if he touch he must beget
And you must bear his murderer.
Deaf! Both deaf! If I should throw
A stick or a stone they would not hear;
And that's a proof my wits are out.

But there's a problem: she must live
Through everything in exact detail,
Driven to it by remorse, and yet   150
Can she renew the sexual act
And find no pleasure in it, and if not,
If pleasure and remorse must both be there,
Which is the greater?
                              I lack schooling.
Go fetch Tertullian; he and I
Will ravel all that problem out
Whilst those two lie upon the mattress
Begetting me.
                    Come back! Come back!
And so you thought to slip away,
My bag of money between your fingers,   160
And that I could not talk and see!
You have been rummaging in the pack.

[*The light in the window has faded out.*]

BOY. You never gave me my right share.
OLD MAN. And had I given it, young as you are,
    You would have spent it upon drink.
BOY. What if I did? I had a right
    To get it and spend it as I chose.
OLD MAN. Give me that bag and no more words.
BOY. I will not.
OLD MAN.   I will break your fingers.

[*They struggle for the bag. In the struggle it drops, scattering the money. The Old Man staggers but does not fall. They stand looking at each other. The window is lit up. A man is seen pouring whiskey into a glass.*]

BOY. What if I killed you? You killed my grand-dad,   170
    Because you were young and he was old.
    Now I am young and you are old.
OLD MAN. [*staring at window*] Better-looking, those sixteen years—
BOY. What are you muttering?
OLD MAN.   Younger—and yet
    She should have known he was not her kind.
BOY. What are you saying? Out with it! [*Old man points to window.*]
    My God! The window is lit up
    And somebody stands there, although
    The floorboards are all burnt away.

OLD MAN. The window is lit up because my father 180
    Has come to find a glass for his whiskey.
    He leans there like some tired beast.
BOY. A dead, living, murdered man!
OLD MAN. "Then the bride-sleep fell upon Adam":
    Where did I read those words?
                  And yet
    There's nothing leaning in the window
    But the impression upon my mother's mind;
    Being dead she is alone in her remorse.
BOY. A body that was a bundle of old bones
    Before I was born. Horrible! Horrible! [*He covers his eyes.*] 190
OLD MAN. That beast there would know nothing, being nothing,
    If I should kill a man under the window
    He would not even turn his head. [*He stabs the* BOY.]
    My father and my son on the same jack-knife!
    That finishes—there—there—there—

[*He stabs again and again. The window grows dark.*]

    "Hush-a-bye baby, father's a knight,
    Thy mother a lady, lovely and bright."
    No, that is something that I read in a book,
    And if I sing it must be to my mother,
    And I lack rhyme.

[*The stage has grown dark except where the tree stands in white light.*]

            Study that tree. 200
    It stands there like a purified soul,
    All cold, sweet, glistening light.
    Dear mother, the window is dark again,
    But you are in the light because
    I finished all that consequence.
    I killed that lad because had he grown up
    He would have struck a woman's fancy,
    Begot, and passed pollution on.
    I am a wretched foul old man
    And therefore harmless. When I have stuck 210
    This old jack-knife into a sod
    And pulled it out all bright again,
    And picked up all the money that he dropped,
    I'll to a distant place, and there
    Tell my old jokes among new men.

[*He cleans the knife and begins to pick up money.*]

Hoof-beats! Dear God,
How quickly it returns—beat—beat—!

Her mind cannot hold up that dream.
Twice a murderer and all for nothing,
And she must animate that dead night   220
Not once but many times!
              O God,
Release my mother's soul from its dream!
Mankind can do no more. Appease
The misery of the living and the remorse of the dead.

      THE END

Chapter Five

Poetry as Description and Vision

A popular narrative poem of the middle nineteenth century begins with the following description:

> Long lines of cliff breaking have left a chasm;
> And in the chasm are foam and yellow sands;
> Beyond, red roofs about a narrow wharf
> In cluster; then a moulder'd church; and higher
> A long street climbs to one tall tower'd mill;
> And high in heaven behind it a gray down
> With Danish barrows; and a hazelwood,
> By autumn nutters haunted, flourishes
> Green in a cuplike hollow of the down.[1]

This rather prosaic passage exhibits some of the simplest and most characteristic devices of description. It breaks up what the eye sees into a pattern of shapes and colors. It selects, names, enumerates, distributes, and reorganizes a series of sense impressions. These are for the most part presented directly as color (here yellow, red, gray, and green) or shape (long, narrow, tall-tower'd, cuplike); and sometimes—though this, of course, is not description at all but the rejection of description as unnecessary—they are not presented save by the all-inclusive defining name that the mind substitutes for the sum of the sensations. It is the frequency with which things are merely named instead of being shown that is responsible for the lack of intensity and precision here and that makes these lines somewhat mediocre, for too much is taken for granted in them.

If we place beside them some lines in William Carlos Williams's *Spring and All*, we shall see how much is gained by the precise, detailed description of specific concrete objects, analyzed minutely and sharply.

[1] *Enoch Arden*, by Alfred, Lord Tennyson.

By the road to the contagious hospital
under the surge of the blue
mottled clouds driven from the
northeast—a cold wind. Beyond, the
waste of broad, muddy fields
brown with dried weeds, standing and fallen

patches of standing water
the scattering of tall trees

All along the road the reddish
purplish, forked, upstanding, twiggy
stuff of bushes and small trees
with dead, brown leaves under them
leafless vines. . . .

Here, by severe economy and searching selection, we get a description that, though it has little charm, does have strength, intensity, and a certain dignity. Two points are worth remarking: first, that this is a poetry of direct statement—there are no figures, similes, or metaphors of any kind; and second, that the poet as observer rejects the vagueness that results from a reliance upon names. He does not name the shrubs he places before us; he presents them through their physical qualities alone: "the reddish, purplish, forked, upstanding, twiggy *stuff* of bushes and small trees."

This is the most elementary and in a way the most unadventurous and least risky kind of description. Its merit is its accuracy and unpretentiousness; its limitation will become clearer as we consider some more complex types of descriptive verse.

We shall find, however, that severe economy and the searching selection of specific detail is also the method of the most vivid and precise descriptive poets—Chaucer, for example, and Dante, and the modern poet who has most nearly achieved a similar sort of stylistic distinction, Ezra Pound. To make us see how a crowd of the damned in Hell peered at visitors from above, knitting their brows in the dim light, Dante says they "sharpened their vision, like an old tailor peering at the eye of a needle." And again, to make us see how the lost lovers are blown about eternally on the winds of Hell, he uses another simple and very vivid comparison:

And as the cranes in long line streak the sky
    And in procession chant their mournful call,
    So I saw come with sound of wailing by
The shadows fluttering in the tempest's brawl.

Modern poets have read their Dante to good effect, and it is easy to demonstrate how surely the selection of significant detail can convey a sense of immediacy and reality when the presentation is concise, concentrated, and concrete:

> Suddenly I saw the cold and rook-delighting heaven
> That seemed as though ice burned and was but the more ice. . . .
> W. B. YEATS

> The fire that stirs about her when she stirs. . . .
> W. B. YEATS

> Her limbs are delicate as an eyelid. . . .
> W. B. YEATS

> Over roads twisted like sheep's guts. . . .
> EZRA POUND

> In the turn of the hill; in hard steel
> The road like a slow screw's thread. . . .
> EZRA POUND

> Without, there was a cold moon up,
>   Of winter radiance sheer and thin;
>   The hollow halo it was in
> Was like an icy crystal cup.
> D. G. ROSSETTI

What all these passages have in common is concentration upon *simple visual images,* stated nakedly, with the utmost directness. The only figures of speech are similes, the most explicit and clear of all types of figures, and these, for the most part, are concerned with presenting a purely visual comparison.

One should notice in these descriptive passages the importance of certain key words—epithets and action words. Such words concentrate a complex of impressions into one sharp and well-fused image. A few brief and striking illustrations of their effectiveness can do more to open the eyes of the uninitiated reader than pages of explanation. Consider in the following passages the sensuous implications, the telescoping of various sense impressions, and the active richness of suggestion in the italicized words.

> A cry that *shivered* to the *tingling* stars.
> ALFRED, LORD TENNYSON

Fade far away, *dissolve*, and quite forget.
JOHN KEATS

Melting melodious words to lutes of *amber*.
ROBERT HERRICK

The sun-beams *trembling* on the floating tides.
ALEXANDER POPE

Now more than ever seems it *rich* to die.
JOHN KEATS

A remarkable feature of the method illustrated in some of these lines is the fact that the quality or action singled out for our attention applies at once to the thing being described and to the sensibility that is perceiving the thing. Thus it is not only the cry that shivers and the stars that tingle but the one who hears the cry and sees the stars. It is not only the melodious words that melt in the music of the lute but the charmed listener also.

Another aspect of the effectiveness of such lines is the unexpected and paradoxical juxtaposition of qualities not easily associated together. Sunbeams might more conventionally be expected to dance on the floating tides. But if we put Pope's line in its place in the second canto of *The Rape of the Lock*, we will find that the sunbeams' trembling is a subtle foreshadowing, almost a fearful anticipation of the unknown danger awaiting Belinda. And when we read the two lines of Keats in their context in *Ode to a Nightingale* (pages 370–372), we realize how much they contribute to Keats's passionate absorption into the visionary world of the midnight garden. Everything is concentrated in the complex sense image of *dissolve*, and it is the whole conscious being of the poet that loses its identity and mingles with the scents and sounds of the enchanted night. This dissolution is a kind of dying, and its luxurious sweetness is transferred to the act of dying and concentrated in the key word *rich*, which here among its other connotations has the sensuous meaning of rich— as whipped cream is rich.

In each of these lines, too, the suddenness and sharpness with which the effect is gained depends to a great extent on a single significant word, dynamic and sensuous. A striking example of such an effect appears in Emily Dickinson's vivid description of a snake moving through the grass:

I more than once at Noon
Have passed, I thought, a Whip lash
Unbraiding in the Sun
When stooping to secure it
It wrinkled, and was gone—

The quickness, the quietness, and the characteristic peculiarity of the movement itself here are concentrated in the one word *wrinkled*. Tennyson, we might note, used the same word to give the suggestion of immense height and distance in his six-line picture of the eagle (pages 75–76):

> The *wrinkled* sea beneath him crawls.

The poet who wishes to make us *see* and to make us *feel* selects a few significant details and presents them as sharply as possible, often directly and nakedly, sometimes with the aid of figurative language, and always with the aid of appropriate variations in rhythm and sound. In Thomas Hardy's lyric narrative *The Five Students* (pages 129–130), the seasons of the year and the ages of man's life are presented progressively in a series of carefully selected vivid details. First, summer:

> The sparrow dips in his wheel-rut bath,
> > The sun grows passionate-eyed,
> And boils the dew to smoke by the paddock path. . . .

Then,

> Autumn moulds the hard fruit mellow. . . .

> The leaf drops: earthworms draw it in
> > At night time noiselessly,
> The fingers of birch and beech are skeleton-thin. . . .

And last, winter, age, and death:

> Icicles tag the church-aisle leads,
> > The flag-rope gibbers hoarse,
> The home-bound foot-folk wrap their snow-flaked heads. . . .

These vivid sketches are not, of course, presented for their own sake. They are intended to harmonize with and to help express the dramatic movement of the poem—to be a part of its "plot." They could not fulfill this function, however, if they were not accurate, clear, and suggestive, each in its own appropriate key. A similar key to that in which Hardy's autumn picture is presented can be noted in the remarkable evocation of the season's ruins that opens Part III of Eliot's *The Waste Land*:

> The river's tent is broken: The last fingers of leaf
> Clutch and sink into the wet bank. The wind
> Crosses the brown land, unheard.

The image of the streaky, refuse-laden, muddy river as a collapsed tent is of a boldness and imaginative appropriateness that the careless reader who fails to read with his eyes and all his senses alert might fail to recognize. The summer leaves, arched out and nearly meeting from both sides of the river in the shape of a tent roof, are now gone. They have fallen to the wet bank; the wind no longer rustles through them but is unheard. In many of these intensely concentrated lines we have been considering, the effect of a quality is presented simultaneously with the quality itself. We are in the presence here of that heightened kind of psychological realism so often found in art at its best.

In modern poetry we often find richly suggestive, visual figures that appeal to an intellectual as well as a sensuous and emotional understanding. Such imagery has contributed to the difficulty and complexity that face the reader but has also contributed much that is rewarding in the subtlety and accuracy with which complex strata of experience can be rendered and examined. Here, to give only one example, is the way in which Marianne Moore describes a snake—not almost invisibly slinking through the grass as in Emily Dickinson, but rearing up out of a snake-charmer's basket.

> Thick, not heavy, it stands up from its travelling-basket,
>   the essentially Greek, the plastic animal all of a piece
>   from nose to tail;
>   one is compelled to look at it as at the shadows of the alps
>   imprisoning in their folds like flies in amber, the rhythms
>   of the skating rink.

This is an impression, recorded in a flash, and by a witty, well-stocked mind. One realizes that it is not the snake that is being described; it is the speaker's impression of the sinuous flashing unfolding gleam. The snake, though curved and moving so that some parts are nearer and others farther away, is all of a piece—like the shadowy mountain range. The glinting, moving light on its folds and scales is conveyed by the distant movement of gleams and lights as if made by skaters imprisoned in the folds of the mountain, and this image is further qualified by another image, "like flies in amber."

Yet this image of "flies in amber" suggests something deadly in the pattern of swift glittering beauty. And the image of "the shadows of the alps" engulfing the rhythmic flashing movements of the skaters is equally sinister, and suggests all the danger and darkness that surround beauty in life. Even the "thick, not heavy" impression of the asp's body carries a foreboding of power—graceful, not awkward power, certainly, but nevertheless *striking-power*, which can make itself felt only too quickly. This underlying conception of lurking death is the clue to the paradoxical alliance in this poem of impressions of brilliance and sinuous movement with those of sculptural repose ("the essentially Greek, the plastic animal all of a piece"). The snake's serenely Grecian simplicity of form almost belies its potential sudden destructiveness. We are "compelled" by this knowledge to remember that, for all its fascinating resemblance to a classically satisfying work of art, it remains a poisonous reptile.

Unexpected as the images of this passage are—in themselves and in relation to one another—their clarity and rightness can hardly be questioned, for what they finally portray is the way the sharply alert mind of the poet assimilates and regroups perceptions. An intellectual concept is revealed only indirectly, through the impressions conveyed by imagery, and the technique is therefore subtle and complex. Miss Moore is a contemporary poet, but this technique is not peculiar to our age. Consider from this point of view a few lines from *The Apparition of His Mistress Calling Him to Elysium*, by the seventeenth-century poet Robert Herrick. In them Herrick is describing a delightful pagan heaven, a kind of earthly paradise of Epicurean delights. It is no place of disembodied shadows but a site of endless pleasures—a living, breathing landscape where every sense is fed.

> This, that, and ev'ry thicket doth transpire
> More sweet than storax from the hallowed fire;
> Where ev'ry tree a wealthy issue bears
> Of fragrant apples, blushing plums, or pears;
> And all the shrubs, with sparkling spangles shew
> Like morning sunshine, tinselling the dew.
> Here in green meadows sits eternal May,
> Purfling the margents, while perpetual day
> So double gilds the air, as that no night
> Can ever rust th' enamel of the light.[1]

In these lines the shine and sparkle of Elysium and the richness and fragrance of an English country summer are combined and caught with a verve that is communicated to all the senses. The ear is titillated with the prickly crackling vitality of the sharp sounds in "And all the shrubs with sparkling spangles show." There is movement everywhere. The perfumes "transpire"—breathe in and out, come in wafts and gusts; and there is movement too in *blushing* plums and *sparkling* dew and the *purfling* of margents.

The strangest triumph, however, is the way in which the whole scene is bathed in light and the way in which the light enriches the whole scene. The

---

[1] *Storax* is a fragrant balsam used in perfumes. *Purfling the margents* means decorating, or embroidering, the outlines of this perfect and beautiful landscape.

dew tinseled by the light is transformed to sparkling spangles. The air, golden in itself (because it is the air of paradise), is doubly gilded by the light of eternal day, and night, in the real world of sense and time, is described as the withdrawal of day which *rusts* the *enamel* of the light. Here is a vivid and original visual image, accounted for perhaps by the fact that Herrick was a countryman and had been a jeweler, but based actually on idea. The light of a summer day is golden; in the evening it turns reddish and darkens; its purity is spoiled ore, the gold changes to dark red, the enamel rusts.

There is a further subtle implication in these lines in that when we try to envision a paradise we imagine the world of the senses at its most beautiful, untouched by change, eternally light, most keenly fragrant and young; and yet all we know of the world of the senses is subject to rust, to change, decay and loss. This paradoxical concept is brought out with such brilliant clarity by Herrick's vivid imagery that no abstract generalization could put the matter with anything like the same conviction and freshness of effect.

This method, which depends upon the combining of wit and sensuousness, is one which Marianne Moore and certain other modern poets, particularly Edith Sitwell, have used with good effect. One need only place beside the ending of the Herrick passage such lines as these by Miss Sitwell:

> The morning light creaks down again

or

> The fire was furry as a bear

or

> The light is braying like an ass

to realize that modern experimentation has been anticipated in the past and that what often seems new and startling is actually a return to a clearer and sharper way of dealing with experience.

It is not always something familiar or, indeed, actually possible that a poet places before our eyes. Puck, the King of Brobdignag, Cerberus, Caliban, the Garden of Adonis, and the Great Rock-Candy Mountain—the strange, the unknown, and the ineffable—can all be given a body, shown to us, and be made real. As Shakespeare expressed it,

> The poet's eye, in a fine frenzy rolling,
> Doth glance from heaven to earth, from earth to heaven,
> And, as imagination bodies forth

> The forms of things unknown, the poet's pen
> Turns them to shapes, and gives to airy nothing
> A local habitation and a name.

That is, the envisioned sight itself is described with all the concrete attributes of an object, and with the bright colors and the jagged edges of things in dreams, and in this way is made convincing and believable, for we can always believe our eyes. This is how Dante tells us he saw the shade of the great Ulysses in Hell:

> The greater horn of the ancient flame was stirred
> To shudder and make a murmur, like a fire
> When in the wind it struggles and is blurred,
> Then tossed upon a flickering crest yet higher,
> As it had been a tongue that spoke, it cast
> A voice forth from the strength of its desire. . . .

Dante's greatest triumph, however, in the realization of vision is properly kept for the climax of the whole great *Divine Comedy*, the vision of God and eternity vouchsafed to the poet at the end of his long pilgrimage through Hell, Purgatory, and Paradise. (See pages 248–249.) As the poet looked into the heart of light, he tells us,

> I beheld leaves within the unfathomed blaze
> Into one volume bound by love, the same
> That the universe holds scattered through its maze.
> Substance and accidents, and their modes, became
> As if together fused, all in such wise
> That what I speak of is one simple flame. . . .
> One moment more oblivion has amassed
> Than five-and-twenty centuries have wrought
> Since Argo's shadow o'er wondering Neptune passed.[2]

"Nowhere in poetry," says T. S. Eliot of this passage, "has experience so remote from ordinary experience been expressed so concretely. . . . One can feel only awe at the power of the master who could thus at every moment realize the inapprehensible in visual images. And I do not know anywhere in poetry a more authentic sign of greatness than the power of association which could in the last line, when the poet is speaking of the divine vision, yet introduce the Argo passing over the head of wondering Neptune."

---

[2] The sense of the third sentence in this passage, very generally, is that once the poet's vision of God is over, it is harder for him to recall its profoundly meaningful reality than it is for men to remember the first sea-voyage of tradition—that of the Argo—which struck wonder into the god of the sea.

It is with images of light and shadow especially that poets and visionaries have tried to convey their intuition of God and eternity. One of the most famous of such images is that with which Henry Vaughan, the seventeenth-century religious poet and Platonist, began his poem *The World*.

> I saw Eternity the other night
> Like a great Ring of pure and endless light,
>   All calm, as it was bright;
> And round beneath it, Time in hours, days, years,
>   Driv'n by the spheres,
> Like a vast shadow mov'd. . . .

The homeliness, familiarity, and almost casualness of "the other night" places the vision in the center of the world of commonplace events and thus adds immeasurably to its convincingness and reality. Like the characteristic imagery of Dante, Vaughan's magnificent picture carries conviction because in it familiar knowledge is unexpectedly linked to an abstract conception in the figure in which time and eternity are seen astronomically. Dante, for example, wants to make us see, and hence believe in, the concourses of blessed spirits that flocked about him in Paradise. He writes:

> As in a fishpond which is still and clear
>   The fishes draw to what comes from outside
>   In such sort that they think their food is there,
> So thousand splendors, ay, and more beside,
>   I saw drawn toward us; and from each was heard
>   "Lo one, by whom our loves are magnified."

(It is interesting that, just as in the Williams poem describing the road to the contagious hospital, the poet used no name but "stuff" and sought out instead vivid specific qualities, so here the poet makes us see the *action* of the thousand unnamed splendors by the vivid and concrete comparison with the fishes.)

There is one great image in modern poetry that especially recalls the method of Dante. It has the concreteness, the vividness, and the element of surprise we have been noting, and a magnificence that almost equals the image of the shadow of the *Argo*. It occurs in the poem *All Souls' Night*, written as an epilogue to W. B. Yeats's *A Vision*. Yeats is telling of a friend whose love for a woman who had died had the clarity and spiritual ardor of Dante's love for Beatrice:

> Two thoughts were so mixed up I could not tell
> Whether of her or God he thought the most,
> But think that his mind's eye,
> When upward turned, on one sole image fell;

And that a slight companionable ghost,
Wild with divinity,
Had so lit up the whole
Immense miraculous house
The Bible promised us,
It seemed a gold fish swimming in a bowl.

The image of the friend's dead love (the "slight companionable ghost")
lights up the concept of Heaven and makes it as lucid and brilliant as the
homely image that closes the passage suggests—clear, comprehensible, and
believable.

Heaven and Hell, the two great visionary concepts of popular religion,
have been made concrete and real in the two most elaborate and successful
poems of the Christian world: Dante's *Divine Comedy* and Milton's
Paradise Lost. Both these works are vast efforts of pure imagination, attempts to visualize supernatural beings in nonmaterial realms. Dante
gives us "pictures" of souls eternally, and in each case appropriately,
tormented in Hell and seeking out their proper punishments in Purgatory,
as well as of absolute innocence and joy in Eden and Paradise. Milton
gives us dazzling pictures of the glory of Heaven, the beauty of angels, the
gentle loveliness of Eden; and he projects gloomy landscapes and vast
arenas of suffering and reverberating debate by Satan and his followers in
Hell. Here is the way he imagines that Hell first appeared to Satan; notice
the image of a flame that throws "no light, but rather darkness visible"
(for light is assumed to be characteristic of God)—a paradoxical picture
that suggests less to the senses than to the emotions; or rather, by suggesting
the utter frustration of the senses, convinces us of the unchangeable hope-
lessness of Satan's condition:

At once as far as Angels ken he views
The dismal Situation waste and wild,
A Dungeon horrible, on all sides round
As one great Furnace flam'd, yet from those flames
No light, but rather darkness visible
Serv'd only to discover sights of woe,
Regions of sorrow, doleful shades, where peace
And rest can never dwell, hope never comes
That comes to all; but torture without end
Still urges, and a fiery Deluge, fed
With ever-burning Sulphur unconsumed. . . .

Just as the best poetry of description re-presents familiar reality to us
more vividly, sharply, and newly than we have ever seen it before, so the
poetry of pure vision exploits the senses to stir our imaginations beyond
actual experience.

Poems: Descriptive and Visionary

The poems here range from a highly compressed, expert description of a fine horse by Shakespeare to poems of pure visionary imagination by Dante, Milton, Coleridge, and Pound. In between, we have first, poems by Browning, Snyder, and Hughes that abound in exuberant, sensuous detail. Hughes's *Pike* sustains an atmosphere of savage terror at the same time, and Emily Dickinson's two poems that follow it suggest—with their subtle response to effects of light—the same atmosphere of terror more quietly but just as intensely. With Thomas and Frost we are back to a sheer delight like that of Browning's poem if on a less magnificent scale. Williams's *Spring and All* ends the group of nature-centered poems with a remarkable evocation of the moment just before spring—the lifeless surface of things, and all the potential energy readying itself for release.

Thomas Kinsella's evocation of dawnlight closing in on a world of human suffering, and Randall Jarrell's repossession of the lost everyday landscape of his childhood, form a kind of transition to a group of human-centered descriptions. Three close-ups of women, by Chaucer, Pope, and MacDiarmid, follow, the first two satirically appreciative and the third zestfully realistic. After these come a group of more complexly meditative descriptions by Marvell, Hopkins, Keats, Crane, Moore, and Auden. In the first of these we hear seventeenth-century Puritan refugees singing of the beauty of the Bermudas in images that suggest a Paradise both earthly and Christian. Hopkins's picture of the effect of the Gulf Stream in blending seasonal tones, as though spring, summer, and winter were colors in a palette, expresses a connoisseur's delight in nature's trickeries. Keats's personification of autumn is at once gently abstract and replete with images of swelling ripeness. Hart Crane's *Repose of Rivers* both captures the movement of the Mississippi through changing landscapes and repossesses a world of childhood experience that might have been lost forever, were it not for the subconscious association made conscious by the experience in the poem. The poems from Crane's *Voyages* have a similar double reference; they project a vastly voluptuous personification of the sea as an irresistible if dangerous woman while at the same time suggesting its literal nature. Marianne Moore's remarkably associative poem is discussed in the text. Auden's *On This Island*, finally, presents the way in which a sensitive responder internalizes the world through sensuous openness and empathy.

Five poems of pure vision end the section. They are projections of the imagination that create, in Pound's *Canto XVI*, a fierce image of William Blake the visionary poet "howling against the evil" that he sees; in Dante's *Paradiso*, the experience of looking directly into godhead; in Milton's *Paradise Lost*, the brilliantly ironic view of Satan's dark presence in the midst of Eden's innocent gaiety; in Coleridge's *Kubla Khan*, a prophetically revelatory succession of dream-images; and in Pound's *Canto XVII*, a vision of the pagan earthly paradise ruled over by Zagreus, the god of ecstatic fertility and wine who speaks here in a voice that is also the poet's—that is, the voice of the fertilizing imagination. This voice merges the figures and symbols of ancient myth, of art—especially that of the Italian Renaissance—and of the modern spirit that sees itself as similar to Odysseus in its heroically exploratory character.

WILLIAM SHAKESPEARE   *A Horse*

(from *Venus and Adonis*)

Round-hoof'd, short-jointed, fetlocks shag and long,
Broad breast, full eye, small head and nostril wide,
High crest, short ears, straight legs and passing strong,
Thin mane, thick tail, broad buttock, tender hide:
    Look, what a horse should have he did not lack,
    Save a proud rider on so proud a back.

JONATHAN SWIFT   *Description of a City Shower*

    Careful observers may foretell the Hour
(By sure Prognostics) when to dread a Show'r:
While Rain depends, the pensive Cat gives o'er
Her Frolics, and pursues her Tail no more.
Returning Home at Night, you'll find the Sink
Strike your offended Sense with double Stink.
If you be wise, then go not far to Dine;
You'll spend in Coach-hire more than save in Wine.
A coming Show'r your shooting Corns presage,
Old Aches throb, your hollow Tooth will rage.   10
Saunt'ring in Coffee-house is Dulman seen;
He damns the Climate, and complains of Spleen.

    Meanwhile the South, rising with dabbled Wings,
A sable Cloud athwart the Welkin flings,
That swill'd more Liquor than it could contain,
And like a Drunkard gives it up again.
Brisk Susan whips her Linen from the Rope,
While the first drizzling Show'r is born aslope,
Such is that Sprinkling which some careless Quean
Flirts on you from her Mop, but not so clean.   20

You fly, invoke the Gods; then turning, stop
To rail; she, singing, still twirls on her Mop.
Not yet the Dust had shunn'd th' unequal Strife
But, aided by the Wind, fought still for Life;
And wafted with its Foe by violent Gust,
'Twas doubtful which was Rain, and which was Dust.
Ah! where must needy Poet seek for Aid,
When Dust and Rain at once his Coat invade,
His only Coat, where Dust, confus'd with Rain,
Roughen the Nap and leave a mingled Stain.   30

    Now in contiguous Drops the Flood comes down,
Threat'ning with Deluge this Devoted Town.
To Shops in Crowds the draggled Females fly,
Pretend to cheapen Goods, but nothing buy.
The Templer spruce, while ev'ry Spout's a-broach,
Stays till 'tis fair, yet seems to call a Coach.
The tuck'd-up Sempstress walks with hasty Strides,
While Streams run down her oil'd Umbrella's Sides.
Here various Kinds by various Fortunes led
Commence Acquaintance underneath a Shed.   40
Triumphant Tories and desponding Whigs
Forget their Feuds, and join to save their Wigs.

    Box'd in a Chair the Beau impatient sits,
While Spouts run clatt'ring o'er the Roof by Fits;
And ever and anon with frightful Din
The Leather sounds; he trembles from within.
So when Troy Chair-men bore the Wooden Steed,
Pregnant with Greeks, impatient to be freed,
(Those Bully Greeks, who, as the Moderns do,
Instead of paying Chair-men, run them thro'.)   50
Laoco'n struck the Outside with his Spear,
And each imprison'd Hero quak'd for Fear.

    Now from all Parts the swelling Kennels flow,
And bear their Trophies with them as they go:
Filth of all Hues and Odours seem to tell
What Street they sail'd from, by their Sight and Smell.
They, as each Torrent drives, with rapid Force
From Smithfield, or St. Pulchre's shape their Course,
And in huge Confluent join at Snow-Hill Ridge,
Fall from the Conduit prone to Holborn-Bridge.   60

Sweepings from Butchers' Stalls, Dung, Guts, and Blood,
Drown'd Puppies, stinking Sprats, all drench'd in Mud,
Dead Cats and Turnip-Tops come tumbling down the Flood.

ROBERT BROWNING   *The Englishman in Italy (Piano di Sorrento)*

Fortù, Fortù, my beloved one,
　Sit here by my side,
On my knees put up both little feet!
　I was sure, if I tried,
I could make you laugh spite of Scirocco.
　Now, open your eyes,
Let me keep you amused till he vanish
　In black from the skies,
With telling my memories over
　As you tell your beads;   10
All the Plain saw me gather, I garland
　—The flowers or the weeds.
Time for rain! for your long hot dry Autumn
　Had net-worked with brown
The white skin of each grape on the bunches,
　Marked like a quail's crown,
Those creatures you make such account of,
　Whose heads,—speckled with white
Over brown like a great spider's back,
　As I told you last night,—   20
Your mother bites off for her supper.
　Red ripe as could be,
Pomegranates were chapping and splitting
　In halves on the tree:
And betwixt the loose walls of great flintstone,
　Or in the thick dust
On the path, or straight out of the rockside,
　Wherever could thrust
Some burnt sprig of bold hardy rock-flower
　Its yellow face up,   30
For the prize were great butterflies fighting,
　Some five for one cup.
So, I guessed, ere I got up this morning,
　What change was in store,
By the quick rustle-down of the quail-nets

Which woke me before
I could open my shutter, made fast
   With a bough and a stone,
And look through the twisted dead vine-twigs,
   Sole lattice that's known.   40
Quick and sharp rang the rings down the net-poles,
   While, busy beneath,
Your priest and his brother tugged at them,
   The rain in their teeth.
And out upon all the flat house-roofs
   Where split figs lay drying,
The girls took the frails under cover:
   Nor use seemed in trying
To get out the boats and go fishing,
   For, under the cliff,   50
Fierce the black water frothed o'er the blind-rock.
   No seeing our skiff
Arrive about noon from Amalfi,
   —Our fisher arrive,
And pitch down his basket before us,
   All trembling alive
With pink and grey jellies, your sea-fruit;
   You touch the strange lumps,
And mouths gape there, eyes open, all manner
   Of horns and of humps,   60
Which only the fisher looks grave at,
   While round him like imps
Cling screaming the children as naked
   And brown as his shrimps;
Himself too as bare to the middle
   —You see round his neck
The string and its brass coin suspended,
   That saves him from wreck.
But to-day not a boat reached Salerno,
   So back, to a man,   70
Came our friends, with whose help in the vineyards
   Grape-harvest began.
In the vat, halfway up in our house-side,
   Like blood the juice spins,
While your brother all bare-legged is dancing
   Till breathless he grins
Dead-beaten in effort on effort
   To keep the grapes under,

Since still when he seems all but master,
    In pours the fresh plunder   80
From girls who keep coming and going
    With basket on shoulder,
And eyes shut against the rain's driving;
    Your girls that are older,—
For under the hedges of aloe,
    And, where, on its bed
Of the orchard's black mould, the love-apple
    Lies pulpy and red,
All the young ones are kneeling and filling
    Their laps with the snails   90
Tempted out by this first rainy weather,—
    Your best of regales,
As to-night will be proved to my sorrow,
    When, supping in state,
We shall feast our grape-gleaners (two dozen,
    Three over one plate)
With lasagne so tempting to swallow
    In slippery ropes,
And gourds fried in great purple slices,
    That colour of popes.   100
Meantime, see the grape bunch they've brought you:
    The rain-water slips
O'er the heavy blue bloom on each globe
    Which the wasp to your lips
Still follows with fretful persistence:
    Nay, taste, while awake,
This half of a curd-white smooth cheese-ball
    That peels, flake by flake,
Like an onion, each smoother and whiter;
    Next, sip this weak wine   110
From the thin green glass flask, with its stopper,
    A leaf of the vine;
And end with the prickly-pear's red flesh
    That leaves thro' its juice
The stony black seeds on your pearl-teeth.
    Scirocco is loose!
Hark! the quick, whistling pelt of the olives
    Which, thick in one's track,
Tempt the stranger to pick up and bite them,
    Tho' not yet half black!   120
How the old twisted olive trunks shudder!

The medlars let fall
Their hard fruit, and the brittle great fig-trees
    Snap off, figs and all,
For here comes the whole of the tempest!
    For refuge, but creep
Back again to my side and my shoulder,
    And listen or sleep.
O how will your country show next week,
    When all the vine-boughs   130
Have been stripped of their foliage to pasture
    The mules and the cows?
Last eve, I rode over the mountains;
    You brother, my guide,
Soon left me, to feast on the myrtles
    That offered, each side,
Their fruit-balls, black, glossy and luscious,—
    Or strip from the sorbs
A treasure, so rosy and wondrous,
    Of hairy gold orbs!   140
But my mule picked his sure, sober path out,
    Just stopping to neigh
When he recognized down in the valley
    His mates on their way
With the faggots, and barrels of water;
    And soon we emerged
From the plain, where the woods could scarce follow;
    And still as we urged
Our way, the woods wondered, and left us,
    As up still we trudged   150
Though the wild path grew wilder each instant,
    And place was e'en grudged
'Mid the rock-chasms and piles of loose stones
    Like the loose broken teeth
Of some monster which climbed there to die
    From the ocean beneath—
Place was grudged to the silver-grey fume-weed
    That clung to the path,
And dark rosemary ever a-dying
    That, 'spite the wind's wrath,   160
So loves the salt rock's face to seaward,
    And lentisks as staunch
To the stone where they root and bear berries,
    And . . . what shows a branch

Coral-coloured, transparent, with circlets
    Of pale seagreen leaves:
Over all trod my mule with the caution
    Of gleaners o'er sheaves,
Still, foot after foot like a lady:
    So, round after round,   170
He climbed to the top of Calvano,
    And God's own profound
Was above me, and round me the mountains,
    And under, the sea,
And within me, my heart to bear witness
    What was and shall be!
Oh, heaven and the terrible crystal!
    No rampart excludes
Your eye from the life to be lived
    In the blue solitudes!   180
Oh, these mountains, their infinite movement!
    Still moving with you:
For, ever some new head and breast of them
    Thrusts into view
To observe the intruder; you see it
    If quickly you turn
And, before they escape you, surprise them:
    They grudge you should learn
How the soft plains they look on, lean over
    And love (they pretend)   190
—Cower beneath them, the flat sea-pine crouches,
    The wild fruit-trees bend,
E'en the myrtle-leaves curl, shrink and shut,
    All is silent and grave,
'Tis a sensual and timorous beauty,
    How fair, but a slave!
So, I turned to the sea; and there slumbered
    As greenly as ever
Those isles of the siren, your Galli;
    No ages can sever   200
The Three, nor enable their sister
    To join them,—halfway
On the voyage, she looked at Ulysses—
    No further today,
Tho' the small one, just launched in the wave,
    Watches breast-high and steady
From under the rock, her bold sister

Swum halfway already.
Fortù, shall we sail there together
  And see from the sides   210
Quite new rocks show their faces, new haunts
  Where the siren abides?
Shall we sail round and round them, close over
  The rocks, tho' unseen,
That ruffle the grey glassy water
  To glorious green?
Then scramble from splinter to splinter,
  Reach land and explore,
On the largest, the strange square black turret
  With never a door,   220
Just a loop to admit the quick lizards;
  Then, stand there and hear
The birds' quiet singing, that tells us
  What life is, so clear?
—The secret they sang to Ulysses
  When ages ago,
He heard and he knew this life's secret
  I hear and I know!

Ah, see! The sun breaks o'er Calvano;
  He strikes the great gloom   230
And flutters it o'er the mount's summit
  In airy gold fume!
All is over! Look out, see the gipsy,
  Our tinker and smith,
Has arrived, set up bellows and forge,
  And down-squatted forthwith
To his hammering, under the wall there;
  One eye keeps aloof
The urchins that itch to be putting
  His jews'-harp to proof,   240
While the other, thro' locks of curled wire,
  Is watching how sleek
Shines the hog, come to share in the windfall
  —An abbot's own cheek.
All is over! Wake up and come out now,
  And down let us go,
And see the fine things got in order
  At Church for the show
Of the Sacrament, set forth this evening;
  To-morrow's the Feast   250

Of the Rosary's Virgin, by no means
    Of Virgins the least,
As you'll hear in the off-hand discourse
    Which (all nature, no art)
The Dominican brother, these three weeks,
    Was getting by heart.

Not a pillar nor post but is dizened
    With red and blue papers;
All the roof waves with ribbons, each altar
    A-blaze with long tapers;   260
But the great masterpiece is the scaffold
    Rigged glorious to hold
All the fiddlers and fifers and drummers
    And trumpeters bold,
Not afraid of Bellini nor Auber,
    Who, when the priest's hoarse,
Will strike us up something that's brisk
    For the feast's second course.
And then will the flaxen-wigged Image
    Be carried in pomp   270
Thro' the plain, while in gallant procession
    The priests mean to stomp.
And all round the glad church lie old bottles
    With gunpowder stopped,
Which will be, when the Image re-enters,
    Religiously popped.
And at night from the crest of Calvano
    Great bonfires will hang,
On the plain will the trumpets join chorus,
    And more poppers bang!   280
At all events, come—to the garden,
    As far as the wall;
See me tap with a hoe on the plaster
    Till out there shall fall
A scorpion with wide angry nippers!

—"Such trifles!" you say?
Fortù, in my England at home,
    Men meet gravely to-day
And debate, if abolishing Corn-laws
    Be righteous and wise   290
—If 'twere proper, Scirocco should vanish
    In black from the skies!

GARY SNYDER   *Floating World Picture: Spring in the Kitagami Mountains*

1

Nobody at the edge of the firepit
snowboots and jute leggings.
white birch flaming
jetting out sour hot sap
—a child sings the kite song
skinning badgers.
housepillars gleaming with soot
    —like shaped with stone axes—
the sheer ceiling
full of the blue smoke of breakfast   10
—vault of a temple—
one shaft of sunlight shooting down and
        all is at the bottom in that
                sensual beam of light.

Spring—at the chilly horsebarn
glimmer of dry hay and snow.
yearning for sunny hills
the horses stamp their hooves.

2

The willow puts out honey flowers
birds flow over hill after hill   20
horses hurry:
        hot-breatht Arab
        glistening light-bodied thoroughbred
invisible cuneiform wind
in the stiff gloomy limbs of the walnut—
a dog rustles in bamboo grass.

        heavy work horse
        flashing his tufty tail
        like a monstrous lizard
                navigating in the sun   30

horses one by one coming,
chewing at the edge of the marl,
climbing along the misty run of snowmelt
under a malachite sky

—bright noisy market—
being led to the
stud inspection center.

TED HUGHES   *Pike*

Pike, three inches long, perfect
Pike in all parts, green tigering the gold.
Killers from the egg: the malevolent aged grin.
They dance on the surface among the flies.

Or move, stunned by their own grandeur,
Over a bed of emerald, silhouette
Of submarine delicacy and horror.
A hundred feet long in their world.

In ponds, under the heat-struck lily pads—
Gloom of their stillness:
Logged on last year's black leaves, watching upwards.   10
Or hung in an amber cavern of weeds

The jaws' hooked clamp and fangs
Not to be changed at this date;
A life subdued to its instrument;
The gills kneading quietly, and the pectorals.

Three we kept behind glass,
Jungled in weed: three inches, four,
And four and a half: fed fry to them—
Suddenly there were two. Finally one   20

With a sag belly and the grin it was born with.
And indeed they spare nobody.
Two, six pounds each, over two feet long,
High and dry and dead in the willow-herb—

One jammed past its gills down the other's gullet:
The outside eye stared: as a vise locks—
The same iron in this eye
Though its film shrank in death.

A pond I fished, fifty yards across,
Whose lilies and muscular tench   30
Had outlasted every visible stone
Of the monastery that planted them—

Stilled legendary depth:
It was as deep as England. It held
Pike too immense to stir, so immense and old
That past nightfall I dared not cast

But silently cast and fished
With the hair frozen on my head
For what might move, for what eye might move.
The still splashes on the dark pond,   40

Owls hushing the floating woods
Frail on my ear against the dream
Darkness beneath night's darkness had freed,
That rose slowly towards me, watching.

EMILY DICKINSON   *A Light exists in Spring*

A Light exists in Spring
Not present on the Year
At any other period—
When March is scarcely here

A Color stands abroad
On Solitary Fields
That Science cannot overtake
But Human Nature feels.

It waits upon the Lawn
It shows the furthest Tree   10
Upon the furthest Slope you know
It almost speaks to you.

Then as Horizons step
Or Noons report away
Without the Formula of sound
It passes and we stay—

A quality of loss
Affecting our Content
As Trade had suddenly encroached
Upon a Sacrament.

EMILY DICKINSON *There's a certain Slant of light*

There's a certain Slant of light,
Winter Afternoons—
That oppresses, like the Heft
of Cathedral Tunes—

Heavenly Hurt, it gives us—
We can find no scar,
But internal difference,
Where the Meanings, are—

None may teach it—Any—
'Tis the Seal Despair—   10
An imperial affliction
Sent us of the Air—

When it comes, the Landscape listens—
Shadows—hold their breath—
When it goes, 'tis like the Distance
On the look of Death—

EDWARD THOMAS *The Manor Farm*

The rock-like mud unfroze a little and rills
Ran and sparkled down each side of the road
Under the catkins wagging in the hedge.
But earth would have her sleep out, spite of the sun;
Nor did I value that thin gliding beam
More than a pretty February thing
Till I came down to the old Manor Farm,
And church and yew-tree opposite, in age
Its equals and in size. The church and yew
And farmhouse slept in a Sunday silentness.   10
The air raised not a straw. The steep farm roof,

With tiles duskily glowing, entertained
The mid-day sun; and up and down the roof
White pigeons nestled. There was no sound but one.
Three cart-horses were looking over a gate
Drowsily through their forelocks, swishing their tails
Against a fly, a solitary fly.

The Winter's cheek flushed as if he had drained
Spring, Summer, and Autumn at a draught
And smiled quietly. But 'twas not Winter—   20
Rather a season of bliss unchangeable
Awakened from farm and church where it had lain
Safe under tile and thatch for ages since
This England, Old already, was called Merry.

ROBERT FROST   *A Hillside Thaw*

To think to know the country and not know
The hillside on the day the sun lets go
Ten million silver lizards out of snow!
As often as I've seen it done before
I can't pretend to tell the way it's done.
It looks as if some magic of the sun
Lifted the rug that bred them on the floor
And the light breaking on them made them run.
But if I thought to stop the wet stampede,
And caught one silver lizard by the tail,   10
And put my foot on one without avail,
And threw myself wet-elbowed and wet-kneed
In front of twenty others' wriggling speed,—
In the confusion of them all aglitter,
And birds that joined in the excited fun
By doubling and redoubling song and twitter,
I have no doubt I'd end by holding none.

It takes the moon for this. The sun's a wizard
By all I tell; but so's the moon a witch.
From the high west she makes a gentle cast   20
And suddenly, without a jerk or twitch,
She has her spell on every single lizard.
I fancied when I looked at six o'clock
The swarm still ran and scuttled just as fast.

The moon was waiting for her chill effect.
I looked at nine: the swarm was turned to rock
In every lifelike posture of the swarm,
Transfixed on mountain slopes almost erect.
Across each other and side by side they lay.
The spell that so could hold them as they were   30
Was wrought through trees without a breath of storm
To make a leaf, if there had been one, stir.
It was the moon's: she held them until day,
One lizard at the end of every ray.
The thought of my attempting such a stay!

WILLIAM CARLOS WILLIAMS   *Spring and All*

By the road to the contagious hospital
under the surge of the blue
mottled clouds driven from the
northeast—a cold wind. Beyond, the
waste of broad, muddy fields
brown with dried weeds, standing and fallen

patches of standing water
the scattering of tall trees

All along the road the reddish
purplish, forked, upstanding, twiggy
stuff of bushes and small trees   10
with dead, brown leaves under them
leafless vines—

Lifeless in appearance, sluggish
dazed spring approaches—

They enter the new world naked,
cold, uncertain of all
save that they enter. All about them
the cold, familiar wind—

Now the grass, tomorrow   20
the stiff curl of wildcarrot leaf
One by one objects are defined—
It quickens: clarity, outline of leaf

But now the stark dignity of
entrance—Still, the profound change
has come upon them: rooted, they
grip down and begin to awaken

THOMAS KINSELLA *First Light*

A prone couple still sleeps.
Light ascends like a pale gas
Out of the sea: dawn-
Light, reaching across the hill
To the dark garden. The grass
Emerges, soaking with grey dew.

Inside, in silence, an empty
Kitchen takes form, tidied and swept,
Blank with marriage—where shrill
Lover and beloved have kept   10
Another vigil far
Into the night, and raved and wept.

Upstairs a whimper or sigh
Comes from an open bedroom door
And lengthens to an ugly wail
—A child enduring a dream
That grows, at the first touch of day,
Unendurable.

RANDALL JARRELL *The Elementary Scene*

Looking back in my mind I can see
The white sun like a tin plate
Over the wooden turning of the weeds;
The street jerking—a wet swing—
To end by the wall the children sang.

The thin grass by the girls' door,
Trodden on, straggling, yellow and rotten,
And the gaunt field with its one tied cow—
The dead land waking sadly to my life—
Stir, and curl deeper in the eyes of time.   10

The rotting pumpkin under the stairs
Bundled with switches and the cold ashes
Still holds for me, in its unwavering eyes,
The stinking shapes of cranes and witches,
Their path slanting down the pumpkin's sky.

Its stars beckon through the frost like cottages
(Homes of the Bear, the Hunter—of that absent star,
The dark where the flushed child struggles into sleep)
Till, leaning a lifetime to the comforter,
I float above the small limbs like their dream: 20

I, I, The future that mends everything.

GEOFFREY CHAUCER   *The Carpenter's Young Wife* [1]

(from *The Canterbury Tales*)

Whilom ther was dwellynge at Oxenford
A riche gnof, that gestes heeld to bord,
And of his craft he was a carpenter. . . .

This carpenter hadde wedded newe a wyf,
Which that he lovede moore than his lyf.
Of eighteteene yeer she was of age.
Jalous he was, and heeld hire narwe in cage,
For she was wylde and yong and he was old,
And demed hymself been lik a cokewold.
He knew nat Catoun, for his wit was rude,   10
That bad man sholde wedden his simylitude.
Men sholde wedden after hire estaat,
For youthe and elde is often at debaat.
But sith that he was fallen in the snare,
He moste endure, as oother folk, his care.
    Fair was this yonge wyf, and therwithal
As any wezele hir body gent and smal.

---

[1] GLOSSARY: *barmclooth* apron; *berne* barn; *boos* boss; *bord* board (table); *bragot* honey; *Catoun* Cato; *ceynt* girdle (wide sash); *cokewold* cuckold; *gestes* guests (boarders); *gnof* crude fellow; *heeth* heather; *latoun* brass; *leggen* lay; *lendes* loins; *likerous* lecherous; *meeth* mead; *noble* British coin worth one-third of a pound; *pere-jonette* pear; *perled* studded; *piggesnye* pig's eye (term of endearment); *popelote*, poppet; *prymerole* primrose; *swalwe* swallow; *thenche* imagine; *tour* tower (the Tower of London, containing the Royal Mint); *voluper* cap; *ye* eye; *yerne* eager.

A ceynt she werede, barred al of silk,
A barmclooth eek as whit as morne milk
Upon her lendes, ful of many a goore,   20
Whit was hir smok, and broyden al bifoore
And eek behynde, on hir coler aboute,
Of col-blak silk, withinne and eek withoute.
The tapes of hir white voluper
Were of the same suyte of hir coler;
Hir filet brood of silk, and set ful hye.
And sikerly she hadde a likerous ye;
Ful smale ypulled were hire browes two,
And tho were bent and blake as any sloo.
She was ful moore blisful on to see   30
Than is the newe pere-jonette tree,
And softer than the wolle is of the wether.
And by hir girdel heeng a purs of lether,
Tasseled with silk, and perled with latoun.
In al this world, to seken up and doun,
There nys no man so wys that koude thenche
So gay a popelote or swich a wenche.
Ful brighter was the shynyng of hir hewe
Than in the tour the noble yforged newe.
But of hir song, it was as loude and yerne   40
As any swalwe sittynge on a berne.
Therto she koude skippe and make game,
As any kyde or calf folwynge his dame.
Hir mouth was sweete as bragot or the meeth,
Or hoord of apples leyd in hey or heeth.
Wynsynge she was, as is a joly colt,
Long as a mast, and upright as a bolt.
A brooch she baar upon hir lowe coler,
As brood as is the boos of a bokeler.
Hir shoes were laced on hir legges hye.   50
She was a prymerole, a piggesnye,
For any lord to leggen in his bedde,
Or yet for any good yeman to wedde.

ALEXANDER POPE   Belinda's Morning

(from The Rape of the Lock)

   And now, unveiled, the Toilet stands displayed,
Each silver Vase in mystic order laid.

First, rob'd in white, the Nymph intent adores,
With head uncovered, the Cosmetic powers.
A heav'nly image in the glass appears,
To that she bends, to that her eyes she rears;
Th' inferior Priestess, at her altar's side,
Trembling begins the sacred rites of Pride.
Unnumbered treasures ope at once, and here
The various off'rings of the world appear;   10
From each she nicely culls with curious toil,
And decks the Goddess with the glitt'ring spoil.
This casket India's glowing gems unlocks,
And all Arabia breathes from yonder box.
The Tortoise here and Elephant unite,
Transformed to combs, the speckled, and the white.
Here files of pins extend their shining rows,
Puffs, Powders, Patches, Bibles, Billet-doux.
Now awful Beauty puts on all its arms;
The fair each moment rises in her charms,   20
Repairs her smiles, awakens every grace,
And calls forth all the wonders of her face;
Sees by degrees a purer blush arise,
And keener lightnings quicken in her eyes. . . .

Not with more glories, in th' etherial plain,
The Sun first rises o'er the purpled main,
Than, issuing forth, the rival of his beams
Launched on the bosom of the silver Thames.
Fair Nymphs, and well-drest Youths around her shone,
But every eye was fixed on her alone.   30
On her white breast a sparkling Cross she wore,
Which Jews might kiss, and Infidels adore.
Her lively looks a sprightly mind disclose,
Quick as her eyes, and as unfixed as those:
Favors to none, to all she smiles extends;
Oft she rejects, but never once offends.
Bright as the sun, her eyes the gazers strike,
And, like the sun, they shine on all alike.
Yet graceful ease, and sweetness void of pride,
Might hide her faults, if Belles had faults to hide: 40
If to her share some female errors fall,
Look on her face, and you'll forget 'em all.
    This Nymph, to the destruction of mankind,
Nourished two Locks, which graceful hung behind

In equal curls, and well conspired to deck
With shining ringlets the smooth iv'ry neck.
Love in these labyrinths his slaves detains,
And mighty hearts are held in slender chains.
With hairy springes we the birds betray,
Slight lines of hair surprise the finny prey,   50
Fair tresses man's imperial race ensnare,
And beauty draws us with a single hair. . . .
  But now secure the painted vessel glides,
The sun-beams trembling on the floating tides:
While melting music steals upon the sky,
And softened sounds along the waters die;
Smooth flow the waves, the Zephyrs gently play,
Belinda smiled, and all the world was gay. . . .

Hugh MacDiarmid (Christopher Grieve) *Old Wife in High Spirits* [1]

In an Edinburgh Pub

An auld wumman cam' in, a mere rickle o' banes, in a faded
                    black dress
And a bonnet wi' beads o' jet rattlin' on it;
A puir-lookin' cratur, you'd think she could haurdly ha'e had less
Life left in her and still lived, but dagonit!

He gied her a stiff whisky—she was nervous as a troot
And could haurdly haud the tumbler, puir cratur;
Syne he gied her anither, joked wi' her, and anither, and syne
Wild as the whisky up cam' her nature.

The rod that struck water frae the rock in the desert
Was naething to the life that sprang oot o' her;   10
The dowie auld soul was twinklin' and fizzin' wi' fire;
You never saw ocht sae souple and kir.

Like a sackful o' monkeys she was, and her lauchin'
Loupit up whiles to incredible heights;
Wi' ane owre the eight her temper changed and her tongue
Flew juist as the forkt lichtnin' skites.

[1] Glossary: *ane owre the eight* one minute after eight; *banes* bones; *carline* hag; *creeshy* fattened; *crippen* hunched up; *dowie* dispirited; *dune* weary; *haud* hold; *heich skeich* wildly gay; *kir* wanton; *kythed* appeared; *loupit* leapt; *muckle* much; *ocht* aught; *rickle* heap; *syne* then; *tashed* ruined; *troot* trout; *whiles* every so often.

The heich skeich auld cat was fair in her element;
Wanton as a whirlwind, and shairly better that way
Than a' crippen thegither wi' laneliness and cauld
Like a foretaste o' the graveyaird clay.   20

Some folk nae doot'll condemn gie'in' a guid spree
To the puir dune body and raither she endit her days
Like some auld tashed copy o' the Bible yin sees
On a street book-barrow's tipenny trays.

A' I ken is weel-fed and weel-put-on though they be
Ninety per cent o' respectable folk never hae
As muckle life in their creeshy carcases frae beginnin' to end
As kythed in that wild auld carline that day!

Andrew Marvell   *Bermudas*

Where the remote Bermudas ride
In th' ocean's bosom unespy'd,
From a small boat that rowed along,
The list'ning winds receiv'd this song:

"What should we do but sing His praise,
That led us through the watery maze,
Unto an isle so long unknown,
And yet far kinder than our own?
Where He the huge sea-monsters wracks,
That lift the deep upon their backs.   10
He lands us on a grassy stage,
Safe from storms, and prelate's rage.
He gave us this eternal spring,
Which here enamels everything,
And sends the fowls to us in care,
On daily visits through the air.
He hangs in shades the orange bright,
Like golden lamps in a green night,
And does in the pomegranates close
Jewels more rich than Ormus shows.   20
He makes the figs our mouths to meet,
And throws the melons at our feet.
But apples plants of such a price,
No tree could ever bear them twice.
With cedars, chosen by His hand,

From Lebanon, he stores the land,
And makes the hollow seas, that roar
Proclaim the ambergris on shore.
He cast (of which we rather boast)
The Gospel's pearl upon our coast   30
And in these rocks for us did frame
A temple, where to sound His name.
Oh let our voice His praise exalt,
Till it arrive at Heaven's vault,
Which thence (perhaps) rebounding, may
Echo beyond the Mexique Bay."

　　Thus sung they, in the English boat,
An holy and a cheerful note;
And all the way, to guide their chime,
With falling oars they kept the time.   40

GERARD MANLEY HOPKINS　*Winter with the Gulf Stream*

The boughs, the boughs are bare enough
But earth has never felt the snow.
Frost-furred our ivies are and rough

With bills of rime the brambles shew.
The hoarse leaves crawl on hissing ground
Because the sighing wind is low.

But if the rain-blasts be unbound
And from dank feathers wring the drops
The clogged brook runs with choking sound

Kneading the mounded mire that stops   10
His channel under clammy coats
Of foliage fallen in the copse.

A simple passage of weak notes
Is all the winter bird dare try.
The bugle moon by daylight floats

So glassy white about the sky,
So like a berg of hyaline,
And pencilled blue so daintily,

I never saw her so divine.
But through black branches, rarely drest   20
In scarves of silky shot and shine,

The webbed and the watery west
Where yonder crimson fireball sits
Looks laid for feasting and for rest.

I see long reefs of violets
In beryl-covered fens so dim,
A gold-water Pactolus frets

Its brindled wharves and yellow brim,
The waxen colours weep and run,
And slendering to his burning rim   30

Into the flat blue mist the sun
Drops out and all our day is done.

John Keats   *Ode to Autumn*

Season of mists and mellow fruitfulness,
    Close bosom-friend of the maturing sun;
Conspiring with him how to load and bless
    With fruit the vines that round the thatch-eaves run;
To bend with apples the moss'd cottage-trees,
    And fill all fruit with ripeness to the core;
        To swell the gourd, and plump the hazel shells
With a sweet kernel; to set budding more,
    And still more, later flowers for the bees,
    Until they think warm days will never cease,   10
        For Summer has o'er brimm'd their clammy cells.

Who hath not seen thee oft amid thy store?
    Sometimes whoever seeks abroad may find
Thee sitting careless on a granary floor,
    Thy hair soft-lifted by the winnowing wind;
Or on a half-reap'd furrow sound asleep,
    Drows'd with the fume of poppies, while thy hook
        Spares the next swath and all its twined flowers:
And sometimes like a gleaner thou dost keep
    Steady thy laden head across a brook;   20
    Or by a cider-press, with patient look,
        Thou watchest the last oozings hours by hours.

Where are the songs of Spring? Ay, where are they?
   Think not of them, thou hast thy music too,—
While barred clouds bloom the soft-dying day,
   And touch the stubble-plains with rosy hue;
Then in a wailful choir the small gnats mourn
   Among the river sallows, borne aloft
      Or sinking as the light wind lives or dies;
And full-grown lambs loud bleat from hilly bourn;   30
   Hedge-crickets sing; and now with treble soft
   The red-breast whistles from a garden-croft;
      And gathering swallows twitter in the skies.

HART CRANE   *Repose of Rivers*

The willows carried a slow sound,
A sarabande the wind mowed on the mead.
I could never remember
That seething, steady leveling of the marshes
Till age had brought me to the sea.

Flags, weeds. And remembrance of steep alcoves
Where cypresses shared the noon's
Tyranny; they drew me into hades almost.
And mammoth turtles climbing sulphur dreams
Yielded, while sun-silt rippled them   10
Asunder . . .

How much I would have bartered! the black gorge
And all the singular nestings in the hills
Where beavers learn stitch and tooth.
The pond I entered once and quickly fled—
I remember now its singing willow rim.

And finally, in that memory all things nurse;
After the city that I finally passed
With scalding unguents spread and smoking darts
The monsoon cut across the delta   20
At gulf gates . . . There, beyond the dykes

I heard wind flaking sapphire, like this summer,
And willows could not hold more steady sound.

Hart Crane   from Voyages

II

—And yet this great wink of eternity,
Of rimless floods, unfettered leewardings,
Samite sheeted and processioned where
Her undinal vast belly moonward bends,
Laughing the wrapt inflections of our love;

Take this Sea, whose diapason knells
On scrolls of silver snowy sentences,
The sceptred terror of whose sessions rends
As her demeanors motion well or ill,
All but the pieties of lovers' hands.   10

And onward, as bells off San Salvador
Salute the crocus lustres of the stars,
In these poinsettia meadows of her tides,—
Adagios of islands, O my Prodigal,
Complete the dark confessions her veins spell.

Mark how her turning shoulders wind the hours,
And hasten while her penniless rich palms
Pass superscription of bent foam and wave,—
Hasten, while they are true,—sleep, death, desire,
Close round one instant in one floating flower.   20

Bind us in time, O Seasons clear, and awe.
O minstrel galleons of Carib fire,
Bequeath us to no earthly shore until
Is answered in the vortex of our grave
The seal's wide spindrift gaze toward paradise.

VI

Where icy and bright dungeons lift
Of swimmers their lost morning eyes,
And ocean rivers, churning, shift
Green borders under stranger skies,

Steadily as a shell secretes
Its beating leagues of monotone,
Or as many waters trough the sun's
Red kelson past the cape's wet stone;

O rivers mingling toward the sky
And harbor of the phoenix' breast—   10
My eyes pressed black against the prow,
—Thy derelict and blinded guest

Waiting, afire, what name, unspoke,
I cannot claim: let thy waves rear
More savage than the death of kings,
Some splintered garland for the seer.

Beyond siroccos harvesting
The solstice thunders, crept away,
Like a cliff swinging or a sail
Flung into April's inmost day—   20

Creation's blithe and petalled word
To the lounged goddess when she rose
Conceding dialogue with eyes
That smile unsearchable repose—

Still fervid covenant, Belle Isle,
—Unfolded floating dais before
Which rainbows twine continual hair—
Belle Isle, white echo of the oar!

The imaged Word, it is, that holds
Hushed willows anchored in its glow.   30
It is the unbetrayable reply
Whose accent no farewell can know.

MARIANNE MOORE   *Snakes, Mongooses, Snake-charmers*
and the Like

I have a friend who would give a price for those long fingers all of one
    length—
those hideous bird's claws, for that exotic asp and the mongoose—
products of the country in which everything is hard work, the country
    of the grass-getter,
the torch-bearer, the dog-servant, the messenger-bearer, the holy-man.
Engrossed in this distinguished worm nearly as wild and as fierce as the
    day it was caught,
he gazes as if incapable of looking at anything with a view to analysis.

"The slight snake rippling quickly through the grass,
the leisurely tortoise with its pied back,
the chameleon passing from twig to stone, from stone to straw,"
lit his imagination at one time; his admiration now converges upon
this.   10
Thick, not heavy, it stands up from its travelling-basket,
the essentially Greek, the plastic animal all of a piece from nose to tail;
one is compelled to look at it as at the shadows of the alps
imprisoning in their folds like flies in amber, the rhythms of the skating
rink.
This animal to which from the earliest times, importance has attached,
fine as its worshippers have said—for what was it invented?
To show that when intelligence in its pure form
has embarked on a train of thought which is unproductive, it will
come back?
We do not know; the only positive thing about it is its shape; but why
protest?
The passion for setting people right is in itself an afflictive disease. 20
Distaste which takes no credit to itself is best.

W. H. Auden   *On This Island*

Look, stranger, on this island now
The leaping light for your delight discovers,
Stand stable here
And silent be,
That through the channels of the ear
May wander like a river
The swaying sound of the sea.

Here at the small field's ending pause
When the chalk wall falls to the foam and its tall ledges
Oppose the pluck   10
And knock of the tide,
And the shingle scrambles after the suck-
-ing surf,
And a gull lodges
A moment on its sheer side.

Far off like floating seeds the ships
Diverge on urgent voluntary errands,
And the full view

Indeed may enter
And move in memory as now these clouds do,
That pass the harbour mirror   20
And all the summer through the water saunter.

EZRA POUND   from *Canto XVI*

And before hell mouth; dry plain
      and two mountains;
On the one mountain, a running form,
      and another
In the turn of the hill; in hard steel
The road like a slow screw's thread,
The angle almost imperceptible,
      so that the circuit seemed hardly to rise;
And the running form, naked, Blake,
Shouting, whirling his arms, the swift limbs,
Howling against the evil,
      his eyes rolling,
Whirling like flaming cart-wheels,
      and his head held backward to gaze on the evil
As he ran from it,   10
      to be hid by the steel mountain,
And when he showed again from the north side;
      his eyes blazing toward hell mouth,
His neck forward. . . .

DANTE ALIGHIERI   *The Vision of God* [1]

(from *Paradiso:* Canto XXXIII)

O supreme Light, who dost thy glory assert
  High over our imagining, lend again
  Memory a little of what to me thou wert.
Vouchsafe unto my tongue such power to attain
  That but one sparkle it may leave behind
  Of thy magnificence to future men.
For by returning somewhat to my mind
  And by a little sounding in this verse

[1] Translated by Laurence Binyon.

More of thy triumph shall be thence divined.
So keenly did the living radiance pierce   10
    Into me, that I think I had been undone
    Had mine eyes faltered, from the light averse.
And I recall that with the more passion
    I clove to it, till my gaze, thereat illumed,
    With the Infinite Good tasted communion.
O Grace abounding, whereby I presumed
    To fix upon the eternal light my gaze
    So deep, that in it I my sight consumed!
I beheld leaves within the unfathomed blaze
    Into one volume bound by love, the same   20
    That the universe holds scattered through its maze.
Substance and accidents, and their modes, became
    As if together fused, all in such wise
    That what I speak of is one simple flame.
Verily I think I saw with mine own eyes
    The form that knits the whole world, since I taste,
    In telling of it, more abounding bliss.
One moment more oblivion has amassed
    Than five-and-twenty centuries have wrought
    Since Argo's shadow o'er wondering Neptune passed.   30
Thus did my mind in the suspense of thought
    Gaze fixedly, all immovable and intent,
    And ever fresh fire from its gazing caught.

JOHN MILTON   *Satan Discovers Eden*

(from *Paradise Lost:* Book IV)

So on he [1] fares, and to the border comes
Of *Eden*, where delicious Paradise,
Now nearer, crowns with her enclosure green,
As with a rural mound the champaign head
Of a steep wilderness, whose hairy sides
With thicket overgrown, grotesque and wild,
Access deni'd; and overhead up grew
Insuperable height of loftiest shade,
Cedar, and Pine, and Fir, and branching Palm,

---

[1] Satan, journeying to Earth to see mankind for the first time.

A Sylvan Scene, and as the ranks ascend   10
Shade above shade, a woody Theatre
Of stateliest view. Yet higher than their tops
The verdurous wall of Paradise upsprung,
Which to our general Sire gave prospect large
Into his nether Empire neighbouring round.
And higher than that Wall a circling row
Of goodliest Trees loaden with fairest Fruit,
Blossoms and Fruits at once of golden hue
Appear'd, with gay enamel'd colours mixt:
On which the Sun more glad impress'd his beams   20
Than in fair Evening Cloud, or humid Bow,
When God hath show'rd the earth; so lovely seem'd
That Landscape: And of pure now purer air
Meets his approach, and to the heart inspires
Vernal delight and joy, able to drive
All sadness but despair. . . .

   Now to th' ascent of that steep savage Hill
Satan had journey'd on, pensive and slow,
But further way found none, so thick entwin'd,
As one continu'd brake, the undergrowth   30
Of shrubs and tangling bushes had perplext
All path of Man or Beast that passed that way.
One Gate there only was, and that look'd East
On th' other side; which, when th' arch-felon saw,
Due entrance he disdained, and in contempt,
At one slight bound high overleap'd all bound
Of Hill or highest Wall, and sheer within
Lights on his feet. As when a prowling Wolf,
Whom hunger drives to seek new haunt for prey,
Watching where Shepherds pen their Flocks at eve   40
In hurdl'd Cotes amid the field secure,
Leaps o'er the fence with ease into the Fold;
Or as a Thief bent to unhoard the cash
Of some rich Burgher, whose substantial doors,
Cross-barr'd and bolted fast, fear no assault,
In at the window climbs, or o'er the tiles;
So clomb this first grand Thief into God's Fold:
So since into his Church lewd Hirelings climb.
Thence up he flew, and on the Tree of Life,
The middle Tree and highest there that grew,
Sat like a Cormorant. . . .   50

Samuel Taylor Coleridge *Kubla Khan*

In Xanadu did Kubla Khan
A stately pleasure-dome decree:
Where Alph, the sacred river, ran
Through caverns measureless to man
    Down to a sunless sea.
So twice five miles of fertile ground
With walls and towers were girdled round:
And here were gardens bright with sinuous rills,
Where blossomed many an incense-bearing tree,
And here were forests ancient as the hills,   10
Enfolding sunny spots of greenery.

But oh! that deep romantic chasm which slanted
Down the green hill athwart a cedarn cover!
A savage place! as holy and enchanted
As e'er beneath a waning moon was haunted
By woman wailing for her demon-lover!
And from this chasm, with ceaseless turmoil seething,
As if this earth in fast thick pants were breathing,
A mighty fountain momently was forced,
Amid whose swift half-intermitted burst   20
Huge fragments vaulted like rebounding hail,
Or chaffy grain beneath the thresher's flail:
And 'mid these dancing rocks at once and ever
It flung up momently the sacred river.
Five miles meandering with a mazy motion
Through wood and dale the sacred river ran,
Then reached the caverns measureless to man,
And sank in tumult to a lifeless ocean:
And 'mid this tumult Kubla heard from far
Ancestral voices prophesying war!   30
    The shadow of the dome of pleasure
    Floated midway on the waves;
    Where was heard the mingled measure
    From the fountain and the caves.
It was a miracle of rare device,
A sunny pleasure-dome with caves of ice!

    A damsel with a dulcimer
    In a vision once I saw:
    It was an Abyssinian maid,

And on her dulcimer she played,   40
Singing of Mount Abora.
Could I revive within me
Her symphony and song,
      To such a deep delight 'twould win me,
That with music loud and long,
I would build that dome in air,
That sunny dome! those caves of ice!
And all who heard should see them there,
And all should cry, Beware! Beware!
His flashing eyes, his floating hair!   50
Weave a circle round him thrice,
And close your eyes with holy dread,
For he on honey-dew hath fed,
And drunk the milk of Paradise.

Ezra Pound *Canto XVII*

So that the vines burst from my fingers
And the bees weighted with pollen
Move heavily in the vine-shoots:
            chirr—chirr—chirr-rikk—a purring sound,
And the birds sleepily in the branches.
            Zagreus! Io Zagreus! [1]
With the first pale-clear of the heaven
And the cities set in their hills,
And the goddess of the fair knees
Moving there, with the oak-woods behind her,   10
The green slope, with white hounds
            leaping about her;
And thence down to the creek's mouth, until evening,
Flat water before me,
            and the trees growing in water,
Marble trunks out of stillness,
On past the palazzi,
                  in the stillness,
The light now, not of the sun.
                  Chrysophrase,   20
And the water green clear, and blue clear;

---

[1] Zagreus! Hail Zagreus! See comment, page 221.

On, to the great cliffs of amber.
Between them,
Cave of Nerea,[2]
she like a great shell curved,
And the boat drawn without sound,
Without odour of ship-work,
Nor bird-cry, nor any noise of wave moving,
Nor splash of porpoise, nor any noise of wave moving,
Within her cave, Nerea, 30
she like a great shell curved
In the suavity of the rock,
cliff green-gray in the far,
In the near, the gate-cliffs of amber,
And the wave
green clear, and blue clear,
And the cave salt-white, and glare-purple,
cool, porphyry smooth,
the rock sea-worn.
No gull-cry, no sound of porpoise, 40
Sand as of malachite, and no cold there,
the light not of the sun.

Zagreus, feeding his panthers,
the turf clear as on hills under light.
And under the almond-trees, gods,
with them, *choros nympharum*.[3] Gods,
Hermes and Athene,
As shaft of compass,
Between them, trembled—
To the left is the place of fauns 50
sylva nympharum; [4]
The low wood, moor-scrub,
the doe, the young spotted deer,
leap up through the broom-plants,
as dry leaf amid yellow.
And by one cut of the hills,
the great alley of Memnons.
Beyond, sea, crests seen over dune,
Night sea churning shingle,

[2] Nerea, Zothar, and Aletha are genuine names of female divinities invented by Pound.
[3] chorus of nymphs
[4] wood of the nymphs

To the left, the alley of cypress.   60
        A boat came,
One man holding her sail,
Guiding her with oar caught over gunwale, saying:
"   There, in the forest of marble,
"   the stone trees—out of water—
"   the arbours of stone—
"   marble leaf, over leaf,
"   silver, steel over steel,
"   silver beaks rising and crossing,
"   prow set against prow,   70
"   stone, ply over ply,
"   the gilt beams flare of an evening."
Borso, Carmagnola,[5] the men of craft, *i vitrei*,[6]
Thither, at one time, time after time,
And the waters richer than glass,
Bronze gold, the blaze over the silver,
Dye-pots in the torch-light,
The flash of wave under prows,
And the silver beaks rising and crossing.
      Stone trees, white and rose-white in the darkness,   80
Cypress there by the towers,
      Drift under hulls in the night.

        "In the gloom the gold
Gathers the light about it." . . .

Now supine in burrow, half over-arched bramble,
One eye for the sea, through that peek-hole,
Gray light, with Athene.
Zothar and her elephants, the gold loin-cloth,
The sistrum, shaken, shaken,
      the cohorts of her dancers.   90
And Aletha, by bend of the shore,
      with her eyes seaward,
     and in her hands sea-wrack

---

[5] Borso d'Este, Carmagnola, and Sigismundo Malatesta were fifteenth-century Italian patrons of art and learning also deeply active in political and military struggles. The poem views them as defeated heroes whose courage and gaiety grew out of a combined earthiness, feeling for craftsmanship, and social intelligence.

[6] *makers of glass*—This was a high art, but also the poet's vision in this poem is presented as life held in stasis—as if created of glass, metal, and marble in a construct that brings together in that one vision experience, history, myth, and imagination.

Salt-bright with the foam,
Koré through the bright meadow,
     with green-gray dust in the grass:
"For this hour, brother of Circe."
Arm laid over my shoulder,
Saw the sun for three days, the sun fulvid,
As a lion lift over sand-plain;
       and that day,
And for three days, and none after,
Splendour, as the splendour of Hermes,
And shipped thence
    to the stone place,
Pale white, over water,
     known water,
And the white forest of marble, bent bough over bough,
The pleached arbour of stone,
Thither Borso, when they shot the barbed arrow at him,
And Carmagnola, between the two columns,
Sigismundo, after that wreck in Dalmatia.
  Sunset like the grasshopper flying.

Chapter Six

Poetry as Intellect and Wit

I

POETIC EXPOSITION

Poetic thought is both an obvious and an elusive presence. On the obvious side, we can always help ourselves "get" a poem by remembering that it is a human act. It is the expression of another human being, and what one person can think someone else can grasp. A poem is made up of sentences or of fragmentary units that, taken in sequence and in relation to one another, present intelligible thoughts or effects. The whole poem, in fact, often unfolds a logical meditation. As with a person, it has wit in proportion to its speed of association and keenness in seeing similarities, incongruities, paradoxes, and dead ends of argument.

The elusive side of poetic thought is that it is an energy or a process and not simply a sequence of rationally related ideas. A poem's real life lies in its dynamics of tone and attitude and feeling and sound—the motion of a mind in action, the mind of the speaker. One cannot define a poem or a person by intellectual abstraction alone. A purposeful illustration of the process may be seen in Robert Duncan's *Strains of Sight* (pages 134–135), where the speaker thinks of Adam and Eve after the Fall and of his own mind meditating on them. Duncan's poem is beautiful and demanding, and the reader will want to return to it often to catch its many facets and implications.

In the present chapter we try to isolate four clear modes of poetry as intellect and wit. These are, first, poetry that presents straightforward exposition or argument; second, "Metaphysical" poetry, which combines its argument subtly and wittily with sensuous and emotional realization; third, poetry that uses wit as a cutting edge of scorn or contempt or even, sometimes, of mild reproof or teasing; and fourth, poetry that plays with ambiguities and complexities both of reality and of our understanding.

All these modes are interrelated. All involve thought as a kind of conceiving and structuring energy rather than something inert and easily summarized. We may begin, then, with direct poetic exposition.

Every poem, no matter how obliquely, presents ideas and in some sense argues for them. The argument may be revealed through a sequence of emotions or the workings of a narrative, or it may be directly and logically stated. In each case, the reader must try to grasp it and follow its thread—indeed, he cannot avoid doing so if he wishes his understanding of the poet's accomplishment to meet the poet's purpose.

Most readers will recognize the difficulty of writing poetry that is explicit in its argument, yet triumphant in its art. Those poets who have done so have proved their skill twice over. Thus, the eighteenth-century masters of intellectual verse (Pope, Prior, Goldsmith, Swift, and others) strove for logical precision as well as brilliance, and succeeded because of their wit, their polished analytical conciseness, and their socially sophisticated mastery of idiom. The neat couplets, each so sharply pointed, of Alexander Pope's *Essay on Man* illustrate their methods:

> Know then thyself, presume not God to scan;
> The proper study of Mankind is Man.
> Placed on this isthmus of a middle state,
> A Being darkly wise, and rudely great;
> With too much knowledge for the Sceptic side,
> With too much weakness for the Stoic's pride,
> He hangs between; in doubt to act, or rest;
> In doubt to deem himself a God, or Beast;
> In doubt his Mind or Body to prefer;
> Born but to die, and reasoning but to err;   10
> Alike in ignorance, his reason such,
> Whether he thinks too little, or too much:
> Chaos of Thought and Passion, all confused;
> Still by himself abused, or disabused;
> Created half to rise, and half to fall;
> Great lord of all things, yet a prey to all;
> Sole judge of Truth, in endless Error hurled:
> The glory, jest and riddle of the world!

Behind the half-scornful satirical tone of this passage is a basic earnestness of thought. A series of parallel assertions and balanced contrasts supports the poet's conception of man's place in the universe wittily, piously, and with confident reiteration. It consists mainly of a number of paradoxical observations to establish the inadequacy of man's nature: He is "darkly wise" and "rudely great"; and though too enlightened by religion to be a skeptic, yet he is weak before temptation. He falls midway between god and beast. The reader might consider any one of Pope's ideas questionable, but together these propositions do make for a consistent, clearly articulated argument. The language itself is intellectual in its philosophic, religious and moral terminology, and the thoughts have been memorably phrased. Whether or not "the proper study of Mankind is Man" may be debated indefinitely, and the paradox interpreted many ways, but the precision, the deft punning, and the air of shrewd wisdom give the couplets the sound of proverbs. These are characteristic virtues of neo-Classic poetry.

The presentation of ideas in verse by Romantic poets, as one might expect, is generally less urban and more emotional.[1] In the following passage from Wordsworth's *The Prelude*, there is a piety equal to that of Pope; and though the speaker may seem to be living in an altogether different world from Pope's, he too is bending all his talents to the precise, controlled formulation of an idea. Yet the lines are much more weighted with emotion than is the *Essay on Man*:

> Dust as we are, the immortal spirit grows
> Like harmony in music; there is a dark
> Inscrutable workmanship that reconciles
> Discordant elements, makes them cling together
> In one society. How strange that all
> The terrors, pains, and early miseries,
> Regrets, vexations, lassitudes interfused
> Within my mind, should e'er have borne a part,
> And that a needful part, in making up
> The calm existence that is mine when I   10
> Am worthy of myself! Praise to the end!
> Thanks to the means which Nature deigned to employ. . . .

This passage too, it is interesting to note, speaks with some humility of the limitations of man's understanding. Both passages, in fact, use forms of the word "dark" to suggest these limitations. But Pope's phrase is one element of a clear-cut antithesis (a balancing of opposed ideas emphasized by the way the words are placed) in a series of antitheses. His main concern has been to appeal to our minds by the force and charm of this series as it rocks the argument back and forth, and to intrigue us by the variety that he so skilfully achieves within this pattern. Wordsworth, on the other hand, uses "dark" to suggest the *mystery* rather than the logical absurdity of the human condition. He follows it up with "inscrutable workmanship," "strange," and then a series of words denoting emotional suffering and confusion. Pope's lines close with a pithy intellectual summary: Man is

---

[1] See pages 405–429 for a more thorough discussion of Classical and Romantic poetry.

"the glory, jest, and riddle of the world!" Wordsworth's, beginning with a musical simile for the divine element in our natures, move through impressions of awe and sadness to an outburst of joyous praise at the end. The argument is clear and logical enough, but its movement is emotional and its tone subjective.

In Metaphysical poetry—to look backward two centuries before Wordsworth—we have writing more abstractly intellectualized than most Romantic poetry, yet more warmly familiar in tone than the elegantly finished Classical mode will ordinarily allow.[2] Although the following poem of George Herbert's lacks the complexity of many other Metaphysical verse-arguments, its four tiny prophecies each shift our attention to a new phase of Herbert's theme, exemplifying perfectly the characteristic Metaphysical technique. That is, the imagery, though intellectually demanding, is strongly emotional in its effect at the same time.

GEORGE HERBERT *Virtue*

> Sweet day, so cool, so calm, so bright,
>   The bridal of the earth and sky,
> The dew shall weep thy fall tonight;
>   For thou must die.
>
> Sweet rose, whose hue angry and brave
>   Bids the rash gazer wipe his eye,
> Thy root is ever in its grave,
>   And thou must die.
>
> Sweet spring, full of sweet days and roses,
>   A box where sweets compacted lie,   10
> My music shows ye have your closes,
>   And all must die.
>
> Only a sweet and virtuous soul,
>   Like seasoned timber, never gives;
> But, though the whole world turn to coal,
>   Then chiefly lives.

What is especially interesting in Herbert's figures of speech here is their developing relation to one another. The day, "bridal of the earth and sky," makes visible the beautiful sights of mortal life. In its calm brightness it seems merely passive, but the rose makes a more defiant show against death. Yet the rose's partial burial, even in life, is a sign that the defiance

---

[2] See pages 280–304 for a more thorough discussion of Metaphysical poetry.

will be quite futile. Nor is the spring, which includes many days and roses and as it were tries to transcend death by multiplying their mortalities within itself, more successful. But the soul unites earth and sky differently from the day, for it joins spirit to flesh; and it defies death more truly though less rashly than the "angry" rose. And like "seasoned timber," it compresses within it all the values of its nature: undying ones, however, rather than dying ones of the earth.

The process of elimination in this poem, incidentally, is characteristic of the emotional way poetic thought often operates: "Try this, and reject it; then this; then this; but accept this last meaning, which has been growing out of all the preceding rejections." In *Virtue*, we "reject" (by mourning for them) the day, the rose, and the spring as impermanent, despite their beauty and sweetness which we love. But we "accept" the soul, whose own beauty and sweetness, though imperishable, has actually been defined for us in the images of the other lovely things mourned.

Poetic argument always leads past the reasoning itself to the vital personality behind it. How elegant and worldly Pope's lines seem, despite their seriousness; how wondering and humbly elated are Wordsworth's; and what a gay, delicate spirit appears, despite the grave theme, in Herbert. His gourmetlike pleasure in the spring, "a box where sweets compacted lie," is as attractive as his quiet punning to leaven his lament that spring must end: "My music shows ye have your closes." The poetry of thought does certainly take seriously the arguments it presents, but it cannot reach us and move us unless the speaking personality it embodies does so at the same time. It is for this reason that some of the most effective verse-arguments ever written appear in narrative and dramatic poetry—in the debates and discussions, for instance, of Milton's *Paradise Lost*, in the soliloquies of Shakespearean tragedy, in the satires of Chaucer and Dryden, and in the best contemplative passages of Wordsworth's *The Prelude*. Such poetry is intellectual and sometimes argumentative, but the development is not always logical, sometimes not logical at all, and never only logical. There is always an emotional fire about the lines, usually perhaps only a faint glow but sometimes a flash or a crackling flame, and there is always the individual voice of the poet.

Poems: Poetic Exposition

The series of poems and passages that follow represent various modes of poetic argument from the Renaissance to the present. They meditate either on the nature of cosmic order or on man's place, if he has one, as a social and spiritual being within that order. Taken together, they present a sort of miniature history of ideas.

The passages by Shakespeare, Donne, Milton, and Pope assume the presence of a conscious, divine scheme in the universe. Ulysses, the speaker in the passage from Shakespeare's play *Troilus and Cressida*, argues for the importance of "degree" or structural order in society as in the greater cosmos— a thought paralleled in Donne's subtler, sadder passage about the intellectual confusions caused by the new science and the new individualism of the seventeenth century: "And new Philosophy calls all in doubt." In the passage by Milton, God explains the paradox of His foreknowledge of all things despite man's freedom to choose his own future. Pope, less rooted in traditional theology than Donne and Milton, stresses the contrast between God's perfect knowledge and the limited awareness of men, using the premises of eighteenth-century rationalism against the very humanism that had created it. His exposition is at once exalted, dogmatic, and satirical.

Later in the eighteenth century, Blake's paradoxes are as vigorous as Pope's, but they emphasize the bitter human predicament far more than an abstract principle. Shelley reaches deep into himself to achieve a visionary state of transcendence and thus overcome that predicament.

We can see the shift to a characteristic nineteenth-century anguish in Tennyson's *In Memoriam*. Science and evolutionary theory have placed the assumptions of Christian orthodoxy on the defensive, and Tennyson feels the pressure of this fact with a deep personal pain in thinking about the reality of a dear friend's death. His poem is an extended elegy in which he faces the issue directly. Although by no means free of similar preoccupations, the twentieth-century poets Rupert Brooke, Wallace Stevens, and X. J. Kennedy are very different from Victorians like Tennyson in point of view and in tone. Brooke makes urbane fun of Tennyson's solemnity by mimicking it; at the same time, he launches an ironic, but quite traditional, attack on man's pride by imagining an optimistic religious faith in the mind of a fish. Stevens treats such faith as a beautiful and seductive but illusory myth; our need is to accept the limits and the glories of our earthly condition and celebrate it as the only paradise we shall ever know. Kennedy presents an amusing reversal of the traditional idea of divine perfection. He sees the notion of perfection itself, in our world of computers and electronics, as a suggestion of "sleek hell," whereas Heaven would be an old-fashioned, pre-Machine Age place of humanly manageable imperfections.

WILLIAM SHAKESPEARE *On Degree*

(from *Troilus and Cressida*)

The heavens themselves, the planets and this centre
Observe degree, priority and place,
Insisture, course, proportion, season, form,
Office and custom, in all line of order;
And therefore is the glorious planet Sol
In noble eminence enthroned and sphered
Amidst the other; whose medicinable eye
Corrects the ill aspects of planets evil,
And posts, like the commandment of a king,
Sans check to good and bad: but when the planets   10
In evil mixture to disorder wander,
What plagues and what portents! what mutiny!
What raging of the sea! shaking of earth!
Commotion in the winds! frights, changes, horrors,
Divert and crack, rend and deracinate
The unity and married calm of states
Quite from their fixture! O, when degree is shaked,
Which is the ladder of all high designs,
Then enterprise is sick! How could communities,
Degrees in schools and brotherhoods in cities,   20
Peaceful commerce from dividable shores,
The primogenitive and due of birth,
Prerogative of age, crowns, sceptres, laurels,
But by degree, stand in authentic place?
Take but degree away, untune that string,
And, hark, what discord follows! each thing meets
In mere oppugnancy: the bounded waters
Should lift their bosoms higher than the shores
And make a sop of all this solid globe:
Strength should be lord of imbecility,   30
And the rude son should strike his father dead:
Force should be right; or rather, right and wrong,
Between whose endless jar justice resides,
Should lose their names, and so should justice too.
Then every thing includes itself in power,
Power into will, will into appetite;
And appetite, an universal wolf,
So doubly seconded with will and power,
Must make perforce an universal prey,
And last eat up himself. . . .   40

John Donne *The New Philosophy*

(from *The First Anniversary*)

And new Philosophy calls all in doubt,
The Element of fire is quite put out;
The Sun is lost, and th'earth, and no man's wit
Can well direct him where to look for it.
And freely men confess that this world's spent,
When in the Planets, and the Firmament
They seek so many new; then see that this
Is crumbled out again to his Atomies.
'Tis all in pieces, all coherence gone;
All just supply, and all Relation: 10
Prince, Subject, Father, Son, are things forgot,
For every man alone thinks he hath got
To be a Phoenix, and that then can be
None of that kind, of which he is, but he.
This is the world's condition now, and now
She that should all parts to reunion bow,
She that had all Magnetic force alone,
To draw, and fasten sund'red parts in one;
She whom wise nature had invented then
When she observ'd that every sort of men   20
Did in their voyage in this world's Sea stray,
And needed a new compass for their way;
She that was best, and first original
Of all faire copies, and the general
Steward to Fate; she whose rich eyes and breast
Gilt the West Indies, and perfum'd the East;
Whose having breath'd in this world, did bestow
Spice on those Isles, and bade them still smell so,
And that rich Indie which doth gold inter,
Is but as single money, coin'd from her: 30
She to whom this world must itself refer,
As Suburbs, or the Microcosm of her,
She, she is dead; she's dead: when thou knowst this
Thou knowst how lame a cripple this world is.
And learn'st thus much of our Anatomy.
That this world's general sickness doth not lie
In any humour, or one certain part;
But as thou sawest it rotten at the heart,
Thou seest a Hectic fever hath got hold
Of the whole substance, not to be controll'd,   40

And that thou hast but one way, not t'admit
The world's infection, to be none of it.
For the world's subtil'st immaterial parts
Feel this consuming wound, and age's darts.
For the world's beauty is decay'd, or gone,
Beauty, that's colour, and proportion.

JOHN MILTON   *Free Will and God's Foreknowledge* [1]

(from *Paradise Lost*)

Only begotten Son, seest thou what rage
Transports our adversary, whom no bounds
Prescrib'd, no bars of Hell, nor all the chains
Heapt on him there, nor yet the main Abyss
Wide interrupt can hold; so bent he seems
On desperate revenge, that shall redound
Upon his own rebellious head. And now
Through all restraint broke loose he wings his way
Not far off Heav'n, in the Precincts of light,
Directly towards the new created World,   10
And Man there plac't, with purpose to assay
If him by force he can destroy, or worse,
By some false guile pervert; and shall pervert,
For man will heark'n to his glozing lies,
And easily transgress the sole Command,
Sole pledge of his obedience: So will fall
He and his faithless Progeny: whose fault?
Whose but his own? ingrate, he had of me
All he could have; I made him just and right,
Sufficient to have stood, though free to fall.   20
Such I created all th' Ethereal Powers
And Spirits, both them who stood and them who fail'd;
Freely they stood who stood, and fell who fell.
Not free, what proof could they have giv'n sincere
Of true allegiance, constant Faith or Love,
Where only what they needs must do, appear'd,
Not what they would? what praise could they receive?
What pleasure I from such obedience paid,

[1] In this passage God explains to Messiah, His son, why although He has foreknowledge of the future, His creatures are free to make their own moral choices. The explanation is occasioned by the sight of Satan on his way to Eden, where he plans to tempt Adam and Eve to disobey God. See pages 249–250.

When Will and Reason (Reason also is choice)
Useless and vain, of freedom both despoil'd,   30
Made passive both, had serv'd necessitie,
Not me. They therefore as to right belong'd,
So were created, nor can justly accuse
Their maker, or their making, or their Fate;
As if Predestination over-rul'd
Their will, dispos'd by absolute Decree
Or high foreknowledge; they themselves decreed
Their own revolt, not I: if I foreknew,
Foreknowledge had no influence on their fault,
Which had no less prov'd certain unforeknown.   40
So without least impulse or shadow of Fate,
Or aught by me immutably foreseen,
They trespass, Authors to themselves in all
Both what they judge and what they choose; for so
I form'd them free, and free they must remain
Till they enthrall themselves: I else must change
Their nature, and revoke the high Decree
Unchangeable, Eternal, which ordain'd
Their freedom; they themselves ordain'd their fall.
The first sort by their own suggestion fell,   50
Self-tempted, self-deprav'd; Man falls deceiv'd
By the other first; Man therefore shall find grace,
The other none: in Mercy and Justice both,
Through Heav'n and Earth, so shall my glorie excel,
But Mercy first and last shall brightest shine.

ALEXANDER POPE   *The Great Chain of Being*

(from *An Essay on Man*)

   Far as Creation's ample range extends,
The scale of sensual,[1] mental powers ascends:
Mark how it mounts, to Man's imperial race,
From the green myriads in the peopled grass:
What modes of sight betwixt each wide extreme,
The mole's dim curtain and the lynx's beam:
Of smell, the headlong lioness between,
And hound sagacious on the tainted green:
Of hearing, from the life that fills the flood,

[1] sensory

To that which warbles through the vernal wood: 10
The spider's touch, how exquisitely fine!
Feels at each thread, and lives along the line:
In the nice bee, what sense so subtly true
From poisonous herbs extracts the healing dew?
How Instinct varies in the grovelling swine,
Compared, half-reasoning elephant, with thine!
'Twixt that, and Reason, what a nice barrier,
Forever separate, yet forever near!
Remembrance and Reflection how allied;
What thin partitions Sense from Thought divide: 20
And Middle natures, how they long to join,
Yet never pass the insuperable line!
Without this just gradation, could they be
Subjected, these to those, or all to thee?
The powers of all subdued by thee alone,
Is not thy reason all these powers in one?
   See, through this air, this ocean, and this earth,
All matter quick,[2] and bursting into birth.
Above, how high progressive life may go!
Around, how wide! how deep extend below! 30
Vast chain of Being! which from God began,
Natures ethereal, human, angel, man,
Beast, bird, fish, insect, what no eye can see,
No glass can reach; from Infinite to thee,
From thee to Nothing.—On superior powers
Were we to press, inferior might on ours:
Or in the full creation leave a void,
Where, one step broken, the great scale's destroyed:
From Nature's chain whatever link you strike,
Tenth or ten thousandth, breaks the chain alike. 40
   And, if each system in gradation roll
Alike essential to the amazing Whole,
The least confusion but in one, not all
That system only, but the Whole must fall.
Let Earth unbalanced from her orbit fly,
Planets and Suns run lawless through the sky;
Let ruling angels from their spheres be hurled,
Being on Being wrecked, and world on world;
Heaven's whole foundations to their centre nod,
And Nature tremble to the throne of God. 50

---

[2] alive

All this dread Order break—for whom? for thee?
Vile worm!—Oh Madness! Pride! Impiety!
  What if the foot, ordained the dust to tread,
Or hand, to toil, aspired to be the head?
What if the head, the eye, or ear repined
To serve mere engines to the ruling Mind?
Just as absurd for any part to claim
To be another, in this general frame:
Just as absurd, to mourn the tasks or pains
The great directing Mind of All ordains.   60
  All are but parts of one stupendous whole,
Whose body Nature is, and God the soul;
That, changed through all, and yet in all the same,
Great in the earth, as in the ethereal frame,
Warms in the sun, refreshes in the breeze,
Glows in the stars, and blossoms in the trees,
Lives through all life, extends through all extent,
Spreads undivided, operates unspent;
Breathes in our soul, informs our mortal part,
As full, as perfect, in a hair as heart: 70
As full, as perfect, in vile Man that mourns,
As the rapt Seraph that adores and burns:
To him no high, no low, no great, no small;
He fills, he bounds, connects, and equals all.
  Cease then, nor Order imperfection name;
Our proper bliss depends on what we blame.
Know thy own point: this kind, this due degree
Of blindness, weakness, Heaven bestows on thee.
Submit.—In this, or any other sphere,
Secure to be as blessed as thou canst bear: 80
Safe in the hand of one disposing Power,
Or in the natal or the mortal hour.
All Nature is but Art, unknown to thee;
All Chance, Direction, which thou canst not see;
All Discord, Harmony not understood;
All partial Evil, universal Good:
And, spite of Pride, in erring Reason's spite,
One truth is clear, WHATEVER IS, IS RIGHT.

  Know then thyself, presume not God to scan;
The proper study of Mankind is Man.   90
Placed on this isthmus of a middle state,
A Being darkly wise, and rudely great:
With too much knowledge for the Sceptic side,

With too much weakness for the Stoic's pride,
He hangs between; in doubt to act, or rest;
In doubt to deem himself a God, or Beast;
In doubt his Mind or Body to prefer;
Born but to die, and reasoning but to err;
Alike in ignorance, his reason such,
Whether he thinks too little, or too much: 100
Chaos of Thought and Passion, all confused;
Still by himself abused, or disabused;
Created half to rise, and half to fall;
Great lord of all things, yet a prey to all;
Sole judge of Truth, in endless Error hurled:
The glory, jest, and riddle of the world!
   Go, wondrous creature! mount where Science guides;
Go, measure earth, weigh air, and state the tides;
Instruct the planets in what orbs to run,
Correct old Time, and regulate the Sun;   110
Go, soar with Plato to the empyreal sphere,
To the first good, first perfect, and first fair;
Or tread the mazy round his followers trod,
And quitting sense call imitating God;
As Eastern priests in giddy circles run,
And turn their heads to imitate the Sun.
Go, teach Eternal Wisdom how to rule—
Then drop into thyself, and be a fool!

WILLIAM BLAKE   *The Human Abstract*

Pity would be no more
If we did not make somebody Poor;
And Mercy no more could be
If all were as happy as we.

And mutual fear brings peace,
Till the selfish loves increase:
Then Cruelty knits a snare,
And spreads his baits with care.

He sits down with holy fears,
And waters the ground with tears;   10
Then Humility takes its root
Underneath his foot.

Soon spreads the dismal shade
Of Mystery over his head;
And the Catterpiller and Fly
Feed on the Mystery.

And it bears the fruit of Deceit,
Ruddy and sweet to eat;
And the Raven his nest has made
In its thickest shade.   20

The Gods of the earth and sea
Sought thro' Nature to find this Tree;
But their search was all in vain:
There grows one in the Human Brain.

PERCY BYSSHE SHELLEY   *Hymn to Intellectual Beauty*

I

The awful shadow of some unseen Power
    Floats tho' unseen among us; visting
    This various world with as inconstant wing
As summer winds that creep from flower to flower;
Like moonbeams that behind some piny mountain shower,
    It visits with inconstant glance
    Each human heart and countenance;
Like hues and harmonies of evening,
    Like clouds in starlight widely spread,
    Like memory of music fled,   10
    Like aught that for its grace may be
Dear, and yet dearer for its mystery.

II

Spirit of BEAUTY, that dost consecrate
    With thine own hues all thou dost shine upon
    Of human thought or form, where art thou gone?
Why dost thou pass away and leave our state,
This dim vast vale of tears, vacant and desolate?
    Ask why the sunlight not for ever
    Weaves rainbows o'er yon mountain river,
Why aught should fail and fade that once is shown;   20
    Why fear and dream and death and birth
    Cast on the daylight of this earth
    Such gloom, why man has such a scope
For love and hate, despondency and hope?

III

No voice from some sublimer world hath ever
  To sage or poet these responses given:
  Therefore the names of Demon, Ghost, and Heaven,
Remain the records of their vain endeavour:
Frail spells, whose uttered charm might not avail to sever,
    From all we hear and all we see,   30
    Doubt, chance, and mutability.
Thy light alone, like mist o'er mountains driven,
    Or music by the night wind sent
    Thro' strings of some still instrument,
    Or moonlight on a midnight stream,
Gives grace and truth to life's unquiet dream.

IV

Love, Hope, and Self-esteem, like clouds, depart
  And come, for some uncertain moments lent.
  Man were immortal and omnipotent,
Didst thou, unknown and awful as thou art,   40
Keep with thy glorious train firm state within his heart.
    Thou messenger of sympathies
    That wax and wane in lovers' eyes;
Thou, that to human thought art nourishment,
    Like darkness to a dying flame!
    Depart not as thy shadow came:
    Depart not, lest the grave should be,
Like life and fear, a dark reality.

V

While yet a boy I sought for ghosts, and sped
  Thro' many a listening chamber, cave and ruin,   50
  And starlight wood, with fearful steps pursuing
Hopes of high talk with the departed dead.
I called on poisonous names with which our youth is fed:
    I was not heard: I saw them not:
    When musing deeply on the lot
Of life, at that sweet time when winds are wooing
    All vital things that wake to bring
    News of birds and blossoming,
    Sudden, thy shadow fell on me;
I shrieked, and clasped my hands in ecstacy!   60

VI

I vowed that I would dedicate my powers
 To thee and thine: have I not kept the vow?
 With beating heart and streaming eyes, even now
I call the phantoms of a thousand hours
Each from his voiceless grave: they have in visioned bowers
  Of studious zeal or love's delight
  Outwatched with me the envious night:
They know that never joy illumed my brow,
  Unlinked with hope that thou wouldst free
  This world from its dark slavery,   70
  That thou, O awful LOVELINESS,
Wouldst give whate'er these words cannot express.

VII

The day becomes more solemn and serene
  When noon is past: there is a harmony
  In autumn, and a lustre in its sky,
Which thro' the summer is not heard or seen,
As if it could not be, as if it had not been!
  Thus let thy power, which like the truth
  Of nature on my passive youth
Descended, to my onward life supply   80
  Its calm, to one who worships thee,
  And every form containing thee,
  Whom, SPIRIT fair, thy spells did bind
To fear himself, and love all human kind.

ALFRED, LORD TENNYSON   from *In Memoriam*

LIV

Oh yet we trust that somehow good
  Will be the final goal of ill,
  To pangs of nature, sins of will,
Defects of doubt, and taints of blood;

That nothing walks with aimless feet;
  That not one life shall be destroyed,
  Or cast as rubbish to the void,
When God hath made the pile complete;

That not a worm is cloven in vain;
   That not a moth with vain desire   10
   Is shriveled in a fruitless fire,
Or but subserves another's gain.

Behold, we know not anything;
   I can but trust that good shall fall
   At last—far off—at last, to all,
And every winter change to spring.

So runs my dream: but what am I?
   An infant crying in the night:
   An infant crying for the light:
And with no language but a cry.   20

LV

The wish, that of the living whole
   No life may fail beyond the grave,
   Derives it not from what we have
The likest God within the soul?

Are God and Nature then at strife,
   That Nature lends such evil dreams?
   So careful of the type she seems,
So careless of the single life;

That I, considering everywhere
   Her secret meaning in her deeds,   10
   And finding that of fifty seeds
She often brings but one to bear,

I falter where I firmly trod,
   And falling with my weight of cares
   Upon the great world's altar-stairs
That slope thro' darkness up to God,

I stretch lame hands of faith, and grope,
   And gather dust and chaff, and call
   To what I feel is Lord of all,
And faintly trust the larger hope.   20

LVI

"So careful of the type?" but no.
  From scarpèd cliff and quarried stone
  She cries, "A thousand types are gone:
I care for nothing, all shall go.

"Thou makest thine appeal to me:
  I bring to life, I bring to death:
  The spirit does but mean the breath:
I know no more." And he, shall he,

Man, her last work, who seem'd so fair,
  Such splendid purpose in his eyes,   10
  Who roll'd the psalm to wintry skies,
Who built him fanes of fruitless prayer,

Who trusted God was love indeed
  And love Creation's final law—
  Tho' Nature, red in tooth and claw
With ravine, shriek'd against his creed—

Who loved, who suffer'd countless ills,
  Who battled for the True, the Just,
  Be blown about the desert dust,
Or seal'd within the iron hills?   20

No more? A monster then, a dream,
  A discord. Dragons of the prime,
  That tare each other in their slime,
Were mellow music match'd with him.

O life as futile, then, as frail!
  O for thy voice to soothe and bless!
  What hope of answer, or redress?
Behind the veil, behind the veil.

RUPERT BROOKE   *Heaven*

Fish (fly-replete, in depth of June,
Dawdling away their wat'ry noon)
Ponder deep wisdom, dark or clear,

Each secret fishy hope or fear.
Fish say, they have their Stream and Pond;
But is there anything Beyond?
This life cannot be All, they swear,
For how unpleasant, if it were!
One may not doubt that, somehow, Good
Shall come of Water and of Mud;   10
And, sure, the reverent eye must see
A purpose in Liquidity.
We darkly know, by Faith we cry,
The future is not Wholly Dry.
Mud unto mud!—Death eddies near—
Not here the appointed End, not here!
But somewhere, beyond Space and Time,
Is wetter water, slimier slime!
And there (they trust) there swimmeth One
Who swam ere rivers were begun,   20
Immense, of fishy form and mind,
Squamous, omnipotent, and kind;
And under that Almighty Fin,
The littlest fish may enter in.
Oh! never fly conceals a hook,
Fish say, in the Eternal Brook,
But more than mundane weeds are there,
And mud, celestially fair;
Fat caterpillars drift around,
And Paradisal grubs are found;   30
Unfading moths, immortal flies,
And the worm that never dies.
And in that Heaven of all their wish,
There shall be no more land, say fish.

WALLACE STEVENS   *Sunday Morning*

I

Complacencies of the peignoir, and late
Coffee and oranges in a sunny chair,
And the green freedom of a cockatoo
Upon a rug mingle to dissipate
The holy hush of ancient sacrifice.
She dreams a little, and she feels the dark
Encroachment of that old catastrophe,

As a calm darkness among water-lights.
The pungent oranges and bright, green wings
Seem things in some procession of the dead,   10
Winding across wide water, without sound.
The day is like wide water, without sound,
Stilled for the passing of her dreaming feet
Over the seas, to silent Palestine,
Dominion of the blood and sepulchre.

II

Why should she give her bounty to the dead?
What is divinity if it can come
Only in silent shadows and in dreams?
Shall she not find in comforts of the sun,
In pungent fruit and bright, green wings, or else   20
In any balm or beauty of the earth,
Things to be cherished like the thought of heaven?
Divinity must live within herself:
Passions of rain, or moods in falling snow;
Grievings in loneliness, or unsubdued
Elations when the forest blooms; gusty
Emotions on wet roads on autumn nights;
All pleasures and all pains, remembering
The bough of summer and the winter branch.
These are the measures destined for her soul.   30

III

Jove in the clouds had his inhuman birth.
No mother suckled him, no sweet land gave
Large-mannered motions to his mythy mind.
He moved among us, as a muttering king,
Magnificent, would move among his hinds,
Until our blood, commingling, virginal,
With heaven, brought such requital to desire
The very hinds discerned it, in a star.
Shall our blood fail? Or shall it come to be
The blood of paradise? And shall the earth   40
Seem all of paradise that we shall know?
The sky will be much friendlier then than now,
A part of labor and a part of pain,
And next in glory to enduring love,
Not this dividing and indifferent blue.

IV

She says, "I am content when wakened birds,
Before they fly, test the reality
Of misty fields, by their sweet questionings;
But when the birds are gone, and their warm fields
Return no more, where, then, is paradise?"   50
There is not any haunt of prophecy,
Nor any old chimera of the grave,
Neither the golden underground, nor isle
Melodious, where spirits gat them home,
Nor visionary south, nor cloudy palm
Remote on heaven's hill, that has endured
As April's green endures; or will endure
Like her remembrance of awakened birds,
Or her desire for June and evening, tipped
By the consummation of the swallow's wings.   60

V

She says, "But in contentment I still feel
The need of some imperishable bliss."
Death is the mother of beauty; hence from her,
Alone, shall come fulfilment to our dreams
And our desires. Although she strews the leaves
Of sure obliteration on our paths,
The path sick sorrow took, the many paths
Where triumph rang its brassy phrase, or love
Whispered a little out of tenderness,
She makes the willow shiver in the sun   70
For maidens who were wont to sit and gaze
Upon the grass, relinquished to their feet.
She causes boys to pile new plums and pears
On disregarded plate. The maidens taste
And stray impassioned in the littering leaves.

VI

Is there no change of death in paradise?
Does ripe fruit never fall? Or do the boughs
Hang always heavy in that perfect sky,
Unchanging, yet so like our perishing earth,
With rivers like our own that seek for seas   80
They never find, the same receding shores
That never touch with inarticulate pang?

Why set the pear upon those river-banks
Or spice the shores with odors of the plum?
Alas, that they should wear our colors there,
The silken weavings of our afternoons,
And pick the strings of our insipid lutes!
Death is the mother of beauty, mystical,
Within whose burning bosom we devise
Our earthly mothers waiting, sleeplessly.   90

VII

Supple and turbulent, a ring of men
Shall chant in orgy on a summer morn
Their boisterous devotion to the sun,
Not as a god, but as a god might be,
Naked among them, like a savage source.
Their chant shall be a chant of paradise,
Out of their blood, returning to the sky;
And in their chant shall enter, voice by voice,
The windy lake wherein their lord delights,
The trees, like serafin, and echoing hills,   100
That choir among themselves long afterward.
They shall know well the heavenly fellowship
Of men that perish and of summer morn.
And whence they came and whither they shall go
The dew upon their feet shall manifest.

VIII

She hears, upon that water without sound,
A voice that cries, "The tomb in Palestine
Is not the porch of spirits lingering.
It is the grave of Jesus, where he lay."
We live in an old chaos of the sun,   110
Or old dependency of day and night,
Or island solitude, unsponsored, free,
Of that wide water, inescapable.
Deer walk upon our mountains, and the quail
Whistle about us their spontaneous cries;
Sweet berries ripen in the wilderness;
And, in the isolation of the sky,
At evening, casual flocks of pigeons make
Ambiguous undulations as they sink,
Downward to darkness, on extended wings.   120

X. J. KENNEDY   *Nothing in Heaven functions as it ought*

Nothing in Heaven functions as it ought:
Peter's bifocals, blindly sat on, crack;
His gates lurch with the cackle of a cock,
Not turn with a hush of gold as Milton had thought;
Gangs of the slaughtered innocents keep huffing
The nimbus off the Venerable Bede
Like that of an old dandelion gone to seed;
And the beatific choir keep breaking up, coughing.

But Hell, sleek Hell hath no freewheeling part:
None takes his own sweet time, none quickens pace.   10
Ask anyone, How come you here, poor heart?—
And he will slot a quarter through his face,
You'll hear an instant click, a tear will start
Imprinted with an abstract of his case.

II

Metaphysical Poetry

Intellect and wit are not the exclusive property of the metaphysical poet, but they are inseparable from his work. Successful metaphysical verse, indeed, so interweaves these qualities with its emotional effects as to make clearer than any other mode of poetry the tremendous importance of thought in poetic achievement. Perhaps the best definition or description of metaphysical wit is still that of the great eighteenth-century critic, Samuel Johnson. "Wit," wrote Johnson in his *Life of Cowley*, "may be more rigorously and philosophically considered as a kind of *discordia concors*; a combination of dissimilar images, or discovery of occult resemblances in things apparently unlike."

Two poems by John Donne—*The Sun Rising* and *Good Friday, 1613. Riding Westward*—will illustrate the "development by rapid association of thought" [1] and the mature, analytical, and complex personality that characterize this poetry at its best. Donne is its classic representative—a man whose instinct compelled him to bring the whole of experience into his verse and to choose the most direct and, for his learned and fantastic mind, the most natural form of expression. (Donne was roughly of the same generation as Shakespeare, Ben Jonson, and the dramatists of the Mermaid Tavern, but he was not, like them, a man of the people, the son of a yeoman or a bricklayer, but a representative of the gentry. He was Catholic by birth, educated at the university, trained for the law and the Church, and closely attached to the Court.) He is colloquial, elevated, slangy, rhetorical, erudite, familiar—all in the same brief poem; and he takes his language from the court and the camp, from the jargon of the law, from the study, and from the marketplace.

This curious combination of qualities, it is interesting to note, can be found alike in his youthful "profane" love poems and in the passionate religious poems of his later life. This can be made clear by a detailed examination of a characteristic example of each group. Here is one of the early poems.

John Donne *The Sun Rising*

> Busy old fool, unruly Sun,
> Why dost thou thus,

---

[1] T. S. Eliot, "The Metaphysical Poets." (*Selected Essays*)

Through windows, and through curtains, call on us?
Must to thy motions lovers' seasons run?
　　Saucy pedantic wretch, go chide
　　Late school-boys and sour prentices,
　Go tell court-huntsmen that the king will ride,
　Call country ants to harvest offices;
Love, all alike, no season knows nor clime,
Nor hours, days, months, which are the rags of time.　　　　10

　　　Thy beams so reverend and strong
　　　Why shouldst thou think?
I could eclipse and cloud them with a wink,
But that I would not lose her sight so long.
　　If her eyes have not blinded thine,
　　Look, and to-morrow late tell me,
　Whether both th' Indias of spice and mine
　Be where thou left'st them, or lie here with me.
Ask for those kings whom thou saw'st yesterday,
And thou shalt hear, "All here in one bed lay."　　　　20

　　　She's all states, and all princes I;
　　　Nothing else is;
Princes do but play us; compared to this,
All honour's mimic, all wealth alchemy.
　　Thou, Sun, art half as happy as we,
　　In that the world's contracted thus;
　Thine age asks ease, and since thy duties be
　To warm the world, that's done in warming us.
Shine here to us, and thou art everywhere;
This bed thy centre is, these walls thy sphere.　　　　30

The Sun Rising is, in the first place, intended to be an amusing, witty, "clever" poem. It is light verse, but it is also, as we shall see, intensely serious—a good demonstration of the fact that seriousness has nothing to do with solemnity and can be accompanied by a good deal of levity. The poem, of course, is addressed to a somewhat sophisticated audience—sophisticated not so much with respect to manners and morals as with respect to literary convention. The poet is reacting against the artificiality and absurdity of the fashionable love poetry of courtly chivalry in which the conceit of the beloved's eyes outshining the sun had long become a tedious cliché. Donne laughs at the hyperboles (the fantastic exaggerations) of the courtly poetry by pretending to accept them. He piles hyperbole on hyperbole and praises his mistress in the most extravagant manner.

But the poem is not intended to be merely literary satire or criticism.

It is a genuine and deeply felt expression of the poet's sense of the beauty and perfection of his loved one. Its final purpose is to express the poet's sense of happiness and completeness in the possession of his mistress. *She* is so all-perfect, all-lovely, all-complete that she, and she alone, makes the fantastic hyperboles of the courtly poets sober truth.

From the first line we must be aware that the *tone* of the poem and the changes and developments of the tone are of the first importance. The poem begins with a ranting, swashbuckling, arrogant address to the sun. Like many of Donne's poems this one begins suddenly, with a sharp, surprising colloquial exclamation:

> Busy old fool, unruly Sun. . . .

Why this tone? And why the contempt so harshly expressed all through this first stanza—"saucy pedantic wretch," "court-huntsmen," "country ants"?

The reason is that in the happy and complete possession of his mistress the poet feels that he possesses, rules, and controls the whole world, and therefore is superior to the sun itself. The lover complaining against the sun at morning for ending a night of happiness was, of course, one of the traditional themes of courtly love poetry, but Donne treats it familiarly, colloquially, irreverently. One of the most concentrated paradoxes of the poem is the application in the first line of the epithet "unruly" to the sun. The sun is actually the standard of order, regulation, and law; but order, rule, and law in the field of nature, of society, of business, and of the court threaten the interests and pleasures of love. So the poet-lover rails against them all. Love transcends time, and the lovers cannot help regarding the sun, which makes time, as a busybody to be scorned and triumphed over.

In the second stanza the poet, still ranting and swaggering, proceeds to develop the thought of the present good fortune that makes him superior to the world-dominating sun. And he does so in terms that also manage to pay exquisite compliments to his mistress. The girl sums up in herself all the riches and perfume of the Orient and the West; she is the glory of the whole world, concentrated and epitomized. Also, the setting of the scene, only implied in the first stanza, is now made more specific.

One of the strangest and most powerful effects of the poem is the progressive softening of the tone until the outrageous and amusing hyperboles of the opening stanza and the air of extravagant enthusiasm with which they are delivered modulate, in the final stanza, into a hushed and serious (though still fantastic and half-playful) expression of the happiness and trust of a completely satisfied devotion.

The Sun Rising is characteristic of Donne's youthful secular love poetry. It is lighter in texture but not essentially different in method from the deeply felt and sometimes terror-stricken religious poems of his maturity and old age. In fact, if we compare it with *Good Friday, 1613,* a poem of greater complexity and scope written after Donne was forty, we find some startling parallels. The earlier poem proudly mocks the sun and the principle of universal order it represents. It argues satirically against the imperious demands that time and the powers that be make upon the happy, self-contained world of the two lovers. *Good Friday, 1613,* on the other hand, is humble and pious if even more passionate. In it the image of the sun is approached with absolute awe and respect. Christ, the *son* of God, is pictured as the *sun* (the pun is deliberate on Donne's part) around which the poet's soul, in the figure of a heavenly "sphere," should properly revolve. A deeply serious though wittily imaginative argument, ending in a prayer, reverses the relation between the speaker and the sun that we remember in *The Sun Rising.* The poems are indeed unlike in their literal themes and in their feeling toward the central images of universal authority, but the similarity in technique should be apparent:

JOHN DONNE *Good Friday, 1613. Riding Westward*

> Let man's soul be a sphere, and then in this
> The intelligence that moves, devotion is;
> And as the other spheres, by being grown
> Subject to foreign motion, lose their own,
> And being by others hurried every day,
> Scarce in a year their natural form obey:
> Pleasure or business so, our souls admit
> For their first mover, and are whirled by it.
> Hence is 't that I am carried towards the west
> This day, when my soul's form bends towards the east.   10
> There I should see a sun, by rising set,
> And by that setting, endless day beget;
> But that Christ on this cross did rise and fall,
> Sin had eternally benighted all.
> Yet dare I'almost be glad I do not see
> That spectacle of too much weight for me.
> Who sees God's face, that is self life, must die;
> What a death were it then to see God die!
> It made his own lieutenant, nature, shrink;
> It made his footstool crack, and the sun wink.   20
> Could I behold those hands which span the poles
> And tune all spheres at once, pierced with those holes?
> Could I behold that endless height, which is
> Zenith to us and our antipodes,
> Humbled below us? or that blood which is

The seat of all our souls, if not of his,
Made dirt of dust, or that flesh which was worn
By God for his apparel, ragg'd and torn?
If on these things I durst not look, durst I
Upon his miserable mother cast mine eye,   30
Who was God's partner here, and furnished thus
Half of that sacrifice which ransomed us?
Though these things, as I ride, be from mine eye,
They are present yet unto my memory,
For that looks towards them; and thou look'st towards me,
O Savior, as thou hang'st upon the tree;
I turn my back to thee but to receive
Corrections, till thy mercies bid thee leave.
Oh, think me worth thine anger, punish me,
Burn off my rusts, and my deformity;   40
Restore thine image, so much, by thy grace,
That thou mayst know me, and I'll turn my face.

A brief summary of the progress of thought in this poem should be useful. Good Friday is part of Holy Week, the week preceding Easter Sunday.
On Good Friday the Crucifixion of Christ is commemorated, and on
Easter His Resurrection is celebrated. The poet is thinking in a vein
appropriate to the day that makes the most solemn religious symbol of the
Christian faith: the sacrifice of Jesus. At the same time, he very strikingly
applies the language of traditional science and philosophy to this contemplation. Hence the special terms and concepts used in this poem: the
medieval concept of an "intelligence," for instance—a guiding spirit or
angel who governs the laws by which heavenly bodies move; the Aristotelian
terms "form" (the essential nature of a thing) and "first mover" (a
philosophical, secular phrase for denoting the creative aspect of God); or
the notion, from medieval physiology, of blood as the vehicle uniting the
soul to the body—hence, in line 26, "the seat of all our souls." Donne's
beginning is at once "scientific" and religious: "Let man's soul," he says,
"be a sphere"—almost the language of a geometry text book—and its
guiding spirit be devotion.

But the heavenly bodies all have distorted orbits because of the influence
of the motions of other spheres; and so it is with the soul, which is often
"whirled" from its true course by business or pleasure instead of holding
to it through piety. On Good Friday, the soul's whole attention should be
bent eastward—that is, toward the place where the Crucifixion occurred.
Instead, the less essential concerns that take up most of our time are bearing
it away from contemplation of divine sacrifice—"westward." Besides, the
poet admits, he is afraid of such contemplation. It would be a terrible thing
to see the living God directly, and therefore even more terrible to gaze upon
Him dying, humbled, and tortured, and upon the suffering of Mary,

His mother. The poet does, however, even as he is being borne away from direct contact with these tragic events, remember them and pray for Christ's grace, so that he may be purged of his sins and hence be enabled to hope for final salvation. Thus, he implies, the influence of divine mercy may prove stronger than that of the secular world and help his weak soul to find its proper orbit once more.

The movement of thought in *Good Friday*, then, has been projected by a series of images: the image of the moving of spheres around a magnetic center, and of contrary forces at work on them; the image of Jesus on the cross—first pictured as a rising and setting sun, and later as a vast paradox containing infinite space and yet subject to infinite humbling and reduction; the image of Mary; and finally, the image of the speaker in his own person appealing directly to Christ. Paralleling this movement, the tone of the language develops from that of intellectual and scientific reasoning (lines 1–10) to one of earnest prayer at the end. In between, the subtle reasoner of the opening lines has become the factual observer (11–14), the humble and awestruck apologist for himself (15–32), the object of God's attention (35–36) and the humble penitent (37–38). The statement has grown increasingly personal, as though with the development of his poetic theme the author had actually come closer to God and God become more particularly attentive to him, until he is emboldened to make the final appeal of the closing couplet.

The Metaphysical poets have had a lasting influence, reflected in the writings of Emerson, Thoreau, and Emily Dickinson in the last century and of Yeats, Eliot, and many others in this one. While the importance of a mature and informed intelligence in poetry should be obvious, this principle is not always understood. In poetry as in life, intelligence is an active force, one that is comparable to emotional and physical vitality, and is essential to the pursuit of the fullest human awareness. Intelligence understood in this way is anything but dry and pedantic, and it enters poetry as inevitably as it enters any other human activity. Men and women cannot help thinking about what they do, however they may feel themselves driven by feeling and passion, and this is not only a matter of being logical but of observing, considering, and meditating in the very midst of experience and afterward.

We have given special attention to Metaphysical poetry because of its highly developed fusion of intellect and emotion. A metaphysical poet— like Donne or Marvell in the seventeenth century and Eliot or Empson in the twentieth—is usually a complex personality, widely and deeply read in philosophy, science, and the political, psychological, and religious ideas current in his time. He approaches his subject with wit and subtlety, and with an engaged responsibility. At best, his is an intelligence that cares and feels as well as thinks.

There are, however, many romantic, impressionistic, and even surrealist poems that show or suggest a considerable pressure of thought without bringing the motions of the mind to the surface. Dylan Thomas's *The force that through the green fuse drives the flower* is one such poem.

DYLAN THOMAS *The force that through the green fuse drives the flower*

> The force that through the green fuse drives the flower
> Drives my green age; that blasts the roots of trees
> Is my destroyer.
> And I am dumb to tell the crooked rose
> My youth is bent by the same wintry fever.
>
> The force that drives the water through the rocks
> Drives my red blood; that dries the mouthing streams
> Turns mine to wax.
> And I am dumb to mouth unto my veins
> How at the mountain spring the same mouth sucks.   10
>
> The hand that whirls the water in the pool
> Stirs the quicksand; that ropes the blowing wind
> Hauls my shroud sail.
> And I am dumb to tell the hanging man
> How of my clay is made the hangman's lime.
>
> The lips of time leech to the fountain head;
> Love drips and gathers, but the fallen blood
> Shall calm her sores.
> And I am dumb to tell a weather's wind
> How time has ticked a heaven round the stars.   20
>
> And I am dumb to tell the lover's tomb
> How at my sheet goes the same crooked worm.

Here the poet keeps asserting over and over again his inability to communicate with the beings and objects of nonhuman nature. The mind within the poem faces the anguished shock of an intense realization of his identity in birth, growth, and death with flower, water, and star. He is young, in his "green age"; the life-force explodes him into flowering growth, and he knows that it will eventually leave him blasted and destroyed as it does the flowers and trees. But other, inorganic forces also, the second stanza says, drive his blood—and will dry it eventually—as they do the mountain spring.

This thought is carried a step further in the third stanza, where whirlpools, quicksand, and dangerous winds are seen as images of the way that natural processes control the doomed whirling of the speaker through life and into death. Here the language grows more involved than before, for the poet wishes to associate the "roping" of the wind with the tackle used in sailing and with the hangman's noose. (The image of a "shroud sail" combines the nautical meaning of "shroud"—certain ropes used to support the mast—with its other meaning of "winding sheet." It suggests the fantastic notion of the human body as a sailing ship bound for death.) The fourth stanza, the most demanding of all, presents an elaborate sexual image of the cosmos. "The lips of time"—the whole realm of physical existence within time and subject to our consciousness—offer themselves to impregnation from a divine phallic "fountainhead" outside our knowledge. From this imagined intercourse that "calms our sores" and reconciles us to death comes our conception of eternity—"heaven." Then, in the closing couplet, this whole primitive notion of a universal sexual principle enabling us to transcend death and time collapses. The final image that identifies the sheets of the marriage bed with the winding sheet in which the dead are wrapped and the grave worm with the lover's phallus is a powerful and concentrated one—a metaphysical conceit that conforms exactly to the definition by Dr. Johnson quoted on page 306.

The poet's thoughts are inseparable from his rage of realization, his frustration at not being able to share his insights with subhuman nature and with the dead. The poem, with its highly patterned stanzas and effective half-rhymes and refrain, is passionately incantatory, and its thoughts are utterances in a desperate yet inspired prayer. In these respects, despite the strained associations in some of the imagery, it is far from being a poem in the Metaphysical tradition. But there is obviously a good deal of ingenuity, and wit of a very serious kind in those associations.

Poems: Metaphysical Poetry

The following poems show something of the variety of tone and method found in Metaphysical poetry. Imaginative comparisons, concentrated or expanded and developed, are used in surprising and fantastic ways to express an intense, unified emotional and intellectual excitement.

In the two opening poems, Donne's *The Apparition* and Milton's *On His Deceased Wife,* love and death are contemplated, in the first with a kind of cold fury and in the second with tenderness, humility, and a truly tragic despair. The dramatic concentration of Milton's closing line gains immensely in power when we realize that the blind poet had never seen his wife except in imagination; when her ghost withdrew as he awoke from his happy dream, he was returned to the double darkness of his blindness and her absence. In Donne's poem the situation is reversed. The poet imagines *himself* dead—an apparition who will return to curse his faithless and scornful mistress. An active sense of real sensuous experience is conveyed by both poems, enhanced in Milton by the Classical allusions and Christian belief so central to his thinking.

The intellectual and moral background of a Metaphysical poem is, because of its full deployment of a mature and subtle vocabulary, unmistakable even when not explicitly stated. Thus, in Andrew Marvell's picture of a lovely aristocratic little girl in a country garden, we have a portrait painted with sophisticated and courtly gallantry. But then at the very end an almost impatient tone of harsh foreboding brings in the eternal theme of the fragility of beauty and innocence. The courtly tone of deference with just the slightest hint of irony is also found in Yeats's sharp and gently mocking rebuke to the proud young beauty, Anne Gregory. The wit of the poem lies in the fact that the rebuke turns in the final stanza into a magnificent compliment. Although all of these poems have to do with very human themes and subjects, their complex awareness and refusal to oversimplify reality illustrate the appeal of Metaphysical poetry to an adult intelligence. It is for this reason that Donne's *The Ecstasy* may be thought of as the Metaphysical poem *par excellence.* It takes a normal human situation—two people who have fallen in love and feel that they have experienced a union of souls but have not yet made love physically—and explores it with all the combined awareness, playfulness, philosophical clarity, and strong desire of a mature and cultivated personality.

The next four poems after these, beginning with Marvell's *The Garden,* deal with philosophical and religious matters: Marvell's sense of bliss in the garden, conceived as an image of how Eden must once have been; Shakespeare's contemplation of the tremendous risks of power and of seeming to achieve a state approaching ideal character or beauty; Jonson's comparable contemplation of how all thought of God's perfection leads him into a state of humility; and Donne's remarkably passionate and personal thoughts on the paradoxical actual condition of the Christian believer. The five modern poems that end the section all play, with varying intensity, on the human desire to transcend our mortal limits. Eliot is wryly ironic about himself and his seventeenth-century Metaphysical predecessors. Graves and Auden are more good-humoredly tolerant of mankind's limitations, and Empson is deeply absorbed in the mind's vast possibilities despite the sense of loneliness and of surrounding darkness he suggests. Wilbur attempts a difficult reconciliation of two opposed moods—joy at the vision of the morning world and depression over the letdown that every day brings because of the soul's "bitter love" of the real world.

JOHN DONNE   *The Apparition*

When by thy scorn, O murd'ress, I am dead,
And that thou think'st thee free
From all solicitation from me,
Then shall my ghost come to thy bed,
And thee, feign'd vestal, in worse arms shall see:
Then thy sick taper will begin to wink,
And he, whose thou art then, being tir'd before,
Will, if thou stir, or pinch to wake him, think
      Thou call'st for more,
And in false sleep, will from thee shrink: 10
And then, poor aspen wretch, neglected thou
Bath'd in a cold quicksilver sweat wilt lie
      A verier ghost than I.
What I will say, I will not tell thee now,
Lest that preserve thee; and since my love is spent,
I'd rather thou shouldst painfully repent,
Than by my threatenings rest still innocent.

JOHN MILTON   *On His Deceased Wife*

Methought I saw my late espoused Saint
  Brought to me like Alcestis from the grave,
  Whom Jove's great Son to her glad Husband gave,
  Rescu'd from death by force though pale and faint.
Mine as whom washt from spot of child-bed taint,
  Purification in the old Law did save,
  And such, as yet once more I trust to have
  Full sight of her in Heaven without restraint,
Came vested all in white, pure as her mind:
  Her face was veil'd; yet to my fancied sight,   10
  Love, sweetness, goodness, in her person shin'd

So clear, as in no face with more delight.
   But O as to embrace me she enclin'd
   I wak'd, she fled, and day brought back my night.

ANDREW MARVELL   *The Picture of Little T. C. in a
Prospect of Flowers*

See with what simplicity
This nymph begins her golden days!
In the green grass she loves to lie,
And there with her fair aspect tames
The wilder flowers, and gives them names,
But only with the roses plays,
      And them does tell
What colour best becomes them, and what smell.

Who can foretell for what high cause
This darling of the gods was born?   10
Yet this is she whose chaster laws
The wanton Love shall one day fear,
And, under her command severe,
See his bow broke and ensigns torn.
      Happy, who can
Appease this virtuous enemy of man!

O then let me in time compound
And parley with those conquering eyes,
Ere they have tried their force to wound;
Ere with their glancing wheels they drive   20
In triumph over hearts that strive,
And them that yield but more despise:
      Let me be laid
Where I may see thy glories from some shade.

Meantime, whilst every verdant thing
Itself does at thy beauty charm,
Reform the errors of the Spring:
Make that the tulips may have share
Of sweetness, seeing they are fair;
And roses of their thorns disarm;   30
      But most procure
That violets may a longer age endure.

But O, young beauty of the woods,
Whom nature courts with fruits and flowers,
Gather the flowers, but spare the buds,
Lest Flora, angry at thy crime
To kill her infants in their prime,
Do quickly make th' example yours;
      And, ere we see,
Nip in the blossom all our hopes and thee.   40

WILLIAM BUTLER YEATS   *For Anne Gregory*

"Never shall a young man,
Thrown into despair
By those great honey-coloured
Ramparts at your ear,
Love you for yourself alone
And not your yellow hair."

"But I can get a hair-dye
And set such colour there,
Brown, or black, or carrot,
That young men in despair   10
May love me for myself alone
And not my yellow hair."

"I heard an old religious man
But yesternight declare
That he had found a text to prove
That only God, my dear,
Could love you for yourself alone
And not your yellow hair."

JOHN DONNE   *The Ecstasy*

Where, like a pillow on a bed,
  A pregnant bank swell'd up, to rest
The violet's reclining head,
  Sat we two, one another's best.

Our hands were firmly cemented
  With a fast balm, which thence did spring;
Our eye-beams twisted, and did thread
  Our eyes upon one double string;

So t' entergraft our hands, as yet
  Was all the means to make us one;   10
And pictures in our eyes to get
  Was all our propagation.

As, 'twixt two equal armies, Fate
  Suspends uncertain victory,
Our souls (which to advance their state
  Were gone out) hung 'twixt her, and me.

And whilst our souls negotiate there,
  We like sepulchral statues lay;
All day, the same our postures were,
  And we said nothing, all the day.   20

If any, so by love refin'd,
  That he soul's language understood,
And by good love were grown all mind,
  Within convenient distance stood,

He (though he knew not which soul spake,
  Because both meant, both spake the same)
Might thence a new concoction take,
  And part far purer than he came.

This ecstasy doth unperplex
  (We said) and tell us what we love;   30
We see by this, it was not sex;
  We see, we saw not what did move:

But as all several souls contain
  Mixture of things, they know not what,
Love, these mix'd souls, doth mix again,
  And makes both one, each this and that.

A single violet transplant,
  The strength, the colour, and the size
(All which before was poor and scant)
  Redoubles still, and multiplies.   40

When love with one another so
   Interinanimates two souls,
That abler soul, which thence doth flow,
   Defects of loneliness controls.

We then, who are this new soul, know,
   Of what we are compos'd, and made,
For th'atomies of which we grow,
   Are souls, whom no change can invade.

But, O alas! so long, so far
   Our bodies why do we forbear?   50
They are ours, though they are not we; we are
   Th'intelligences, they the spheres.

We owe them thanks, because they thus
   Did us, to us, at first convey,
Yielded their forces, sense, to us,
   Nor are dross to us, but allay.

On man heaven's influence works not so,
   But that it first imprints the air;
For soul into the soul may flow,
   Though it to body first repair.   60

As our blood labours to beget
   Spirits, as like souls as it can,
Because such fingers need to knit
   That subtle knot, which makes us man;

So must pure lovers' souls descend
   T' affections, and to faculties,
Which sense may reach and apprehend,
   Else a great prince in prison lies.

To'our bodies turn we then, that so
   Weak men on love reveal'd may look;   70
Love's mysteries in souls do grow,
   But yet the body is his book.

And if some lover, such as we,
   Have heard this dialogue of one,
Let him still mark us, he shall see
   Small change when we're to bodies gone.

ANDREW MARVELL   *The Garden* [1]

How vainly men themselves amaze
To win the Palm, the Oak, or Bays;
And their uncessant Labours see
Crown'd from some single Herb or Tree,
Whose short and narrow-verged Shade
Does prudently their Toils upbraid;
While all Flow'rs and all Trees do close
To weave the Garlands of repose.

Fair quiet, have I found thee here,
And Innocence thy Sister dear!   10
Mistaken long; I sought you then
In busy Companies of Men.
Your sacred Plants, if here below,
Only among the Plants will grow.
Society is all but rude,
To this delicious Solitude.

No white nor red was ever seen
So am'rous as this lovely green.
Fond Lovers, cruel as their Flame,
Cut in these Trees their Mistress' name.   20
Little, Alas, they know, or heed,
How far these Beauties Hers exceed!
Fair Trees! where s'eer your barks I wound,
No Name shall but your own be found.

When we have run our Passion's heat,
Love hither makes his best retreat.
The *Gods*, that mortal Beauty chase,
Still in a Tree did end their race.
Apollo hunted *Daphne* so,
Only that She might Laurel grow.   30
And *Pan* did after *Syrinx* speed,
Not as a nymph, but for a Reed.

What wond'rous Life is this I lead!
Ripe Apples drop about my head;
The Luscious Clusters of the Vine

[1] See comment in Chapter One, Section I (pp. 2–3).

Upon my Mouth do crush their Wine;
The Nectarine, and curious Peach,
Into my hands themselves do reach;
Stumbling on Melons, as I pass,
Insnar'd with Flow'rs, I fall on Grass.   40

Meanwhile the Mind, from pleasure less,
Withdraws into its happiness:
The Mind, that Ocean where each kind
Does straight its own resemblance find;
Yet it creates, transcending these,
Far other Worlds, and other Seas;
Annihilating all that's made
To a green Thought in a green Shade.

Here at the Fountain's sliding foot,
Or at some Fruit-tree's mossy root,   50
Casting the Body's Vest aside,
My Soul into the boughs does glide:
There like a Bird it sits, and sings,
Then whets, and combs its silver Wings;
And, till prepar'd for longer flight,
Waves in its Plumes the various Light.

Such was that happy Garden-state,
While Man there walk'd without a Mate:
After a Place so pure, and sweet,
What other Help could yet be meet!   60
But 'twas beyond a Mortal's share
To wander solitary there:
Two Paradises 'twere in one
To live in Paradise alone.

How well the skilfull Gard'ner drew
Of flow'rs and herbs this Dial new;
Where from above the milder Sun
Does through a fragrant Zodiack run;
And, as it works, th'industrious Bee
Computes its time as well as we.   70
How could such sweet and wholesome Hours
Be reckon'd but with herbs and flow'rs!

WILLIAM SHAKESPEARE　*Sonnet XCIV*

They that have power to hurt, and will do none,
That do not do the thing they most do show,
Who, moving others, are themselves as stone,
Unmoved, cold, and to temptation slow:
They rightly do inherit heaven's graces,
And husband nature's riches from expense.
They are the Lords and owners of their faces;
Others, but stewards of their excellence.
The summer's flower is to the summer sweet
Though to itself it only live and die,　　　　　　　　　　10
But if that flower with base infection meet,
The basest weed outbraves his dignity:
　　　For sweetest things turn sourest by their deeds,
　　　Lilies that fester smell far worse then weeds.

BEN JONSON　*To Heaven*

Good, and great God, can I not think of thee,
　　But it must, straight, my melancholy be?
Is it interpreted in me disease,
　　That, laden with my sins, I seek for ease?
O, be thou witness, that the reins dost know,
　　And hearts of all, if I be sad for show,
And judge me after: if I dare pretend
　　To aught but grace, or aim at other end.
As thou art all, so be thou all to me,
　　First, midst, and last, converted one, and three;　　10
My faith, my hope, my love: and in this state,
　　My judge, my witness, and my advocate.
Where have I been this while exil'd from thee?
　　And whither rap'd, now thou but stoop'st to me?
Dwell, dwell here still: O, being every-where,
　　How can I doubt to find thee ever, here?
I know my state, both full of shame, and scorn,
　　Conceiv'd in sin, and unto labour born,
Standing with fear, and must with horror fall,
　　And destin'd unto judgement, after all.　　　　　　20
I feel my griefs too, and there scarce is ground,
　　Upon my flesh t'inflict another wound.

Yet dare I not complain, or wish for death
  With holy Paul, lest it be thought the breath
Of discontent; or that these prayers be
  For weariness of life, not love of thee.

JOHN DONNE   from *Holy Sonnets*

VII

At the round earth's imagin'd corners blow
Your trumpets, angels, and arise, arise
From death, you numberless infinities
Of souls, and to your scatter'd bodies go,
All whom the flood did, and fire shall o'erthrow,
All whom war, dearth, age, agues, tyrannies,
Despair, law, chance, hath slain, and you whose eyes
Shall behold God and never taste death's woe.
But let them sleep, Lord, and me mourn a space;
For, if above all these my sins abound,   10
'Tis late to ask abundance of Thy grace,
When we are there. Here on this lowly ground,
Teach me how to repent, for that's as good
As if Thou hadst seal'd my pardon with Thy blood.

X

Death, be not proud, though some have called thee
Mighty and dreadful, for, thou are not so;
For those whom thou think'st thou dost overthrow
Die not, poor Death, nor yet canst thou kill me.
From rest and sleep, which but thy pictures be,
Much pleasure, then from thee, much more must flow,
And soonest our best men with thee do go,
Rest of their bones, and soul's delivery.
Thou art slave to Fate, Chance, kings, and desperate men,
And dost with poison, war, and sickness dwell,   10
And poppy, or charms can make us sleep as well,
And better than thy stroke; why swell'st thou then?
One short sleep past, we wake eternally,
And Death shall be no more; Death, thou shalt die.

XIII

What if this present were the world's last night?
Mark in my heart, O Soul, where thou dost dwell,
The picture of Christ crucified, and tell

Whether that countenance can thee affright:
Tears in his eyes quench the amazing light,
Blood fills his frowns, which from his pierc'd head fell,
And can that tongue adjudge thee unto hell,
Which pray'd forgiveness for his foes' fierce spite?
No, no; but as in my idolatry
I said to all my profane mistresses,   10
Beauty, of pity, foulness only is
A sign of rigour: so I say to thee,
To wicked spirits are horrid shapes assign'd,
This beauteous form assures a piteous mind.

XIV

Batter my heart, three personed God; for you
As yet but knock, breathe, shine, and seek to mend;
That I may rise and stand, o'erthrow me and bend
Your force to break, blow, burn and make me new.
I, like an usurped town, to another due,
Labour to admit you, but Oh, to no end;
Reason, your viceroy in me, me should defend,
But is captived and proves weak or untrue.
Yet dearly I love you and would be loved fain,
But am betrothed unto your enemy: 10
Divorce me, untie or break that knot again,
Take me to you, imprison me, for I
Except you enthrall me, never shall be free,
Nor ever chaste, except you ravish me.

XVIII

Show me, dear Christ, thy Spouse so bright and clear.
What! is it She, which on the other shore
Goes richly painted? or which rob'd and tore
Laments and mourns in Germany and here?
Sleeps she a thousand, then peeps up one year?
Is she self truth and errs? now new, now outwore?
Doth she, and did she, and shall she evermore
On one, on seven, or on no hill appear?
Dwells she with us, or like adventuring knights
First travail we to seek and then make Love?   10
Betray, kind husband, thy spouse to our sights,
And let mine amorous soul court thy mild Dove,
Who is most true, and pleasing to thee, then
When she' is embrac'd and open to most men.

T. S. ELIOT Whispers of Immortality

Webster was much possessed by death
And saw the skull beneath the skin;
And breastless creatures under ground
Leaned backward with a lipless grin.

Daffodil bulbs instead of balls
Stared from the sockets of the eyes!
He knew that thought clings round dead limbs
Tightening its lusts and luxuries.

Donne, I suppose, was such another
Who found no substitute for sense,   10
To seize and clutch and penetrate;
Expert beyond experience,

He knew the anguish of the marrow
The ague of the skeleton;
No contact possible to flesh
Allayed the fever of the bone.

*   *   *

Grishkin is nice: her Russian eye
Is underlined for emphasis;
Uncorseted, her friendly bust
Gives promise of pneumatic bliss.   20

The couched Brazilian jaguar
Compels the scampering marmoset
With subtle effluence of cat;
Grishkin has a maisonette;

The sleek Brazilian jaguar
Does not in its arboreal gloom
Distil so rank a feline smell
As Grishkin in a drawing-room.

And even the Abstract Entities
Circumambulate her charm;   30
But our lot crawls between dry ribs
To keep our metaphysics warm.

ROBERT GRAVES   *The Thieves*

Lovers in the act dispense
With such meum-teum sense
As might warningly reveal
What they must not pick or steal,
And their nostrum is to say:
"I and you are both away."

After, when they disentwine
You from me and yours from mine,
Neither can be certain who
Was that I whose mine was you.   10
To the act again they go
More completely not to know.

Theft is theft and raid is raid
Though reciprocally made.
Lovers, the conclusion is,
Doubled sighs and jealousies
In a single heart that grieves
For lost honour among thieves.

WILLIAM EMPSON   *Legal Fiction*

Law makes long spokes of the short stakes of men.
Your well fenced out real estate of mind
No high flat of the nomad citizen
Looks over, or train leaves behind.

Your rights extend under and above your claim
Without bound; you own land in Heaven and Hell;
Your part of earth's surface and mass the same,
Of all cosmos' volume, and all stars as well.

Your rights reach down where all owners meet, in Hell's
Pointed exclusive conclave, at earth's centre   10
(Your spun farm's root still on that axis dwells);
And up, through galaxies, a growing sector.

You are nomad yet; the lighthouse beam you own
Flashes, like Lucifer, through the firmament.
Earth's axis varies; your dark central cone
Wavers, a candle's shadow, at the end.

W. H. Auden *In Praise of Limestone*

If it form the one landscape that we, the inconstant ones,
    Are consistently homesick for, this is chiefly
Because it dissolves in water. Mark these rounded slopes
    With their surface fragrance of thyme and, beneath,
A secret system of caves and conduits; hear the springs
    That spurt out everywhere with a chuckle,
Each filling a private pool for its fish and carving
    Its own little ravine whose cliffs entertain
The butterfly and the lizard; examine this region
    Of short distances and definite places: 10
What could be more like Mother or a fitter background
    For her son, the flirtatious male who lounges
Against a rock in the sunlight, never doubting
    That for all his faults he is loved; whose works are but
Extensions of his power to charm? From weathered outcrop
    To hill-top temple, from appearing waters to
Conspicuous fountains, from a wild to a formal vineyard,
    Are ingenious but short steps that a child's wish
To receive more attention than his brothers, whether
    By pleasing or teasing, can easily take.   20

Watch, then, the band of rivals as they climb up and down
    Their steep stone gennels in twos and threes, at times
Arm in arm, but never, thank God, in step; or engaged
    On the shady side of a square at midday in
Voluble discourse, knowing each other too well to think
    There are any important secrets, unable
To conceive a god whose temper-tantrums are moral
    And not to be pacified by a clever line
Or a good lay: for, accustomed to a stone that responds,
    They have never had to veil their faces in awe   30
Of a crater whose blazing fury could not be fixed;
    Adjusted to the local needs of valleys
Where everything can be touched or reached by walking,
    Their eyes have never looked into infinite space
Through the lattice-work of a nomad's comb; born lucky,
    Their legs have never encountered the fungi
And insects of the jungle, the monstrous forms and lives
    With which we have nothing, we like to hope, in common.
So, when one of them goes to the bad, the way his mind works
    Remains comprehensible: to become a pimp   40

Or deal in fake jewellery or ruin a fine tenor voice
   For effects that bring down the house, could happen to all
But the best and the worst of us . . .
                            That is why, I suppose,
   The best and worst never stayed here long but sought
Immoderate soils where the beauty was not so external,
   The light less public and the meaning of life
Something more than a mad camp. "Come!" cried the granite wastes,
   "How evasive is your humour, how accidental
Your kindest kiss, how permanent is death." (Saints-to-be
   Slipped away sighing.) "Come!" purred the clays and gravels.   50
"On our plains there is room for armies to drill; rivers
   Wait to be tamed and slaves to construct you a tomb
In the grand manner: soft as the earth is mankind and both
   Need to be altered." (Intendant Caesars rose and
Left, slamming the door.) But the really reckless were fetched
   By an older colder voice, the oceanic whisper:
"I am the solitude that asks and promises nothing;
   That is how I shall set you free. There is no love;
There are only the various envies, all of them sad."
   They were right, my dear, all those voices were right   60
And still are; this land is not the sweet home that it looks,
   Nor its peace the historical calm of a site
Where something was settled once and for all: A backward
   And dilapidated province, connected
To the big busy world by a tunnel, with a certain
   Seedy appeal, is that all it is now? Not quite:
It has a worldly duty which in spite of itself
   It does not neglect, but calls into question
All the Great Powers assume; it disturbs our rights. The poet,
   Admired for his earnest habit of calling   70
The sun the sun, his mind Puzzle, is made uneasy
   By these marble statues which so obviously doubt
His antimythological myth; and these gamins,
   Pursuing the scientist down the tiled colonnade
With such lively offers, rebuke his concern for Nature's
   Remotest aspects: I, too, am reproached, for what
And how much you know. Not to lose time, not to get caught,
   Not to be left behind, not, please! to resemble
The beasts who repeat themselves, or a thing like water
   Or stone whose conduct can be predicted, these   80
Are our Common Prayer, whose greatest comfort is music
   Which can be made anywhere, is invisible,

And does not smell. In so far as we have to look forward
　To death as a fact, no doubt we are right: But if
Sins can be forgiven, if bodies rise from the dead,
　These modifications of matter into
Innocent athletes and gesticulating fountains,
　Made solely for pleasure, make a further point:
The blessed will not care what angle they are regarded from,
　Having nothing to hide. Dear, I know nothing of   90
Either, but when I try to imagine a faultless love
　Or the life to come, what I hear is the murmur
Of underground streams, what I see is a limestone landscape.

Richard Wilbur *Love Calls Us to the Things
of This World*

　　The eyes open to a cry of pulleys,
And spirited from sleep, the astounded soul
Hangs for a moment bodiless and simple
As false dawn.
　　　　　　Outside the open window
The morning air is all awash with angels.

　　Some are in bed-sheets, some are in blouses,
Some are in smocks: but truly there they are.
Now they are rising together in calm swells
Of halcyon feeling, filling whatever they wear   10
With the deep joy of their impersonal breathing;

　　Now they are flying in place, conveying
The terrible speed of their omnipresence, moving
And staying like white water; and now of a sudden
They swoon down into so rapt a quiet
That nobody seems to be there.
　　　　　　　　The soul shrinks

　　From all that it is about to remember,
From the punctual rape of every blessèd day,
And cries,   20
　　　　"Oh, let there be nothing on earth but laundry,
Nothing but rosy hands in the rising steam
And clear dances done in the sight of heaven."

Yet, as the sun acknowledges
With a warm look the world's hunks and colors,
The soul descends once more in bitter love
To accept the waking body, saying now
In a changed voice as the man yawns and rises,

    "Bring them down from their ruddy gallows;
Let there be clean linen for the backs of thieves;   30
Let lovers go fresh and sweet to be undone,
And the heaviest nuns walk in a pure floating
Of dark habits,
                keeping their difficult balance."

III

Irony, Invective, and Satire

In examining the intellectual aspect of poetry, we have again and again emphasized the role of *wit*. Although in general usage this term is a technical one of some exactness, the word implies more than a heightened perceptiveness and mastery of language such as all good poets possess. Originally it meant intellectual power; gradually the meaning changed to something nearer intellectual *alertness*, with an ability to see unfamiliar connections between words and ideas in a manner often surprising and amusing. The surprise need not be stunning, the humor need not be hilarious; in fact, either or both may be almost invisible, hidden in the felicitous phrasing a writer employs. As Dr. Johnson put it, wit strikes us as "at once natural and new," and "though not obvious, is, upon its first production, acknowledged to be just."

We have observed in a number of instances how varied the surprising justness of witty writing may be. Let us consider a little further this element of poetic thought. As we have seen in Dylan Thomas's lyric, wit may be present in poems that are not only absolutely serious but are for the most part musical, incantatory, and nonintellectual. In A. E. Housman's *To an Athlete Dying Young* (pages 415–416), it is discovered in the wry turn by which the poet finds consolation in praising the dead youth for his *ingenuity*, as though he had *decided* to die young to avoid disillusionment:

> Smart lad, to slip betimes away
> From fields where glory does not stay. . . .

Even more striking for its wryness, because one does not ordinarily think of Death as a courteous visitor, is Emily Dickinson's famous opening effect

> Because I could not stop for Death—
> He kindly stopped for me. . . .

And wit can show itself through an image that, through its grotesqueness, startles us by revealing a frank, unconventional, unexpected directness of thought, as at the end of Emerson's *Hamatreya*:

> When I heard the Earth-song,
> I was no longer brave;
> My avarice cooled
> Like lust in the chill of the grave.

This last image, with its daring leap of association, recalls another definition of wit, also by Dr. Johnson. In writing about the seventeenth-century Metaphysical poets, he noted that wit could be considered "a kind of *discordia concors*: a combination of dissimilar images, or discovery of occult resemblances in things apparently unlike." In Metaphysical verse, he wrote, "the most heterogeneous ideas are yoked by violence together; nature and art are ransacked for illustrations, comparisons, and allusions; their learning instructs, and their subtlety surprises. . . ." Dr. Johnson was not altogether pleased with this quality, thinking it made for writing too labored, or special, and more extravagant than his typically neo-Classical theory that "great thoughts are always general" allowed for. Nevertheless, he granted that the Metaphysical conceit has its values: "If their greatness seldom elevates, their acuteness often surprises."[1] Indeed, the successful conceit, with its intellectual daring, its concise aptness, and its disconcerting suddenness, brings the essence of wit into the poetic image.

It is in satirical writing, as we might expect, that wit comes most openly and fully into its own. It may manifest itself here quite gently, almost fondly, as in Lord Byron's lines on the dissembling of women:

> The charming creatures lie with such a grace,
> There's nothing so becoming to the face.

But how cruelly accurate a weapon wit can be in showing up human vice or folly, the following passage from Pope's *Moral Essays*, with its contemptuous yet tragic picture of London's fashionable elderly dowagers in the early eighteenth century, will reveal:

> As Hags hold Sabbaths, less for joy than spight,
> So these their merry, miserable Night;
> Still round and round the Ghosts of Beauty glide,
> And haunt the places where their Honour dy'd.
>   See how the World its Veterans rewards!
> A Youth of frolicks, an old Age of Cards,
> Fair to no purpose, artful to no end,
> Young without Lovers, old without a Friend,
> A Fop their Passion, but their Prize a Sot,
> Alive, ridiculous, and dead, forgot!   10

---

[1] See pages 68–70 for a discussion of the conceit. Donne's image, discussed there, of separated lovers in the figure of the legs of a compass, is an excellent example. So is his picture, in *The Ecstasy*, of two lovers gazing at one another:

> Our eye-beams twisted, and did thread
> Our eyes, upon one double string. . . .

Pope compares the frivolous social rounds of these aged beauties to the Witches' Sabbaths of medieval tradition in which witches, sorcerers, and demons were believed to gather in unholy, orgiastic, and blasphemous communion. Calling these ladies "ghosts of beauty" in one of the most biting satirical couplets in English verse, he then describes them as unrewarded "veterans" (of the campaigns of society), and goes on to picture the emptiness of their memories of the past and the pointlessness of their pathetic, absurd lives now that they are old. If we observe how the passage builds up its impressions, we then see that the poet's unsentimental ridicule of these old "hags," "ghosts," "veterans," whose lives were cheated of meaning from the start, is not without sardonic pity. And we realize that a whole way of life is under attack, that there is hatred and disgust for the attitudes toward life represented by the targets of Pope's wit. As one critic, William Empson, has accurately observed, "An impression of febrile and uncontrollable hatred is given to the terrible climax of this passage by the flat, indifferent little words, *fop, sot*, which . . . must be hurled at a person conceived as in front of you, to whom you know they are intolerable."

We may compare this passage with a gentler one by Pope, still unmincingly critical of a social class—the country gentry—but more light-hearted and mocking. In his poem *To a Young Lady*, Pope teases a young woman who must return home after an exciting visit to London by picturing the "delights" of country life and the kind of "romantic" wooing to which she may look forward there.

> Some Squire, perhaps, you take a delight to rack;
> Whose game is Whisk, whose treat a toast in sack;
> Who visits with a gun, presents you birds,
> Then gives a smacking buss, and cries,—No words!
> Or with his hound comes hallowing from the stable,
> Makes love with nods, and knees beneath a table;
> Whose laughs are hearty, tho' his jests are coarse,
> And loves you best of all things—but his horse.

Social types are not the only object of the satirist's wit. Certain aspects of human nature, and foolish or wicked ideas, can be made to look ridiculous by the same sort of surprising comparisons and contrasts and by the same emphasis on extravagant manner and behavior, ignorance, and thoughtlessness. In the seventeenth century, John Wilmot, Earl of Rochester, employed these methods in his bitterly sarcastic *A Satire Against Mankind*:

> Were I, who to my Cost already am
> One of those strange, prodigious Creatures *Man*,
> A spirit free, to chuse for my own share,

What sort of Flesh and Blood I pleas'd to wear,
I'd be a Dog, a Monkey, or a Bear,
Or any thing, but that vain Animal
Who is so proud of being Rational.
The Senses are too gross; and he'll contrive
A sixth, to contradict the other Five:
And before certain Instinct, will prefer   10
Reason, which Fifty times for One does err.
Reason, an *Ignis Fatuus* of the Mind,
Which leaves the Light of Nature, Sense, behind.
Pathless, and dang'rous, wand'ring ways it takes,
Through Error's fenny Bogs, and thorny Brakes. . . .

Rochester's great contemporary, John Dryden, used satire to destroy
the reputation of a dull, inferior poet, Thomas Shadwell. (The effective
satirizing in verse of a particular individual has been familiar since the
ancient Greeks and Romans.) Dryden made Shadwell the butt of *Mac-
Flecknoe*, a mock-epic poem in which the king of the realms of Nonsense
selects him as his heir apparent. The essence of the wit in this poem lies
in its topsy-turvy praise of Shadwell, as when, for instance, he is called
"mature in dulness." We have, consequently, a series of momentarily
concealed insults which reveal themselves, delightfully and devastatingly,
in a succession of "double-takes" or minor explosions:

This aged Prince, now flourishing in peace,
And blest with issue of a large increase;
Worn out with business, did at length debate
To settle the succession of the State;
And pond'ring which of all his sons was fit
To reign, and wage immortal war with wit,
Cried: " 'Tis resolved; for Nature pleads, that he
Should only rule, who most resembles me.
Sh——— alone my perfect image bears,
Mature in dulness from his tender years: 10
Sh——— alone, of all my sons, is he
Who stands confirm'd in full stupidity.
The rest to some faint meaning make pretense,
But Sh——— never deviates into sense.
Some beams of wit on other souls may fall,
Strike thro', and make a lucid interval;
But Sh———'s genuine night admits no ray,
His rising fogs prevail upon the day.

There are some famous personal attacks in English verse in which wit
and emotion are powerfully fused. (The only emotion Dryden had wasted
on Shadwell was a rather cold contempt.) The sharpest, most venomous of

all is without doubt Pope's characterization of Lord Hervey in his *Epistle to Arbuthnot*. Here Lord Hervey, a court favorite, is given the name "Sporus," after a favorite eunuch of Nero's. Although granting that he is not worthy of notice—being a "thing of silk," a "mere white curd of Ass's milk," and an insensitive insect ("Who breaks a butterfly upon a wheel?")—Pope launches his jeering couplets so fiercely that they have been called "screams" of hatred and contempt:

> Yet let me flap this bug with gilded wings,
> This painted child of dirt, that stinks and stings;
> Whose buzz the witty and the fair annoys,
> Yet Wit ne'er tastes, and Beauty ne'er enjoys;
> So well-bred spaniels civilly delight
> In mumbling of the game they dare not bite.
> Eternal smiles his emptiness betray,
> As shallow streams run dimpling all the way,
> Whether in florid impotence he speaks,
> And, as the prompter breathes, the puppet squeaks,   10
> Or at the ear of Eve, familiar Toad,
> Half froth, half venom, spits himself abroad,
> In puns, or politics, or tales, or lies,
> Or spite, or smut, or rhymes, or blasphemies;
> His wit all see-saw between *that* and *this,*
> Now high, now low, now master up, now miss,
> And he himself one vile Antithesis.
> Amphibious thing! that acting either part,
> The trifling head, or the corrupted heart;
> Fop at the toilet, flatt'rer at the board,   20
> Now trips a Lady, and now struts a Lord.
> Eve's tempter thus the Rabbins have exprest,
> A cherub's face, a reptile all the rest;
> Beauty that shocks you, Parts that none will trust,
> Wit that can creep, and Pride that licks the dust.

Another savage sketch is Jonathan Swift's *A Satyrical Elegy* (page 314), written at the death of the Duke of Marlborough. A few lines will show the bluntness of Swift's language, the clear intention to heap insult on the name of a hated enemy:

> Behold, his funeral appears,
> Nor widow's sighs, nor orphan's tears,
> Wont at such times each heart to pierce,
> Attend the progress of his hearse.
> And what of that? his friends may say.
> He had those honours in his day.
> True to his profit and his pride,
> He made them weep before he died.

The wit here, of course, derives from the shifting meaning of "widow"
and "orphan." At first they denote the fact that Marlborough left no
wife or child of his own; then they are reminders of his ruthless policy of
war.

Similar are the attacks of Shelley and Byron on Lord Castlereagh, the
Prime Minister who bore so much responsibility for crushing the European
struggles for popular freedom after the French Revolution. In *The Masque
of Anarchy*, Shelley cries out,

> I met Murder on the way—
> He had a mask like Castlereagh. . . .

And Byron, hearing of Castlereagh's madness and suicide, set down this
harsh judgment:

Lord Byron *Epigrams on Castlereagh*

I

> So Castlereagh had cut his throat! The worst
> Of this is,—that his own was not the first.

II

> So *He* has cut his throat at last! He? Who?
> The man who cut his country's long ago.

Another kind of poetic invective, purely personal in character, appears
from time to time simply because poets naturally express themselves most
readily in verse. When Elizabeth Barrett Browning died, an occasion for
such invective was thoughtlessly provided by Edward Fitzgerald, the
translator of Omar Khayyam. He wrote a letter to a friend about her death,
and the letter was eventually published (twenty-eight years later, in 1889)
in a posthumous volume of his correspondence. In it he had written:
"Mrs. Browning's death is rather a relief to me, I must say: no more
Aurora Leighs, thank God! A woman of real genius, I know: but what is
the upshot of it all? She and her Sex had better mind the Kitchen and
their Children; and perhaps the Poor: except in such things as little
Novels, they can only devote themselves to what Men do much better,
leaving that which Men do worse or not at all."

By our contemporary standards, the ideas here set forth appear savagely
antediluvian, although the implied criticism of Mrs. Browning's long poem
Aurora Leigh has merit. But when Browning read this letter in the new
book, his reaction was not ideological in any sense. It was simply the
natural helpless fury of an old man who was himself close to death. He
published the following poem almost at once:

Robert Browning *To Edward Fitzgerald*

> I chanced upon a new book yesterday:
> I opened it, and where my finger lay
> 'Twixt page and uncut page those words I read,
> Some six or seven at most, and learned thereby
> That you, Fitzgerald, whom by ear and eye
> She never knew, "thanked God my wife was dead."
> Ay, dead! and were yourself alive, good Fitz,
> How to return you thanks would pass my wits.
> Kicking you seems the common lot of curs—
> While more appropriate greeting lends you grace:
> Surely to spit there glorifies your face—
> Spitting from lips once sanctified by hers.

Attacks and appeals such as these, in their eagerness to win the reader's emotional assent, are often more rhetorical than satiric. The poetry of our own century is rich in examples of both sorts and includes bitter sallies against intellectual vulgarization or social injustice, acid portraits, and angry jibes at cruel or absurd aspects of our culture. Such poetry has been sometimes direct, sometimes subtle, and sometimes also grossly all-inclusive. Contemporary poets, like many contemporary novelists, dramatists, and philosophers, are oppressed by the mechanization and standardization of modern life, and by the sense of uncontrollable violence in an increasingly volatile social situation. "Things fall apart, the centre cannot hold," and it seems, as Yeats expressed it in his great poem *The Second Coming*, as if "Mere anarchy is loosed upon the world." Yeats's poem is not satire but prophetic vision. Most satire, though not all, is lighter, witty, and even comic, as in these urbane lines in which John Betjeman's *In Westminster Abbey* ridicules the moral hypocrisy of some upper-class "patriots" in England during the last war:

> Gracious Lord, oh bomb the Germans.
>   Spare their women for Thy sake,
> And if that is not too easy
>   We will pardon Thy mistake.
> But gracious Lord, whate'er shall be,
> Don't let anyone bomb me.
>
> Keep our empire undismembered,
>   Guide our Forces by Thy hand,
> Gallant blacks from far Jamaica,
>   Honduras and Togoland;
> Protect them Lord in all their fights,
> And even more, protect the whites.

10

Compare this light but very effective mockery with the hammer blows in Robert Lowell's angry description of what has happened to a modern American city, once perhaps the moral and intellectual capital of the nation:

> on Boylston Street, a commercial photograph
> shows Hiroshima boiling
>
> over a Mosler safe, the "Rock of Ages"
> that survived the blast. Space is nearer.
> When I crouch to my television set,
> the drained faces of Negro school-children rise like balloons. . . .
>
> The Aquarium is gone. Everywhere,
> giant finned cars nose forward like fish;
> a savage servility
> slides by on grease.   10

Betjeman's satire depends on the obvious incongruity between a self-centered and unconsciously hypocritical callousness and the humility and compassion Christian prayer should, ideally, express. The satire in Lowell, too, is based on incongruity, though not in such a way as to make it amusing—in spite of the near pun in "Boylston" and "boiling." The incongruity lies in the matter-of-fact acceptance of atomic horror and social injustice by a culture fed on advertising, television, and journalism. "A savage servility" that "slides by on grease" has been substituted for the natural and humane values cherished in the past.

Poems: Irony, Invective, and Satire

The satirical poems that begin this section are self-explanatory. Those of Rochester and Harington have become proverbial, and Swift's verses on the death of Marlborough reflect the bitter scorn of a powerful mind for a man whose "ill-got honours" were at the expense of so many helpless victims. (He is echoed by the tragic satire of Yeats that closes the section.) Pope is more brilliant on the death of Buckingham; he cuts more by his pity, his accuracy about Buckingham's misery, than by direct invective. ("In the worst inn's worst room" is among the most memorably telling of Pope's phrases.) Again, in his disgusted picture of wealthy "Timon's" showy wastefulness, Pope shows his satiric power. Mingling mock-admiration with a few lines of explicit criticism, he tempers his effect with the observation that, after all, Timon does help the poor in his own vain and unintentional way. The closing lines suggest the pathos of a presumptuous and contemptible life like Timon's.

Robinson's twentieth-century satirical poem, *Cassandra*, is spoken by the prophetess of the title, unheeded here as she was in Aeschylus's play *Agamemnon*, where she appeared almost twenty-five centuries ago. Robinson wrote his poem on the eve of America's entrance into World War I, attacking our complacent, self-betraying blindness to the limitations of our wealth, power, and right to impose our wills on others. More recently, we find Robert Lowell making the same point more subtly, vigorously, and concretely, with much allusion to American history and the contemporary American scene. The poems of Pound, Cummings, Graves, and Ginsberg jeer at set attitudes and official pomposity. They are accompanied by more purely comic satirical pieces, each with a wry or self-ironic tone, by Reed, MacNeice, Amis, and Fearing.

JOHN WILMOT, EARL OF ROCHESTER   *On Charles II*

> Here lies our Sovereign Lord the King,
>   Whose word no man relies on,
> Who never said a foolish thing,
>   Nor ever did a wise one.

SIR JOHN HARINGTON   *Of Treason*

> Treason doth never prosper—what's the reason?
> If it doth prosper, none dare call it treason.

JONATHAN SWIFT *A Satyrical Elegy on the Death of a
Late Famous General,*[1] *1722*

His Grace! impossible! what, dead!
Of old age, too, and in his bed!
And could that mighty warrior fall,
And so inglorious, after all?
Well, since he's gone, no matter how,
The last loud trump must wake him now;
And, trust me, as the noise grows stronger,
He'd wish to sleep a little longer.
And could he be indeed so old
As by the newspapers we're told?   10
Threescore, I think, is pretty high;
'Twas time, in conscience he should die!
This world he cumber'd long enough;
He burnt his candle to the snuff;
And that's the reason, some folks think,
He left behind so great a stink.
Behold his funeral appears,
Nor widow's sighs, nor orphan's tears,
Wont at such times each heart to pierce,
Attend the progress of his hearse.   20
And what of that? his friends may say,
He had those honours in his day.
True to his profit and his pride,
He made them weep before he died.
   Come hither, all ye empty things,
Ye bubbles raised by breath of kings!
Who float upon the tide of state;
Come hither, and behold your fate.
Let Pride be taught by this rebuke,
How very mean a thing's a duke;   30
From all his ill-got honours flung,
Turn'd to that dirt from whence he sprung.

ALEXANDER POPE *The Death of the Duke of Buckingham*

(from *Moral Essays*, Epistle III)

In the worst inn's worst room, with mat half-hung,
The floors of plaister, and the walls of dung,

[1] the Duke of Marlborough.

On once a flock-bed, but repair'd with straw,
With tape-ty'd curtains, never meant to draw,
The George and Garter dangling from that bed
Where tawdry yellow strove with dirty red,
Great Villiers lies—alas! how chang'd from him,
That life of pleasure, and that soul of whim!
Gallant and gay, in Cliveden's proud alcove,
The bow'r of wanton Shrewsbury and love;   10
Or just as gay, at Council, in a ring
Of mimic'd Statesmen, and their merry King.
No Wit to flatter left of all his store!
No Fool to laugh at, which he valu'd more.
There, Victor of his health, of fortune, friends,
And fame, this lord of useless thousands ends.

ALEXANDER POPE *On the Collar of a Dog Presented by Mr. Pope to the Prince of Wales*

I am his Highness' dog at Kew;
Pray tell me, sir, whose dog are you?

ALEXANDER POPE *At Timon's Villa*

(from *Epistle to Burlington*)

At Timon's Villa let us pass a day,
Where all cry out, "What sums are thrown away!"
So proud, so grand; of that stupendous air,
Soft and agreeable come never there.
Greatness, with Timon, dwells in such a draught
As brings all Brobdignag before your thought.
To compass this, his building is a town,
His pond an ocean, his parterre a down:
Who but must laugh, the master when he sees,
A puny insect, shivering at a breeze!   10
Lo, what huge heaps of littleness around!
The whole, a laboured quarry above ground;
Two cupids squirt before; a lake behind
Improves the keenness of the northern wind.
His gardens next your admiration call,
On every side you look, behold the wall!
No pleasing intricacies intervene,

No artful wildness to perplex the scene;
Grove nods at grove, each alley has a brother,
And half the platform just reflects the other.   20
The suffering eye inverted nature sees,
Trees cut to statues, statues thick as trees;
With here a fountain, never to be played;
And there a summer-house that knows no shade;
Here Amphitrite sails through myrtle bowers;
There gladiators fight, or die, in flowers;
Unwatered see the drooping sea-horse mourn,
And swallows roost in Nilus' dusty urn.
    My lord advances with majestic mien,
Smit with the mighty pleasure, to be seen: 30
But soft,—by regular approach,—not yet,—
First through the length of yon hot terrace sweat;
And when up ten steep slopes you've dragged your thighs,
Just at his study door he'll bless your eyes.
    His study! with what authors is it stored?
In books, not authors, curious is my lord;
To all their dated backs he turns you round:
These Aldus printed, those Du Sueil has bound.
Lo, some are vellum, and the rest as good
For all his lordship knows, but they are wood.   40
For Locke or Milton 'tis in vain to look,
These shelves admit not any modern book.
    And now the chapel's silver bell you hear,
That summons you to all the pride of prayer;
Light quirks of music, broken and uneven,
Make the soul dance upon a jig to Heaven.
On painted ceilings you devoutly stare,
Where sprawl the saints of Verrio or Laguerre,
On gilded clouds in fair expansion lie,
And bring all paradise before your eye.   50
To rest, the cushion and soft dean invite,
Who never mentions hell to ears polite.
    But hark! the chiming clocks to dinner call;
A hundred footsteps scrape the marble hall;
The rich buffet well-coloured serpents grace,
And gaping Tritons spew to wash your face.
Is this a dinner? this a genial room?
No, 'tis a temple, and a hecatomb.
A solemn sacrifice, performed in state,
You drink by measure, and to minutes eat.   60

So quick retires each flying course, you'd swear
Sancho's dread doctor and his wand were there.
Between each act the trembling salvers ring,
From soup to sweet-wine, and God bless the King.
In plenty starving, tantalized in state,
And complaisantly helped to all I hate,
Treated, caressed, and tired, I take my leave,
Sick of his civil pride from morn to eve;
I curse such lavish cost, and little skill,
And swear no day was ever passed so ill.   70
    Yet hence the poor are clothed, the hungry fed;
Health to himself, and to his infants bread
The labourer bears: What his hard heart denies,
His charitable vanity supplies.
    Another age shall see the golden ear
Embrown the slope, and nod on the parterre,
Deep harvests bury all his pride has planned,
And laughing Ceres re-assume the land.

EZRA POUND   *The Seeing Eye*

The small dogs look at the big dogs;
They observe unwieldly dimensions
And curious imperfections of odor.
Here is a formal male group:
The young men look upon their seniors,
They consider the elderly mind
And observe its inexplicable correlations.

Said Tsin-Tsu:
It is only in small dogs and the young
That we find minute observation.   10

EDWIN ARLINGTON ROBINSON   *Cassandra* [1]

I heard one who said: "Verily,
    What word have I for children here?
Your Dollar is your only Word,
    The wrath of it your only fear.

----

[1] Cassandra, the Trojan prophetess, was doomed to know the truth but never be heeded.

"You build it altars tall enough
    To make you see, but you are blind;
You cannot leave it long enough
    To look before you or behind.

"When Reason beckons you to pause,
    You laugh and say that you know best;   10
But what it is you know, you keep
    As dark as ingots in a chest.

"You laugh and answer, 'We are young;
    Oh, leave us now, and let us grow:'
Not asking how much more of this
    Will Time endure or Fate bestow.

"Because a few complacent years
    Have made your peril of your pride,
Think you that you are to go on
    Forever pampered and untried?   20

"What lost eclipse of history,
    What bivouac of the marching stars,
Has given the sign for you to see
    Millenniums and last great wars?

"What unrecorded overthrow
    Of all the world has ever known,
Or ever been, has made itself
    So plain to you, and you alone?

"Your Dollar, Dove and Eagle make
    A Trinity that even you   30
Rate higher than you rate yourselves;
    It pays, it flatters, and it's new.

"And though your very flesh and blood
    Be what your Eagle eats and drinks,
You'll praise him for the best of birds,
    Not knowing what the Eagle thinks.

"The power is yours, but not the sight;
    You see not upon what you tread;
You have the ages for your guide,
    But not the wisdom to be led.   40

"Think you to tread forever down
    The merciless old verities?
And are you never to have eyes
    To see the world for what it is?

"Are you to pay for what you have
    With all you are?"—No other word
We caught, but with a laughing crowd
    Moved on. None heeded, and few heard.

E. E. Cummings   "next to of course god america i

"next to of course god america i
love you land of the pilgrims' and so forth oh
say can you see by the dawn's early my
country 'tis of centuries come and go
and are no more what of it we should worry
in every language even deafanddumb
thy sons acclaim your glorious name by gorry
by jingo by gee by gosh by gum
why talk of beauty what could be more beautiful than these heroic happy dead   10
who rushed like lions to the roaring slaughter
they did not stop to think they died instead
then shall the voice of liberty be mute?"

He spoke. And drank rapidly a glass of water.

Robert Graves   *The Persian Version*

Truth-loving Persians do not dwell upon
The trivial skirmish fought near Marathon.
As for the Greek theatrical tradition
Which represents that summer's expedition
Not as a mere reconnaissance in force
By three brigades of foot and one of horse
(Their left flank covered by some obsolete
Light craft detached from the main Persian fleet)
But as a grandiose, ill-starred attempt
To conquer Greece—they treat it with contempt;   10
And only incidentally refute
Major Greek claims, by stressing what repute

The Persian monarch and the Persian nation
Won by this salutary demonstration:
Despite a strong defence and adverse weather
All arms combined magnificently together.

HENRY REED *Naming of Parts*

Today we have naming of parts. Yesterday,
We had daily cleaning. And tomorrow morning,
We shall have what to do after firing. But today,
Today we have naming of parts. Japonica
Glistens like coral in all the neighboring gardens,
    And today we have naming of parts.

This is the lower sling swivel. And this
Is the upper sling swivel, whose use you will see,
When you are given your slings. And this is the piling swivel,
Which in your case you have not got. The branches   10
Hold in the gardens their silent, eloquent gestures,
    Which in our case we have not got.

This is the safety-catch, which is always released
With an easy flick of the thumb. And please do not let me
See anyone using his finger. You can do it quite easy
If you have any strength in your thumb. The blossoms
Are fragile and motionless, never letting anyone see
    Any of them using their finger.

And this you can see is the bolt. The purpose of this
Is to open the breech, as you see. We can slide it   20
Rapidly backwards and forwards: we call this
Easing the spring. And rapidly backwards and forwards
The early bees are assaulting and fumbling the flowers:
    They call it easing the Spring.

They call it easing the Spring: it is perfectly easy
If you have any strength in your thumb: like the bolt,
And the breech, and the cocking-piece, and the point of balance,
Which in our case we have not got; and the almond-blossom
Silent in all of the gardens and the bees going backwards and
                            forwards,
    For today we have naming of parts.   30

Louis MacNeice *Bagpipe Music*

It's no go the merrygoround, it's no go the rickshaw,
All we want is a limousine and a ticket for the peepshow.
Their knickers are made of crêpe-de-chine, their shoes are made of
  python,
Their halls are lined with tiger rugs and their walls with heads of
  bison.

John MacDonald found a corpse, put it under the sofa,
Waited till it came to life and hit it with a poker,
Sold its eyes for souvenirs, sold its blood for whiskey,
Kept its bones for dumb-bells to use when he was fifty.

It's no go the Yogi-Man, it's no go Blavatsky,
All we want is a bank balance and a bit of skirt in a taxi.   10

Annie MacDougall went to milk, caught her foot in the heather,
Woke to hear a dance record playing of Old Vienna.
It's no go your maidenheads, it's no go your culture,
All we want is a Dunlop tyre and the devil mend the puncture.

The Laird o' Phelps spent Hogmannay declaring he was sober;
Counted his feet to prove the fact and found he had one foot over.
Mrs. Carmichael had her fifth, looked at the job with repulsion,
Said to the midwife "Take it away; I'm through with over-
  production."

It's no go the gossip column, it's no go the Ceilidh,
All we want is a mother's help and a sugar-stick for the baby.   20

Willie Murray cut his thumb, couldn't count the damage,
Took the hide of an Ayrshire cow and used it for a bandage.
His brother caught three hundred cran when the seas were lavish,
Threw the bleeders back in the sea and went upon the parish.

It's no go the Herring Board, it's no go the Bible,
All we want is a packet of fags when our hands are idle.

It's no go the picture palace, it's no go the stadium,
It's no go the country cot with a pot of pink geraniums.
It's no go the Government grants, it's no go the elections,
Sit on your arse for fifty years and hang your hat on a pension.   30

It's no go my honey love, it's no go my poppet;
Work your hands from day to day, the winds will blow the profit.
The glass is falling hour by hour, the glass will fall for ever,
But if you break the bloody glass you won't hold up the weather.

KINGSLEY AMIS   *A Dream of Fair Women*

The door still swinging to, and girls revive,
Aeronauts in the utmost altitudes
   Of boredom fainting, dive
Into the bright oxygen of my nod;
Angels as well, a squadron of draped nudes,
   They rear towards their god.

Militant all, they fight to take my hat,
No more as yet; the other men retire
   Insulted, gestured at;
Each girl presses on me her share of what   10
Makes up the barn-door target of desire:
   And I am a crack shot.

Speech fails them, amorous, but each one's look,
Endorsed in other ways, begs me to sign
   Her body's autograph-book;
"Me first, Kingsley; I'm cleverest" each declares,
But no gourmet races downstairs to dine,
   Nor will I race upstairs.

Feigning aplomb, perhaps for half an hour,
I hover, and am shown by each princess   20
   The entrance to her tower;
Open, in that its tenant throws the key
At once to anyone, but not unless
   The anyone is me.

Now from the corridor their fathers cheer,
Their brothers, their young men; the cheers increase
   As soon as I appear;
From each I win a handshake and sincere
Congratulations; from the chief of police
   A nod, a wink, a leer.   30

This over, all delay is over too;
The first eight girls (the roster now agreed)
   Leap on me, and undo . . .
But honesty impels me to confess
That this is "all a dream," which was, indeed,
   Not difficult to guess.

But wait; not "just a dream," because, though good
And beautiful, it is also true, and hence
   Is rarely understood;
Who would choose any feasible ideal   40
In here and now's giant circumference,
   If that small room were real?

Only the best; the others find, have found
Love's ordinary distances too great,
   And, eager, stand their ground;
Map-drunk explorers, dry-land sailors, they
See no arrival that can compensate
   For boredom on the way;

And, seeming doctrinaire, but really weak,
Limelighted dolls guttering in their brain,   50
   They come with me, to seek
The halls of theoretical delight,
The women of that ever-fresh terrain,
   The night after to-night.

KENNETH FEARING   *Thirteen O'Clock*

Why do they whistle so loud, when they walk past the graveyard late
    at night?
Why do they look behind them when they reach the gates? Why do
    they have any gates? Why don't they go through the wall?
But why, O why do they make that horrible whistling sound?

GO AWAY, LIVE PEOPLE, STOP HAUNTING THE DEAD.

If they catch you, it is said, they make you rap, rap, rap on a table all
    night,
And blow through a trumpet and float around the room in long white
    veils,

While they ask you, and ask you: Can you hear us, Uncle Ted?
Are you happy, Uncle Ted? Should we buy or should we sell? Should
    we marry, Uncle Ted?   10
What became of Uncle Ned, Uncle Ted, and is he happy, and ask
    him if he knows what became of Uncle Fred?

KEEP AWAY, LIVE PEOPLE, KEEP FAR AWAY,
STAY IN THE WORLD'S OTHER WORLD WHERE YOU REALLY BELONG, YOU
    WILL PROBABLY BE MUCH HAPPIER THERE.

And who knows what they are hunting for, always looking, looking,
    looking with sharp bright eyes where they ought to have sockets?
Whoever saw them really grin with their teeth?
Who knows why they worry, or what they scheme, with a brain where
    there should be nothing but good, damp air?

STAY AWAY, LIVE PEOPLE, STAY AWAY, STAY AWAY,
YOU MEAN NO HARM, AND WE AREN'T AFRAID OF YOU, AND WE DON'T
    BELIEVE SUCH PEOPLE EXIST,
BUT WHAT ARE YOU LOOKING FOR? WHO DO YOU WANT?
WHO? WHO? WHO? O WHO?   20

ALLEN GINSBERG   *America* [1]

America I've given you all and now I'm nothing.
America two dollars and twentyseven cents January 17, 1956.
I can't stand my own mind.
America when will we end the human war?
Go fuck yourself with your atom bomb.
I don't feel good don't bother me.
I won't write my poem till I'm in my right mind.
America when will you be angelic?
When will you take off your clothes?
When will you look at yourself through the grave?   10
When will you be worthy of your million Trotskyites?
America why are your libraries full of tears?
America when will you send your eggs to India?
I'm sick of your insane demands.
When can I go into the supermarket and buy what I need with my
    good looks?

[1] See comments in Chapter One, Section II, (p. 29).

America after all it is you and I who are perfect not the next world.
Your machinery is too much for me.
You made me want to be a saint.
There must be some other way to settle this argument.
Burroughs is in Tangiers I don't think he'll come back it's sinister. 20
Are you being sinister or is this some form of practical joke?
I'm trying to come to the point.
I refuse to give up my obsession.
America stop pushing I know what I'm doing.
America the plum blossoms are falling.
I haven't read the newspapers for months, everyday somebody goes on
      trial for murder.
America I feel sentimental about the Wobblies.
America I used to be a communist when I was a kid I'm not sorry.
I smoke marijuana every chance I get. 30
I sit in my house for days on end and stare at the roses in the closet.
When I go to Chinatown I get drunk and never get laid.
My mind is made up there's going to be trouble.
You should have seen me reading Marx.
My psychoanalyst thinks I'm perfectly right.
I won't say the Lord's Prayer.
I have mystical visions and cosmic vibrations.
America I still haven't told you what you did to Uncle Max after he
      came over from Russia.

I'm addressing you. 40
Are you going to let your emotional life be run by Time Magazine?
I'm obsessed by Time Magazine.
I read it every week.
Its cover stares at me every time I slink past the corner candystore.
I read it in the basement of the Berkeley Public Library.
It's always telling me about responsibility. Businessmen are serious.
      Movie producers are serious. Everybody's serious but me.
It occurs to me that I am America.
I am talking to myself again.

Asia is rising against me.
I haven't got a chinaman's chance. 50
I'd better consider my national resources.
My national resources consist of two joints of marijuana millions of
      genitals an unpublishable private literature that goes 1400
      miles an hour and twentyfive-thousand mental institutions.

I say nothing about my prisons nor the millions of underprivileged
     who live in my flowerpots under the light of five hundred
     suns.
I have abolished the whorehouses of France, Tangiers is the next to go.
My ambition is to be President despite the fact that I'm a Catholic.

America how can I write a holy litany in your silly mood?
I will continue like Henry Ford my strophes are as individual as his
     automobiles more so they're all different sexes.
America I will sell you strophes $2500 apiece $500 down on your old
     strophe
America free Tom Mooney
America save the Spanish Loyalists   60
America Sacco & Vanzetti must not die
America I am the Scottsboro boys.
America when I was seven Momma took me to Communist Cell
     meetings they sold us garbanzos a handful per ticket a ticket
     costs a nickel and the speeches were free everybody was
     angelic and sentimental about the workers it was all so
     sincere you have no idea what a good thing the party was in
     1835 Scott Nearing was a grand old man a real mensch
     Mother Bloor made me cry I once saw Israel Amter plain.
     Everybody must have been a spy.
America you don't really want to go to war.
America it's them bad Russians.
Them Russians them Russians and them Chinamen. And them
     Russians.
The Russia wants to eat us alive. The Russia's power mad. She wants
     to take our cars from out our garages.
Her wants to grab Chicago. Her needs a Red Readers' Digest. Her
     wants our auto plants in Siberia. Him big bureaucracy run-
     ning our fillingstations.
That no good. Ugh. Him make Indians learn read. Him need big black
     niggers. Hah. Her make us all work sixteen hours a day.
     Help.
America this is quite serious.   70
America this is the impression I get from looking in the television set.
America is this correct?
I'd better get right down to the job.
It's true I don't want to join the Army or turn lathes in precision parts
     factories, I'm nearsighted and psychopathic anyway.
America I'm putting my queer shoulder to the wheel.

Robert Lowell   *For the Union Dead*

"Relinquunt omnia servare rem publicam." [1]

The old South Boston Aquarium stands
in a Sahara of snow now. Its broken windows are boarded.
The bronze weathervane cod has lost half its scales.
The airy tanks are dry.

Once my nose crawled like a snail on the glass;
my hand tingled
to burst the bubbles
drifting from the noses of the cowed, compliant fish.

My hand draws back. I often sigh still
for the dark downward and vegetating kingdom   10
of the fish and reptile. One morning last March,
I pressed against the new barbed and galvanized

fence on the Boston Common. Behind their cage,
yellow dinosaur steamshovels were grunting
as they cropped up tons of mush and grass
to gouge their underworld garage.

Parking-spaces luxuriate like civic
sandpiles in the heart of Boston.
A girdle of orange, Puritan-pumpkin colored girders
braces the tingling Statehouse,   20

shaking over the excavations, as it faces Colonel Shaw
and his bell-cheeked Negro infantry
on St. Gaudens' shaking Civil War relief,
propped by a plank splint against the garage's earthquake.

Two months after marching through Boston,
half the regiment was dead;
at the dedication,
William James could almost hear the bronze Negroes breathe.

Their monument sticks like a fishbone
in the City's throat.   30
Its Colonel is as lean
as a compass-needle.

[1] "They forsake everything to save the republic."

He has an angry wrenlike vigilance,
a greyhound's gentle tautness;
he seems to wince at pleasure,
and suffocate for privacy.

He is out of bounds now. He rejoices in man's lovely,
peculiar power to choose life and die—
when he leads his black soldiers to death,
he cannot bend his back.   40

On a thousand small town New England greens,
the old white churches hold their air
of sparse, sincere rebellion; frayed flags
quilt the graveyards of the Grand Army of the Republic.

The stone statues of the abstract Union Soldier
grow slimmer and younger each year—
wasp-waisted, they doze over muskets
and muse through their sideburns . . .

Shaw's father wanted no monument
except the ditch,   50
where his son's body was thrown
and lost with his "niggers."

The ditch is nearer.
There are no statues for the last war here;
on Boylston Street, a commercial photograph
shows Hiroshima boiling

over a Mosler Safe, the "Rock of Ages"
that survived the blast. Space is nearer.
When I crouch to my television set,
the drained faces of Negro school-children rise like balloons.   60

Colonel Shaw
is riding on his bubble,
he waits
for the blessèd break.

The Aquarium is gone. Everywhere,
giant finned cars nose forward like fish;
a savage servility
slides by on grease.

WILLIAM BUTLER YEATS   *Nineteen Hundred and Nineteen: V*

Come let us mock at the great
That had such burdens on the mind
And toiled so hard and late
To leave some monument behind,
Nor thought of the levelling wind.

Come let us mock at the wise;
With all those calendars whereon
They fixed old aching eyes,
They never saw how seasons run,
And now but gape at the sun.   10

Come let us mock at the good
That fancied goodness might be gay,
And sick of solitude
Might proclaim a holiday:
Wind shrieked—and where are they?

Mock mockers after that
That would not lift a hand maybe
To help good, wise or great
To bar that foul storm out, for we
Traffic in mockery.   20

IV

AMBIGUITY AND IMPLICATION

One of the most potent intellectual resources of a poet is irony—the use of language to imply the precise opposite of what is actually stated. In its clearest form, irony is the handmaiden of satire. Dryden's *MacFlecknoe* was a case in point, and so are the following tongue-in-cheek lines by Arthur Hugh Clough that purport to interpret the Ten Commandments in an "up-to-date" way and make them more businesslike. The effect of these lines depends upon the apparent solemnity with which they recommend a superficial religious conformity as the high road not to heavenly glory but to commercial and social success. *The Latest Decalogue* is a satire on Victorian respectability and utilitarianism.

ARTHUR HUGH CLOUGH from *The Latest Decalogue*

Thou shalt have one God only; who
Would be at the expense of two?

No graven images may be
Worshipped, except the currency:

Swear not at all; for, for thy curse
Thine enemy is none the worse:

At church on Sunday to attend
Will serve to keep the world thy friend:

Honour thy parents; that is, all
From whom advancement may befall;   10

Thou shalt not kill; but need'st not strive
Officiously to keep alive:

Do not adultery commit;
Advantage rarely comes of it:

Thou shalt not steal; an empty feat,
When it's so lucrative to cheat:

Bear not false witness; let the lie
Have time on its own wings to fly:

> Thou shalt not covet, but tradition
> Approves all forms of competition. 20

But irony may be used *without* satire. It may, instead, be employed to give edge to the emotion of a lyric poem. In Marvell's *To His Coy Mistress* (pages 436–437), it underlines a lover's impatience. The speaker has been presenting the conventional argument that if we do not seize the joys of life when we are young, old age and death will deprive us of them forever. At one point he pretends to consider the advantages of existence in the grave, *as if* he were thinking the problem over seriously, from every point of view. We know that no one really thinks this way; philosophers have discussed the relative value of life and death, but not in terms that are more suitable to the renting of living quarters than to religion and metaphysics:

> The Grave's a fine and private place,
> But none, I think, do there embrace.

Irony may be even more subtle, and certainly very serious in its effects, when it implies not a denial of a pretended attitude but a sense of the discrepancy between human desires and the tragic realities of life. This kind of irony is found in the climax of Milton's sonnet *On His Deceased Wife*, in which he tells of dreaming that he has once again seen his young wife who died in childbirth. The effect of irony here lies in the brutality with which truth breaks in on his dream. This effect is increased for us if we note Milton's reference to his blindness in the words "veil'd" and "fancied" and the restraint with which he suggests, through the frustration of the moment of waking, his deeper misery because of her death:

> Her face was veil'd; yet to my fancied sight,
> Love, sweetness, goodness, in her person shin'd
> So clear, as in no face with more delight.
> But O as to embrace me she enclin'd
> I wak'd, she fled, and day brought back my night.

In its usefulness for opening up the relation between illusion and reality, irony is closely related to ambiguity. Indeed, irony is a special instance of ambiguity, the expression in a single term of more than one meaning. Ambiguity, when it is intentionally and skilfully used, modifies, enriches, compares, illustrates, and even undermines or denies an idea at the same time as it expresses it, and thus is a subtle way of suggesting the complexity and variability—the "ambiguity"—of things. Irony and ambiguity can exist in a single word or a brief figure, or they may be extended throughout the development and denouement of a complete plot.

A passage in Chaucer's *The Pardoner's Tale* will illustrate this relationship. The tale itself is a rollicking yet tragic account of three foolish drunkards who stagger out one morning to catch and kill Death! Of course, they find only their own deaths, which they themselves, unwittingly, have contrived through their greed. The person telling this ironic story is himself exceedingly avaricious; yet it is he, again ironically, who proclaims its moral—that greed for wealth is the root of all evil. The passage we are concerned with now, however—the most moving in the tale—is the great transition point between the rollicking satire of the beginning and the tragic insight of the ending. The drunks have met and insulted an old man because of his great age. As part of his reply, before he directs them to the place where they will find Death, he utters a complaint in which he describes his own terrible longing to die. No irony could be greater than that which lies in the difference between the superficial hatred of the roisterers for death and the old man's profound desire for it.

> Thus walke I, lyk a restelees caityf,
> And on the ground, which is my modres gate,
> I knokke with my staf, both erly and late,
> And seye, "Leve moder, leet me in!
> Lo, how I vanysshe, flessh, and blood, and skyn!
> Allas! when shul my bones been at reste!" [1]

[1] A rough translation into modern English follows:

> Thus walk I, like a restless prisoner,
> And on the ground, which is my mother's gate,
> I knock with my staff, both early and late,
> And say, "Dear Mother, let me in!
> Lo, how I vanish, flesh and blood and skin!
> Alas. when shall my bones be at rest?"

A profound idea wells up in this passage—the idea that we cannot conceive of bringing an end to death without at the same time destroying the principle of the life-cycle here symbolized by Mother Earth. The complaint becomes a devastating comment on the vanity of the human desire to circumvent the destiny of man, which includes death as well as birth and growth. In his deep knowledge and weariness of life, the old man wishes to complete his own cycle as nature intended it to be completed.

But who is the old man? The most direct answer is that he is simply a very wise and aged person, and that when he refers to the earth as his mother he is merely speaking figuratively. Nevertheless, this explanation does not account for his being *unable* to die, or for the assurance with which he describes the place where the men can find Death. There is something about him of the magical and the supernatural; and his calling the earth his mother summons up, actually, the beliefs and fears embodied in primitive mythology.

Chaucer does not pause to explain just who the old man is; hence the ambiguity of this character, who can be seen in several different ways. The most obvious explanation, and the most satisfying one, is that he is Death himself—and what a crowning irony, to find Death complaining that he cannot die, even while he is arranging for the self-destruction of the poor fools who have set out to tamper with things better left alone! Even if we do not see him as Death, however, he can at least be seen as a passionately conceived spirit of old age, speaking for the natural order of things as opposed to the younger men's desire to defy that natural order. He is in any case a mystical and prophetic figure, and Chaucer's deliberate avoidance of explanatory comment deepens the mystery and awe that surround him.

A different sort of ambiguity and irony can be found in a seemingly light poem of William Blake's:

WILLIAM BLAKE *I askèd a thief*

> I askèd a thief to steal me a peach:
> He turned up his eyes.
> I ask'd a lithe lady to lie her down:
> Holy and meek she cries.
> As soon as I went an angel came:
> He wink'd at the thief
> And smil'd at the dame,
> And without one word spoke
> Had a peach from the tree,
> And 'twixt earnest and joke   10
> Enjoy'd the Lady.

Whereas the ambiguity of Chaucer's poem is centered in one character and one incident that deepen the meaning of the whole work, Blake's poem is ambiguous in its intent rather than in its characterization and action. We know just what has happened and who has done it. The thief and the lady have refused—on supposedly ethical grounds—the speaker's request for their services. But the angel seems to have an unspoken understanding with them, and easily makes them forget their pious pretensions. How are we to explain this poem? On the surface it is simply a joke, deriving its humor from a reversal of what one would ordinarily expect— a joke which may be tartly suggesting that the successful profligate must *pretend* to be an angel. But the author does not *say* the angel is not really one. Indeed, if we push into the poem a bit further, he seems rather to be suggesting that only some supernatural being can free us to behave spontaneously and unselfconsciously, and in this suggestion he is castigating conventional morality as hypocritical and unnatural. There is a powerful lesson hidden in the implication that angels and ordinary human beings live by entirely different rules, and rightly so—that "you can do anything if you're an angel." Although the pleasure of the poem lies first of all in the comic characterizations of lady and thief, in the debonair dexterity of the angel, and in the amusing paradox of the situation, this unorthodox and exciting concept goes far beyond either playful whimsy, conventional moralizing, or commonplace cynicism.

In Blake's deceptively light poem, as elsewhere in his writings, there is a searching analysis of popular beliefs, both economic and sexual. The "I" of the poem is a "natural man," who desires to have what is simply good and gratifying to the senses. Those who could get it for him or give it to him are prevented from responding by what transpires to be a hypocritical and conventional morality. It is only the "angel," who paradoxically seems to have all the suave and adept worldliness of the devil, whose neat and accomplished approach overcomes their scruples without a word spoken.

But the "moral" of this poem—for it *is* a poem that impresses us as having a moral, however ambivalent it may be—is probably not that it is important to be an "angel" because then you can do anything or take anything. It is true that for the timid ordinary being who must ask, his natural desires are thwarted by uncertainty and overseriousness; and it is true that the angel has none of this uncertainty, and none of the solemnity with which philosophers and moralists deal with problems of conduct. But the true meaning of angels is seen in the fact that only they are gay, innocent, and convincing enough—and now the angel is seen to be more like a real angel and less like a limb of Satan—to overcome the scruples of the thief and the lady and *set them free* to perform the services they are ideally created to perform as human beings. The point of view is familiar in this poet's other work—for instance, in these more explicit lines:

> Abstinence sows sand all over
> The ruddy limbs & flaming hair,
> But Desire Gratified
> Plants fruits of life & beauty there.

When we begin to think of the angel not as the slick accomplished seducer, but as the liberator of the senses and the instincts from the bondage of respectability and fear, we are in a position to appreciate the truly critical and original force of this dynamic poem.[2]

---

[2] Even this line of thought does not exhaust the richness of suggestion. There are also undoubted parallels between the fable here and the story of the temptation and the fall in the Garden of Eden. This may lead us too far astray, but the unorthodox nature of Blake's genuinely religious thought could be demonstrated were we to follow out the possible identifications: the thief with Adam, the lady with Eve, the angel with the Serpent, and, perhaps, the "I" with Everyman. But we are concerned here only to illustrate the richness of ambiguity and irony that adheres to a short and apparently light and even comic poem.

In its oblique handling of a very touchy matter, *I asked a thief* resembles many modern poems that challenge accepted standards of thought and behavior. It is unlike the characteristic work of the day, however, in its surface clarity. The poem becomes difficult and ambiguous only when we probe beneath this surface. Modern poets, on the other hand, often put on a kind of protective armor of imagery that, once penetrated, is seen to have covered a sense of isolation from the orthodox world and its beliefs.

Hart Crane's *Passage* (pages 337–338) is an instance. Perhaps the most pervasive fear of thinking people, and the most difficult to contemplate, is that all our values are illusory. *Passage* approaches this problem by giving us an "autobiographical" account in a series of metaphors and other images. This account tells how the speaker sought "an improved infancy"—a rebirth in a more beautiful and sunnier life—through a deliberate putting-aside of the sordid, petty, diseased "night" memories of actual human experience. The "sapphire" brilliance of sky and sea in the open daylight would lead him, he thought, to the purer arena of artistic vision. But the laws of life could not be circumvented, and the vision of his art was seen to be furtive, evasive—the "stolen book" of a "thief." Seeing himself thus—not as the laurel-crowned hero of the human spirit but as a "split" being, half thief and half death-messenger—he is overwhelmed by a new and terrible vision of the impersonal, nonhuman nature of the universe in which he lives.

It would be impossible directly to express the ideas implied by *Passage* without seeming to most people frightened and oversensitive. The oblique method of Hart Crane helps him avoid creating this impression before the precise character of his attitude has been made clear to the reader who must take the trouble of penetrating the imagery of each stanza. Of course, there is a risk that a poet like Hart Crane takes. The reader may not be willing to go along with him to the end. On the other hand, Blake's risk was that the reader would be satisfied with the easier and less complete meaning of his poem. Every poet, certainly, runs the risk of being misunderstood by the hasty, lazy, or wrongheaded reader.

In these poems, ambiguity—the suggestion of more than one valid interpretation for the feelings and experiences presented (and for the words through which they are communicated)—has done its enriching work. It has enabled the poet to awaken our sensibilities and awareness on the broadest possible scale without vagueness or didacticism.

Poems: Ambiguity and Implication

Each of the following poems presents a situation at once specific and suggestive of more than one interpretation. The most ambiguous of them, perhaps, is Crane's *Passage*, discussed in the text. The opening lines of Emily Dickinson's poem are paradoxical yet clear and touching; by themselves they make a sharply aphoristic little poem. At the same time, they hold the germ of the striking idea that whenever God "grasps" someone, "hope and he part company." It is an idea with reverberations of meaning that the poem suggests but does not spell out. Stevie Smith's poem, too, presents what at first seems a literal situation but then is seen to be symbolic, for a dead man could hardly have been "moaning." By the end of the poem we see that the grim witticism in line four characterizes a whole life-condition of the supposed "dead man."

Hardy's *Channel Firing* deliberately confuses the realms of the living and the dead. Hardy imagines a grotesque and macabre scene and dialogue before the final stanza extends its implications backward in time toward the remotest past, from that of known history to that of primitive and mythical ancient Britain. Margaret Avison's "nameless" insect becomes herself and her own life as well, suggesting that any sort of life is a making-do, for undefined purposes, out of difficult materials and limited circumstances. John Donne's Metaphysical poem, chivalrous and erotic, is based on a suggestive conceit concerning the true relation of lovers. Empson's poem moves among many thoughts and images seeking out elusive links between "bliss" and "despair." Fearing's ambiguity has a different source; he gives us a series of verbs and descriptive phrases—almost all desolate—but omits the subjects of his sentences (except for an undefined "it"). His poem projects a state of feeling rather than a defined situation or attitude. In Jarrell's poem, the speaker is a girl whose sister has died and who now cannot sort out her dream and fantasy life from literal reality. Most challenging of all is Baraka's (Jones's) poem. Here the speaker, possibly expressing the feeling of many black people in a culture dominated by whites, struggles against a painful, imposed identity that distorts his real self and needs.

EMILY DICKINSON *Drowning is not so pitiful*

Drowning is not so pitiful
As the attempt to rise.
Three times, 'tis said, a sinking man
Comes up to face the skies,
And then declines forever

To that abhorred abode,
Where hope and he part company—
For he is grasped of God.
The Maker's cordial visage,
However good to see,   10
Is shunned, we must admit it,
Like an adversity.

STEVIE SMITH *Not Waving but Drowning*

Nobody heard him, the dead man,
But still he lay moaning:
I was much further out than you thought
And not waving but drowning.

Poor chap, he always loved larking
And now he's dead
It must have been too cold for him his heart gave way,
They said.

Oh, no no no, it was too cold always
(Still the dead one lay moaning)   10
I was much too far out all my life
And not waving but drowning.

HART CRANE *Passage*

Where the cedar leaf divides the sky
I heard the sea.
In sapphire arenas of the hills
I was promised an improved infancy.

Sulking, sanctioning the sun,
My memory I left in a ravine,—
Casual louse that tissues the buckwheat,
Aprons rocks, congregates pears
In moonlit bushels
And wakens alleys with a hidden cough.   10

Dangerously the summer burned
(I had joined the entrainments of the wind).

The shadows of boulders lengthened my back:
In the bronze gongs of my cheeks
The rain dried without odour.

"It is not long, it is not long;
See where the red and black
Vine-stanchioned valleys—": but the wind
Died speaking through the ages that you know
And hug, chimney-sooted heart of man!   20
So was I turned about and back, much as your smoke
Compiles a too well-known biography.

The evening was a spear in the ravine
That throve through very oak. And had I walked
The dozen particular decimals of time?
Touching an opening laurel, I found
A thief beneath, my stolen book in hand.

"Why are you back here—smiling an iron coffin?"
"To argue with the laurel," I replied:
"Am justified in transience, fleeing   30
Under the constant wonder of your eyes—."

He closed the book. And from the Ptolemies
Sand troughed us in a glittering abyss.
A serpent swam a vertex to the sun
—On unpaced beaches leaned its tongue and drummed.
What fountains did I hear? what icy speeches?
Memory, committed to the page, had broke.

THOMAS HARDY   *Channel Firing* [1]

That night your great guns, unawares,
Shook all our coffins as we lay,
And broke the chancel window-squares,
We thought it was the Judgment-day

And sat upright. While drearisome
Arose the howl of wakened hounds:
The mouse let fall the altar-crumb,
The worms drew back into the mounds,

[1] See comment in Chapter One, Section I, (p. 8).

The glebe cow drooled. Till God called, "No;
It's gunnery practice out at sea   10
Just as before you went below;
The world is as it used to be:

"All nations striving strong to make
Red war yet redder. Mad as hatters
They do no more for Christés sake
Than you who are helpless in such matters.

"That this is not the judgment-hour
For some of them's a blessed thing,
For if it were they'd have to scour
Hell's floor for so much threatening. . . .   20

"Ha, ha. It will be warmer when
I blow the trumpet (if indeed
I ever do; for you are men,
And rest eternal sorely need)."

So down we lay again, "I wonder,
Will the world ever saner be,"
Said one, "than when He sent us under
In our indifferent century!"

And many a skeleton shook his head.
"Instead of preaching forty year,"   30
My neighbour Parson Thirdly said,
"I wish I had stuck to pipes and beer."

Again the guns disturbed the hour,
Roaring their readiness to avenge,
As far inland as Stourton Tower,
And Camelot, and starlit Stonehenge.

MARGARET AVISON *A Nameless One*

Hot in June a narrow winged
long-elbowed-three-legged
living insect lived
and died within
the lodgers' second-floor bathroom here.

At six a.m.
wafting ceilingward,
no breeze but what it living made there;

at noon standing
still as a constellation of spruce needles   10
before the moment of
making it, whirling;

at four a
wilted flotsam, cornsilk, on the linoleum:

now that it is
over, I
look with new eyes
upon this room
adequate for one to
be, in.   20

Its insect-day
has threaded a needle
for me for my eyes dimming
over rips and tears and
thin places.

JOHN DONNE   *A Valediction Forbidding Mourning*

As virtuous men pass mildly away,
    And whisper to their souls to go,
Whilst some of their sad friends do say,
    The breath goes now, and some say, No:

So let us melt, and make no noise,
    No tear-floods, nor sigh-tempests move;
'Twere profanation of our joys
    To tell the laity our love.

Moving of th' earth brings harms and fears,
    Men reckon what it did, and meant;   10
But trepidation of the spheres,
    Though greater far, is innocent.

Dull sublunary lovers' love
　—Whose soul is sense—cannot admit
Absence, because it doth remove
　Those things which elemented it.

But we by a love so much refined
　That ourselves know not what it is,
Inter-assurèd of the mind,
　Care less eyes, lips and hands to miss.　　20

Our two souls therefore, which are one,
　Though I must go, endure not yet
A breach, but an expansion,
　Like gold to airy thinness beat.

If they be two, they are two so
　As stiff twin compasses are two;
Thy soul, the fix'd foot, makes no show
　To move, but doth, if th' other do.

And though it in the centre sit,
　Yet, when the other far doth roam,　　30
It leans, and hearkens after it,
　And grows erect, as that comes home.

Such wilt thou be to me, who must,
　Like th' other foot, obliquely run;
Thy firmness makes my circle just,
　And makes me end where I begun.

WILLIAM EMPSON　*This Last Pain*

This last pain for the damned the Fathers found:
"They knew the bliss with which they were not crowned."
　Such, but on earth, let me foretell,
　Is all, of heaven or of hell.

Man, as the prying housemaid of the soul,
May know her happiness by eye to hole:
　He's safe; the key is lost; he knows
　Door will not open, nor hole close.

"What is conceivable can happen too,"
Said Wittgenstein, who had not dreamt of you;   10
    But wisely; if we worked it long
    We should forget where it was wrong.

Those thorns are crowns which, woven into knots,
Crackle under and soon boil fool's pots;
    And no man's watching, wise and long,
    Would ever stare them into song.

Thorns burn to a consistent ash, like man;
A splendid cleanser for the frying-pan:
    And those who leap from pan to fire
    Should this brave opposite admire.   20

All those large dreams by which men long live well
Are magic-lanterned on the smoke of hell;
    This then is real, I have implied,
    A painted, small, transparent slide.

These the inventive can hand-paint at leisure,
Or most emporia would stock our measure;
    And feasting in their dappled shade
    We should forget how they were made.

Feign then what's by a decent tact believed
And act that state is only so conceived,   30
    And build an edifice of form
    For house where phantoms may keep warm.

Imagine, then, by miracle, with me,
(Ambiguous gifts, as what gods give must be)
    What could not possibly be there,
    And learn a style from a despair.

KENNETH FEARING *Green Light*

Bought at the drug store, very cheap; and later pawned.
After a while, heard on the street; seen in the park.
Familiar, but not quite recognized.
Followed and taken home and slept with.
Traded or sold. Or lost.

Bought again at the corner drug store,
At the green light, at the patient's demand, at nine o'clock.
Re-read and memorized and re-wound.
Found unsuitable.
Smashed, put together, and pawned.   10

Heard on the street, seen in a dream, heard in the park, séen by the
    light of day;
Carefully observed one night by a secret agent of the Greek Hydraulic
    Mining Commission, in plain clothes, off duty.
The agent, in broken English, took copious notes. Which he lost.
Strange, and yet not extraordinary.
Sad, but true.

True, or exaggerated, or true;
As it is true that the people laugh and the sparrows fly;
As it is exaggerated that the people change, and the sea stays;
As it is that the people go;
As the lights go on and it is night and it is serious, and just the
    same;   20
As some one dies and it is serious, and the same;
As a girl knows and it is small, and true;
As the corner hardware clerk might know and it is true, and
    pointless;
As an old man knows and it is grotesque, but true;
As the people laugh, as the people think, as the people change,
It is serious and the same, exaggerated or true.

Bought at the drug store down the street
Where the wind blows and the motors go by and it is always night,
    or day;
Bought to use as a last resort,
Bought to impress the statuary in the park.   30
Bought at a cut rate, at the green light, at nine o'clock.
Borrowed or bought. To look well. To ennoble. To prevent disease.
    To entertain. To have.
Broken or sold. Or given away. Or used and forgotten. Or lost.

RANDALL JARRELL   *The Black Swan*

When the swans turned my sister into a swan
    I would go to the lake, at night, from milking:

The sun would look out through the reeds like a swan,
    A swan's red beak; and the beak would open
And inside there was darkness, the stars and the moon.

Out on the lake a girl would laugh.
    "Sister, here is your porridge, sister,"
I would call; and the reeds would whisper,
    "Go to sleep, go to sleep, little swan."
My legs were all hard and webbed, and the silky   10

Hairs of my wings sank away like stars
    In the ripples that ran in and out of the reeds:
I heard through the lap and hiss of water
    Someone's "Sister . . . sister," far away on the shore,
And then as I opened my beak to answer

I heard my harsh laugh go out to the shore
    And saw—saw at last, swimming up from the green
Low mounds of the lake, the white stone swans:
    The white, named swans . . . "It is all a dream,"
I whispered, and reached from the down of the pallet   20

To the lap and hiss of the floor.
    And "Sleep, little sister," the swans all sang
From the moon and stars and frogs of the floor.
    But the swan my sister called, "Sleep at last, little sister,"
And stroked all night, with a black wing, my wings.

IMAMU AMIRI BARAKA (LEROI JONES)   *An Agony. As Now.*

I am inside someone
who hates me. I look
out from his eyes. Smell
what fouled tunes come in
to his breath. Love his
wretched women.

Slits in the metal, for sun. Where
my eyes sit turning, at the cool air
the glance of light, or hard flesh
rubbed against me, a woman, a man,   10
without shadow, or voice, or meaning.

This is the enclosure (flesh,
where innocence is a weapon. An
abstraction. Touch. (Not mine.
Or yours, if you are the soul I had
and abandoned when I was blind and had
my enemies carry me as a dead man
(if he is beautiful, or pitied.

It can be pain. (As now, as all his
flesh hurts me.) It can be that. Or   20
pain. As when she ran from me into
that forest.
              Or pain, the mind
silver spiraled whirled against the
sun, higher than even old men thought
God would be. Or pain. And the other. The
yes. (Inside his books, his fingers. They
are withered yellow flowers and were never
beautiful.) The yes. You will, lost soul, say
'beauty.' Beauty, practiced, as the tree. The
slow river. A white sun in its wet sentences.   30
Or, the cold men in their gale. Ecstasy. Flesh
or soul. The yes. (Their robes blown. Their bowls
empty. They chant at my heels, not at yours.) Flesh
or soul, as corrupt. Where the answer moves too quickly.
Where the God is a self, after all.)

Cold air blown through narrow blind eyes. Flesh,
white hot metal. Glows as the day with its sun.
It is a human love, I live inside. A bony skeleton
you recognize as words or simple feeling.

But it has no feeling. As the metal, is hot, it is not,   40
given to love.

It burns the thing
inside it. And that thing
screams.

Chapter Seven

Poetry as Symbol and Evocation

I

VARIETIES OF SYMBOLISM

"Man," says the philosopher Ernst Cassirer, "lives in a symbolic universe. Language, myth, art, and religion are parts of this universe. They are the varied threads which weave the symbolic net, the tangled web of human experience." [1]

Even our most prosaic thinking is dominated by symbols—coins, trademarks, directional signals on cars, for example. And our emotional lives are full of such symbols as engagement rings, gifts, meaningful looks and gestures, diplomas and prizes. Insofar as one thing is used to represent something else, we may call it a symbol. A symbol may be quite without emotional connotation—witness the numbers and signs used in mathematics to denote relationships and quantities. But it may also be charged with feeling: the Flag, the Cross, the Statue of Liberty. The latter kind of symbol not only denotes an idea but also connotes, and evokes, an attitude toward it and an emotion that surrounds it. The symbols of poetry fall in this second class.

In the most general sense, all poetry is symbolic. It has the power to control our imaginations by suggesting new associations for familiar ideas and experiences. From this point of view, Shakespeare's metaphor beginning his *Sonnet LXXIII* is symbolic:

> That time of year thou mayst in me behold
> When yellow leaves, or none, or few do hang
> Upon those boughs which shake against the cold. . . .[2]

[1] Ernst Cassirer, *An Essay on Man.*
[2] See pages 112–115 for this poem and a discussion of it.

The association of the barren, abandoned, chilled look of trees in late autumn with old age is a visible and generally sensuous representation of something not itself directly present to the senses.

But more precisely, we do not use the word "symbol" merely as a synonym for "figure of speech." An image is a symbol, first, when it comes already fraught with literary, historical, or popular associations; its emotional power will be most strongly felt, of course, when it is placed in the right context and so phrased as to be unusually startling and significant. Three lines by the Elizabethan poet Thomas Nashe will illustrate this principle:

> Brightness falls from the air,
> Queens have died young and fair,
> Dust hath closed Helen's eye. . . .

Nowhere in these lines does the poet explicitly state his melancholy underlying theme that death must come to all things, even the most beautiful. It is the unusual, brilliant effect of the beginning that especially takes the imagination. The notion is so unexpected that at first we may get the *wrong* impression, an impression of heavenly brightness descending and illuminating us—a happy and blessed picture. Then the true picture takes shape, of bright daylight that disappears and leaves the air dark, dull, and cold. The shock of this belated realization adds to its power and intensity, to the effect of irredeemable loss. And finally therefore, aided by the lines that follow "Brightness falls from the air," we will think of the universal fact of death, applicable to all things however glorious and lovely.

Supporting this striking image that so takes us unawares, we have first the simple pathos—half folk-wisdom and half a "truth" of fairy-tale lore—of "Queens have died young and fair." The fresh, naïve directness of the statement saves it from triteness and provides an emotional frame for the preceding line. And afterward, the full elegiac note of sadness is struck in the reminder of the death of Helen of Troy, the great popularly accepted symbol of erotic feminine beauty in all ages since Homer. It is hard to think of Helen dead, and the somewhat surprising use of her name with all its evocative power in this way helps give the passage its reverberating richness. The second and third lines lend to the extraordinary image they follow the quality of a traditional symbol, for they bring to it their own connotations of fallen brightness from mythology and popular legendry.

Images become symbols in yet other ways. If a poet lays emphasis on an image by pointing out that it has a special meaning and perhaps even defining that meaning for us, it then becomes a symbol almost by main force. The following passage from Wordsworth's *The Prelude* contains two examples of this second, more obvious, and often more static type of poetic symbolism. Notice how explicitly the poet makes clear what his symbolic clues are, and how we are to interpret them. Wordsworth, in this passage, tells how he would gaze at the faces on London's crowded streets, trying to fathom the mysterious meaning behind each of them. The blind beggar he once saw there, wearing his pathetic "written paper" that told his life story, signifies the futile superficiality of all men's supposed knowledge. Similarly, the poet's vision of a "second-sight procession" is a sign of the vagueness with which, at best, essential truth presents itself to our limited human understanding. It should be clear from these lines that even such interpreted symbols vary greatly in their intensity of evocation.

> How oft, amid those overflowing streets,
> Have I gone forward with the crowd, and said
> Unto myself, "The face of every one
> That passes by me is a mystery!"
> Thus have I looked, nor ceased to look, oppressed
> By thoughts of what and whither, when and how,
> Until the shapes before my eyes became
> A second-sight procession, such as glides
> Over still mountains, or appears in dreams;
> And once, far-travelled in such mood, beyond   10
> The reach of common indication, lost
> Amid the moving pageant, I was smitten
> Abruptly, with the view (a sight not rare)
> Of a blind Beggar, who, with upright face,
> Stood, propped against a wall, upon his chest
> Wearing a written paper, to explain
> His story, whence he came, and who he was.
> Caught by the spectacle my mind turned round
> As with the might of waters; an apt type
> This label seemed of the utmost we can know,   20
> Both of ourselves and of the universe;
> And, on the shape of that unmoving man,
> His steadfast face and sightless eyes, I gazed,
> As if admonished from another world.

Wordsworth's symbolism here is effective, both in clarifying his conception and in suggesting the feeling with which he associated it. But one of his symbols, the blind beggar with his piece of paper, is far inferior in emotional power to the symbol that precedes it—the dim, visionary procession gliding in the distance, elusive and significant as a dream. One reason is that the poet comments on the obvious meaning of the beggar-symbol so quickly and explicitly that it is hard for us to catch its special evocation from the image alone. Unlike the purer symbol it follows, it is overly dominated by its intended didactic function. Were it not for the grave and compelling seriousness of "steadfast face and sightless eyes," it would serve this function very poorly; it would merely illustrate an idea, mechanically and without being itself the embodiment of a living meaning.

Many popular poems are really pictorial arguments or parables of a sort, with a single important difference. The symbols they present usually do not arise from the poet's search for illustrations to illuminate his theme and viewpoint. On the contrary, the symbols came first, and the poet then sought for a "noble" way of interpreting them. A good example is Bryant's *To a Waterfowl*. Moved by the distant sight of a solitary bird flying in the sky, the poet felt the universal significance of the certain, unwavering flight of the small creature toward its proper destination in the midst of vastness and danger:

> All day thy wings have fanned,
> At that far height, the cold, thin atmosphere,
> Yet stoop not, weary, to the welcome land,
> Though the dark night is near.

Pondering the significance of the bird in its flight, Bryant discovers "the lesson thou hast given"—the guidance of God in which all of us, in our lonely life-journeys, must trust. Poetry like this really consists of two independent aspects—the imagery, or story, as such, which is often original and moving, and the "moral," generally contrived and obvious but sometimes appropriate and effective in its own right.

In allegorical writing, which generally takes a narrative form, the picture-story with an interpretation reaches its extreme form. But an allegory, unlike a parable, is not merely a story consistent with an attached moral. This most elaborate form of symbolic didactic argument makes a point through everything that appears in it; every image, character, and incident, as well as the entire plot, signifies a definable abstraction. The abstraction may be a doctrine, a psychological conflict, a social type, even a particular individual's character—anything that can be stated as a general proposition. One of the allegorist's chief devices is personification—the representation of ideas and inanimate things as though they were human beings; and together with this device, he will use other, related types of metaphor in which an abstract idea is seen as a concrete object. When, as in Dante, the pictures are thoroughly alive and compelling in themselves, even though at the same time they represent abstract principles, current politics, or other implied meanings, we approach the state of pure symbolism in the sense discussed below, on pages 353–356. But in any case, the narrative form gets the symbols moving in active relation with one another, and thus clarifies the intended meaning of all of them, as well as the meaning of the whole sequence of events. The symbols, quite static in themselves, come to life through their interplay, which is essential to the success of an allegorical work.

Thus, the hero of the first book of Spenser's *The Faerie Queene* is the Red Cross Knight who symbolizes, among other things, the idea of holiness and the mission of the Anglican Church. His armor is that of a true Christian, for he is clad

> . . . . in mightie armes and silver shielde,
> Wherein old dints of deepe wounds did remaine,

and on this shield there is the image of Christ on the Cross, fashioned there

> For soveraine hope, which in his helpe he had:
> Right faithfull true he was in deede and word.

(The description of the knight's armor was also a definite reminder, to Spenser's Bible-conscious sixteenth-century readers, of St. Paul's allegorical figure of "putting on the breastplate of faith and love; and for a helmet, the hope of salvation.")

This knight fights for the lady Una, who represents the one true faith as the Protestant poet conceives it. She is lovely, pure, innocent, "and by descent from royal lineage"—that is, she represents genuine Christianity as it is derived from the kingdom of God by way of the Gospels. The knight's chief adversary, on the other hand, represents the Catholic Church and the hypocrisy that Spenser—a zealous Puritan—attributed to it. The adversary, Archimago, seems a pious, simple hermit. He dresses in sober black and walks humbly with his eyes cast down,

> And all the way he prayèd, as he went,
> And often knockt his breast, as one that did repent.

But in reality he is

> A bold bad man, that dared to call by name
> Great Gorgon, Prince of darkness and dead night. . . .

The knight tears himself free of Archimago's influence, as was foreshadowed in his earlier victory over the foul dragon of erroneous religious doctrine—"a monster vile, whom God and man does hate."

An allegory, then, is a quite elaborate pictorial dramatization of relationships among ideas, attitudes, institutions, and other abstract concepts. Of necessity, therefore, it must be a work of considerable length. But many shorter pieces are allegorical in a more limited sense; they use one or another typical feature of allegory, and it is clear that the symbols in them are more important for their implied significance than they are for themselves. Thus, Collins's brief eighteenth-century *Ode* in praise of all soldiers who have died in their country's service (pages 447–448) employs allegorical personification. When such soldiers die, we are told, they are blessed and mourned by the principles for which they fought:

> There Honour comes, a Pilgrim grey,
> To bless the Turf that wraps their Clay,
> And Freedom shall awhile repair,
> To dwell a weeping Hermit there!

Closely allied in purpose, and different only in small degree from allegory, is the kind of poem in which a writer describes an adventure or a scene and then explains its inherent significance or makes his characters do so. Because it is so clearly about an imaginary and symbolic incident, the following poem is even nearer to allegory than most such work.

WILFRED OWEN *Strange Meeting*

> It seemed that out of battle I escaped
> Down some profound dull tunnel, long since scooped
> Through granites which titanic wars had groined.
> Yet also there encumbered sleepers groaned,
> Too fast in thought or death to be bestirred.
> Then, as I probed them, one sprang up, and stared
> With piteous recognition in fixed eyes,
> Lifting distressful hands as if to bless.
> And by his smile I knew that sullen hall,
> By his dead smile I knew we stood in Hell.   10
> With a thousand pains that vision's face was grained;
> Yet no blood reached there from the upper ground,
> And no guns thumped, or down the flues made moan.
> "Strange friend," I said, "here is no cause to mourn."
> "None," said the other, "save the undone years,
> The hopelessness. Whatever hope is yours,
> Was my life also; I went hunting wild
> After the wildest beauty in the world,
> Which lies not calm in eyes, or braided hair,
> But mocks the steady running of the hour,
> And if it grieves, grieves richlier than here.   20

For by my glee might many men have laughed,
And of my weeping something had been left,
Which must die now. I mean the truth untold,
The pity of war, the pity war distilled.
Now men will go content with what we spoiled,
Or, discontent, boil bloody and be spilled.
They will be swift with swiftness of the tigress,
None will break ranks, though nations trek from progress.
Courage was mine, and I had mystery,   30
Wisdom was mine, and I had mastery;
To miss the march of this retreating world
Into vain citadels that are not walled.
Then, when much blood had clogged their chariot wheels
I would go up and wash them from sweet wells,
Even with truths that lie too deep for taint.
I would have poured my spirit without stint
But not through wounds; not on the cess of war.
Foreheads of men have bled where no wounds were.
I am the enemy you killed, my friend.   40
I knew you in this dark; for so you frowned
Yesterday, through me as you jabbed and killed.
I parried, but my hands were loath and cold.
Let us sleep now. . . ."

Wilfred Owen, the author of *Strange Meeting*, was killed in the first World War before he could quite complete the poem. His meaning, however, is clear enough. The speaker has had a vision of meeting, in Hell, a man he had killed in battle, one with aspirations like his own to serve mankind in some high way. The war, he learns, has, by making him the destroyer of other men's hopes and ideals, also corrupted his own. War is thus seen as a spoiler of men and of societies. The passionate speech of the "strange friend," with its consonantal rhymes such as *wild-world* or *killed-cold*, is the heart of the poem. The rocking music of the rhymes helps set the theme hypnotically—the bitter frustration by war of the ecstatic creativity of the human spirit. The narrative provides only the slightest of dramatic frameworks, but it does help us to see that the "I" of the poem stands not for the poet only but for any soldier in any army of any war, while the strange friend represents both the nobler aspects of the average man and the special group of sensitive and idealistic persons to be found in any society.

Strange Meeting thus stands midway between the didactic, often contrived symbolism of allegory and parable and the pure symbolism discussed in the following pages. A brief poem by Randall Jarrell will remind us of how ideas are embodied in the latter kind of writing.

RANDALL JARRELL *The Death of the Ball Turret Gunner*

From my mother's sleep I fell into the State,
And I hunched in its belly till my wet fur froze.
Six miles from earth, loosed from its dream of life,
I woke to black flak and the nightmare fighters.
When I died they washed me out of the turret with a hose.

The thought behind this poem, although much less explicit than that of *Strange Meeting*, is a great deal more concrete and forceful. The reason is that the two final lines present nightmare reality with a physical directness that simultaneously shocks and convinces. We are not told in so many words that there is such a thing as what Owen calls "the pity of war" or that it has stunted the growth of the free and creative spirit. Instead, the poem provides a series of images in which birth and death are linked. From his mother's womb the speaker "fell into" that of the State. There is a similar wrenching away from nature in his being carried up into the world of air-combat and away from earth (the old familiar "Mother Earth" of tradition). The womb and birth imagery is horribly reversed in the final line. We note that the true mother is warm, personal, protective; the State is cold, uninterested, and its womb is one in which the developing personality is neither cherished nor awakened intellectually—in which the "wet fur" of the embryo human intelligence freezes before it realizes its own misery of existence. From the instinctive, mindless, natural care of the mother ("my mother's sleep") the young human animal has been drafted into the orbit of the impersonal State; the earth contains a dream of life, but does not know how to keep her charges true to that dream. Death itself comes to the man in a virtual nightmare while he is curled up like a foetus in the ball turret. Both the pathos and the meaning, then, derive from this unawakened dream-quality, this unrealized consciousness; it is as if a child should die before coming to any awareness of itself or its possibilities in life. All these ideas and suggestions are concentrated in the symbol of the womb.

The intellectual implications of such symbolism, as in the symbolic dialogue of *Strange Meeting*, are an essential ingredient of the poem in which they appear. It is true that in Owen's poem we are closer to allegory—which, as Yeats once observed, requires "right information" for its interpretation rather than the "right intuition" which pure symbolism demands of the reader. But both Owen and Jarrell are bringing attitudes to light and life—however different the forms in which they appear, and however important it is to remember that a good poem is never merely the vehicle for an idea. The abhorrence of war and the other allied ideas we find in the two pieces by Owen and Jarrell are the durable intellectual cement of these poems.

We should not lose sight of the essential technical difference between a symbol and an ordinary figure of speech: the greater magnetic power in the former to evoke many psychological associations. This magnetic power is most completely felt in the purest poetic symbols, in which a figure of speech is *implied but not stated*. In this kind of image, the poet does not, for example, say that his love is like a rose; he does not say, even, that she *is* a rose.[3] Rather, perhaps, he will treat the rose itself as his subject, but in a special way. Omitting any reference to the woman who would ordinarily be his main topic, he may yet attribute to the rose qualities he feels belong both to it and to her, and other qualities arising from the association itself. The result, if successful, will produce not only the effect an ordinary metaphor would have produced but also the transcendent, subtle, and vital connotations that William Butler Yeats has called "perfectly symbolical." [4] Once again we may turn to Blake for an example:

WILLIAM BLAKE *The Sick Rose*

O Rose, thou art sick!
The invisible worm,
That flies in the night,
In the howling storm,

Has found out thy bed
Of crimson joy;
And his dark secret love
Does thy life destroy.

In this poem we have the purest sort of symbolism, in which we feel a precise, concentrated, terrifyingly significant meaning. The atmosphere is tragic; the imagery suggests the corruption of life and joy by death or by some force hostile to them yet needing them for its own nourishment. The "worm" suggests both the snake that corrupted Eden and the worms of the grave; darkness and terror attend it. The rose suggests full-blown womanliness, beautiful and vulnerable. Something in the world has infected and blighted this joyous presence in life, and is destroying it. We may read a number of possible interpretations, all actually present, into this symbolism; however, its power will be explained not by any one interpretation, nor yet by the flash of perception in the implied metaphors, but by the violent, self-contained life of the symbol itself: the flower possessed and being killed by the worm.

[3] See the discussion of simile and metaphor and the references to Burns's *O my luve is like a red, red rose*, on page 484.

[4] William Butler Yeats, "The Symbolism of Poetry." (*Essays*) The passage referred to is quoted and discussed, pages 390–391.

Why should "natural" symbols like the rose and the "brightness" that "falls from the air" strike us as purer in their evocative power than most traditional symbols? Logically, it would seem that symbols of the latter type, trailing their inherited associations behind them as they enter a poem, carry a greater suggestiveness from the start than those the poet himself has brought into significant focus for the first time. We remember the aura about the name of Helen of Troy, in Nashe's lines. And when Spenser writes of a knight that

> . . . . on his breast a bloody Cross he bore,
> The dear remembrance of his dying Lord,

we respond at once to the knight's character and to the virtues he represents.

Yet the poet who depends on traditional symbols runs the great risk of finding himself with a stereotyped set of images. Or else he has a team of runaway images whose powerful general associations force him to lose sight of his own attitudes once he gets behind them. If the poet is as steeped in classical literature and learning as Milton, and as gifted, he can use such symbols freshly. But for all his learning Milton, like Dante, knew the value and force of images drawn from ordinary human experience—birds, animals, flowers, sun and stars, sickness, birth, and all the other many familiar yet emotionally significant data of daily life. Amid the mythological and Biblical figures that dominate his elegy *Lycidas* (pages 365–370), we find such homely images as the following ones (intended to symbolize greedy and incompetent priests and their neglected congregations):

> . . . . such as for their bellies' sake
> Creep and intrude, and climb into the fold. . . .
> Blind mouths! that scarce themselves know how to hold
> A sheep-hook, or have learn'd aught else the least
> That to the faithful herdsman's art belongs!
> What recks it them? What need they? They are sped;
> And when they list, their lean and flashy songs
> Grate on their scrannel pipes of wretched straw,
> The hungry sheep look up, and are not fed,
> But swoln with wind, and the rank mist they draw,   10
> Rot inwardly, and foul contagion spread. . . .

It is, of course, traditional to view priests as shepherds (pastors) and those to whom they minister as their flocks. What renders the symbolism here memorable, however, is not Milton's use of conventional associations but the way he transmutes them through the passionate sense of reality revealed in the pictures of the corrupt clergy and their effect on their "sheep." In the context of the poem, this is no mere generalized painting but a furious attack on the practices of the established church by a fiery Puritan of the 1630's. Without the sense of common realities here displayed, the attack could not have been so overwhelmingly managed. When Milton wishes to suggest the beauty and simplicity of character of his friend, Edward King, whose death the poem laments, and the affection he inspired, he does so indirectly by describing the common but lovely English flowers that will be strewed on his hearse by the mourners—

> . . . . the rathe primrose that forsaken dies,
> The tufted crow-toe, and pale jessamine,
>
> The white pink, and the pansy freaked with jet,
> The glowing violet,
> The musk rose, and the well-attired woodbine,
> With cowslips wan that hang the pensive head. . . .

This symbolism is not only appropriate to the character ascribed to Milton's friend; it is also, like the symbolism of the sick and hungry sheep, drawn from the pervasive but usually undefined associations that lie deep in the recurrent observations, joys, and difficulties of people in their everyday life. A natural symbol is really halfway to being a traditional symbol, from this point of view. Its advantage lies in the greater leeway it allows the poet to draw on one or another of its familiar associations in his own unique fashion, because it has never been popularly viewed as representative of an institution or a creed, and is not therefore surrounded by fierce loyalties and taboos and authorized interpretations.

Thus, when Walt Whitman, in his elegy for Lincoln (pages 372–379), wished to create appropriate symbols for the greatness of the dead President, for the love with which he cherished his memory, and for his own role as a poet singing a message of consolation and courage, he chose three natural objects: the western star, the lilac, and the hermit thrush. Instead of counting on the accumulated richness of traditional symbols, he gained something of the same effect through accumulative presentation. His symbols emerge most fully at the end of the poem, after he has driven them home to us in many ways. By the time we reach the final lines with their final tribute—

> . . . . for the dead I loved so well,
> For the sweetest, wisest soul of all my days and lands, and this for his
> dear sake,
> Lilac and star and bird twined with the chant of my soul,
> There in the fragrant pines and the cedars dusk and dim.

—the star, the flower, and the bird have become carriers of universal meanings that go far beyond the specific occasion that led to their use in this poem.

A poet using a traditional symbol will often elaborate on it by adding details of action, atmosphere, and sense-impression that suggest his own response to it. He hopes thus to gain from its initial advantages and at the same time to re-create it into something newly discovered, like the symbols of Whitman. Keats's *Ode to a Nightingale* (pages 370–372) employs certain traditional symbols such as the Roman god Bacchus and his leopards—symbols of intoxication through wine-drinking—in a quite conventional fashion. But they have a relatively minor function in the poem. The major symbol, the sweet-singing nightingale with its mythological associations of suffering and desire, is exalted through the concentrated pressure of emotion and imagination. We do not have here the brilliant realistic visualization with which Milton reawakens meanings latent in symbolic language: instead, an old symbol is redefined for us in the light of the feelings and imagined states of being the poet attaches to it. The bird's song is made first of all a sense-experience. But as the poet's mood that has been brought to light by it develops and changes, it takes on meanings that are neither in nature nor in tradition, meanings arising from his uniquely personal sense of the abyss between reality and joyous self-transformation.

Keats's *Ode* begins with an impassioned, almost physical statement of painful depression:

> My heart aches, and a drowsy numbness pains
> My sense, as though of hemlock I had drunk. . . .

We then learn what has induced this feeling—the nightingale singing in the richly scented summer woodlands. And we learn also that it is *excess of happiness* that is responsible for the poet's anguish. Pleasure too intense is pain. The Classical references to *Lethe*, the river of forgetfulness from which the dead must drink, and *dryad*, a wood spirit, here the nightingale, are in keeping with the reference to the hemlock, the drug used to kill Socrates.

How can the poet, he asks himself, enter into the happy world where the nightingale dwells? He suggests the cool, fragrant, intoxicating wine of Provence—a province in the south of France associated with the troubadours and medieval love poetry. This is a happier and more enticing draught than the hemlock of the previous stanza. But the poet's desire is to escape from the limitations and frustrations of the world of fact in which his waking life is spent.

The third stanza makes clear why he wishes to escape—or what he wishes to escape from. It is Time—as in Donne's *The Sun Rising*—that is the destroyer of youth and beauty and the corrupter of love.[5] But the tone is much more intense than in Donne's brilliant and witty poem, for it is of his own approaching death and wasted youth that Keats is thinking. He knew at the time the poem was composed that he was touched with consumption.

The poet rejects escape through the medium of opiates or wine. "Bacchus and his pards" refers to the god of wine, followed by his train of revelers and his sacred leopards. Instead it is with the aid of poetry, i.e., the creative imagination, the emotions and the senses, that he will escape into the world of eternal happiness and beauty, of which we should now realize the bird has become the symbol. And in the fourth stanza the magical change does come about, suddenly:

> Already with thee! Tender is the night. . . .

The tone is one of surprise. The spell has worked. The poet is transported from the world of sick thought and numbing pain into the eternal, ever-youthful world of the imagination. All is a Midsummer Night's dream of rich and exquisite music, which is presented in the rest of this stanza and in the next with an intensity and precision that perfectly realize the aim of the artist to endow the world of imagination with reality.

The almost purely descriptive and very beautiful fifth stanza, we should realize, presents not an escape from reality but an immersion in it. All the imagery comes from the actual natural world experienced with the utmost sensuousness, but it is a changing and fleeting world where the seasons come and go and the flowers are "fast fading." Phrases such as "soft incense," "embalmèd darkness," and "violets cover'd up in leaves" distill a funereal and deathlike atmosphere—all in the midst of an exquisitely pleasurable sensation.

This passage prepares us for the deeply emotional and intensely personal development in the sixth. Here is the expression of perfect ecstasy; but how is it to be retained? How can the inevitable relapse that terminates it be escaped? Is there no way to thwart the ebbing back of the sorrows of the sick world of reality? Only one way suggests itself, and it has suggested itself before: to die at the moment of intensest ecstasy—

> To cease upon the midnight with no pain.

Indeed, in the mood of excitement that the bird has induced, death itself is a sensuous experience—

[5] Discussed on pages 280–283.

Now more than ever seems it *rich* to die.

In the seventh—the most famous and wonderful stanza—the bird as a symbol of eternal, superhuman beauty and as a liberator of the heart into the fairyland of the imagination is presented with the greatest directness and in ringing tones that are sharply contrasted to the yearning desperation of the stanza before.

But suddenly, almost unconsciously, at the height of his excitement the poet has stumbled on a word—the word "forlorn"—and the vision so magically and intensely presented in the lines that begin "Already with thee!" (line 35) collapses like a bubble. The poet is left forsaken with no resource but his own lonely and inadequate self. The total experience the poem presents is not the ecstatic vision of its central section with its *seeming* escape into the eternal world of the imagination but the melancholy and disillusioned awakening to the fact that "the fancy" (he does not call it imagination, which to him was man's highest faculty for perceiving truth) "cannot cheat so well as she is famed to do." But with what skill the song of the bird fading in the distance is equated to the gradual fading away of the happy vision and the return of the harsh world where but to think is to be full of sorrow!

An interesting example of the transmuting of a traditional symbol by a modern poet may be found in T. S. Eliot's vision, in *The Waste Land*, of London as a hellish place, the abode of the living dead. His method is to describe the crowds on the street as though they were passing through the mysteriously "unreal" landscape of Hell, in an atmosphere of murk and filth, with an unwilled, pointless, flowing movement. Eliot's picture is based on the oldest traditions of European literature and mythology, and especially on Dante's *Inferno*. It is the unexpected literalness with which he describes the actual city, London, in terms of Hell that turns his symbolism into something completely new:

Unreal City,
Under the brown fog of a winter dawn,
A crowd flowed over London Bridge, so many,
I had not thought death had undone so many.
Sighs, short and infrequent, were exhaled,
And each man fixed his eyes before his feet.

The final three lines of this quotation closely echo lines in Canto III of the *Inferno*, in which Dante describes his entrance into Hell. Here, near the very gates, he sees the horde of souls who "lived without blame, and without praise," who never committed themselves to good or evil causes but were only "for themselves," who never made a decision nor entered into life and consequently have no being or personality that can know either salvation or damnation. They are the hollow men, the vast multitudes of the mediocre and the timidly selfish. Dante is overwhelmed by their number: "I had not thought death had undone so many." Death has "undone" them in the elementary sense that they have died. But the word itself has a certain rich ambiguity, for it also suggests, as part of this ruin that death has brought them, the unwrapping of flesh and bones from the bodiless spirits. And more than this, it suggests the special misery of their present indefinite status. We are told that they have passed into utter oblivion; even "deep Hell receives them not, for the wicked would have some glory over them," and "they are envious of every other lot."

The shock of Eliot's lines echoing Dante lies in the sudden apparition of the big-city multitudes as misery-driven creatures, so uninspired and characterless that they are like these forgotten shades, excluded from further damnation as well as from glory, envisioned in the *Inferno*. Of course, Eliot does not say they are "like" the shades, or that they are suffering spirits wavering on the edge of Hell. Rather, he creates his own symbol in which all the suggestions of unreality, suffering, and pity converge: Here is the Unreal City, and here are its inhabitants. The reader should compare this brief passage with that by Wordsworth quoted on pages 349–350. He will see that they share the essential evocativeness of all symbolism, but that the Eliot passage omits explanation, transition, everything that will not contribute to the purest evocative effect.

In reviewing these various forms the symbol may take—simple and complex, natural and traditional, static and pure and poet-transmuted—we must always remember the special evocative character of the poetic symbol. It is the kind of image that directs our sensibilities, magnetically, toward a deep emotional awareness that includes but goes beyond in-tellectual concepts. It may appear in a single line or group of lines only. It may, by itself or in relation to other symbols, dominate the structure of a whole poem. Or it may, in the purest and most concentrated poetry, actually be inseparable from the poem as a whole. (The lines from Nashe will illustrate the first of these possibilities; Whitman's *When lilacs last in the dooryard bloom'd*, the second of them; and Blake's *The Sick Rose*, the third.)

Poems: Varieties of Symbolism

The workings of symbolism in the poems in this section should be fairly clear. We begin with two poems, by Blake and by Yeats, that present pure symbolic situations. Blake's sunflower "aspires" toward a realm beyond this world, and yet in that realm aspiration does not cease—a suggestion of a universe made up of endless unfulfillment, although Blake makes no effort to read an abstract meaning into the pictures he presents. Yeats's poem presents the cat and the moon in an intimate, reciprocal relationship suggesting a constant interplay between our animal natures and the cold cosmic forces that define our fate—again, however, without explicit interpretation beyond a playfully mystical tone in the comment offered.

The poems that follow, however, are emphatically explicit. Those by Lawrence and Herbert take some of their force from a kind of prophetic revelation of universal meanings. *Lycidas* has some of the allegorical symbolism of Herbert's *Redemption* but derives its energy equally from symbols out of Classical mythology and from a number of natural and even pure symbols as well. Many of its figures and images are characteristically present in the traditional elegy, yet the mourning tone, the angry notes, and the spirit of renewal at the end have a freshness of feeling that organizes the symbols around them and keeps the poem vividly alive. This poem, and those by Keats and by Whitman, have been discussed in the text. All three are different from Hart Crane's *Proem*, which centers on a symbol of the industrial age as a token of man's divine creativity instead of on Classical and natural symbols. These latter types of symbol are present as well, though, in Crane's subtly and intricately developed poem, which is finally not really optimistic after all. Eberhart and Nemerov focus our attention on two symbols: Eberhart's the dead groundhog in its various stages of decay and Nemerov's the dead goose fish grinning at the lovers on the beach. Both symbols arouse terror, confusion, and a sense of diminution in the speakers.

WILLIAM BLAKE Ah! Sun-flower

> Ah! sun-flower, weary of time,
> Who countest the steps of the Sun,
> Seeking after that sweet golden clime
> Where the traveller's journey is done;
>
> Where the Youth pined away with desire,
> And the pale Virgin shrouded in snow,
> Arise from their graves, and aspire
> Where my Sun-flower wishes to go.

WILLIAM BUTLER YEATS   *The Cat and the Moon*

The cat went here and there
And the moon spun round like a top,
And the nearest kin of the moon,
The creeping cat, looked up.
Black Minnaloushe stared at the moon,
For, wander and wail as he would,
The pure cold light in the sky
Troubled his animal blood.
Minnaloushe runs in the grass
Lifting his delicate feet.   10
Do you dance, Minnaloushe, do you dance?
When two close kindred meet
What better than call a dance?
Maybe the moon may learn,
Tired of that courtly fashion,
A new dance turn.
Minnaloushe creeps through the grass
From moonlit place to place,
The sacred moon overhead
Has taken a new phase.   20
Does Minnaloushe know that his pupils
Will pass from change to change,
And that from round to crescent,
From crescent to round they range?
Minnaloushe creeps through the grass
Alone, important and wise,
And lifts to the changing moon
His changing eyes.

D. H. LAWRENCE   *Tortoise Shell*

The Cross, the Cross
Goes deeper in than we know,
Deeper into life;
Right into the marrow
And through the bone.

Along the back of the baby tortoise
The scales are locked in an arch like a bridge,
Scale-lapping, like a lobster's sections

Or a bee's.
Then crossways down his sides   10
Tiger-stripes and wasp-bands.

Five, and five again, and five again,
And round the edges twenty-five little ones,
The sections of the baby tortoise shell.

Four, and a keystone;
Four, and a keystone;
Four, and a keystone;
Then twenty-four, and a tiny little keystone.

It needed Pythagoras to see life playing with counters on the living
    back
Of the baby tortoise;   20
Life establishing the first eternal mathematical tablet,
Not in stone, like the Judean Lord, or bronze, but in life-clouded,
    life-rosy tortoise shell.

The first little mathematical gentleman
Stepping, wee mite, in his loose trousers
Under all the eternal dome of mathematical law.

Fives, and tens,
Threes and fours and twelves,
All the *volte face* of decimals,
The whirligig of dozens and the pinnacle of seven.

Turn him on his back,   30
The kicking little beetle,
And there again, on his shell-tender, earth-touching belly,
The long cleavage of division, upright of the eternal cross
And on either side count five,
On each side, two above, on each side, two below
The dark bar horizontal.

The Cross!
It goes right through him, the sprottling insect,
Through his cross-wise cloven psyche,
Through his five-fold complex-nature.   40

So turn him over on his toes again;
Four pin-point toes, and a problematical thumb-piece,
Four rowing limbs, and one wedge-balancing head,
Four and one makes five, which is the clue to all mathematics.

The Lord wrote it all down on the little slate
Of the baby tortoise.
Outward and visible indication of the plan within,
The complex, manifold involvedness of an individual creature
Plotted out
On this small bird, this rudiment,   50
This little dome, this pediment
Of all creation,
This slow one.

GEORGE HERBERT   *Redemption*

Having been tenant long to a rich lord,
Not thriving, I resolved to be bold,
And make a suit unto him, to afford
A new small-rented lease, and cancel the old.
In heaven at his manor I him sought:
They told me there, that he was lately gone
About some land, which he had dearly bought
Long since on earth to take possession.
I straight returned, and knowing his great birth,
Sought him accordingly in great resorts;   10
In cities, theatres, gardens, parks, and courts:
At length I heard a ragged noise and mirth
Of thieves and murderers: there I him espied,
Who straight, *Your suit is granted*, said, and died.

JOHN MILTON   *Lycidas*

   In this Monody the Author bewails a learned Friend, unfortunately
drowned in his passage from Chester on the Irish Seas, 1637; and, by
occasion, foretells the ruin of our corrupted Clergy, then in their height.

Yet once more, O ye laurels, and once more,
Ye myrtles brown, with ivy never-sear,
I come to pluck your berries harsh and crude,

And with forc'd fingers rude
Shatter your leaves before the mellowing year.
Bitter constraint and sad occasion dear
Compels me to disturb your season due;
For Lycidas is dead, dead ere his prime,
Young Lycidas, and hath not left his peer:
Who would not sing for Lycidas? he knew   10
Himself to sing, and build the lofty rhyme.
He must not float upon his watery bier
Unwept, and welter to the parching wind,
Without the meed of some melodious tear.
    Begin then, Sisters of the sacred well,
That from beneath the seat of Jove doth spring,
Begin, and somewhat loudly sweep the string.
Hence with denial vain, and coy excuse:
So may some gentle Muse
With lucky words favour my destin'd urn,   20
And as he passes turn,
And bid fair peace be to my sable shroud!
For we were nurst upon the self-same hill,
Fed the same flock, by fountain, shade, and rill.
    Together both, ere the high lawns appear'd
Under the opening eye-lids of the morn,
We drove a-field, and both together heard
What time the gray-fly winds her sultry horn,
Batt'ning our flocks with the fresh dews of night,
Oft till the star that rose, at ev'ning bright   30
Toward heav'n's descent had slop'd his westering wheel.
Meanwhile the rural ditties were not mute;
Temper'd to the oaten flute,
Rough Satyrs danc'd, and Fauns with clov'n heel
From the glad sound would not be absent long;
And old Damœtas lov'd to hear our song.
    But, O the heavy change, now thou art gone,
Now thou art gone and never must return!
Thee, Shepherd, thee the woods, and desert caves,
With wild thyme and the gadding vine o'ergrown,   40
And all their echoes mourn.
The willows, and the hazel copses green,
Shall now no more be seen,
Fanning their joyous leaves to thy soft lays.
As killing as the canker to the rose,
Or taint-worm to the weanling herds that graze,

Or frost to flowers, that their gay wardrobe wear,
When first the white-thorn blows;
Such, Lycidas, thy loss to shepherd's ear.
   Where were ye, Nymphs, when the remorseless deep   50
Clos'd o'er the head of your lov'd Lycidas?
For neither were ye playing on the steep
Where your old bards, the famous Druids, lie,
Nor on the shaggy top of Mona high,
Nor yet where Deva spreads her wizard stream.
Ay me! I fondly dream!
Had ye been there—for what could that have done?
What could the Muse herself that Orpheus bore,
The Muse herself for her enchanting son,
Whom universal nature did lament,   60
When by the rout that made the hideous roar,
His gory visage down the stream was sent,
Down the swift Hebrus to the Lesbian shore?
   Alas! what boots it with uncessant care
To tend the homely slighted shepherd's trade,
And strictly meditate the thankless Muse?
Were it not better done as others use,
To sport with Amaryllis in the shade,
Or with the tangles of Neæra's hair?
Fame is the spur that the clear spirit doth raise   70
(That last infirmity of noble mind)
To scorn delights, and live laborious days;
But the fair guerdon when we hope to find,
And think to burst out into sudden blaze,
Comes the blind Fury with th' abhorred shears,
And slits the thin-spun life. "But not the praise,"
Phœbus replied, and touched my trembling ears:
"Fame is no plant that grows on mortal soil,
Nor in the glistering foil
Set off to th' world, nor in broad rumour lies,   80
But lives and spreads aloft by those pure eyes
And perfect witness of all-judging Jove;
As he pronounces lastly on each deed,
Of so much fame in Heav'n expect thy meed."
   O fountain Arethuse, and thou honour'd flood,
Smooth-sliding Mincius, crown'd with vocal reeds,
That strain I heard was of a higher mood.
But now my oat proceeds,
And listens to the Herald of the Sea,

That came in Neptune's plea.   90
He ask'd the waves, and ask'd the felon winds,
What hard mishap hath doom'd this gentle swain?
And question'd every gust of rugged wings
That blows from off each beaked promontory.
They knew not of his story;
And sage Hippotades their answer brings,
That not a blast was from his dungeon stray'd:
The air was calm, and on the level brine
Sleek Panope with all her sisters play'd.
It was that fatal and perfidious bark,   100
Built in th' eclipse, and rigg'd with curses dark,
That sunk so low that sacred head of thine.
   Next Camus, reverend sire, went footing slow,
His mantle hairy, and his bonnet sedge,
Inwrought with figures dim, and on the edge
Like to that sanguine flower inscrib'd with woe.
Ah! who hath reft (quoth he) my dearest pledge?
Last came, and last did go,
The Pilot of the Galilean Lake;
Two massy keys he bore of metals twain,   110
(The golden opes, the iron shuts amain)
He shook his miter'd locks, and stern bespake:
How well could I have spar'd for thee, young swain,
Enow of such as for their bellies' sake,
Creep and intrude, and climb into the fold!
Of other care they little reck'ning make
Than how to scramble at the shearer's feast,
And shove away the worthy bidden guest.
Blind mouths! that scarce themselves know how to hold
A sheep-hook, or have learn'd ought else the least   120
That to the faithful herdsman's art belongs!
What recks it them? What need they? They are sped;
And when they list, their lean and flashy songs
Grate on their scrannel pipes of wretched straw,
The hungry sheep look up, and are not fed,
But swoln with wind, and the rank mist they draw,
Rot inwardly, and foul contagion spread:
Besides what the grim wolf with privy paw
Daily devours apace, and nothing said,
But that two-handed engine at the door,   130
Stands ready to smite once, and smite no more.
   Return, Alpheus, the dread voice is past,

That shrunk thy streams; return, Sicilian Muse,
And call the vales, and bid them hither cast
Their bells, and flow'rets of a thousand hues.
Ye valleys low where the mild whispers use
Of shades and wanton winds, and gushing brooks,
On whose fresh lap the swart star sparely looks,
Throw hither all your quaint enamel'd eyes,
That on the green turf suck the honied show'rs,   140
And purple all the ground with vernal flow'rs.
Bring the rathe primrose that forsaken dies,
The tufted crow-toe, and pale jessamine,
The white pink, and the pansy freaked with jet,
The glowing violet,
The musk-rose, and the well-attir'd woodbine,
With cowslips wan that hang the pensive head,
And every flower that sad embroidery wears;
Bid amaranthus all his beauty shed,
And daffadillies fill their cups with tears,   150
To strew the laureate hearse where Lycid lies.
For so, to interpose a little ease,
Let our frail thoughts dally with false surmise.
Ay me! whilst thee the shores, and sounding seas
Wash far away, where'er thy bones are hurl'd;
Whether beyond the stormy Hebrides,
Where thou perhaps under the whelming tide
Visit'st the bottom of the monstrous world;
Or whether thou, to our moist vows deny'd,
Sleep'st by the fable of Bellerus old,   160
Where the great Vision of the guarded mount
Looks toward Namancos and Bayona's hold.
Look homeward Angel now, and melt with ruth:
And, O ye dolphins, waft the hapless youth.
    Weep no more, woeful shepherds, weep no more,
For Lycidas, your sorrow, is not dead,
Sunk though he be beneath the wat'ry floor,
So sinks the day-star in the ocean bed,
And yet anon repairs his drooping head,
And tricks his beams, and with new-spangled ore   170
Flames in the forehead of the morning sky:
So Lycidas sunk low, but mounted high,
Through the dear might of him that walk'd the waves,
Where other groves, and other streams along,
With nectar pure his oozy locks he laves,

And hears the unexpressive nuptial song,
In the blest kingdoms meek of joy and love.
There entertain him all the Saints above,
In solemn troops, and sweet societies
That sing, and singing in their glory move,   180
And wipe the tears for ever from his eyes.
Now, Lycidas, the shepherds weep no more;
Henceforth thou art the Genius of the shore,
In thy large recompense, and shalt be good
To all that wander in that perilous flood.

    Thus sang the uncouth swain to th' oaks and rills,
While the still morn went out with sandals gray:
He touch'd the tender stops of various quills,
With eager thought warbling his Doric lay:
And now the sun had stretch'd out all the hills,   190
And now was dropt into the western bay;
At last he rose, and twitch'd his mantle blue:
To-morrow to fresh woods, and pastures new.

JOHN KEATS   *Ode to a Nightingale*

My heart aches, and a drowsy numbness pains
    My sense, as though of hemlock I had drunk,
Or emptied some dull opiate to the drains
    One minute past, and Lethe-wards had sunk:
'Tis not through envy of thy happy lot,
    But being too happy in thine happiness,—
        That thou, light-winged Dryad of the trees,
            In some melodious plot
Of beechen green, and shadows numberless,
    Singest of summer in full-throated ease.   10

O, for a draught of vintage! that hath been
    Cool'd a long age in the deep-delved earth,
Tasting of Flora and the country green,
    Dance, and Provençal song, and sunburnt mirth!
O for a beaker full of the warm South,
    Full of the true, the blushful Hippocrene,
        With beaded bubbles winking at the brim,
            And purple-stained mouth;
That I might drink, and leave the world unseen,
    And with thee fade away into the forest dim: 20

Fade far away, dissolve, and quite forget
  What thou among the leaves hast never known,
The weariness, the fever, and the fret
  Here, where men sit and hear each other groan;
Where palsy shakes a few, sad, last gray hairs,
    Where youth grows pale, and spectre-thin, and dies;
      Where but to think is to be full of sorrow
          And leaden-eyed despairs,
  Where Beauty cannot keep her lustrous eyes,
    Or new Love pine at them beyond to-morrow.   30

Away! away! for I will fly to thee,
  Not charioted by Bacchus and his pards,
But on the viewless wings of Poesy,
  Though the dull brain perplexes and retards:
Already with thee! tender is the night,
    And haply the Queen-Moon is on her throne,
      Cluster'd around by all her starry Fays;
          But here there is no light,
  Save what from heaven is with the breezes blown
    Through verdurous glooms and winding mossy ways.   40

I cannot see what flowers are at my feet,
  Nor what soft incense hangs upon the boughs,
But, in embalmed darkness, guess each sweet
  Wherewith the seasonable month endows
The grass, the thicket, and the fruit-tree wild:
    White hawthorn, and the pastoral eglantine;
      Fast fading violets cover'd up in leaves;
          And mid-May's eldest child,
  The coming musk-rose, full of dewy wine,
    The murmurous haunt of flies on summer eves.   50

Darkling I listen; and, for many a time
  I have been half in love with easeful Death,
Call'd him soft names in many a mused rhyme,
  To take into the air my quiet breath;
Now more than ever seems it rich to die,
    To cease upon the midnight with no pain,
      While thou are pouring forth thy soul abroad
          In such an ecstacy!
  Still wouldst thou sing, and I have ears in vain—
    To thy high requiem become a sod.   60

Thou wast not born for death, immortal Bird!
  No hungry generations tread thee down;
The voice I hear this passing night was heard
  In ancient days by emperor and clown:
Perhaps the self-same song that found a path
  Through the sad heart of Ruth, when, sick for home,
    She stood in tears amid the alien corn;
          The same that oft-times hath
Charm'd magic casements, opening on the foam
  Of perilous seas, in faery lands forlorn.   70

Forlorn! the very word is like a bell
  To toll me back from thee to my sole self!
Adieu! the fancy cannot cheat so well
  As she is fam'd to do, deceiving elf.
Adieu! adieu! thy plaintive anthem fades
  Past the near meadows, over the still stream,
    Up the hill-side; an now 'tis buried deep
          In the next valley-glades:
  Was it a vision, or a waking dream?
    Fled is that music:—Do I wake or sleep?   80

WALT WHITMAN   *When lilacs last in the dooryard bloom'd* [1]

1

When lilacs last in the dooryard bloom'd,
And the great star early droop'd in the western sky in the night,
I mourn'd, and yet shall mourn with ever-returning spring.

Ever returning spring, trinity sure to me you bring,
Lilac blooming perennial and drooping star in the west,
And thought of him I love.

2

O powerful western fallen star!
O shades of night—O moody, tearful night!
O great star disappear'd—O the black murk that hides the star!
O cruel hands that hold me powerless—O helpless soul of me!   10
O harsh surrounding cloud that will not free my soul.

[1] See comment in Chapter Two, Section III (pp. 87–88).

3

In the dooryard fronting an old farm-house near the white-wash'd
    palings,
Stands the lilac-bush tall-growing with heart-shaped leaves of rich
    green,
With many a pointed blossom rising delicate, with the perfume strong
    I love,
With every leaf a miracle—and from this bush in the dooryard,
With delicate-colour'd blossoms and heart-shaped leaves of rich green,
A sprig with its flower I break.

4

In the swamp in secluded recesses,
A shy and hidden bird is warbling a song.

Solitary the thrush,   20
The hermit withdrawn to himself, avoiding the settlements,
Sings by himself a song.

Song of the bleeding throat,
Death's outlet song of life (for well, dear brother, I know
If thou was not granted to sing thou would'st surely die).

5

Over the breast of the spring, the land, amid cities,
Amid lanes and through old woods, where lately the violets peep'd
    from the ground, spotting the grey débris,
Amid the grass in the fields each side of the lanes, passing the endless
    grass,
Passing the yellow-spear'd wheat, every grain from its shroud in the
    dark-brown fields uprisen,
Passing the apple-tree blows of white and pink in the orchards,   30
Carrying a corpse to where it shall rest in the grave,
Night and day journeys a coffin.

6

Coffin that passes through lanes and streets,
Through day and night with the great cloud darkening the land,
With the pomp of the inloop'd flags with the cities draped in black,
With the show of the States themselves as of crape-veil'd women
    standing,
With processions long and winding and the flambeaus of the night,

With the countless torches lit, with the silent sea of faces and the
    unbared heads,
With the waiting depôt, the arriving coffin, and the sombre faces,
With dirges through the night, with the shout and voices rising strong
    and solemn,   40
With all the mournful voices of the dirges pour'd around the coffin,
The dim-lit churches and the shuddering organs—where amid these
    you journey,
With the tolling, tolling bells' perpetual clang,
Here, coffin that slowly passes,
I give you my sprig of lilac.

7

(Nor for you, for one alone,
Blossoms and branches green to coffins all I bring,
For fresh as the morning, thus would I chant a song for you, O sane
    and sacred death.

All over bouquets of roses,
O death, I cover you over with roses and early lilies,   50
But mostly and now the lilac that blooms the first,
Copious I break, I break the sprigs from the bushes,
With loaded arms I come, pouring for you,
For you and the coffins all of you, O death.)

8

O western orb, sailing the heaven,
Now I know what you must have meant as a month since I walk'd,
As I walk'd in silence the transparent shadowy night,
As I saw you had something to tell as you bent to me night after night,
As you droop'd from the sky low down as if to my side (while the
    other stars all look'd on),
As we wander'd together the solemn night (for something I know not
    what kept me from sleep),   60
As the night advanced, and I saw on the rim of the west how full you
    were of woe,
As I stood on the rising ground in the breeze in the cool transparent
    night,
As I watch'd where you pass'd and was lost in the netherward black
    of the night,
As my soul in its trouble dissatisfied sank, as where you, sad orb,
Concluded, dropt in the night, and was gone.

9

Sing on there in the swamp,
O singer, bashful and tender, I hear your notes, I hear your call,
I hear, I come presently, I understand you,
But a moment I linger, for the lustrous star has detain'd me,
The star my departing comrade holds and detains me.   70

10

O how shall I warble myself for the dead one there I loved?
And how shall I deck my song for the large sweet soul that has gone?
And what shall my perfume be for the grave of him I love?

Sea-winds blown from east and west,
Blown from the Eastern sea and blown from the Western sea, till
    there on the prairies meeting,
These and with these and the breath of my chant,
I'll perfume the grave of him I love.

11

O what shall I hang on the chamber walls?
And what shall the pictures be that I hang on the walls,
To adorn the burial-house of him I love?   80

Pictures of growing spring and farms and homes,
With the Fourth-month eve at sundown, and the grey smoke lucid
    and bright,
With floods of the yellow gold of the gorgeous, indolent sinking sun,
    burning, expanding the air,
With the fresh sweet herbage under foot, and the pale green leaves of
    the trees prolific,
In the distance the flowing glaze, the breast of the river, with a wind-
    dapple here and there,
With ranging hills on the banks, with many a line against the sky,
    and shadows,
And the city at hand with dwellings so dense, and stacks of chimneys,
And all the scenes of life and the workshops, and the workmen
    homeward returning.

12

Lo, body and soul—this land,
My own Manhattan with spires, and the sparkling and hurrying tides,
    and the ships,   90

The varied and ample land, the South and the North in the light,
   Ohio's shores and flashing Missouri,
And ever the far-spreading prairies cover'd with grass and corn.

Lo, the most excellent sun so calm and haughty,
The violet and purple morn with just-felt breezes,
The gentle soft-born measureless light,
The miracle spreading bathing all, the fulfill'd noon,
The coming eve delicious, the welcome night and the stars,
Over my cities shining all, enveloping man and land.

13

Sing on, sing on, you grey-brown bird,
Sing from the swamps, the recesses, pour your chant from the
   bushes,   100
Limitless out of the dusk, out of the cedars and pines.

Sing on, dearest brother, warble your reedy song.
Loud human song, with voice of uttermost woe.

O liquid and free and tender!
O wild and loose to my soul—O wondrous singer!
You only I hear—yet the star holds me (but will soon depart),
Yet the lilac with mastering odour holds me.

14

Now while I sat in the day and look'd forth,
In the close of the day with its light and the fields of spring and the
   farmers preparing their crops,
In the large unconscious scenery of my land with its lakes and
   forests,   110
In the heavenly aerial beauty (after the perturb'd winds and the
   storms),
Under the arching heavens of the afternoon swift passing, and the
   voices of children and women,
The many-moving sea-tides, and I saw the ships how they sail'd,
And the summer approaching with richness, and the fields all busy
   with labour,
And the infinite separate houses, how they all went on, each with its
   meals and minutia of daily usages,
And the streets how their throbbings throbb'd, and the cities pent—
   lo, then and there,

Falling upon them all and among them all, enveloping me with the
    rest,
Appear'd the cloud, appear'd the long black trail,
And I knew death, its thought, and the sacred knowledge of death.

Then with the knowledge of death as walking one side of me,   120
And the thought of death close-walking the other side of me,
And I in the middle as with companions, and as holding the hands of
    companions,
I fled forth to the hiding receiving night that talks not,
Down to the shores of the water, the path by the swamp in the
    dimness,
To the solemn shadowy cedars and ghostly pines so still.

And the singer so shy to the rest receiv'd me,
The grey-brown bird I know receiv'd us comrades three,
And he sang the carol of death, and a verse for him I love.

From deep secluded recesses,
From the fragrant cedars and the ghostly pines so still,
Came the carol of the bird.   130

And the charm of the carol rapt me,
As I held as if by their hands my comrades in the night,
And the voice of my spirit tallied the song of the bird.

Come lovely and soothing death,
Undulate round the world, serenely arriving, arriving,
In the day, in the night, to all, to each,
Sooner or later delicate death.

Prais'd be the fathomless universe,
For life and joy, and for objects and knowledge curious,   140
And for love, sweet love—but praise! praise! praise!
For the sure-enwinding arms of cool-enfolding death.

Dark mother always gliding near with soft feet,
Have none chanted for thee a chant of fullest welcome?
Then I chant it for thee, I glorify thee above all,
I bring thee a song that when thou must indeed come, come
    unfalteringly.

Approach strong deliveress,
When it is so, when thou hast taken them I joyously sing the dead,
Lost in the loving floating ocean of thee,
Laved in the flood of thy bliss, O death.   150

From me to thee glad serenades,
Dances for thee I propose saluting thee, adornments and feastings
      for thee,
And the sights of the open landscape and the high-spread sky are
      fitting,
And life and the fields, and the huge and thoughtful night.

The night in silence under many a star,
The ocean shore and the husky whispering wave whose voice I know,
And the soul turning to thee, O vast and well-veil'd death,
And the body gratefully nestling close to thee.

Over the tree-tops I float thee a song,
Over the rising and sinking waves, over the myriad fields and the
      prairies wide,   160
Over the dense-pack'd cities and all the teeming wharves and ways,
O float this carol with joy, with joy to thee, O death.

15

To the tally of my soul,
Loud and strong kept up the grey-brown bird,
With pure deliberate notes spreading filling the night.

Loud in the pines and cedars dim,
Clear in the freshness moist and the swamp-perfume,
And I with my comrades there in the night.

While my sight that was bound in my eyes unclosed,
As to long panoramas of visions.   170

And I saw askant the armies,
I saw as in noiseless dreams hundreds of battle-flags,
Borne through the smoke of the battles and pierc'd with missiles I
      saw them,
And carried hither and yon through the smoke, and torn and bloody,

And at last but a few shreds left on the staffs (and all in silence),
And the staffs all splinter'd and broken.

I saw battle-corpses, myriads of them,
And the white skeletons of young men, I saw them,
I saw the débris and débris of all the slain soldiers of the war,
But I saw they were not as was thought,   180
They themselves were fully at rest, they suffer'd not,
The living remain'd and suffer'd, the mother suffer'd,
And the wife and the child and the musing comrade suffer'd,
And the armies that remain'd suffer'd.

16

Passing the visions, passing the night,
Passing, unloosing the hold of my comrades' hands,
Passing the song of the hermit bird and the tallying song of my soul,
Victorious song, death's outlet song, yet varying ever-altering song,
As low and wailing, yet clear the notes, rising and falling, flooding
    the night,
Sadly sinking and fainting, as warning and warning, and yet again
    bursting with joy,   190
Covering the earth and filling the spread of heaven,
As that powerful psalm in the night I heard from recesses,
Passing, I leave thee lilac with heart-shaped leaves,
I leave thee there in the door-yard, blooming, returning with spring.

I cease from my song for thee,
From my gaze on thee in the west, fronting the west, communing with
    thee,
O comrade lustrous with silver face in the night.

Yet each to keep and all, retrievements out of the night,
The song, the wondrous chant of the grey-brown bird,
And the tallying chant, the echo arous'd in my soul,   200
With the lustrous and drooping star with the countenance full of woe,
With the holders holding my hand nearing the call of the bird,
Comrades mine and I in the midst, and their memory ever to keep,
    for the dead I loved so well,
For the sweetest, wisest soul of all my days and lands—and this for
    his dear sake,
Lilac and star and bird twined with the chant of my soul,
There in the fragrant pines and the cedars dusk and dim.

HART CRANE   from *The Bridge*[1]

Proem: To Brooklyn Bridge

How many dawns, chill from his rippling rest
The seagull's wings shall dip and pivot him,
Shedding white rings of tumult, building high
Over the chained bay waters Liberty—

Then, with inviolate curve, forsake our eyes
As apparitional as sails that cross
Some page of figures to be filed away;
—Till elevators drop us from our day . . .

I think of cinemas, panoramic sleights
With multitudes bent toward some flashing scene   10
Never disclosed, but hastened to again,
Foretold to other eyes on the same screen;

And Thee, across the harbor, silver-paced
As though the sun took step of thee, yet left
Some motion ever unspent in thy stride,—
Implicitly thy freedom staying thee!

Out of some subway scuttle, cell or loft
A bedlamite speeds to thy parapets,
Tilting there momently, shrill shirt ballooning,
A jest falls from the speechless caravan.   20

Down Wall, from girder into street noon leaks,
A rip-tooth of the sky's acetylene;
All afternoon the cloud-flown derricks turn . . .
Thy cables breathe the North Atlantic still.

And obscure as that heaven of the Jews,
Thy guerdon . . . Accolade thou dost bestow
Of anonymity time cannot raise:
Vibrant reprieve and pardon thou dost show.

[1] This "proem" (preface) serves as the invocation to the sequence *The Bridge*, which Hart Crane conceived of as a modern epic poem. In the traditional epic, the poet exalts his Muse or guiding deity and prays to be the humble conveyor of divine inspiration. *Does the same thing happen here? Are there indications that the poet is looking for a secular symbol, in nature or in man's own constructive and imaginative energy, to replace or add to the symbols of traditional religion? What do the shifts of tone, intensity, and relative joy or sadness in the poem have to do with this search?*

O harp and altar, of the fury fused,
(How could mere toil align thy choiring strings!)   30
Terrific threshold of the prophet's pledge,
Prayer of pariah, and the lover's cry,—

Again the traffic lights that skim thy swift
Unfractioned idiom, immaculate sigh of stars,
Beading thy path—condense eternity:
And we have seen night lifted in thine arms.

Under thy shadow by the piers I waited;
Only in darkness is thy shadow clear.
The City's fiery parcels all undone,
Already snow submerges an iron year . . .   40

O Sleepless as the river under thee,
Vaulting the sea, the prairies' dreaming sod,
Unto us lowliest sometime sweep, descend
And of the curveship lend a myth to God.

D. H. LAWRENCE *Whales Weep Not!*

They say the sea is cold, but the sea contains
the hottest blood of all, and the wildest, the most urgent.
All the whales in the wider deeps, hot are they, as they urge
on and on, and dive beneath the ice-bergs.
The right whales, the sperm-whales, the hammer-heads, the killers
there they blow, there they blow, hot wild white breath out of the sea!

And they rock and they rock, through the sensual ageless ages
on the depths of the seven seas,
and through the salt they reel with drunk delight
and in the tropics tremble they with love   10
and roll with massive, strong desire, like gods.
Then the great bull lies up against his bride
in the blue deep of the sea
as mountain pressing on mountain, in the zest of life:
and out of the inward roaring of the inner red ocean of whale blood
the long tip reaches strong, intense, like the maelstrom-tip, and comes
     to rest
in the clasp and the soft, wild clutch of a she-whale's fathomless body.

And over the bridge of the whale's strong phallus, linking the wonder
  of whales
the burning archangels under the sea keep passing, back and forth,
keep passing archangels of bliss   20
from him to her, from her to him, great Cherubim
that wait on whales in mid-ocean, suspended in the waves of the sea
great heaven of whales in the waters, old hierarchies.

And enormous mother whales lie dreaming suckling their whale-
  tender young
and dreaming with strange whale eyes wide open in the waters of the
  beginning and the end.

And bull-whales gather their women and whale-calves in a ring
when danger threatens, on the surface of the ceaseless flood
and range themselves like great fierce Seraphim facing the threat
encircling their huddled monsters of love.
and all this happiness in the sea, in the salt   30
where God is also love, but without words:
and Aphrodite is the wife of whales
most happy, happy she!

and Venus among the fishes skips and is a she-dolphin
she is the gay, delighted porpoise sporting with love and the sea
she is the female tunny-fish, round and happy among the males
and dense with happy blood, dark rainbow bliss in the sea.

RICHARD EBERHART   *The Groundhog*

In June, amid the golden fields,
I saw a groundhog lying dead.
Dead lay he; my senses shook,
And mind outshot our naked frailty.
There lowly in the vigorous summer
His form began its senseless change,
And made my senses waver dim
Seeing nature ferocious in him.
Inspecting close his maggots' might
And seething cauldron of his being,   10
Half with loathing, half with a strange love,
I poked him with an angry stick.
The fever arose, became a flame
And Vigour circumscribed the skies,

Immense energy in the sun,
And through my frame a sunless trembling.
My stick had done nor good nor harm.
Then stood I silent in the day
Watching the object, as before;
And kept my reverence for knowledge   20
Trying for control, to be still,
To quell the passion of the blood;
Until I had bent down on my knees
Praying for joy in the sight of decay.
And so I left: and I returned
In Autumn strict of eye, to see
The sap gone out of the groundhog,
But the bony sodden hulk remained.
But the year had lost its meaning,
And in intellectual chains   30
I lost both love and loathing,
Mured up in the wall of wisdom.
Another summer took the fields again
Massive and burning, full of life,
But when I chanced upon the spot
There was only a little hair left,
And bones bleaching in the sunlight
Beautiful as architecture;
I watched them like a geometer,
And cut a walking stick from a birch.   40
It has been three years, now.
There is no sign of the groundhog.
I stood there in the whirling summer,
My hand capped a withered heart,
And thought of China and of Greece,
Of Alexander in his tent;
Of Montaigne in his tower,
Of Saint Theresa in her wild lament.

HOWARD NEMEROV   *The Goose Fish*

On the long shore, lit by the moon
To show them properly alone,
Two lovers suddenly embraced
So that their shadows were as one.
The ordinary night was graced
For them by the swift tide of blood

That silently they took at flood,
And for a little time they prized
            Themselves emparadised.

Then, as if shaken by stage-fright   10
Beneath the hard moon's bony light,
They stood together on the sand
Embarrassed in each other's sight
But still conspiring hand in hand,
Until they saw, there underfoot,
As though the world had found them out,
The goose fish turning up, though dead,
            His hugely grinning head.

There in the china light he lay,
Most ancient and corrupt and grey.   20
They hesitated at his smile,
Wondering what it seemed to say
To lovers who a little while
Before had thought to understand,
By violence upon the sand,
The only way that could be known
            To make a world their own.

It was a wide and moony grin
Together peaceful and obscene;
They knew not what he would express,   30
So finished a comedian
He might mean failure or success,
But took it for an emblem of
Their sudden, new and guilty love
To be observed by, when they kissed,
            That rigid optimist.

So he became their patriarch,
Dreadfully mild in the half-dark.
His throat that the sand seemed to choke,
His picket teeth, these left their mark   40
But never did explain the joke
That so amused him, lying there
While the moon went down to disappear
Along the still and tilted track
            That bears the zodiac.

II

The Symbol as a Directive Force

The magnetism of poetic symbols is their most striking quality. Within poems, they provide a vital emotional center around which a pattern may coalesce. (Indeed, poetry is always in some sense compressed and patterned symbolic statement.) At the same time they place in focus emotional attitudes toward important questions of all kinds. Though these symbols are born of the pressure of tradition and experience on the *poet's* imagination, they evoke a similar emotional attitude in the responsive reader. He may not agree with the poet's view of life, but he will understand better than before how it is possible to hold such a view and have genuinely deep feelings about it.

A simple example of this double directive power may be seen in Shelley's *Ozymandias* (page 396). The scattered pieces of a broken statue in the desert wastes of "an antique land" hold the stage here. We see one part of the statue at a time, and then the "lone and level sands" that engulf it. This sequence determines the structure of the poem and its meaning; it is also the key to the larger theme—the vanity of pride in material power, especially as it manifests itself in rulers and empires. It is curious how the poet's description of the great sneering sculptured head dominates the imagination and makes what might otherwise be merely obvious seem startlingly significant.

A more complex example is found in Yeats's *Leda and the Swan* (page 399). Here a mythical incident, the ravishment of the girl Leda by the Greek god Zeus in the form of a swan, is brought to violent, sensuous life at the climactic moment. We are shown how the experience, with all its mystery, would have felt to Leda and we are reminded of the subsequent legendary events: the birth of Helen of Troy, the Trojan War, the tragic return afterward to Greece of King Agamemnon. The literature and art around these events, of course, are high points in Western culture; we might almost say they created it. The poem ends with the interesting question whether Leda, having been impregnated by the god with his power to create the future, had any awareness of how the future was now working through her. The symbolic incident, its results, its meaning to the human being involved—these make the ordering of the poem. But this poem brings us not to a set attitude but to a problem: Is man merely the creature of impersonal forces that use him and pass on, a creature that can be excited when seized by them for their own purposes but himself only a passive vehicle of an "indifferent" divinity? Or does he have a portion of divine intelligence within himself? After all, the myths of Leda and Helen and the Trojan War are *man*-created. The problem has many religious, historical, and philosophical reverberations. The mystery of the union of Zeus and Leda becomes the mystery of the source of human creativity.

Whether simple or complex, then, the poetic symbol that gives direction to a poem is at the same time organizing a conception of reality or of the approach to some problem concerning it. Inside the poem and out, the new and special light thrown by the symbol makes familiar sights and thoughts seem new and special too. The symbolic poem that has this effect reveals to us a view of the world so complete, so consistent within itself, that it must somehow remain part of our own view henceforth.

A detailed examination of the following poem by Yeats will reveal how profound the connection can be between the place of symbols in the structure of poetry and their relation to reality. The symbols of this poem are self-contained; the poem has an intense life of its own. Nevertheless, they also shed an unusually brilliant light on a myriad of real-life problems as the term is ordinarily understood—such problems as the usefulness of art, the predicament of old age, and the proper aims of human thought and action.

WILLIAM BUTLER YEATS   *Sailing to Byzantium*

I

That is no country for old men. The young
In one another's arms, birds in the trees
—Those dying generations—at their song,
The salmon-falls, the mackerel-crowded seas,
Fish, flesh, or fowl, commend all summer long
Whatever is begotten, born, and dies.
Caught in that sensual music all neglect
Monuments of unageing intellect.

II

An aged man is but a paltry thing,
A tattered coat upon a stick, unless   10
Soul clap its hands and sing, and louder sing
For every tatter in its mortal dress,
Nor is there singing school but studying
Monuments of its own magnificence;
And therefore I have sailed the seas and come
To the holy city of Byzantium.

III

O sages standing in God's holy fire
As in the gold mosaic of a wall,
Come from the holy fire, perne in a gyre,[1]
And be the singing-masters of my soul.   20
Consume my heart away; sick with desire
And fastened to a dying animal
It knows not what it is; and gather me
Into the artifice of eternity.

IV

Once out of nature I shall never take
My bodily form from any natural thing,
But such a form as Grecian goldsmiths make
Of hammered gold and gold enamelling
To keep a drowsy Emperor awake;
Or set upon a golden bough to sing   30
To lords and ladies of Byzantium
Of what is past, or passing, or to come.

To begin with the first symbols of the poem, the speaker is an old man describing an uncongenial country. In the very first line we look at that country—the world of nature—through his eyes. The exceptionally observant and self-analytical protagonist tells us that it is "no country for old men." Nature belongs to the young, and to the animal world—or rather, they to it—for it is characterized by mating and giving birth, processes interrupted only by death, which, in turn, makes room for more "dying generations" caught in the round of "sensual music." The speaker does not despise the sensual life; the language he uses to describe it shows this fact. But he feels that an old man is merely a cast-off remnant of that life ("a tattered coat upon a stick," a scarecrow,) and can never again take any satisfaction from it.

All the images used to picture the sensual world evoke both its power of enchantment and the pathetic transience of the life within it. The young lovers, the singing birds that must die soon, the fish swarming in the waters, all make a music in praise of fertility and natural mortality. And it *is* a "music," with all the connotations of beauty and value that the word must have for us. But the only part of the life-cycle now applicable to the old man is death. (Notice that the idea of dying is brought into the first stanza three times.) After all, however, there is apparently something

---

[1] swoop down (and gather me up) in a hawklike movement

else available—something to which only those not hypnotized and caught up in the natural cycle can pay attention: another world of intelligence, spirituality, and art suggested by the phrase "monuments of unageing intellect."

This new idea, brought in at the very close of the first stanza, seems at first to offer only the weakest, most pedantic alternative for the speaker. But as the poet develops it in later stanzas, we see it in images as intense and poignant as those of the sensual world, and we soon realize that two sets of symbols are being played against one another in a very telling way. Thus, the second stanza speaks of a soul's music that must be learnt instead of the "sensual music" of the beginning. It is a music to be studied in the "singing-school" of man's greatest creative achievements in religion and thought and especially art. In the same way, and for the same reasons, the speaker turns from the country of entranced fleshly life to Byzantium— the symbol of the ideal, esthetic, transformed existence he longs for. (Byzantium suggests a far-off, unfamiliar civilization, whose art is non-representational and whose religion has taken an exotic form because of the merging of Western and Eastern churches and religious traditions.)

The interplay of the two opposing sets of symbols is intricate and rich despite the shortness of the poem. Note, for instance, that there are old men in Byzantium too— the "sages standing in God's holy fire" to whom the speaker appeals. But in them the last remnants of sensuality have long been purged away, and he begs them to do the same for him. Again, instead of the flesh-and-blood birds ("those dying generations") of the first stanza, there are golden birds in Byzantium; the speaker would be one of these, artificial, precious, durable beyond time. "I have read somewhere," Yeats's note to this poem tells us, "that in the Emperor's palace at Byzantium was a tree made of gold and silver, and artificial birds that sang." His song, when *he* is a golden bird, will be that of spiritual ecstasy (the soul "clapping its hands and singing"). And he will be surrounded, not by the heedless, hypnotized young lovers and other animal creatures of the sexual cycle, but by an audience that is elegant, abstract, and like the beings of the sensual life only in the way that a work of art is like life—that is, there are resemblances but each has its own unique laws. There, he will have no age; past, present, and future are all one there.

But though the poem is so complex in its patterns, it never moves away from its central, directing symbol. As we have seen, it brings us again and again to view life in terms of music. The opposed kinds of music define the subject of the poem for us in their own way; they make the symbol around which the poem grows and from which it takes its life. Against the naked rhythms of the sensual life, enmeshed in the sharp, helpless, tragically limited ecstasy of the life-cycle, is set the loud, strong, deliberately created music of soul and will. Music means life, and the protagonist will be but a lifeless scarecrow if he cannot supplant the music of nature with that of the singing-masters of the soul.

And so he forsakes all allegiance to nature and commits himself entirely to their tutelage. But will they accept him into their "Byzantium," where the "holy fire" of divine inspiration is the only atmosphere breathed? We do not know. He has sailed to Byzantium, and he has prayed to be released from the deathly taint of his old associations, but whether his prayer is to be granted we do not know. Perhaps it will be, since in the final stanza the poet imagines what the new life in the "artifice of eternity" will be like. Its music will not be of that intensely rapturous yet tragic sort associated with procreation and the death of the old to make way for the new; it will be calm, and the audience will be a part of perfection and therefore not desperate in its clutching for transient joys, for experience without form. Yet perhaps the transformation will not come to pass (in the literal sense, of course, it cannot)—in which case the whole poem is but the pathetic song of an old man excluded from the only two kinds of music that mean richness and life, the music of youthful passion and that of pure soul's achievement. It is, if this be true, a song of desolation, impure because his heart is still "fastened to a dying animal" and sterile because his vision is not yet realized.

In either case, the poem is a song which sets the music of one kind of desire against that of another, possibly to be created in the future. There is the ceaseless round of the first stanza (almost a monotone, except for the cyclical character of the music and the intensity), implied by the cataloguing of kinds of creatures and the inclusiveness of the fifth, sixth, and seventh lines. (One almost overlooks the suggestion that this is the music of but a single season—"all summer long"—and the implication that it is therefore inferior in kind and illusory.) Next there is the vision of the soul rising joyously away from this:

> . . . unless
> Soul clap its hands and sing, and louder sing
> For every tatter in its mortal dress. . . .

Following up this vision, the third stanza is pure prayer and incantation, in which the speaker transfers the language of desire to the realm of eternity, so that the two kinds of music seem to intermingle for a moment before the calm, formal music of the concluding stanza brings the poem to a close. In the third stanza, too, as throughout the poem, the rhythm, rhyme, and imagery themselves symbolize the poem's larger qualities. Here the "sages," the agents of the soul, are set into action against the sick, animal heart of man, their cycles (the "gyres" in which they swing away from their centers to seize upon the stuff of human experience and transform it into the substance of art) are eternal, whereas those of the lower world are temporary. The eighth line (with a fraction of the seventh) foreshadows the mood of the concluding stanza. The *s*'s, long *a*-sounds, long *i*-sounds, and *r*'s carry echoes of each of these opposites into the images of the other. Thus there is a music of sound and image within the larger music of emotions and ideas, and this inner music reinforces the clash and resolution of the poem's guiding symbols.

Sailing to Byzantium is one of those poems which have strongly influenced the thinking and feelings of a good many readers. It has, at the least, sharpened their sense of the seriousness and reality of the motivations of creative minds. It is a poem of the sort that redirects our attention to the basic choices of our lives, and to the way in which these choices affect our long-range perspectives. Curiously, it helps us to see the very weaknesses of the human condition in a light that lends them dignity and high significance. It presents unchallengeable proof of the power of the poetic symbol to create relationships and meanings around itself that seem to depend on nothing else but the intensity and depth with which the symbol is conceived, and at the same time to rearrange our understanding of what the real world is and of what our individual places are in it.

A Note on the Symbolist Movement

Often the term *symbolism* is used in a rather special sense to denote the characteristic methods and theories of the nineteenth-century movement called French Symbolism. This movement has had a marked influence on the modern poets of many countries, including the English-speaking ones. Baudelaire, Verlaine, Mallarmé and others, feeling that modern utilitarianism and science-mindedness were alien to the traditions and aims of art, sought to create a verse that could rise, as C. M. Bowra has written, "through scent, colour, and sound to raptures of the spirit." [2] The essence of this movement is "its insistence on a world of ideal beauty, and its conviction that this is realised through art. The ecstasies which religion claims for the devout through prayer and contemplation are claimed by the Symbolist for the poet through the exercise of his craft."

Intensity, concentrated richness, musical suggestiveness, evocativeness—these were the qualities especially valued by the Symbolists and those whom they influenced. From their point of view, any image, any figure of speech, any literary or mythological or historical allusion, any turn of speech even, may be symbolic, carrying us toward a mystical realization beyond immediate experience. In a famous passage, Yeats illustrates what

[2] C. M. Bowra, *The Heritage of Symbolism.*

he calls "the continuous indefinable symbolism which is the substance of all style":

> There are no lines with more melancholy beauty than these by Burns—
>> The white moon is setting behind the white wave,
>> And Time is setting with me, O!
>
> and these lines are perfectly symbolical. Take from them the whiteness of the moon and of the wave, whose relation to the setting of Time is too subtle for the intellect, and you take from them their beauty. But when all are together, moon and wave and whiteness and setting Time and the last melancholy cry, they evoke an emotion which cannot be evoked by any other arrangement of colours and sounds and forms.[3]

In the early poems of Yeats, we find many passages that strive for this kind of evocation, for example:

> . . . . the shadows of the wood,
> And the white breast of the dim sea
> And all dishevelled wandering stars.[4]

and:

> We sat grown quiet at the name of love;
> We saw the last embers of daylight die;
> And in the trembling blue-green of the sky
> A moon, worn as if it had been a shell
> Washed by time's waters as they rose and fell
> About the stars and broke in days and years.[5]

The Symbolists' idealization of artistic sensibility and the artistic symbol has not only been sustained in some of the most powerful tendencies of modern literature but has also helped create a veritable "religion of art" in much contemporary criticism.

---

[3] William Butler Yeats, "The Symbolism of Poetry."
[4] William Butler Yeats, *Who Goes with Fergus?*
[5] William Butler Yeats, *Adam's Curse.*

Poems: The Symbol as a Directive Force

Dryden's sardonically gay masque (a form allowing for music, dance, and allegorical characters as well as poetry) focuses on the failure of the seventeenth century to fulfill its ideals. Diana, Mars, and Venus symbolize the pointless, bestial aims the age hunted after, the wars that ravaged it, and the failure of love to prevail in it. The symbolism, pointed up by the final song of the Chorus, is redeemed from sourness by a festive atmosphere and by the exuberant movement of the speeches and quick succession of stage-effects.

Shelley too characterizes his age in the prophetic Chorus from his poetic play *Hellas*. He borrows symbols from the Classical tradition that the first-century B.C. Roman poet Vergil had used in his fourth Eclogue, to foretell the coming of a golden age. At first Shelley expresses the revolutionary idealism of a nineteenth-century romantic idealist. Finally, though, he betrays his fear that, should such portents recur, they must also bring back the tragic side—stated very directly in his *Ozymandias*—of the past.

Yeats's *Two Songs from a Play* (see the notes that follow it) echoes Vergil's and Shelley's language to affirm the inevitability of what Shelley feared. To Shelley's symbols Yeats adds the figures of Dionysus and Christ, whose sacrificial deaths show an inevitable cyclical process in history and emphasize man's inability to sustain any moment of triumph or transcendence. The same theme is presented by Yeats in a more concentrated form in *Leda and the Swan* discussed in the text, and in *The Second Coming*. The sheer terror of transcendence, of possession by a force beyond oneself, is most purely expressed by Mary's speech in *The Mother of God*.

Auden's two poems present symbols of comparable import. In the sonnet, the demons long thought vanquished by civilization return by a Freudian path to strike us down psychologically. In *The Shield of Achilles*, the goddess Thetis observes with dismay that the ancient dream of a rich and innocently ceremonious life has been replaced by a murderous and bleak reality, imaged on the shield of her son Achilles. Thus Auden suggests the degeneration and loss of a cherished, precious traditional human ideal. (Homer had described the shield differently, in the light of that ideal.) A. J. M. Smith's brief poem suggests the same modern situation in a wry mimicry of official language that belies the theme of the loss of an ancient symbolic vision of hope and rebirth. Richard Wilbur's *Advice to a Prophet* then suggests the way in which the danger of atomic annihilation can be brought home to people—not through argument or statistics but by imagining the absence of everything in nature. This poem suddenly focuses our attention on the fact that everything in nature, from the "white-tailed deer" to some mountain stream, embodies and symbolizes the character of life on earth. The allegorical phrasing of the final three stanzas shows how man uses nature as the mirror of "all we mean or wish to mean." Wilbur's poem well illustrates Ezra

Pound's principle that "the best symbol is the natural symbol." Notice, however, that Pound's brilliantly dynamic poem *The Return*, which is haunted by envisioned figures out of the heroic past who long to return to the foreground of consciousness, takes its force from mythical, Homeric, and psychological sources rather than from literal nature.

JOHN DRYDEN   *The Secular Masque* [1]

(*Enter Janus.*)

JANUS: Chronos, Chronos, mend thy pace:
An hundred times [1] the rolling Sun
Around the Radiant Belt has run
   In his revolving race.
Behold, behold, the goal in sight;
Spread thy fans, and wing thy flight.

(*Enter Chronos, with a scythe in his hand, and a great globe on his back, which he sets down at his entrance.*)

CHRONOS: Weary, weary of my weight,
Let me, let me drop my freight,
   And leave the World behind.
     I could not bear   10
     Another year,
   The load of human-kind.

(*Enter Momus, laughing.*)

MOMUS: Ha! ha! ha! Ha! ha! ha! well hast thou done
   To lay down thy pack,
   And lighten thy back.
The World was a fool, e'er since it begun,
And since neither Janus, nor Chronos, nor I
   Can hinder the crimes
   Or mend the bad times,
'Tis better to laugh than to cry.   20

Cho. of all 3.   *'Tis better to laugh than to cry.*

JANUS: Since Momus comes to laugh below,
Old Time, begin the show,
That he may see, in every Scene,

---

[1] This poem celebrates the ending of the seventeenth century. "Secular" is from the Latin *saeculum*, meaning "age" or "century."

| | What changes in this Age have been. |
| CHRONOS: | Then, Goddess of the Silver Bow, begin. |

(Horns, or Hunting-music within. Enter Diana.)

DIANA:	With horns and with hounds I waken the day,
	And hye to my woodland walks away:
	I tuck up my robe, and am buskined soon,
	And tie to my forehead a waxing Moon. 30
	I course the fleet stag, unkennel the fox,
	And chase the wild goats o'er summits of rocks:
	With shouting and hooting we pierce thro' the sky,
	And Echo turns hunter, and doubles the cry.

| Cho. of all: | *With shouting and hooting, &c.* |

JANUS:	Then our age was in its prime:
CHRONOS:	Free from rage.
DIANA:	And free from crime.
MOMUS:	A very merry, dancing, drinking,
	Laughing, quaffing, and unthinking time. 40

| Cho. of all: | *Then our age, &c.* |

(Dance of Diana's attendants.)

(Enter Mars.)

MARS:	Inspire the vocal brass, inspire;
	The World is past its infant age:
	Arms and honour,
	Arms and honour,
	Set the martial mind on fire,
	And kindle manly rage.
	Mars has looked the sky to red;
	And Peace, the lazy Good, is fled.
	Plenty, Peace, and Pleasure fly; 50
	The sprightly green
	In woodland-walks no more is seen;
	The sprightly green has drunk the Tyrian dye.

| Cho. of all: | *Plenty, Peace, &c.* |

MARS:	Sound the trumpet, beat the drum;
	Through all the World around,
	Sound a Reveille, sound, sound,
	The Warrior-God is come.

| Cho. of all: | *Sound the trumpet, &c.* |

MOMUS: Thy sword within the scabbard keep,   60
           And let Mankind agree;
        Better the World were fast asleep,
           Than kept awake by thee.
        The fools are only thinner,
           With all our cost and care;
        But neither side a winner,
           For things are as they were.

Cho. of all: *The fools are only, &c.*

        (Enter Venus.)

VENUS: Calms appear when storms are past;
        Love will have his hour at last: 70
        Nature is my kindly care;
        Mars destroys, and I repair;
        Take me, take me, while you may,
        Venus comes not ev'ry day.

Cho. of all: *Take her, take her, &c.*

CHRONOS: The World was then so light,
          I scarcely felt the weight;
        Joy rul'd the day, and Love the night.
        But since the Queen of Pleasure left the ground,
          I faint, I lag,   80
          And feebly drag
        The pond'rous Orb around.

MOMUS: All, all of a piece throughout:
  Pointing to Diana: Thy chase had a beast in view;
       to Mars: Thy wars brought nothing about;
      to Venus: Thy lovers were all untrue.
JANUS: 'Tis well an old Age is out.
CHRONOS: And time to begin a new.

Cho. of all: *All, all of a piece throughout:*
         Thy chase had a beast in view;   90
      Thy wars brought nothing about;
         Thy lovers were all untrue.
     'Tis well an old Age is out,
         And time to begin a new.

     (Dance of Huntsmen, Nymphs, Warriors, and Lovers.)

PERCY BYSSHE SHELLEY *Ozymandias*

I met a traveller from an antique land
Who said: two vast and trunkless legs of stone
Stand in the desert . . . Near them, on the sand,
Half sunk, a shattered visage lies, whose frown,
And wrinkled lip, and sneer of cold command,
Tell that its sculptor well those passions read
Which yet survive, stamped on these lifeless things,
The hand that mocked them, and the heart that fed:
And on the pedestal these words appear:
"My name is Ozymandias, king of kings: 10
Look on my works, ye Mighty, and despair!"
Nothing beside remains. Round the decay
Of that colossal wreck, boundless and bare
The lone and level sands stretch far away.

PERCY BYSSHE SHELLEY *Chorus* from *Hellas*

The world's great age begins anew,
    The golden years return,
The earth doth like a snake renew
    Her winter weeds outworn:
Heaven smiles, and faiths and empires gleam,
Like wrecks of a dissolving dream.

A brighter Hellas rears its mountains
    From waves serener far;
A new Peneus rolls his fountains
    Against the morning star.   10
Where fairer Tempes bloom, there sleep
Young Cyclads on a sunnier deep.

A loftier Argo cleaves the main,
Fraught with a later prize;
Another Orpheus sings again,
    And loves, and weeps, and dies.
A new Ulysses leaves once more
Calypso for his native shore.

Oh, write no more the tale of Troy,
   If earth Death's scroll must be!   20
Nor mix with Laian rage the joy
   Which dawns upon the free:
Although a subtler Sphinx renew
Riddles of death Thebes never knew.

Another Athens shall arise,
   And to remoter time
Bequeath, like sunset to the skies,
   The splendour of its prime;
And leave, if nought so bright may live,
All earth can take or Heaven can give.   30

Saturn and Love their long repose
   Shall burst, more bright and good
Than all who fell, than One who rose,
   Than many unsubdued:
Not gold, not blood, their altar dowers,
But votive tears and symbol flowers.

Oh, cease! must hate and death return?
   Cease! must men kill and die?
Cease! drain not to its dregs the urn
   Of bitter prophecy.
The world is weary of the past,   40
Oh, might it die or rest at last!

WILLIAM BUTLER YEATS   *Two Songs from a Play* [1]

I

I saw a staring virgin stand
Where holy Dionysus died,

---

[1] The "staring virgin" of line 1 is Athene, associated with the myth of the killing and rebirth of Dionysus. The "fierce virgin" of line 15 refers specifically to Mary, the mother of Jesus, but to Athene and to the goddess Astraea as well. Yeats, in his play *The Resurrection* in which these songs appear, presents Dionysus and Christ as manifestations of a recurrent process of the rise and fall of religions and civilizations, each occuring over a period of a "great year" lasting thousands of years (*Magnus Annus*). The age of Greek rationalism was ending; that of Christian compassion was being born, at the time of the Crucifixion and Resurrection.

And tear the heart out of his side,
And lay the heart upon her hand
And bear that beating heart away;
And then did all the Muses sing
Of Magnus Annus at the spring,
As though God's death were but a play.

Another Troy must rise and set,
Another lineage feed the crow,   10
Another Argo's painted prow
Drive to a flashier bauble yet.
The Roman Empire stood appalled:
It dropped the reins of peace and war
When that fierce virgin and her Star
Out of the fabulous darkness called.

II

In pity for man's darkening thought
He walked that room and issued thence
In Galilean turbulence;
The Babylonian starlight brought
A fabulous, formless darkness in;
Odor of blood when Christ was slain
Made all Platonic tolerance vain
And vain all Doric discipline.

Everything that man esteems
Endures a moment or a day.
Love's pleasure drives his love away,   10
The painter's brush consumes his dreams;
The herald's cry, the soldier's tread
Exhaust his glory and his might:
Whatever flames upon the night
Man's own resinous heart has fed.

Ezra Pound   *The Return*

See, they return; ah, see the tentative
Movements, and the slow feet,
The trouble in the pace and the uncertain
Wavering!

See, they return, one, and by one,
With fear, as half-awakened;
As if the snow should hesitate
And murmur in the wind,
        and half turn back;
These were the "Wing'd-with-Awe,"   10
      Inviolable,

Gods of the wingèd shoe!
With them the silver hounds,
        sniffing the trace of air!
Haie! Haie!
     These were the swift to harry;
These the keen-scented;
These were the souls of blood.

Slow on the leash,
        pallid the leash-men!   20

WILLIAM BUTLER YEATS *Leda and the Swan*

A sudden blow: the great wings beating still
Above the staggering girl, her thighs caressed
By the dark webs, her nape caught in his bill,
He holds her helpless breast upon his breast.

How can those terrified vague fingers push
The feathered glory from her loosening thighs?
And how can body, laid in that white rush,
But feel the strange heart beating where it lies?

A shudder in the loins engenders there
The broken wall, the burning roof and tower   10
And Agamemnon dead.
                Being so caught up,
So mastered by the brute blood of the air,
Did she put on his knowledge with his power
Before the indifferent beak could let her drop?

WILLIAM BUTLER YEATS *The Mother of God*

The threefold terror of love; a fallen flare
Through the hollow of an ear;

Wings beating about the room;
The terror of all terrors that I bore
The Heavens in my womb.

Had I not found content among the shows
Every common woman knows,
Chimney corner, garden walk,
Or rocky cistern where we tread the clothes
And gather all the talk?   10

What is this flesh I purchased with my pains,
This fallen star my milk sustains,
This love that makes my heart's blood stop
Or strikes a sudden chill into my bones
And bids my hair stand up?

WILLIAM BUTLER YEATS   *The Second Coming* [1]

Turning and turning in the widening gyre
The falcon cannot hear the falconer:
Things fall apart; the centre cannot hold;
Mere anarchy is loosed upon the world,
The blood-dimmed tide is loosed, and everywhere
The ceremony of innocence is drowned;
The best lack all conviction, while the worst
Are full of passionate intensity.

Surely some revelation is at hand;
Surely the Second Coming is at hand.   10
The Second Coming! Hardly are those words out
When a vast image out of *Spiritus Mundi*
Troubles my sight: somewhere in the sands of the desert
A shape with lion body and the head of a man,
A gaze blank and pitiless as the sun,
Is moving its slow thighs, while all about it
Reel shadows of the indignant desert birds.
The darkness drops again; but now I know

---

[1] See note to *Two Songs from a Play* (p. 397). In this poem the Christian era is ending and there are signs of the return of ancient savagery and "fabulous formless darkness." The Second Coming will not be of Christ but of a bestial harbinger of the post-twentieth-century world. *Why does the poem end with a question rather than with an outright assertion?*

That twenty centuries of stony sleep
Were vexed to nightmare by a rocking cradle,   20
And what rough beast, its hour come round at last,
Slouches towards Bethlehem to be born?

W. H. AUDEN *So an age ended*

So an age ended, and its last deliverer died
In bed, grown idle and unhappy; they were safe:
The sudden shadow of a giant's enormous calf
Would fall no more at dusk across their lawns outside.

They slept in peace: in marshes here and there no doubt
A sterile dragon lingered to a natural death,
But in a year the slot had vanished from the heath;
A kobold's knocking in the mountain petered out.

Only the sculptors and the poets were half-sad,
And the pert retinue from the magician's house   10
Grumbled and went elsewhere. The vanquished powers were glad

To be invisible and free; without remorse
Struck down the silly sons who strayed into their course,
And ravished the daughters, and drove the fathers mad.

A. J. M. SMITH *News of the Phoenix*

They say the Phoenix is dying, some say dead.
Dead without issue is what one message said,
But that has been suppressed, officially denied.

I think myself the man who sent it lied.
In any case, I'm told, he has been shot,
As a precautionary measure, whether he did or not.

W. H. AUDEN *The Shield of Achilles*

She looked over his shoulder
    For vines and olive trees,
Marble well-governed cities

And ships upon untamed seas,
But there on the shining metal
His hands had put instead
An artificial wilderness
And a sky like lead.

A plain without a feature, bare and brown,
No blade of grass, no sign of neighbourhood,   10
Nothing to eat and nowhere to sit down,
Yet, congregated on its blankness, stood
An unintelligible multitude,
A million eyes, a million boots in line,
Without expression, waiting for a sign.

Out of the air a voice without a face
Proved by statistics that some cause was just
In tones as dry and level as the place:
No one was cheered and nothing was discussed;
Column by column in a cloud of dust   20
They marched away enduring a belief
Whose logic brought them, somewhere else, to grief.

She looked over his shoulder
For ritual pieties,
White flower-garlanded heifers,
Libation and sacrifice,
But there on the shining metal
Where the altar should have been,
She saw by his flickering forge-light
Quite another scene.   30

Barbed wire enclosed an arbitrary spot
Where bored officials lounged (one cracked a joke)
And sentries sweated for the day was hot:
A crowd of ordinary decent folk
Watched from without and neither moved nor spoke
As three pale figures were led forth and bound
To three posts driven upright in the ground.

The mass and majesty of this world, all
That carries weight and always weighs the same
Lay in the hands of others; they were small   40
And could not hope for help and no help came:

What their foes liked to do was done, their shame
Was all the worst could wish; they lost their pride
And died as men before their bodies died.

> She looked over his shoulder
>   For athletes at their games,
> Men and women in a dance
>   Moving their sweet limbs
> Quick, quick, to music,
>   But there on the shining shield
> His hands had set no dancing-floor
>   But a weed-choked field.

A ragged urchin, aimless and alone,
    Loitered about that vacancy, a bird
Flew up to safety from his well-aimed stone:
    That girls are raped, that two boys knife a third,
    Were axioms to him, who'd never heard
Of any world where promises were kept,
Or one could weep because another wept.

> The thin-lipped armourer,
>   Hephaestos hobbled away,
> Thetis of the shining breasts
>   Cried out in dismay
> At what the god had wrought
>   To please her son, the strong
> Iron-hearted man-slaying Achilles
>   Who would not live long.

RICHARD WILBUR   *Advice to a Prophet*

When you come, as you soon must, to the streets of our city,
    Mad-eyed from stating the obvious,
    Not proclaiming our fall but begging us
In God's name to have self-pity,

Spare us all word of the weapons, their force and range,
    The long numbers that rocket the mind;
    Our slow, unreckoning hearts will be left behind,
Unable to fear what is too strange.

Nor shall you scare us with talk of the death of the race.
How should we dream of this place without us?—   10
The sun mere fire, the leaves untroubled about us,
A stone look on the stone's face?

Speak of the world's own change. Though we cannot conceive
Of an undreamt thing, we know to our cost
How the dreamt cloud crumbles, the vines are blackened by frost,
How the view alters. We could believe,

If you told us so, that the white-tailed deer will slip
Into perfect shade, grown perfectly shy,
The lark avoid the reaches of our eye,
The jack-pine lose its knuckled grip   20

On the cold ledge, and every torrent burn
As Xanthus once, its gliding trout
Stunned in a twinkling. What should we be without
The dolphin's arc, the dove's return,

These things in which we have seen ourselves and spoken?
Ask us, prophet, how we shall call
Our natures forth when that live tongue is all
Dispelled, that glass obscured or broken

In which we have said the rose of our love and the clean
Horse of our courage, in which beheld   30
The singing locust of the soul unshelled,
And all we mean or wish to mean.

Ask us, ask us whether with the worldless rose
Our hearts shall fail us; come demanding
Whether there shall be lofty or long standing
When the bronze annals of the oak-tree close.

Chapter Eight

Tradition and the Sense of the Present

I

CLASSICISM AND ROMANTICISM

A poem, we have seen, may have many meanings at once, particularly since the poet's intention cannot be altogether a conscious one. One reason —apart from the human mind's stubborn complexities—is that words and ideas are never any one person's property; they carry along with them all the connotations and varying meanings that the history of man's thought has given them. The sum of all these connotations and possible meanings is the poem's whole "frame of reference." In a narrative poem, for instance, the hero will be a new version of many other heroes resembling each other in their virtues, abilities, and deficiencies. (Think back, for a moment, over the many heroes of motion-pictures you have seen. Do they not, for the most part, bear very strong resemblances to one another? Similar resemblances can be found among the heroes of epic and other narrative poems, and among the speaking personalities of lyric poems.) And however successfully it says what he wants it to say, the language a poet uses will also suggest the kind of thinking common to his times and something of his own private character. The very form he writes in—ballad, dramatic monologue, or any other—will suggest other works written in the same form. His images, too, are part of a history of such images. Thus, a poem using a flower-image reminds us of a whole tradition, perhaps, of love-poems. Because such associations are always present, a poem is always, more or less subtly, emphasizing certain ideas and attitudes and minimizing others, justifying a set of assumptions of some kind—in short, working upon our beliefs.

So it is that many poems, in addition to what they say on the surface, point to certain implied assumptions that may be just as important as their apparent meaning. It is part of the "game," the method of art, that one thing should be done in terms of another. Narrative catches and holds our attention more easily than logic, and often serves as a façade for it. And "logic," in turn, is often mainly a way of getting at an emotional or moral insight. When we have become accustomed to such transfers of meaning within a poem, we trouble ourselves less about final interpretation and more about the relation between any possible interpretation and the underlying assumptions of the poem as a whole. For we see that the argument is important, but that its importance lies in its contribution to the poem's felt meaning rather than in the abstract theme.

Let us see how, in each of two poems about a woman's beauty, the narrative structure resolves itself into a kind of argument, which in turn is absorbed into a set of values and attitudes implied by the sounds and images of the poem. The first is a nineteenth-century Romantic poem.

Edgar Allan Poe *To Helen*

> Helen, thy beauty is to me
>   Like those Nicèan barks of yore,
> That gently, o'er a perfumed sea,
>   The weary, way-worn wanderer bore
>   To his own native shore.
>
> On desperate seas long wont to roam,
>   Thy hyacinth hair, thy classic face,
> Thy Naiad airs have brought me home
>   To the glory that was Greece
> And the grandeur that was Rome.   10
>
> Lo! in yon brilliant window-niche
>   How statue-like I see thee stand,
>   The agate lamp within thy hand!
> Ah, Psyche, from the regions which
>   Are Holy Land!

One hardly notices the fact here that the speaker is telling a "story"— that is, recounting something that has "happened" to him. (Helen's beauty has brought him to an appreciation of the magnificent, serene security of the values of classical art and thought, and to a realization of the mysterious significance of her nature.) Helen's face—perhaps the reader is expected to make an association with Marlowe's famous line: "Was this the face that launched a thousand ships?"—reminds him of the vessels by which weary travelers would return home in the long-distant, the mythic past. Since the name Helen evokes the legend of the beautiful woman over whom Homer tells us the Trojan War was fought, and since the next stanza praises the glories of classical Greece and Rome, it would be a fair guess that the speaker is thinking of the Grecian warriors—very possibly Odysseus, the weariest "way-worn wanderer" in literature—returning home from Troy.

Helen's beauty, the speaker says, has borne him "homeward" gently and pleasurably—"o'er a perfumed sea." Now such a statement cannot be read literally. If the poem had ended with the second stanza, we might believe it was intended to argue, rather too blatantly, that the beauty of the woman the speaker is addressing (if, indeed, he is not directly addressing the original Helen of Troy) has led him to appreciate the kindred beauty of classical art. Such art, and the standards embodied in it, he might be arguing, is calm, reassuring, nobly beautiful—a true port for such stormy, uncontrolled natures as his own.

In the third stanza, however—the most intense one in this poem—the emphasis on classical beauty is minimized. Now that Helen's beauty has brought the voyager to a vision of calm and security after violent despair, she is nevertheless still remote, a strange, statuelike, though brilliant figure in the window-niche. He calls her Psyche—"soul"—thus endowing her with a spiritual, unreachable quality. The name Psyche also recalls the heroine of the Greek myth who married Cupid but spoiled the marriage by attempting to look directly into his face. She is then a symbol both of beauty and of frustration from the ancient world, which the speaker calls the "Holy Land"; and "Holy Land," of course, has a sacred Biblical association, although it is Greece of which he is speaking.

Clearly, though the poem does have to do with the values of classical art symbolized by Helen, this is not really its major theme. Rather, the last stanza suggests a kind of mystery, as we have seen, at the heart of the poem, instead of an intellectual purpose. One could argue that the poem is actually about the speaker's feeling for a particular woman; or that it is a confession of failure in love or in poetic achievement; or that Helen, and the "native shore," and classical Greece and Rome, and Psyche, and "Holy Land" all symbolize a long-lost, much-desired security, such as a mother gives her infant child. At any rate, the general "argument" that we have followed through seems to blend with the speaker's private associations (just as the *h*'s, *l*'s, and *n*'s in "Helen" and "Holy Land," together with a few other sounds almost equally widespread throughout the poem, blend the two motifs in a musical way).

Some of the more salient characteristics of Romanticism may be found in *To Helen*. We feel a conflict in it between the clear line of the argument and the emotional content of the images, with the latter element dominating. The poet is trying to convey, partly through an appeal to subconscious emotions, a sense of a compelling, ideal vision—to *make* it come to life through the intensity of his presentation of it. William

Blake's *The Tyger* has a similar objective, and we have suggested its closeness to the spirit of the primitive magician. Romantic poetry does preoccupy itself with the magical. It fastens on the mystery hidden in ordinary existence. It also seeks to make experiences seem real that are purely imaginary or associated with spiritual life only or with exotic times and places. The aim of the Romantic writer is closely related to the attempts, in such modern poems as *The Love Song of J. Alfred Prufrock*, to evoke our sense of the human meaning of experience through images rather than through logical presentation. The "argument" of a romantic poem tends to imply a rejection of the world as it is, or seems to be, in favor of some more idealized or "deeper" understanding of it.

The second of our poems about a woman's beauty is written in the Classical tradition:

EDMUND WALLER *Song*

> Go lovely Rose
> Tell her that wastes her time and me,
>   That now she knows
> When I resemble her to thee,
>   How sweet and fair she seems to be.
>
> Tell her that's young,
> And shuns to have her graces spy'd,
>   That hadst thou sprung
> In Desarts, where no men abide,
>   Thou must have uncommended dy'd.   10
>
> Small is the worth
> Of Beauty from the light retir'd;
>   Bid her come forth,
> Suffer her self to be desir'd,
>   And not blush so to be admir'd.
>
> Then die, that she,
> The common fate of all things rare,
>   May read in thee;
> How small a part of time they share,
>   That are so wondrous sweet and fair.   20

Here, as in *To Helen*, there is a chronological sequence—a "story," as it were, foretold in a series of commands to the rose. The lover directs it to "go" to his desired mistress with a series of symbolic "messages." It is to represent her own sweetness and beauty to her; it is to persuade her to make herself available to the speaker, for otherwise her loveliness will be wasted; and it is to die, symbolizing life's brevity and the urgency of seizing joy while we may.

This chronological sequence is inseparable from the argument, which develops an extremely familiar seventeenth-century poetic theme with unusual grace and masculine persuasive force. The argument is clear and sharp, rising to passionate directness in the closing lines of the third stanza and falling into a genuinely sad mood over the mutability of "all things rare" recalled at the end. It moves through four definite stages: First comes the "proof," by way of the rose, of the lover's sincerity in praising his lady's beauty. Then, through the image of the desert flower, he makes the further point that this beauty must not be wasted. The same point is asserted more urgently and directly, in terms of the lady herself and not in the imagery of flowers, in the third stanza. And in the fourth, it is once again reinforced by the reminder of the brevity of youth and beauty.

Go lovely Rose does not reject the values of this world as *To Helen* does. But like other worldly poems in the Classical tradition it is preoccupied with that which is most desirable in life and presents it with such zest and elegance as to idealize it. To the Classical standards of intellectual clarity and stylistic grace it adds the special interest of the seventeenth-century Cavalier poet in writing songs for music. This poem was, in fact, set to music by the famous seventeenth-century composer Henry Lawes. The modern poet Ezra Pound esteemed Waller's poem so highly that, in the *Envoi* (or closing poem) of his sequence *Hugh Selwyn Mauberley*, he refers to "that song of Lawes" and employs a stanza-form and specific allusions that recall it and set it up as a model of beauty:

> *Tell her that goes*
> *With song upon her lips*
> *But sings not out the song, nor knows*
> *The maker of it, some other mouth*
> *May be as fair as hers,*
> *Might, in new ages, gain her worshippers,*
> *When our two dusts with Waller's shall be laid,*
> *Siftings on siftings in oblivion,*
> *Till change hath broken down*
> *All things save Beauty alone.*   10

From these examples, we see the way in which poems imply the assumptions behind the traditions they embody. In the Romantic tradition of Poe's poem, high value is placed on escape from the humdrum and the familiar, and on the search for some ideal, ineffable, and, especially, *mysterious* beauty usually associated with the feminine principle. In the

Classical tradition of the Cavalier poet Waller, other values appear: an elegant, worldly gallantry, and the union of manliness with grace and of art with ardor. It is interesting that Pound, in the quoted stanza from *Envoi*, idealizes Waller's Classical perfectionism but does so in language suggestive of Poe's less tough-minded thinking. Pound is romanticizing an esthetic conception of pure Beauty, rigorously achieved through art. His viewpoint is a relatively modern one, but he uses a modification of Waller's stanza-form (longer, more intellectually developed, but with a comparable variation of rhyme and line-length) to emphasize the presence of the living past in what he is doing. It is as if he were saying: "If Waller were alive and writing today, with our modern preoccupations, he would write as I do."

The Romantic poets of the late eighteenth and early nineteenth centuries introduced a preoccupation with their own private personalities and inward moods and disturbances that has remained an important tendency in poetry ever since, We have seen how Keats's *Ode to a Nightingale* begins with the very personal outcry: "My heart aches. . . ." Coleridge speaks in one of his poems, which has the revealing title *Dejection: An Ode*, of feeling

> A grief without a pang, void, dark, and drear,
>   A stifled, drowsy, unimpassioned grief,
>   Which find no natural outlet, no relief. . . .

And Wordsworth devotes his *Ode: Intimations of Immortality from Recollections of Early Childhood* to thinking about the melancholy fact that he no longer can experience the spontaneous delight he once felt in nature. These are but a very few instances of the poetry of self-awareness cultivated by the Romantics. In our own day, the tendency has been carried much farther.

The Romantic poet usually presented himself as a rather generalized sensitive spirit, without explicitly personal details, pondering his feelings in relation to something, most often something in nature, outside himself—the nightingale and its song, a beautiful landscape, moonlight on a tranquil evening. Then, by a series of gradations marking the history of poetry over the past century and a half, an ever-greater absorption developed in effects of keen, accurate sensation, intensely projected psychological states, and complex states of awareness or sensibility. To take some ready examples, Browning's dramatic monologues and certain of his more subjectively developed poems like *Two in the Campagna* and *The Englishman in Italy* may be compared with Eliot's *The Love Song of J. Alfred Prufrock* (discussed on pages 152–153). Eliot's poem is not *better* than the ones by Browning, but the inward condition of his speaker is exposed to the world mercilessly. The past decade or so has seen the emergence of a body of poetry in which the poet, in his own right, talks far more intimately and frankly about himself than most poetry in English has ever done. The "Confessional" poetry of Robert Lowell, Sylvia Plath, and others would seem to be the culmination of this trend. One reason, perhaps, may be the ever more difficult question of personal identity and individual difference in a world becoming more crowded with people and more impersonal in its organization. Perhaps it is this situation that underlies the following poem by Denise Levertov, in which a woman thinks about who, exactly, she is in relation to the man she loves:

DENISE LEVERTOV *Losing Track*

    Long after you have swung back
    away from me
    I think you are still with me:

    you come in close to the shore
    on the tide
    and nudge me awake the way

    a boat adrift nudges the pier:
    am I a pier
    half-in half-out of the water?

    and in the pleasure of that communion   10
    I lose track,
    the moon I watch goes down, the

    tide swings you away before
    I know I'm
    alone again long since,

    mud sucking at gray and black
    timbers of me,
    a light growth of green dreams drying.

The woman who speaks in this poem defines herself only in terms of the presence or absence of the man. Although real and present, she is ordinarily hardly conscious of her own nature until the man's love "nudges" her awake. Then, long after this has happened, the sense of achieved communion remains with her. She has "lost track," not only of time but of her separate identity. Eventually, however, she must know herself "alone" again. But what she *is* has been made clearer in the image of the pier in the last stanza.

    There are three centers of attention in the poem: the image of the woman as a pier, the image of the man as a boat, and the transformed, awakened consciousness of the woman. The most striking discovery she makes is of the relation of these three points of attention in the figure of the boat coming in on the tide and nudging the pier—a sensuous, revealing figure. When, however, the poet focuses attention on the pier image itself, in its own right, the question of identity is brought into the open:

> am I a pier
> half-in half-out of the water?

But that way, the image makes her seem rather inert; when the boat recedes again, this inertness is combined with associations of a slightly brackish sort:

> mud sucking at gray and black
> timbers of me,
> a light growth of green dreams drying.

The ultimate projection of the poet's view of herself as an inert, isolated being whose psychological existence has a desolate quality approaching self-disgust except when she is touched into life by the man's love is deeply personal in its impact. At the same time, it reflects the Romantic belief that one must seek within oneself for the unknown meaning of life. No poem, of course, is ever simply personal. Miss Levertov, as any poet must, uses traditional motifs and prevailing modes of thought despite the intimately individual tone of the poem. For instance, allegory (the use of the boat and pier to symbolize the love-relationship) is an ancient poetic device for the representation of abstract principles and psychological processes. A more modern tradition Miss Levertov employs is that of imagist technique: the evocation of emotional states through concrete images rather than through generalized statement. As the combining of these three modes—Romantic, allegorical, and imagist—demonstrates, poetry itself is the product of a continuing tradition that has been renewed many times by fresh perspectives and starting points.

Poems: Classicism and Romanticism

In Classical writing, ideas and feelings tend to be sharp, clear, direct, and untrammeled. If not always cool, their temper is controlled and self-possessed. The writer asserts his mastery of his images and his subject, and is never carried away by them. Romantic writing, on the other hand, is iridescent, emotional, and filled with personal enthusiasm. The Romantic poet seeks the unattainable, the strange, and the new beyond the limits of mundane reason and the circumscriptions of time. His motto is Browning's "A man's reach should exceed his grasp/Or what's a Heaven for?" He thinks it nobler to fail in attempting something great than to achieve the limited perfection that is the Classical writer's goal.

We begin with six Classical poems. Starting with Jonson's self-castigating, biting *Ode*, it is easy to see their simplicity, directness, universality, and human sympathy. One should notice, however, that their real impact comes through implication and irony; far beyond their sharp surface clarity, they communicate a mood and an attitude. In Herrick's and Hardy's brief, concentrated lyric poems we see, in one instance, the futility and yet the inevitability (in the face of man's faithlessness) of woman's tears and, in the other, the brevity of human love when measured in the scale of the stars. Housman's poem conveys the pathetic tentativeness of all human triumph, and Davie's more personal elegy (for the poet Theodore Roethke) struggles with the difficulty of holding on to the living personality of a writer who has died. Yvor Winters's poem reminds us that a poet is often a judge and lawgiver who exposes the folly of corruption of anyone who distorts the values of the public mind for his own gain.

The Romantic poems that follow should make very clear the contrast we have been outlining. After Winters's Classical ode come four poems by Shelley, Byron, Jeffers, and Spender that reveal a more intimate sense of political commitment, and perhaps a more insistent exhortation to action, than Winters allows his poem to show. The rest of the Romantic group deal with the most common themes of Romanticism: sexual love and nature. All are deeply involved emotionally with their themes and illustrate the imaginative transcendence of the literal and the exclusively rational. Shelley's *The Indian Serenade* and Tennyson's *Now sleeps the crimson petal* reveal a mood of hushed rapture, created not only by music and image but by appeals to all the senses. These two nocturnes are unique and thrilling evocations of a mood of tremulous excitement such as is only rarely experienced even in passionate love.

It should be noted here that, whereas Classicism deals usually with the normal and the general, Romanticism seeks to express the unique and different, sometimes with an emotional subjectivity the Classicist might consider morbid. Keats's *Ode to Melancholy*, like his *Ode to a Nightingale*, is

a beautiful illustration of this aspect of Romanticism in its preoccupation
with intensity of feeling for its own sake and with the relationship between
death and ecstasy. The comparative calmness and clarity of exposition in a
great part of Wordsworth's *Tintern Abbey*, contrasting with the exalted
emotional tone of certain climactic passages, makes this poem an example
of some of the virtues of both modes of poetry. On a smaller scale, Graves's
Sick Love paradoxically presents a Romantic viewpoint with Classical precision and conciseness; and Hopkins's *The Starlight Night* attempts, as this
poet does so often, to discipline an extreme responsiveness to sense-impressions
by translating natural imagery into religious symbolism. The contemporary
verses of Anne Sexton and John Berryman, on the other hand, are extreme
examples of the poetry of Romantic confessionalism, centered on the speakers'
private personalities. The words *Classical* and *Romantic* are, of course, purely
descriptive. They are not terms of praise or abuse, although some critics have
so used them.

1. Classical Poems

Ben Jonson   *An Ode to Himself*

> Where dost thou careless lie,
>   Buried in ease and sloth?
> Knowledge that sleeps doth die;
> And this security,
>   It is the common moth
> That eats on wits and arts, and oft destroys them both.
>
> Are all the Aonian springs
>   Dried up? Lies Thespia waste?
> Doth Clarius' harp want strings,
> That not a nymph now sings?   10
>   Or droop they as disgraced,
> To see their seats and bowers by chattering pies defaced?
>
> If hence thy silence be,
>   As 'tis too just a cause,
> Let this thought quicken thee:
> Minds that are great and free
>   Should not on fortune pause;
> 'Tis crown enough to virtue still, her own applause.
>
> What though the greedy fry
>   Be taken with false baits   20
> Of worded balladry,

And think it poesy?
    They die with their conceits,
And only piteous scorn upon their folly waits.

Then take in hand thy lyre;
    Strike in thy proper strain;
With Japhet's line aspire
Sol's chariot for new fire
    To give the world again;
Who aided him will thee, the issue of Jove's brain.   30

And, since our dainty age
    Cannot endure reproof,
Make not thyself a page
To that strumpet the stage;
    But sing high and aloof,
Safe from the wolf's black jaw, and the dull ass's hoof.

ROBERT HERRICK   *Upon Julia Weeping*

She by the River sate, and sitting there,
She wept, and made it deeper by a tear.

THOMAS HARDY   *The Comet at Yell'ham*

I

It bends far over Yell'ham Plain,
    And we, from Yell'ham Height,
Stand and regard its fiery train,
    So soon to swim from sight.

II

It will return long years hence, when
    As now its strange swift shine
Will fall on Yell'ham; but not then
    On that sweet form of thine.

A. E. HOUSMAN   *To an Athlete Dying Young*

The time you won your town the race
We chaired you through the market-place;
Man and boy stood cheering by,
And home we brought you shoulder-high.

Today, the road all runners come,
Shoulder-high we bring you home,
And set you at your threshold down,
Townsman of a stiller town.

Smart lad, to slip betimes away
From fields where glory does not stay,   10
And early though the laurel grows
It withers quicker than the rose.

Eyes the shady night has shut
Cannot see the record cut,
And silence sounds no worse than cheers
After earth has stopped the ears:

Now you will not swell the rout
Of lads that wore their honors out,
Runners whom renown outran
And the name died before the man.   20

So set, before its echoes fade,
The fleet foot on the sill of shade,
And hold to the low lintel up
The still-defended challenge-cup.

And round that early-laureled head
Will flock to gaze the strengthless dead,
And find unwithered on its curls
The garland briefer than a girl's.

DONALD DAVIE   *July, 1964*

I smell a smell of death.
Roethke, who died last year
with whom I drank in London,
wrote the book I am reading;
a friend, of a firm mind,
has died or is dying now,
a telegram informs me;
the wife of a neighbour died
in three quick months of cancer.

Love and art I practise;   10
they seem to be worth no more
and no less than they were.
The firm mind practised neither.
It practised charity
vocationally and
yet for the most part truly.
Roethke, who practised both,
was slack in his art by the end.

The practice of an art
is to convert all terms   20
into the terms of art.
By the end of the third stanza
death is a smell no longer;
it is a problem of style.
A man who ought to know me
wrote in a review
my emotional life was meagre.

YVOR WINTERS   *An Ode on the Despoilers of Learning
in an American University (1947)*

This was our heritage:
In Learning's monument
To study, and teach the young,
Until our days were spent;
To reëmbody mind
In age succeeding age,
That some few men might see,
Though, mostly, men were blind;
To hold what men had wrung
From struggle to atone   10
For man's stupidity,
In labor and alone.

But now the insensate, calm
Performers of the hour,
Cold, with cold eye and palm,
Desiring trivial power,
And terror-struck within
At their own emptiness,

Move in. As they move in,
Slow and invidious,   20
They pause and calculate,
Then, as such beings use,
With long-perfected hate,
Strike the immortal Muse.

What art of prose or verse
Should bring their like to book?
What consecrated curse
And pious rhetoric?
No one: we need but look.
For these have come too far: 30
They stand here, coarse and lined,
And permanent as stone,
In the final light of mind.
The body politic
Of Learning is its own
Inscrutable old Bar.

2. *Romantic Poems*

PERCY BYSSHE SHELLEY   *Song to the Men of England*

Men of England, wherefore plough
For the lords who lay ye low?
Wherefore weave with toil and care
The rich robes your tyrants wear?

Wherefore feed, and clothe, and save,
From the cradle to the grave,
Those ungrateful drones who would
Drain your sweat—nay, drink your blood?

Wherefore, Bees of England, forge
Many a weapon, chain, and scourge,   10
That these stingless drones may spoil
The forced produce of your toil?

Have ye leisure, comfort, calm,
Shelter, food, love's gentle balm?
Or what is it ye buy so dear
With your pain and with your fear?

The seed ye sow, another reaps;
The wealth ye find, another keeps;
The robes ye weave, another wears;
The arms ye forge, another bears. 20

Sow seed,—but let no tyrant reap;
Find wealth,—let no impostor heap;
Weave robes,—let not the idle wear;
Forge arms,—in your defence to bear.

Shrink to your cellars, holes, and cells;
In halls ye deck, another dwells.
Why shake the chains ye wrought? Ye see
The steel ye tempered glance on ye.

With plough and spade, and hoe and loom,
Trace your grave, and build your tomb, 30
And weave your winding-sheet, till fair
England be your sepulchre.

GEORGE GORDON, LORD BYRON   *Sonnet on Chillon* [1]

Eternal spirit of the chainless Mind!
   Brightest in dungeons, Liberty! thou art,
   For there thy habitation is the heart—
The heart which love of thee alone can bind;
And when thy sons to fetters are consign'd—
   To fetters, and the damp vault's dayless gloom,
   Their country conquers with their martyrdom,
And Freedom's fame finds wings on every wind.
Chillon! thy prison is a holy place,
   And thy sad floor an altar—for 'twas trod, 10
Until his very steps have left a trace
   Worn, as if thy cold pavement were a sod,
By Bonnivard!—May none those marks efface!
   For they appeal from tyranny to God.

[1] place of the dungeon where François de Bonnivard, the sixteenth-century Swiss
patriot, was imprisoned for his political and religious opinions

ROBINSON JEFFERS   *Shine, Perishing Republic*

While this America settles in the mould of its vulgarity, heavily
    thickening to empire,
And protest, only a bubble in the molten mass, pops and sighs
    out, and the mass hardens,

I sadly smiling remember that the flower fades to make fruit, the
    fruit rots to make earth.
Out of the mother; and through the spring exultances, ripeness
    and decadence; and home to the mother.

You making haste haste on decay; not blameworthy; life is good,
    be it stubbornly long or suddenly
A mortal splendor: meteors are not needed less than mountains:
    shine, perishing republic.

But for my children, I would have them keep their distance from
    the thickening center; corruption
Never has been compulsory, when the cities lie at the monster's
    feet there are left the mountains.

And boys, be in nothing so moderate as in love of man, a clever
    servant, insufferable master.
There is the trap that catches noblest spirits, that caught—they   10
    say—God, when he walked on earth.

STEPHEN SPENDER   *Not Palaces, an Era's Crown*

Not palaces, an era's crown
Where the mind dwells, intrigues, rests;
Architectural gold-leaved flower
From people ordered like a single mind,
I build. This only what I tell:
It is too late for rare accumulation,
For family pride, for beauty's filtered dusts;
I say, stamping the words with emphasis,
Drink from here energy and only energy,
As from the electric charge of a battery,   10
To will this Time's change.
Eye, gazelle, delicate wanderer,
Drinker of horizon's fluid line;

Ear that suspends on a chord
The spirit drinking timelessness;
Touch, love, all senses;
Leave your gardens, your singing feasts,
Your dreams of suns circling before our sun,
Of heaven after our world.
Instead, watch images of flashing glass   20
That strike the outward sense, the polished will,
Flag of our purpose which the wind engraves.
No spirit seek here rest. But this: No one
Shall hunger: Man shall spend equally.
Our goal which we compel: Man shall be man.
    That programme of the antique Satan
Bristling with guns on the indented page,
With battleship towering from hilly waves:
For what? Drive of a ruining purpose
Destroying all but its age-long exploiters.   30
Our programme like this, but opposite,
Death to the killers, bringing light to life.

PERCY BYSSHE SHELLEY   *The Indian Serenade*

I arise from dreams of thee
In the first sweet sleep of night,
When the winds are breathing low,
And the stars are shining bright:
I arise from dreams of thee,
And a spirit in my feet
Hath led me—who knows how?
To thy chamber window, Sweet!

The wandering airs they faint
On the dark, the silent stream—   10
The Champak odours fail
Like sweet thoughts in a dream;
The nightingale's complaint,
It dies upon her heart;
As I must on thine,
Oh, belovèd as thou art!

Oh lift me from the grass!
I die! I faint! I fail!

Let thy love in kisses rain
On my lips and eyelids pale.   20
My cheek is cold and white, alas!
My heart beats loud and fast;
Oh! press it to thine own again,
Where it will break at last.

WILLIAM WORDSWORTH   *Lines Composed a Few Miles
above Tintern Abbey*

On revisiting the bank of the Wye during a tour, July 13, 1798

Five years have past; five summers, with the length
Of five long winters! and again I hear
These waters, rolling from their mountain-springs
With a soft inland murmur.—Once again
Do I behold these steep and lofty cliffs,
That on a wild secluded scene impress
Thoughts of more deep seclusion; and connect
The landscape with the quiet of the sky.
The day is come when I again repose
Here, under this dark sycamore, and view   10
These plots of cottage-ground, these orchard-tufts,
Which at this season, with their unripe fruits,
Are clad in one green hue, and lose themselves
'Mid groves and copses. Once again I see
These hedge-rows, hardly hedge-rows, little lines
Of sportive wood run wild: these pastoral farms,
Green to the very door; and wreaths of smoke
Sent up, in silence, from among the trees!
With some uncertain notice, as might seem
Of vagrant dwellers in the houseless woods,   20
Or of some Hermit's cave, where by his fire
The Hermit sits alone.

                        These beauteous forms,
Through a long absence, have not been to me
As is a landscape to a blind man's eye:
But oft, in lonely rooms, and 'mid the din
Of towns and cities, I have owed to them,
In hours of weariness, sensations sweet,
Felt in the blood, and felt along the heart;

And passing even into my purer mind,
With tranquil restoration:—feelings too   30
Of unremembered pleasure: such, perhaps,
As have no slight or trivial influence
On that best portion of a good man's life,
His little, nameless, unremembered acts
Of kindness and of love. Nor less, I trust,
To them I may have owed another gift,
Of aspect more sublime; that blessed mood,
In which the burthen of the mystery,
In which the heavy and the weary weight
Of all this unintelligible world,   40
Is lightened:—that serene and blessed mood,
In which the affections gently lead us on,—
Until, the breath of this corporeal frame
And even the motion of our human blood
Almost suspended, we are laid asleep
In body, and become a living soul:
While with an eye made quiet by the power
Of harmony, and the deep power of joy,
We see into the life of things.
                            If this
Be but a vain belief, yet, oh! how oft—   50
In darkness and amid the many shapes
Of joyless daylight; when the fretful stir
Unprofitable, and the fever of the world,
Have hung upon the beatings of my heart—
How oft, in spirit, have I turned to thee,
O sylvan Wye! thou wanderer thro' the woods,
How often has my spirit turned to thee!

And now, with gleams of half-extinguished thought,
With many recognitions dim and faint,
And somewhat of a sad perplexity,   60
The picture of the mind revives again:
While here I stand, not only with the sense
Of present pleasure, but with pleasing thoughts
That in this moment there is life and food
For future years. And so I dare to hope,
Though changed, no doubt, from what I was when first
I came among these hills; when like a roe
I bounded o'er the mountains, by the sides
Of the deep rivers, and the lonely streams,

Wherever nature led: more like a man   70
Flying from something that he dreads than one
Who sought the thing he loved. For nature then
(The coarser pleasures of my boyish days,
And their glad animal movements all gone by)
To me was all in all.—I cannot paint
What then I was. The sounding cataract
Haunted me like a passion: the tall rock,
The mountain, and the deep and gloomy wood,
Their colours and their forms, were then to me
An appetite; a feeling and a love,   80
That had no need of a remoter charm,
By thought supplied, nor any interest
Unborrowed from the eye.—That time is past,
And all its aching joys are now no more,
And all its dizzy raptures. Not for this
Faint I, nor mourn nor murmur; other gifts
Have followed; for such loss, I would believe,
Abundant recompense. For I have learned
To look on nature, not as in the hour
Of thoughtless youth; but hearing oftentimes   90
The still, sad music of humanity,
Nor harsh nor grating, though of ample power
To chasten and subdue. And I have felt
A presence that disturbs me with the joy
Of elevated thoughts; a sense sublime
Of something far more deeply interfused,
Whose dwelling is the light of setting suns,
And the round ocean and the living air,
And the blue sky, and in the mind of man:
A motion and a spirit, that impels   100
All thinking things, all objects of all thought,
And rolls through all things. Therefore am I still
A lover of the meadows and the woods,
And mountains; and of all that we behold
From this green earth; of all the mighty world
Of eye, and ear,—both what they half create,
And what perceive; well pleased to recognise
In nature and the language of the sense
The anchor of my purest thoughts, the nurse,
The guide, the guardian of my heart, and soul   110
Of all my moral being.

                                    Nor perchance,
If I were not thus taught, should I the more
Suffer my genial spirits to decay:
For thou art with me here upon the banks
Of this fair river; thou my dearest Friend,
My dear, dear Friend; and in thy voice I catch
The language of my former heart, and read
My former pleasures in the shooting lights
Of thy wild eyes. Oh! yet a little while
May I behold in thee what I was once,   120
My dear, dear Sister! and this prayer I make,
Knowing that Nature never did betray
The heart that loved her! 'tis her privilege,
Through all the years of this our life, to lead
From joy to joy; for she can so inform
The mind that is within us, so impress
With quietness and beauty, and so feed
With lofty thoughts, that neither evil tongues,
Rash judgments, nor the sneers of selfish men,
Nor greetings where no kindness is, nor all   130
The dreary intercourse of daily life,
Shall e'er prevail against us, or disturb
Our cheerful faith, that all which we behold
Is full of blessings. Therefore let the moon
Shine on thee in thy solitary walk;
And let the misty mountain-winds be free
To blow against thee; and, in after years,
When these wild ecstasies shall be matured
Into a sober pleasure; when thy mind
Shall be a mansion for all lovely forms,   140
Thy memory be as a dwelling-place
For all sweet sounds and harmonies; oh! then,
If solitude, or fear, or pain, or grief,
Should be thy portion, with what healing thoughts
Of tender joy wilt thou remember me,
And these my exhortations! Nor, perchance—
If I should be where I no more can hear
Thy voice, nor catch from thy wild eyes these gleams
Of past existence—wilt thou then forget
That on the banks of this delightful stream   150
We stood together; and that I, so long
A worshipper of Nature, hither came

Unwearied in that service: rather say
With warmer love—oh! with far deeper zeal
Of holier love. Nor wilt thou then forget
That after many wanderings, many years
Of absence, these steep woods and lofty cliffs,
And this green pastoral landscape, were to me
More dear, both for themselves and for thy sake!

ALFRED, LORD TENNYSON   Song: *Now sleeps the crimson
petal, now the white*

Now sleeps the crimson petal, now the white;
Nor waves the cypress in the palace walk;
Nor winks the gold fin in the porphyry font:
The fire-fly wakens; waken thou with me.

Now droops the milk-white peacock like a ghost,
And like a ghost she glimmers on to me.

Now lies the Earth all Danaë to the stars,
And all thy heart lies open unto me.

Now slides the silent meteor on, and leaves
A shining furrow, as thy thoughts in me.   10

Now folds the lily all her sweetness up,
And slips into the bosom of the lake:
So fold thyself, my dearest, thou, and slip
Into my bosom and be lost in me.

JOHN KEATS   *Ode on Melancholy*

No, no, go not to Lethe, neither twist
    Wolf's-bane, tight-rooted, for its poisonous wine;
Nor suffer thy pale forehead to be kiss'd
    By nightshade, ruby grape of Proserpine;
Make not your rosary of yew-berries,
    Nor let the beetle, nor the death-moth be
        Your mournful Psyche, nor the downy owl
A partner in your sorrow's mysteries;
    For shade to shade will come too drowsily,
        And drown the wakeful anguish of the soul.   10

But when the melancholy fit shall fall
  Sudden from heaven like a weeping cloud,
That fosters the droop-headed flowers all,
  And hides the green hill in an April shroud;
Then glut thy sorrow on a morning rose,
  Or on the rainbow of the salt sandwave,
    Or on the wealth of globed peonies;
Or if thy mistress some rich anger shows,
  Emprison her soft hand, and let her rave,
    And feed deep, deep upon her peerless eyes.   20

She dwells with Beauty—Beauty that must die;
  And Joy, whose hand is ever at his lips
Bidding adieu; and aching Pleasure nigh,
  Turning to poison while the bee-mouth sips:
Ay, in the very temple of Delight
  Veil'd Melancholy has her sovran shrine,
    Though seen of none save him whose strenuous tongue
Can burst Joy's grape against his palate fine:
  His soul shall taste the sadness of her might,
    And be among her cloudy trophies hung.   30

ROBERT GRAVES   *Sick Love*

O Love, be fed with apples while you may,
And feel the sun and go in royal array,
A smiling innocent on the heavenly causeway,

Though in what listening horror for the cry
That soars in outer blackness dismally,
The dumb blind beast, the paranoiac fury:

Be warm, enjoy the season, lift your head,
Exquisite in the pulse of tainted blood,
That shivering glory not to be despised.

Take your delight in momentariness,   10
Walk between dark and dark—a shining space
With the grave's narrowness, though not its peace.

GERARD MANLEY HOPKINS   *The Starlight Night*

Look at the stars! look, look up at the skies!
    O look at all the fire-folk sitting in the air!
    The bright boroughs, the circle-citadels there!
Down in dim woods and diamond delves! the elves'-eyes!
The grey lawns cold where gold, where quickgold lies!
    Wind-beat whitebeam! airy abeles set on a flare!
    Flake-doves sent floating forth at a farmyard scare!—
Ah well! it is all a purchase, all is a prize.

Buy then! bid then!—What?—Prayer, patience, alms, vows.
Look, look: a May-mess, like on orchard boughs!   10
    Look! March-bloom, like on mealed-with-yellow sallows!
These are indeed the barn; withindoors house
The shocks. This piece-bright paling shuts the spouse
    Christ home, Christ and his mother and all his hallows.

ANNE SEXTON   *The Starry Night*

*That does not keep me from having a terrible need of—shall I say the
word—religion. Then I go out at night to paint the stars.*

                    —VINCENT VAN GOGH in a letter to his brother

The town does not exist
except where one black-haired tree slips
up like a drowned woman into the hot sky.
The town is silent. The night boils with eleven stars.
O starry starry night! This is how
I want to die.

It moves. They are all alive.
Even the moon bulges in its orange irons
to push children, like a god, from its eye.
The old unseen serpent swallows up the stars.   10
Oh starry starry night! This is how
I want to die:

into that rushing beast of the night,
sucked up by that great dragon, to split
from my life with no flag,
no belly,
no cry.

JOHN BERRYMAN   *Dream Song 29*

There sat down, once, a thing on Henry's heart
só heavy, if he had a hundred years
& more, & weeping, sleepless, in all them time
Henry could not make good.
Starts again always in Henry's ears
the little cough somewhere, an odour, a chime.

And there is another thing he has in mind
like a grave Sienese face a thousand years
would fail to blur the still profiled reproach of. Ghastly,
with open eyes, he attends, blind.   10
All the bells say: too late. This is not for tears;
thinking.

But never did Henry, as he thought he did,
end anyone and hacks her body up
and hide the pieces, where they may be found.
He knows: he went over everyone, & nobody's missing.
Often he reckons, in the dawn, them up.
Nobody is ever missing.

II

Two Abiding Themes: Love and War

Besides such literary and intellectual traditions as Classicism and Romanticism, poetry also embodies basic attitudes of its creator and his age. Through the microscope of these attitudes the poet subjects the great universal themes—love, war, death, morality, truth, religion, and the others —to sharp private scrutiny. The "private" aspect of the picture is essential— the poet's special talent and sensitivity exist apart from the broader meanings he expresses through them. Thus, it was a special sensitivity to *touch* that gave Walt Whitman's poetry much of its force: "Blind, loving wrestling touch, sheath'd hooded sharp-tooth'd touch!" he wrote in *Song of Myself*. But it was his attitude toward the genteel, repressive moral code of his era that led him to employ this sensitivity as he often did. An example can be seen in his *Twenty-eight young men bathe by the shore* (page 442). Here we have a sympathetic, accurate description of a frustrated woman's feelings that is an excellent clue to hidden needs and struggles of spirit in midnineteenth-century America and England, just as Denise Levertov's *Losing Track* (pages 411–412) shows the self-realization and self-questioning of a modern woman. (She might, indeed, be the same woman as the one in Whitman's poem—but one living in the completely changed world of social attitudes existing a century later.)

If we selected one of the universal themes of poetry—love or war, let us say—and traced it throughout the history of English verse we would not find that all the poets of a given era approached it in just the same way. Yet certain key relationships would exist. We may instance the sonnets by Edmund Spenser and Michael Drayton on pages 122 and 123 and Shakespeare's sonnets *Let me not to the marriage of true minds* (page 435) and *Th'expense of spirit in a waste of shame* (pages 435–436), all written in the age of Elizabeth I. In these poems we find a common seriousness and a Platonic Christian idealism, whereas other poems, such as the earlier anonymous *O westron wind* or Sir Thomas Wyatt's also earlier *They flee from me* are more worldly, perhaps more natural and, while lighter in tone, actually quite as serious.

The surprising but very satisfying union of lightness—what T. S. Eliot even calls levity—with an intense seriousness can be seen in Andrew Marvell's *To His Coy Mistress*. This is a perfect example of how the passionate intellectualism of much seventeenth-century verse allowed room for levity, courtly love-making, satirical realism, and intense seriousness in the same poem. Marvell first idealizes a lady's beauty and virtue in bantering, sometimes sardonic language. Then he describes piercingly—though still wittily and banteringly—the frightening vistas of death ahead. (The "tomorrow we die" argument is itself a longstanding convention.) Finally, its humor and irony sloughed off behind it, we find the argument rising to its most passionate and serious tone, projecting a vision of the man and woman transformed by ecstatic love—superior to time and death, and themselves like gods.

It is interesting to compare the elegantly refined moral sentiments of Oliver Goldsmith's *Stanzas on Woman* (pages 438–439) with the intense poetry of Shakespeare's *Sonnet CXXIX* and Marvell's *To His Coy Mistress*. The expression of such general and rather artificial sentiments was one of the fashions of the eighteenth century, and Goldsmith's poem was highly successful as an "affectingly" high-toned comment on the social meaning of love and desire:

> When lovely Woman stoops to folly,
>   And finds too late that men betray,
> What charm can soothe her melancholy,
>   What art can wash her guilt away?

With sympathetic restraint, Goldsmith then goes on to tell "lovely Woman" that her only escape from shame "—is to die." He does not at any point suggest that life is not always as simple as he here makes it out to be. In this sense, his poem is itself almost as flippant if not as satirical as T. S. Eliot's parody, in *The Waste Land*, of its opening lines. Eliot's parody is also, of course, a caustic comment on the amorality of many people in our own day:

> When lovely woman stoops to folly and
> Paces about her room again, alone,
> She smoothes her hair with automatic hand,
> And puts a record on the gramophone.

Eliot's lines and the long poem in which they occur are a contemptuous dismissal of spiritless and automatic sex. They are not, of course, the last or the whole word. Whatever moral judgment Eliot's poetry implies, it reflects also the candor and psychological probing that mark twentieth-century thought and literature generally. The new atmosphere has permitted many woman poets to accept and explore their own feminine nature while questioning conventional expectations concerning morality and human nature in general.

The poetry of war is easier to see in relation to its time. Primitive war-poets, for example, were uncritical reporters who treated war as a fact of life dreadful only as death at sea or in some natural catastrophe could be called dreadful. When the West Saxons defeated the invading Scots and Danes at Brunanburh in the tenth century, their poet sang of how fiercely they had "hacked at the flyers before us" and of how the enemy were "shamed in their souls." Without pity, he painted the bleak terror of the carnage that had been wrought:

> Many a carcase they left to be carrion . . .
> Gave to the garbaging war-hawk to gorge it, and
> That gray beast, the wolf of the weald.

Such poetry has none of the patriotic fervor of a poem like Drayton's *Agincourt*, written at the height of Elizabethan England's newborn national pride. This poem celebrates the exploits of a fifteenth-century monarch as a glorious background for the still more glorious present. The first stanza is unforgettable in its freshness and enthusiasm:

> Fair stood the wind for France
> 　　When we our sails advance,
> Nor now to prove our chance
> 　　Longer will tarry;
> But putting to the main,
> At Caux, the mouth of Seine,
> With all his martial train
> 　　Landed King Harry.

Toward the end, the poem mingles this ardent patriotism with a medieval delight in the prowess of individual noblemen and with a still more ancient relish for the sheer clash and brutality of battle:

> Warwick in blood did wade,
> 　　Oxford the foe invade,
> And cruel slaughter made
> 　　Still as they ran up;
> Suffolk his axe did ply,
> Beaumont and Willoughby
> Bare them right doughtily,
> 　　Ferrers and Fanhope.

Compare this inspired doggerel or Richard Lovelace's much subtler *To Lucasta, Going to the Wars* (page 447), which in its way justifies war on grounds of personal honor, with two post-Restoration poems: Anne Winchilsea's *Trail all your pikes* (page 447) and William Collins's *Ode Written in the Beginning of the Year 1746* (page 447). The Countess of Winchilsea's poem marks both a common-sense reaction against extravagantly chivalric conceptions inherited from the Middle Ages and an emergence of modern questioning, humane values. Her point of view is feminine, with a realistic frame of reference that subverts, not without pity, men's pretensions to martial glory and their insistence that women admire these pretensions. Had *Trail all your pikes* only been written by some Lucasta half a century earlier, it would certainly have made the gallant Lovelace wince. Collins's brief, perfect allegorical poem is not critical, yet it too marks a shift from simple acceptance of war, whether fatalistic or enthusiastic, to a concern with its larger meanings. This poem is as patriotic as *Agincourt*, but its nationalism is abstract, it avoids swashbuckling, and it is consolatory rather than exultant in its gentle affirmation that those who die for their country perish nobly.

Although poems critical of war have been composed in earlier ages, the closer we come to our own day the more we find a special emphasis on personal *experience* of war itself, and very often on the death and the suffering involved in it. Whitman's *A sight in camp in the daybreak gray and dim* (page 448), for instance, is consolatory, like Collins's *Ode*. But Collins's dead soldiers, though he says they have preserved the nation and now sweeten the earth, are still anonymous. Whitman's poem is an unaffected expression of love for particular soldiers in the Civil War whose still bodies he comes upon in the early morning. He refuses to dismiss them as lost to the meanings of life and love, describing them in detail and stressing the divinity of their being. Had he not been so ardently concerned to deny the possible meaninglessness of any death, and also so imbued with his sense of the North's evangelical mission in the Civil War, Whitman's personal feelings for these soldiers might have led him to write a poem like Jarrell's *Death of the Ball Turret Gunner* (page 354), which, as we have seen, turns the spotlight with unwavering realism on death in war. This poem of World War II recalls the characteristically shocked response of many poets—Wilfred Owen, Isaac Rosenberg, Herbert Read, and many others—to the first World War, a response similar to that expressed in such a novel as Hemingway's *A Farewell to Arms*. Over the past century and a half, indeed, as wars have become more devastating and society less willing to accept them as necessary and inevitable, our poetry has increasingly stressed the horror, the pity, and the irony of their occurrence. Saturation bombing and the atomic bomb destroyed any illusion of glamor that might have been left. Moreover the fact that so much of modern warfare involves an "impersonal" distance between the soldier and his unseen victims or killers, and between armies or airmen and civilian populations, has introduced new feelings of terror as well as of guilt and revulsion. Many poets such as Keith Douglas, Randall Jarrell, and James Dickey have given voice to new sets of feelings that carry over into psychological states in which war is not directly involved.

Poems: Two Abiding Themes: Love and War

Here we have a sequence of poems on two of the oldest and most universal themes: love and war. They are arranged more or less chronologically to illustrate both variety and continuity. The love poems extend from the simple, deeply felt medieval cry O *westron wind, when will thou blow* to the sophisticated twentieth-century lyrics of Cummings and Auden. Two of Shakespeare's serious affirmations of the power of love and sex are found in his sonnets CXVI and CXXIX. They are followed by three more directly personal poems that are at once witty and intensely serious. This fusion of tones is clearest in the combined scorn, pride, and anguished memory of Wyatt's realistic and very modern-sounding evocation of love passages at the court of Henry VII, and in Marvell's sudden intensifying of the delicate fooling of the first half of *To His Coy Mistress* by his introduction of the great traditional theme of Death and Time as enemies of love. Cummings's *ponder,darling* is a modern rewriting of the seventeenth-century poem, a parody that presents the lovers as American tourists visiting the Forum in Rome. What these poems have in common, beyond the obvious identity of situation and structure, is the man's complex attitude toward the woman. Humorous, tender, impatient, and conscious of his greater experience and practical wisdom, he means—half ironically and half seriously—to exalt and praise her, and to seduce her. Goldsmith's sentimental and conventional portrayal of eighteenth-century social morality is in sharp contrast to the other poems here.

Romanticism is especially illustrated in the love poems of this section by the passionate aspiration of Keats's great lonely sonnet (more exalted than O *westron wind*; more inward than the poems by Wyatt, Marvell, and Cummings) and by the fierce though understated emotionalism of Yeats's poem. A gentle psychological realism marks Browning's surprisingly modern *Two in the Campagna*. Browning's lovers, like Cummings's, are in Rome, and here too the man alone speaks. But how different is the tone and treatment! A thoroughly modern psychological realism is found, again, in the strange and powerful poems by Whitman, Hardy, and Lawrence.

When we come to the poems on war, some of the same comparisons and contrasts can be drawn. Peacock's early nineteenth-century re-creation of the wild spirit of the barbarian Welsh border cattle raiders, with their ecstatic glorification of bloodshed and war, displays one of the historic and still living attitudes toward war. Lovelace's *To Lucasta, Going to the Wars* gives us the chivalric and courtly concept of war as honor and duty, a concept repudiated by a woman of Lovelace's own time in the Countess of Winchilsea's attack on "the false idol, Honour." William Collins in the eighteenth century and Ralph Waldo Emerson in the nineteenth still pay homage to this idol in its patriotic aspect, but the realistic poems of the Civil War by Whitman and of the two world wars of the twentieth century

by Edward Thomas, Wilfred Owen, Herbert Read, Richard Eberhart, and
W. T. Scott concentrate on the pity, horror, waste, and pain of war that has
become increasingly terrible and obviously useless. Owen's *Greater Love* is a
simultaneous rejection both of chivalry in love and chivalry in war, a sometimes clumsy but piercing mockery of the attitudes that were implicit in
Lovelace's poem. Dickey's *The Performance* suggests, with grotesque pathos,
the dwindling of the ancient image of the warrior-hero in the figure of an
American World War II pilot. The pilot here is a sacrificial victim who
nevertheless "performs" a heroic act as his final gesture.

1. Love

ANONYMOUS   *O westron wind, when will thou blow*

> O westron wind, when will thou blow,
>   The small rain down can rain?
> Christ, if my love were in my arms
>   And I in my bed again!

WILLIAM SHAKESPEARE   *Sonnet CXVI*

> Let me not to the marriage of true minds
> Admit impediments; love is not love
> Which alters when it alteration finds,
> Or bends with the remover to remove.
> O, no! it is an ever-fixed mark
> That looks on tempests and is never shaken;
> It is the star to every wandering bark,
> Whose worth's unknown, although his height be taken.
> Love's not Time's fool, though rosy lips and cheeks
> Within his bending sickle's compass come;   10
> Love alters not with his brief hours and weeks,
> But bears it out even to the edge of doom.
>   If this be error and upon me prov'd,
>   I never writ, nor no man ever lov'd.

WILLIAM SHAKESPEARE   *Sonnet CXXIX*

> Th' expense of Spirit in a waste of shame
> Is lust in action; and, till action, lust
> Is perjur'd, murd'rous, bloody, full of blame,
> Savage, extreme, rude, cruel, not to trust;

Enjoy'd no sooner but despised straight;
Past reason hunted, and no sooner had,
Past reason hated as a swallow'd bait
On purpose laid to make the taker mad:
Mad in pursuit, and in possession so;
Had, having, and in quest to have extreme;   10
A bliss in proof, and prov'd, a very woe;
Before, a joy propos'd; behind, a dream.
    All this the world well knows, yet none knows well
    To shun the heaven that leads men to this hell.

SIR THOMAS WYATT   *They flee from me*

They flee from me, that sometime did me seek
With naked foot, stalking in my chamber:
I have seen them gentle, tame, and meek,
That now are wild, and do not remember
That sometime they put themselves in danger
To take bread at my hand; and now they range
Busily seeking with a continual change.

Thanked be fortune it hath been otherwise
Twenty times better; but once, in special,
In thin array, after a pleasant guise,   10
When her loose gown from her shoulders did fall,
And she me caught in her armes long and small,
Therewithal sweetly did me kiss,
And softly said, "Dear heart, how like you this?"

It was no dream; I lay broad waking:
But all is turnéd, thorough my gentleness,
Into a strange fashion of forsaking;
And I have leave to go of her goodness,
And she also to use new-fangleness.
But since that I so kindély am servéd,   20
I would fain know what she hath deservéd.

ANDREW MARVELL   *To His Coy Mistress* [1]

Had we but World enough, and time,
This coyness, Lady, were no crime.

[1] See comment in Chapter Six, Section IV (p. 331).

We would sit down, and think which way
To walk, and pass our long Love's Day.
Thou by the *Indian Ganges* side
Should'st Rubies find: I by the Tide
Of *Humber* would complain. I would
Love you ten years before the Flood:
And you should if you please refuse
Till the Conversion of the *Jews*.   10
My vegetable Love should grow
Vaster than Empires, and more slow.
An hundred years should go to praise
Thine Eyes, and on thy Forehead Gaze.
Two hundred to adore each Breast:
But thirty thousand to the rest.
An Age at least to every part,
And the last Age should show your Heart.
For Lady, you deserve this State,
Nor would I love at lower rate.   20
   But at my back I always hear
Time's winged Chariot hurrying near:
And yonder all before us lie
Desarts of vast Eternity.
Thy Beauty shall no more be found,
Nor, in thy marble Vault, shall sound
My echoing Song. Then Worms shall try
That long preserv'd Virginity,
And your quaint Honour turn to dust,
And into ashes all my Lust.   30
The Grave's a fine and private place,
But none, I think, do there embrace.
   Now therefore, while the youthful hue
Sits on thy skin like morning dew,
And while thy willing Soul transpires
At every pore with instant Fires,
Now let us sport us while we may;
And now, like am'rous birds of prey,
Rather at once our Time devour,
Than languish in his slow-chapt pow'r.   40
Let us roll all our Strength, and all
Our sweetness, up into one Ball,
And tear our Pleasures with rough strife
Thorough the Iron gates of Life.
Thus, though we cannot make our Sun
Stand still, yet we will make him run.

E. E. Cummings   *(ponder,darling,these busted statues*

(ponder,darling,these busted statues
of yon motheaten forum be aware
notice what hath remained
—the stone cringes
clinging to the stone, how obsolete

lips utter their extant smile . . . .
remark

a few deleted of texture
or meaning monuments and dolls

resist Them Greediest Paws of careful   10
time all of which is extremely
unimportant) whereas Life

matters if or

when the your- and my-
idle vertical worthless
self unite in a peculiarly
momentary

partnership (to instigate
constructive
         Horizontal   20
business . . . . even so, let us make haste
—consider well this ruined aqueduct

lady,
which used to lead something into somewhere)

Oliver Goldsmith   *Stanzas on Woman*

When lovely Woman stoops to folly,
  And finds too late that men betray,
What charm can soothe her melancholy,
  What art can wash her guilt away?

The only art her guilt to cover,
    To hide her shame from every eye,
To give repentance to her lover,
    And wring his bosom—is, to die.

JOHN KEATS   *Bright star! would I were steadfast as thou art*

Bright star! would I were steadfast as thou art—
    Not in lone splendour hung aloft the night
And watching, with eternal lids apart,
    Like Nature's patient, sleepless Eremite,
The moving waters at their priestlike task
    Of pure ablution round earth's human shores,
Or gazing on the new soft fallen mask
    Of snow upon the mountains and the moors—
No—yet still steadfast, still unchangeable,
    Pillow'd upon my fair love's ripening breast,   10
To feel for ever its soft fall and swell,
    Awake for ever in a sweet unrest,
Still, still to hear her tender-taken breath,
And so live ever—or else swoon to death.

ROBERT BROWNING   *Two in the Campagna*

I wonder do you feel to-day,
    As I have felt since, hand in hand,
We sat down on the grass, to stray
    In spirit better through the land,
This morn of Rome and May?

For me, I touched a thought, I know,
    Has tantalized me many times,
(Like turns of thread the spiders throw
    Mocking across our path) for rhymes
To catch at and let go.   10

Help me to hold it! First it left
    The yellowing fennel, run to seed
There, branching from the brickwork's cleft,
    Some old tomb's ruin; yonder weed
Took up the floating weft,

Where one small orange cup amassed
   Five beetles—blind and green they grope
Among the honey-meal; and last,
   Everywhere on the grassy slope
I traced it. Hold it fast!   20

The champaign with its endless fleece
   Of feathery grasses everywhere!
Silence and passion, joy and peace,
   An everlasting wash of air—
Rome's ghost since her decease.

Such life here, through such lengths of hours,
   Such miracles performed in play,
Such primal naked forms of flowers,
   Such letting Nature have her way
While Heaven looks from its towers!   30

How say you? Let us, O my dove,
   Let us be unashamed of soul,
As earth lies bare to heaven above!
   How is it under our control
To love or not to love?

I would that you were all to me,
   You that are just so much, no more,
Nor yours, nor mine, nor slave nor free!
   Where does the fault lie? What the core
Of the wound, since wound must be?   40

I would I could adopt your will,
   See with your eyes, and set my heart
Beating by yours, and drink my fill
   At your soul's springs,—your part my part
In life, for good and ill.

No. I yearn upward, touch you close,
   Then stand away. I kiss your cheek,
Catch your soul's warmth—I pluck the rose
   And love it more than tongue can speak—
Then the good minute goes.   50

Already how am I so far
  Out of that minute? Must I go
Still like the thistle-ball, no bar,
  Onward, whenever light winds blow,
Fixed by no friendly star?

Just when I seemed about to learn!
  Where is the thread now? Off again!
The old trick! Only I discern—
  Infinite passion, and the pain
Of finite hearts that yearn.   60

THOMAS HARDY *After a Journey*

Hereto I come to view a voiceless ghost;
  Whither, O whither will its whim now draw me?
Up the cliff, down, till I'm lonely, lost,
  And the unseen waters' ejaculations awe me.
Where you will next be there's no knowing,
  Facing round about me everywhere,
      With your nut-coloured hair,
And gray eyes, and rose-flush coming and going.

Yes: I have re-entered your olden haunts at last;
  Through the years, through the dead scenes I have tracked you; 10
What have you now found to say of our past—
  Scanned across the dark space wherein I have lacked you?
Summer gave us sweets, but autumn wrought division?
  Things were not lastly as firstly well
      With us twain, you tell?
But all's closed now, despite Time's derision.

I see what you are doing: you are leading me on
  To the spots we knew when we haunted here together,
The waterfall, above which the mist-bow shone
  At the then fair hour in the then fair weather,   20
And the cave just under, with a voice still so hollow
  That it seems to call out to me from forty years ago,
      When you were all aglow,
And not the thin ghost that I now frailly follow!

Ignorant of what there is flitting here to see,
   The waked birds preen and the seals flop lazily,
Soon you will have, Dear, to vanish from me,
   For the stars close their shutters and the dawn whitens hazily.
Trust me, I mind not, though Life lours,
   The bringing me here; nay, bring me here again!   30
       I am just the same as when
Our days were a joy, and our paths through flowers.

WALT WHITMAN   *Twenty-eight young men bathe by the shore*

(from *Song of Myself*)

Twenty-eight young men bathe by the shore,
Twenty-eight young men and all so friendly;
Twenty-eight years of womanly life and all so lonesome.

She owns the fine house by the rise of the bank,
She hides handsome and richly drest aft the blinds of the window.

Which of the young men does she like the best?
Ah the homeliest of them is beautiful to her.

Where are you off to, lady? for I see you,
You splash in the water there, yet stay stock still in your room.

Dancing and laughing along the beach came the twenty-ninth
    bather,   10
The rest did not see her, but she saw them and loved them.

The beards of the young men glisten'd with wet, it ran from their
    long hair,
Little streams pass'd all over their bodies.

An unseen hand also pass'd over their bodies,
It descended tremblingly from their temples and ribs.

The young men float on their backs, their white bellies bulge to the
    sun, they do not ask who seizes fast to them,
They do not know who puffs and declines with pendant and bending
    arch,
They do not think whom they souse with spray.

WILLIAM BUTLER YEATS *A Deep-Sworn Vow* [1]

> Others because you did not keep
> That deep-sworn vow have been friends of mine;
> Yet always when I look death in the face,
> When I clamber to the heights of sleep,
> Or when I grow excited with wine,
> Suddenly I meet your face.

W. H. AUDEN *Lullaby*

> Lay your sleeping head, my love,
> Human on my faithless arm;
> Time and fevers burn away
> Individual beauty from
> Thoughtful children, and the grave
> Proves the child ephemeral:
> But in my arms till break of day
> Let the living creature lie,
> Mortal, guilty, but to me
> The entirely beautiful.   10
>
> Soul and body have no bounds:
> To lovers as they lie upon
> Her tolerant enchanted slope
> In their ordinary swoon,
> Grave the vision Venus sends
> Of supernatural sympathy,
> Universal love and hope;
> While an abstract insight wakes
> Among the glaciers and the rocks
> The hermit's carnal ecstasy.   20
>
> Certainty, fidelity
> On the stroke of midnight pass
> Like vibrations of a bell
> And fashionable madmen raise
> Their pedantic boring cry:
> Every farthing of the cost,
> All the dreaded cards foretell,

[1] See comment in Chapter Two, Section III (p. 90).

Shall be paid, but from this night
Not a whisper, not a thought,
Not a kiss nor look be lost.   30

Beauty, midnight, vision dies:
Let the winds of dawn that blow
Softly round your dreaming head
Such a day of welcome show
Eye and knocking heart may bless,
Find our mortal world enough;
Noons of dryness find you fed
By the involuntary powers,
Nights of insult let you pass
Watched by every human love.   40

D. H. LAWRENCE   *Hymn to Priapus*

My love lies underground
With her face upturned to mine,
And her mouth unclosed in a last long kiss
That ended her life and mine.

I dance at the Christmas party
Under the mistletoe
Along with a ripe, slack country lass
Jostling to and fro.

The big, soft country lass,
Like a loose sheaf of wheat   10
Slipped through my arms on the threshing floor
At my feet.

The warm, soft country lass,
Sweet as an armful of wheat
At threshing-time broken, was broken
For me, and ah, it was sweet!

Now I am going home
Fulfilled and alone,
I see the great Orion standing
Looking down.   20

He's the star of my first beloved
Love-making.
The witness of all that bitter-sweet
Heart-aching.

Now he sees this as well,
This last commission.
Nor do I get any look
Of admonition.

He can add the reckoning up
I suppose, between now and then,   30
Having walked himself in the thorny, difficult
Ways of men.

He has done as I have done
No doubt:
Remembered and forgotten
Turn and about.

My love lies underground
With her face upturned to mine,
And her mouth unclosed in the last long kiss
That ended her life and mine.   40

She fares in the stark immortal
Fields of death;
I in these goodly, frozen
Fields beneath.

Something in me remembers
And will not forget.
The stream of my life in the darkness
Deathward set!

And something in me has forgotten,
Has ceased to care.   50
Desire comes up, and contentment
Is debonair.

I, who am worn and careful,
How much do I care?
How is it I grin then, and chuckle
Over despair?

Grief, grief, I suppose and sufficient
Grief makes us free
To be faithless and faithful together
As we have to be.   60

2. War

Thomas Love Peacock   *The War-Song of Dinas Vawr*

The mountain sheep are sweeter,
But the valley sheep are fatter;
We therefore deemed it meeter
To carry off the latter.
We made an expedition;
We met a host, and quelled it;
We forced a strong position,
And killed the men who held it.

On Dyfed's richest valley,
Where herds of kine were brousing,   10
We made a mighty sally,
To furnish our carousing.
Fierce warriors rushed to meet us;
We met them, and o'erthrew them:
They struggled hard to beat us;
But we conquered them, and slew them.

As we drove our prize at leisure,
The king marched forth to catch us:
His rage surpassed all measure,
But his people could not match us.   20
He fled to his hall-pillars;
And, ere our force we led off,
Some sacked his house and cellars,
While others cut his head off.

We there, in strife bewild'ring,
Spilt blood enough to swim in:
We orphaned many children,
And widowed many women.
The eagles and the ravens
We glutted with our foemen;   30
The heroes and the cravens,
The spearmen and the bowmen.

We brought away from battle,
And much their land bemoaned them,
Two thousand head of cattle,
And the head of him who owned them:
Ednyfed, king of Dyfed,
His head was borne before us;
His wine and beasts supplied our feasts,
And his overthrow, our chorus.   40

RICHARD LOVELACE   *To Lucasta, Going to the Wars*

Tell me not (Sweet) I am unkind,
    That from the Nunnery
Of thy chaste breast, and quiet mind,
    To War and Arms I fly.

True, a new Mistress now I chase,
    The first Foe in the Field;
And with a stronger Faith imbrace
    A Sword, a Horse, a Shield.

Yet this Inconstancy is such,
    As thou too shalt adore;   10
I could not love thee (Dear) so much,
    Lov'd I not Honour more.

ANNE FINCH, COUNTESS OF WINCHILSEA   *Trail all your pikes*

Trail all your pikes, dispirit every drum,
March in a slow procession from afar,
Ye silent, ye dejected, men of war.
Be still the hautboys, and the flute be dumb!
Display no more, in vain, the lofty banner;
For see where on the bier before ye lies
The pale, the fall'n, the untimely sacrifice
To your mistaken shrine, to your false idol **Honour.**

WILLIAM COLLINS   *Ode Written in the Beginning of
the Year 1746*

How sleep the Brave, who sink to Rest,
By all their Country's Wishes blest!

When Spring, with dewy Fingers cold,
Returns to deck their hallow'd Mold,
She there shall dress a sweeter Sod,
Than Fancy's Feet have ever trod.

By Fairy Hands their Knell is rung,
By Forms unseen their Dirge is sung;
There Honour comes, a Pilgrim grey,
To bless the Turf that wraps their Clay,   10
And Freedom shall awhile repair,
To dwell a weeping Hermit there!

RALPH WALDO EMERSON   *Concord Hymn*

By the rude bridge that arched the flood,
    Their flag to April's breeze unfurled,
Here once the embattled farmers stood
    And fired the shot heard round the world.

The foe long since in silence slept;
    Alike the conqueror silent sleeps;
And Time the ruined bridge has swept
    Down the dark stream which seaward creeps.

On this green bank, by this soft stream,
    We set today a votive stone;   10
That memory may their deed redeem,
    When, like our sires, our sons are gone.

Spirit, that made those heroes dare
    To die, and leave their children free,
Bid Time and Nature gently spare
    The shaft we raise to them and thee.

WALT WHITMAN   *A sight in camp in the daybreak gray and dim*

A sight in camp in the daybreak gray and dim,
As from my tent I emerge so early sleepless,
As slow I walk in the cool fresh air the path near by the hospital tent,
Three forms I see on stretchers lying, brought out there untended
    lying,

Over each the blanket spread, ample brownish woolen blanket,
Grey and heavy blanket, folding, covering all.

Curious I halt and silent stand,
Then with light fingers I from the face of the nearest the first just
    lift the blanket;
Who are you elderly man so gaunt and grim, with well-gray'd hair, and
    flesh all sunken about thy eyes?
Who are you my dear comrade?   10

Then to the second I step—and who are you my child and darling?
Who are you sweet boy with cheeks yet blooming?

Then to the third—a face nor child nor old, very calm, as of beautiful
    yellow-white ivory;
Young man I think I know you—I think this face is the face of the
    Christ himself,
Dead and divine and brother of all, and here again he lies.

EDWARD THOMAS   *As the team's head-brass*

As the team's head-brass flashed out on the turn
The lovers disappeared into the wood.
I sat among the boughs of the fallen elm
That strewed the angle of the fallow, and
Watched the plough narrowing a yellow square
Of charlock. Every time the horses turned
Instead of treading me down, the ploughman leaned
Upon the handles to say or ask a word,
About the weather, next about the war.
Scraping the share he faced towards the wood,   10
And screwed along the furrow till the brass flashed
Once more.
          The blizzard felled the elm whose crest
I sat in, by a woodpecker's round hole,
The ploughman said. "When will they take it away?"
"When the war's over." So the talk began—
One minute and an interval of ten,
A minute more and the same interval.
"Have you been out?" "No." "And don't want to, perhaps?"
"If I could only come back again, I should.   20
I could spare an arm. I shouldn't want to lose

A leg. If I should lose my head, why, so,
I should want nothing more. . . . Have many gone
From here?" "Yes." "Many lost?" "Yes, a good few.
Only two teams work on the farm this year.
One of my mates is dead. The second day
In France they killed him. It was back in March,
The very night of the blizzard, too. Now if
He had stayed here we should have moved the tree."
"And I should not have sat here. Everything   30
Would have been different. For it would have been
Another world." "Ay, and a better, though
If we could see all all might seem good." Then
The lovers came out of the wood again:
The horses started and for the last time
I watched the clods crumble and topple over
After the ploughshare and the stumbling team.

WILFRED OWEN   *Insensibility*

Happy are men who yet before they are killed
Can let their veins run cold.
Whom no compassion fleers
Or makes their feet
Sore on the alleys cobbled with their brothers.
The front line withers,
But they are troops who fade, not flowers
For poets' tearful fooling:
Men, gaps for filling:
Losses who might have fought   10
Longer; but no one bothers.

And some cease feeling
Even themselves or for themselves.
Dullness best solves
The tease and doubt of shelling,
And Chance's strange arithmetic
Comes simpler than the reckoning of their shilling.
They keep no check on armies' decimation.

Happy are these who lose imagination:
They have enough to carry with ammunition.   20

Their spirit drags no pack,
Their old wounds save with cold can not more ache.
Having seen all things red,
Their eyes are rid
Of the hurt of the colour of blood for ever.
And terror's first constriction over,
Their hearts remain small-drawn.
Their senses in some scorching cautery of battle
Now long since ironed,
Can laugh among the dying, unconcerned.   30

Happy the soldier home, with not a notion
How somewhere, every dawn, some men attack,
And many sighs are drained.
Happy the lad whose mind was never trained:
His days are worth forgetting more than not.
He sings along the march
Which we march taciturn, because of dusk,
The long, forlorn, relentless trend
From larger day to huger night.

We wise, who with a thought besmirch   40
Blood over all our soul,
How should we seek our task
But through his blunt and lashless eyes?
Alive, he is not vital overmuch;
Dying, not mortal overmuch;
Nor sad, nor proud,
Nor curious at all.
He cannot tell
Old men's placidity from his.

But cursed are dullards whom no cannon stuns,   50
That they should be as stones;
Wretched are they, and mean
With paucity that never was simplicity.
By choice they made themselves immune
To pity and whatever mourns in man
Before the last sea and the hapless stars;
Whatever mourns when many leave these shores;
Whatever shares
The eternal reciprocity of tears.

WILFRED OWEN   *Greater Love*

Red lips are not so red
   As the stained stones kissed by the English dead.
Kindness of wooed and wooer
Seems shame to their love pure.
O Love, your eyes lose lure
   When I behold eyes blinded in my stead!

Your slender attitude
   Trembles not exquisite like limbs knife-skewed,
Rolling and rolling there
Where God seems not to care;   10
Till the fierce love they bear
   Cramps them in death's extreme decrepitude.

Your voice sings not so soft,—
   Though even as wind murmuring through raftered loft,—
Your dear voice is not dear,
Gentle, and evening clear,
As theirs whom none now hear,
   Now earth has stopped their piteous mouths that coughed.

Heart, you were never hot
   Nor large, nor full like hearts made great with shot;   20
And though your hand be pale,
Paler are all which trail
Your cross through flame and hail:
   Weep, you may weep, for you may touch them not.

HERBERT READ   *To a Conscript of 1940*

Qui n'a pas une fois désespéré de l'honneur, ne sera jamais un héros.[1]
                     —GEORGES BERNANOS

A soldier passed me in the freshly fallen snow,
   His footsteps muffled, his face unearthly grey;
And my heart gave a sudden leap
   As I gazed on a ghost of five-and-twenty years ago.

I shouted Halt! and my voice had the old accustomed ring
   And he obeyed it as it was obeyed

---

[1] He who has not at least once despaired of his honor will never be a hero.

In the shrouded days when I too was one
   Of an army of young men marching

Into the unknown. He turned towards me and I said:
   "I am one of those who went before you   10
Five-and-twenty years ago: one of the many who never returned,
   Of the many who returned and yet were dead.

We went where you are going, into the rain and the mud;
   We fought as you will fight
With death and darkness and despair;
   We gave what you will give—our brains and our blood.

We think we gave in vain. The world was not renewed.
   There was hope in the homestead and anger in the streets
But the old world was restored and we returned
   To the dreary field and workshop, and the immemorial feud   20

Of rich and poor. Our victory was our defeat.
   Power was retained where power had been misused
And youth was left to sweep away
   The ashes that the fires had strewn beneath our feet.

But one thing we learned: there is no glory in the deed
   Until the soldier wears a badge of tarnished braid;
There are heroes who have heard the rally and have seen
   The glitter of a garland round their head.

Theirs is the hollow victory. They are deceived.
   But you, my brother and my ghost, if you can go   30
Knowing that there is no reward, no certain use
   In all your sacrifice, then honour is reprieved.

To fight without hope is to fight with grace,
   The self reconstructed, the false heart repaired."
Then I turned with a smile, and he answered my salute
   As he stood against the fretted hedge, which was like white lace.

RICHARD EBERHART   *The Fury of Aerial Bombardment*

You would think the fury of aerial bombardment
Would rouse God to relent; the infinite spaces
Are still silent. He looks on shock-pried faces.
History, even, does not know what is meant.

You would feel that after so many centuries
God would give man to repent; yet he can kill
As Cain could, but with multitudinous will,
No farther advanced than in his ancient furies.

Was man made stupid to see his own stupidity?
Is God by definition indifferent, beyond us all?   10
Is the eternal truth man's fighting soul
'Wherein the Beast ravens in its own avidity?

Of Van Wettering I speak, and Averill,
Names on a list, whose faces I do not recall
But they are gone to early death, who late in school
Distinguished the belt feed lever from the belt holding pawl.

WINFIELD TOWNLEY SCOTT   *The U.S. Sailor with the
Japanese Skull*

Bald-bare, bone-bare, and ivory yellow: skull
Carried by a thus two-headed U.S. sailor
Who got it from a Japanese soldier killed
At Guadalcanal in the ever-present war: our

Bluejacket, I mean, aged 20, in August strolled
Among the little bodies on the sand and hunted
Souvenirs: teeth, tags, diaries, boots; but bolder still
Hacked off this head and under a Ginkgo tree skinned it:

Peeled with a lifting knife the jaw and cheeks, bared
The nose, ripped off the black-haired scalp and gutted   10
The dead eyes to these thoughtful hollows: a scarred
But bloodless job, unless it be said brains bleed.

Then, his ship underway, dragged this aft in a net
Many days and nights—the cold bone tumbling
Beneath the foaming wake, weed-worn and salt-cut
Rolling safe among fish and washed with Pacific;

Till on a warm and level-keeled day hauled in
Held to the sun and the sailor, back to a gun-rest,
Scrubbed the cured skull with lye, perfecting this:
Not foreign as he saw it first: death's familiar cast.   20

Bodiless, fleshless, nameless, it and the sun
Offend each other in strange fascination
As though one of the two were mocked; but nothing is in
This head, or it fills with what another imagines

As: here were love and hate and the will to deal
Death or to kneel before it, death emperor,
Recorded orders without reasons, bomb-blast, still
A child's morning, remembered moonlight on Fujiyama:

All scoured out now by the keeper of this skull
Made elemental, historic, parentless by our   30
Sailor boy who thinks of home, voyages laden, will
Not say, "Alas! I did not know him at all."

JAMES DICKEY *The Performance*

The last time I saw Donald Armstrong
He was staggering oddly off into the sun,
Going down, of the Philippine Islands.
I let my shovel fall, and put that hand
Above my eyes, and moved some way to one side
That his body might pass through the sun,

And I saw how well he was not
Standing there on his hands,
On his spindle-shanked forearms balanced,
Unbalanced, with his big feet looming and waving   10
In the great, untrustworthy air
He flew in each night, when it darkened.

Dust fanned in scraped puffs from the earth
Between his arms, and blood turned his face inside out,
To demonstrate its suppleness
Of veins, as he perfected his role.
Next day, he toppled his head off
On an island beach to the south,

And the enemy's two-handed sword
Did not fall from anyone's hands
At that miraculous sight,   20
As the head rolled over upon
Its wide-eyed face, and fell
Into the inadequate grave

He had dug for himself, under pressure.
Yet I put my flat hand to my eyebrows
Months later, to see him again
In the sun, when I learned how he died,
And imagined him, there,
Come, judged, before his small captors,   30

Doing all his lean tricks to amaze them—
The back somersault, the kip-up—
And at last, the stand on his hands,
Perfect, with his feet together,
His head down, evenly breathing,
As the sun poured up from the sea

And the headsman broke down
In a blaze of tears, in that light
Of the thin, long human frame
Upside down in its own strange joy,   40
And, if some other one had not told him,
Would have cut off the feet

Instead of the head,
And if Armstrong had not presently risen
In kingly, round-shouldered attendance,
And then knelt down in himself
Beside his hacked, glittering grave, having done
All things in this life that he could.

III

THE POEM'S REFLECTION OF ITS TIME AND PLACE

As we have suggested at the start of the present chapter (page 405), a poem's frame of reference is of course not only a matter of its approach to such well-defined themes as love and war. It also influences any description, narrative, or emotional perception—each of which will in its own way encompass an evaluation of the experience of being alive in a certain time and place. Even the simplest description of a scene will suggest, through its selection of detail and its general tone, an attitude toward what the scene itself represents. A modern American poet, Delmore Schwartz, shows a city mourning in its heavy, impervious, recurrent sameness:

> The stony street
> Displayed the stillness in which buildings stand,
> The street-lamp's vigil and the horse's patience.

T. S. Eliot presents a comparably depressing vignette of evening in a deteriorated city neighborhood early in this century.

T. S. ELIOT *Prelude I*

> The winter evening settles down
> With smell of steaks in passageways.
> Six o'clock.
> The burnt-out ends of smoky days.
> And now a gusty shower wraps
> The grimy scraps
> Of withered leaves about your feet
> And newspapers from vacant lots;
> The showers beat
> On broken blinds and chimney-pots,   10
> And at the corner of the street
> A lonely cab-horse steams and stamps.
> And then the lighting of the lamps.

Another city close-up, this time very contemporary, is seen in Gwendolyn Brooks's poem *The Blackstone Rangers.* (page 474) This brief photoflash gives us people rather than buildings or horses (that common sight on city streets until relatively recent times) to contemplate:

> There they are.
> Thirty at the corner.
> Black, raw, ready.
> Sores in the city
> that do not want to heal.

Such apparently uncomplicated descriptions exist within their own specific frames of reference. In the passages by Schwartz and Eliot we feel the whole modern sense of the oppressiveness of the city. In each one, the presence of the horse is a reminder of what happens to natural life amidst the dreary tedium of an unnatural environment, and in Eliot's poem details of shabbiness and unpleasantness are added: the stale smell of food in apartment buildings, newspapers blowing from vacant lots, grime, and broken things. In Miss Brooks's poem the intensified sense of imminent violence and of conditions that actively resist improvement marks the renewed concern of contemporary Americans with a volatile and intractable social problem.

In strong contrast, the opening stanza of Charles Cotton's *Evening Quatrains* (pages 466–467) suggests a happier set of attitudes in the speaker—one appropriate to the rural setting and to the vitality of classical imagery and myth in the seventeenth century:

> The Day's grown old, the fainting Sun
> Has but a little way to run,
> And yet his Steeds, with all his skill,
> Scarce lug the Chariot down the Hill.

The tone of weariness in these lines reflects the natural feeling at the end of a long summer's day rather than anything tiresome in the appearance of the sun itself. In fact, the poem treats the sun "sympathetically," personifying it as Apollo with his steeds reaching journey's end as the day wears on. The frame of reference includes classical mythology, and Apollo is one of the more attractive of the Grecian gods. The image of the slow-moving horses of the sun and their master's anxiety to get home is amusing without being forced. Notice how the succession of stressed syllables in "Dáy's grówn óld" and "Scárce lúg" slows up the movement of the first and fourth lines, while the second and third move much faster—a device that sharpens the contrast between the sun-god's eagerness to speed his horses and their tired reluctance to go at all. This clever pacing makes the description amusing and personal, although the imagery may at first seem only flatly conventional.

That Cotton intended the stanza to have this amusing and personal effect is made clear by a further series of whimsical contrasts:

The Shadows now so long do grow
That Brambles like tall Cedars show,
Mole-hills seem Mountains, and the Ant
Appears a monstrous Elephant.

A very little little Flock
Shades thrice the ground that it would stock;
Whilst the small Stripling following them,
Appears a mighty Polypheme.

The scene is a pastoral one, in which the landscape and all that moves on it change by magic, grotesquely but charmingly distorted. In the last stanza of this poem, the humorous realism and the genial mythological framework come together easily and naturally:

And now on Benches all are sat
In the cool Air to sit and chat,
Till Phoebus, dipping in the West,
Shall lead the World the way to Rest.

Thus, Cotton's world was not a simpler one than that of Eliot, Schwartz, and Miss Brooks, but its way of thinking was different. It looked at things differently. Cotton saw things in the light of a civilization still predominantly rural; his training colored his view of life with a strongly Classical pigmentation, and he was not concerned to evaluate critically either the civilization or the training. Many of our latter-day poets, on the other hand, are oppressed by a burdensome sense of a life deprived of important values—a life that might have been otherwise. Poetry in any era reveals what Shakespeare called the "form and pressure" of "the very age and body of the time." Therefore, it helps us evaluate our own world and its relation to the past.

The poetry of the last hundred years has performed this function more deliberately and certainly more self-consciously than did most poetry before it. Since the middle of the nineteenth century the blows against what seemed the established order have been so many and so severe that there has been an unending search to find new values or to rediscover the old ones. The impact of Darwin, Marx, Freud, and the scientific relativists has caused a confusion more disturbing even than the chaos introduced into the medieval cosmos by the Copernican philosophy. In the wake of this confusion has come the attempt by thinkers and artists, including poets, to compare our civilization with those of past centuries in order to define it clearly and to enable us to envision where we have gone astray, what our strengths and weaknesses are, and the directions in which our best hopes for the future lie.

One of the poets who have most effectively attempted this type of evaluation of our society's unique time and place is T. S. Eliot. The intense sensitivity of his work has bitten deep enough to influence the thinking of at least two generations. His specific religious and philosophical ideas are not on the surface shared by most poets and readers, but his fundamentally critical attitude toward mechanized and impersonal civilization is very widely held indeed. Most important, as a reading of his poem *Gerontion* (pages 476–478) will show, Eliot gives voice to the fear of emptiness and pointlessness that haunts the modern mind.

Gerontion is at first a puzzling and difficult poem because, like abstract painting, it is hard to see what it is about. The form is clear, and there seems to be a plot or action. Characters appear and disappear, a situation is presented, or perhaps merely suggested, and reflections and conclusions are drawn. But everything is so oblique, and the literary and historical references with which the poem abounds are so subtle or erudite, that it is not surprising that *Gerontion* should have been appreciated as great poetry before its complete meaning had been rightly or widely understood. It was felt at once that the loose blank verse in which the poem is written was handled with a mastery of style that recalled the distinction of the late Elizabethan dramatists and, indeed, of Shakespeare himself. And, further, it was clear in a general way that the poem (written in 1920) was about history, that it concerned itself with the breakdown of civilization, culture, and religion in Europe, and that it was an expression of emotional attitudes about the contemporary chaos—and perhaps also that it was an intensely religious poem. But beyond this nothing was certain. The abstract and apparently disconnected method of development, the unfamiliar allusions, and the return to something like the complex traditionalism of Milton's *Lycidas*—all this made the detailed significance of the poem hard to perceive. Not until the poem has been analyzed in detail is it possible to grasp its full significance. Let us suggest the lines this analysis should follow.

To begin with the title, "Gerontion" is a word coined from the Greek and means "shrunken old man." The epigraph is from the Duke's speech in Shakespeare's *Measure for Measure* and asserts that a life empty of heroic ideals and acts is no better than a sleep full of sentimental dreams. Its relevance to the poem becomes quickly apparent.

The poem itself is impersonal and dramatic. The action takes place in an old man's consciousness—an old man who is himself a symbol of the spiritual emptiness of an age of collapsing religious values and cultural confusion. The opening lines give a vivid impressionistic picture of decay and weariness in an age of futile regret for the heroism and certainty of a period of action far in the past. Here, as in *The Waste Land*, rain, the sea, and water are symbols of spiritual vitality, while dryness, sand, rock, and stone symbolize deadness and insensitivity.

As the nightmarelike picture develops we get a view of modern Europe as a bankrupt, decadent, refuse-laden waste, where no heroic action such as once glorified the "hot gates" of Thermopylae is possible. The pictures and allusions suggest the squalid history of the decline in Europe since the Middle Ages of the chivalric, noble, and Christian ideals under the impact of the rise of commerce and materialism in Antwerp, Brussels, and London. This is a point of view shared with Catholic historians and philosophers such as Chesterton, Belloc, and Maritain. (But compare Wordsworth's "getting and spending we lay waste our powers" and Ezra Pound's *Canto XLV*: "With usura hath no man a house of good stone.")

The line "And the jew squats on the window sill" has been found offensive by some, but actually the whole passage in which it occurs is a tour de force of irony and ambiguity. Eliot is at once recording the traditional Renaissance view of the clever and avaricious money-lender as portrayed in the plays of Marlowe and Shakespeare (the many lines of pure Elizabethan blank verse worked into the poem indicate this), and at the same time exposing the hypocrisy of the commercial society that did not scruple to make use of what it condemned and persecuted.

Suddenly (line 15) a suggestion is developed as to the cause of the breakdown. It is the absence or corruption of the religious spirit in the modern world, and particularly the decay of faith in Christianity, that has robbed our culture of significance and meaning. This is suggested indirectly in the phantasmagoric pictures and bitter prophetic words that follow in the lines beginning "Signs are taken for wonders." "We would see a sign!" is the scornful and dubious cry of the Pharisees demanding of Christ that he perform a miracle to prove his divinity.

> The word within a word, unable to speak a word,
> Swaddled with darkness

is an allusion to a Christmas sermon preached by Bishop Lancelot Andrewes at the Court of King James I. The preacher is referring to the divine mystery of the infant Christ in the manger—himself the Word, that is, God, and yet at the same time a human infant in swaddling clothes, unable to speak a word. The effect of this modified quotation is to suggest in the most concentrated way the modern rejection of belief, our Pharisaical demand to be shown proof before we believe and the inability of Jesus to speak to us today. How different in an earlier, fresher age, "the juvescence of the year"! Then Christ came with the power and beauty of a tiger, with the godlike energy and glory that Blake's tiger symbolizes. There is here a conscious, if oblique, reference to Blake's famous lyric,

> Tyger, Tyger, burning bright
> In the forests of the night.

Our spring is simply the spawning rebirth of vegetable and animal matter, not a renewal of spiritual strength or a resurrection of the crucified Christ. Hence May is "depraved," its sign, the flowering judas, recalling not Christ but Christ's betrayer. The host is eaten, divided, and drunk "among whispers" in a sinister and blasphemous celebration of the Mass. Who are the celebrants of the unholy service? They are figures briefly but vividly etched as the empty, slightly decadent, and neurotic denizens of a chaotic cosmopolitan world, shadows in the mind of the symbolic old man whose reverie is the substance of the poem.

Now the nightmarelike reverie, filled with sudden glimpses and half-remembered figures, is replaced by a passage of controlled meditation. The protagonist of the poem, this old man in a dry month, who is filled with the knowledge of evil, if not of good, considers the possibility of redemption: "After such knowledge, what forgiveness?" Can we not from the knowledge of the past and the intelligent study of history learn how to recover faith and wholeness and the human perfection that comes from spiritual health? But alas, vanity, distraction, and confusion subtly distort the lessons of history. Indeed, good and evil, virtue and vice, honesty and hypocrisy are so inextricably mixed that we have lost the means and the power (and perhaps the will) to win forgiveness and return to the life-giving springs of faith.

The tiger springs in the new year. Us he devours.

This completes the cycle of the Christian year, the Great Year of two thousand years of Christianity. Originally ("in the juvescence of the year") Christ came with the power and the beauty of the tiger. But now after the "impudent crimes" and "unnatural vices" he comes again in the new year as a devouring, destroying, punitive force.

Already the destruction has been partially accomplished, and before we can reach any conclusion to our effort to examine the meaning of history, we "stiffen in a rented house"—that is, we grow insensitive, old, unsubtle, and unresponsive, stagnating in a culture we live in but cannot make our own. In this phrase there is a suggestion, too, of the brevity of life. The end of the materialist is to stiffen in death in the coffin he occupies but does not own.

After protesting his sincerity in making these bitter and despairing judgments, the protagonist continues to develop his awareness of the consequences of our condition. Human contact, the life-giving sense of oneness that was once possible in passionate love, has been transformed from beauty to terror, and at last has been adulterated by nervous, destructive probing, until finally the senses themselves have been weakened, distorted, and intellectualized almost out of existence, so that not even these can be used to draw human beings together.

In this part of the poem there is a tone of bitter and disillusioned self-contempt that echoes (not literally but in cadence and rhythm) certain passages from some of the late Elizabethan dramatists, Middleton, Chapman, and the Shakespeare of *Hamlet,* and adds a new dimension of irony and ambiguity. This literary allusiveness suggests a comparison between the complexity and corrupting weariness of the modern intellect and the bitterness and horror with which the late Elizabethan and Jacobean dramatists expressed *their* sense of the spiritual corruption of the later Renaissance.

In the stanza that follows we have a concentrated and very vivid analysis of modern decadence. Indeed, it is almost a definition of our decadence:

> Excite the membrane, when the sense has cooled,
> With pungent sauces, multiply variety
> In a wilderness of mirrors.

Then comes an ominous note. Do we imagine that such a civilization and such a culture will live forever? Already the spider and the weevil are preparing themselves. The time will come when all the frail and empty characters such as those glimpsed for a moment in the early part of the poem will be whirled into existlessness. Other names are mentioned, De Bailhache, Fresca, Mrs. Cammel, but they take their place in the slightly sinister cosmopolitan society inhabited by Fräulein Von Kulp, Madame de Tornquist, Mr. Silvero and the rest.

And now by a process of free association that anticipates the technique of the psychological novel and the film, the poem is filled with images of the open sea, the stinging salt spray, and the untrammeled wind. These are symbols of spiritual vitality in sharply ironic contrast to the poem's overall tone of torpor and regret—a tone that returns in the old man's final dispirited look at himself. He concludes his reverie with a self-mocking, apologetic dismissal of his own thoughts that echoes similar earlier language about himself. At the end of the first stanza, he had called himself "a dull head among windy spaces"; at the end of the fourth stanza, "an old man in a draughty house/Under a windy knob." Now he discounts all the anguished self-searching he has taken us through as

> Tenants of the house,
> Thoughts of a dry brain in a dry season.

The poem as a whole is a supreme act of imagination sizing up the state of Western civilization: its sense of a disintegrating structure of values—religious, moral, and aesthetic—just after World War I. It reflects the persistent desire for a totally meaningful life, passionately realized, despite the paralyzing feeling that the civilization itself has grown sterile and impotent. The poem is about a humiliating and humility-breeding situation, from the point of view of a mind that cherishes the spiritual traditions of the past but ruthlessly faces up to what has become of them. This mind, embattled, knowledgeable, candid, at once idealistic and disillusioned, embodies one kind of sophisticated modern intelligence and speaks largely to the meaning of a good deal of twentieth-century history.

Poems: The Poem's Reflection of Its Time and Place

The poems that follow are intended, for the most part, to provide varied instances of the way that the time and place out of which a poet writes affect the whole quality of his writing. There is, for instance, a long tradition of poems having to do with evening—its coming on, its atmosphere, the meditation it evokes. The two pastoral poems, by the seventeenth-century poet Charles Cotton and the eighteenth-century poet William Collins, are both rural nocturnes. Cotton's poem, while laden with realistic detail, is touched with an occasional mythological allusion that, like its rhyming couplets, summons up an idyllic, Classically colored view of country life. The speaker here is at once charmed, knowledgeable, and slightly condescending. Collins's poem indulges his considerable gift for allegorical and idealized suggestion of an atmosphere, but is nevertheless concretely accurate. It reflects the tendency of the period toward abstract rather than intimate writing. When we move from these poems to T. S. Eliot's and Delmore Schwartz's impressions of night and dawn in a great modern city, the differences are striking. Eliot's poem gives us a nightmare vision of reality in which the psyche has been stripped of the daylight reassurances of ordinary life with its clear, dependable patterns. A series of gross, distorted images, close to the realm of madness, has been substituted. Like Schwartz's sense of a world alien to human needs and feelings, Eliot's projection of a sensibility deprived of all defenses against life's horrors is an expression of modern and urban neurosis.

Two other modern poems, James Dickey's tale of modern rural romance in a junkyard and Gwendolyn Brooks's close-ups of young Blacks in a Chicago gang, may be compared as reflecting different contexts of contemporary American life. The two poets' styles, and the social circumstances about which they write, are so unlike that one might well overlook certain similarities. Both poems are narratives, in detail, about youthful intensity and passion, and both suggest a very modern, if Romantic, aspiration to transcend the tawdry limitations of life through violent action. We have already discussed the way in which Eliot's *Gerontion*—however more sophisticated and intellectually complex than either of these works—presents the same frustrated need for transcendence through a meaningful violence of spirit. Finally, the opening poem of Yeats's sequence *Nineteen Hundred and Nineteen*, written out of the experience of World War I and of Ireland's struggle for independence, considers the disillusionment that follows in the wake of violence. It is one of the great summings-up in modern poetry of the tragic directions and losses of our age.

CHARLES COTTON *Evening Quatrains*

The day's grown old, the fainting Sun
Has but a little way to run,
And yet his Steeds, with all his skill,
Scarce lug the Chariot down the Hill.

With Labour spent, and Thirst opprest,
Whilst they strain hard to gain the West,
From Fetlocks hot drops melted light,
Which turn to Meteors in the Night.

The Shadows now so long do grow
That Brambles like tall Cedars show,   10
Mole-hills seem Mountains, and the Ant
Appears a monstrous Elephant.

A very little little Flock
Shades thrice the ground that it would stock;
Whilst the small Stripling following them
Appears a mighty Polypheme.

These being brought into the Fold
And by the thrifty Master told,
He thinks his Wages are well paid,
Since none are either lost or stray'd.   20

Now lowing Herds are each-where heard,
Chains rattle in the Villain's Yard,
The Cart's on Tail set down to rest,
Bearing on high the Cuckold's crest.

The hedge is stripped, the Clothes brought in;
Nought's left without should be within;
The Bees are hiv'd, and hum their Charm
Whilst every House does seem a Swarm.

The Cock now to the Roost is prest,
For he must call up all the rest;   30
The Sow's fast pegg'd within the Sty
To still her squeaking Progeny.

Each one has had his Supping Mess,
The Cheese is put into the Press,
The Pans and Bowls clean scalded all,
Rear'd up against the Milk-house Wall.

And now on Benches all are sat
In the cool Air to sit and chat,
Till Phoebus, dipping in the West,
Shall lead the World the way to Rest.   40

WILLIAM COLLINS *Ode to Evening*

If ought of Oaten Stop, or Pastoral Song,
May hope, chaste Eve, to soothe thy modest Ear,
    Like thy own solemn Springs,
    Thy Springs, and dying Gales,

O Nymph reserv'd, while now the bright-hair'd Sun
Sits in yon western Tent, whose cloudy Skirts,
    With Brede ethereal wove,
    O'erhang his wavy Bed:

Now Air is hush'd, save where the weak-ey'd Bat,
With short shrill Shriek flits by on leathern Wing,   10
    Or where the Beetle winds
    His small but sullen Horn,

As oft he rises 'midst the twilight Path,
Against the Pilgrim born in heedless Hum:
    Now teach me, Maid compos'd,
    To breathe some soften'd Strain,

Whose Numbers stealing thro' thy dark'ning Vale,
May not unseemly with its Stillness suit,
    As musing slow, I hail
    Thy genial lov'd Return!   20

For when thy folding Star arising shews
His paly Circlet, at his warning Lamp
    The fragrant Hours, and Elves
    Who slept in Flow'rs the Day,

And many a Nymph who wreathes her Brows with Sedge,
And sheds the fresh'ning Dew, and lovelier still,
   The Pensive Pleasures sweet
   Prepare thy shadowy Car.

Then lead, calm Vot'ress, where some sheety Lake,
Cheers the lone Heath, or some time-hallow'd Pile,   30
   Or up-land Fallows grey
   Reflect its last cool Gleam.

But when chill blust'ring Winds, or driving Rain,
Forbid my willing Feet, be mine the Hut,
   That from the Mountain's Side,
   Views Wilds, and swelling Floods,

And Hamlets brown, and dim-discover'd Spires,
And hears their simple Bell, and marks o'er all
   Thy Dewy Fingers draw
   The gradual dusky Veil.   40

While Spring shall pour his Show'rs, as oft he wont,
And bathe thy breathing Tresses, meekest Eve!
   While Summer loves to sport,
   Beneath thy ling'ring Light;

While sallow Autumn fills thy Lap with Leaves,
Or Winter yelling thro' the troublous Air,
   Affrights thy shrinking Train,
   And rudely rends thy Robes,

So long sure-found beneath thy sylvan Shed,
Shall Fancy, Friendship, Science, rose-lip'd Health,   50
   Thy gentlest Influence own,
   And hymn thy fav'rite Name!

T. S. Eliot   *Rhapsody on a Windy Night*

Twelve o'clock.
Along the reaches of the street
Held in a lunar synthesis,
Whispering lunar incantations
Dissolve the floors of memory

And all its clear relations,
Its divisions and precisions,
Every street lamp that I pass
Beats like a fatalistic drum,
And through the spaces of the dark   10
Midnight shakes the memory
As a madman shakes a dead geranium.

   Half-past one,
The street-lamp sputtered,
The street-lamp muttered,
The street-lamp said, "Regard that woman
Who hesitates toward you in the light of the door
Which opens on her like a grin.
You see the border of her dress
Is torn and stained with sand,   20
And you see the corner of her eye
Twists like a crooked pin."

   The memory throws up high and dry
A crowd of twisted things;
A twisted branch upon the beach
Eaten smooth, and polished
As if the world gave up
The secret of its skeleton,
Stiff and white.
A broken spring in a factory yard,   30
Rust that clings to the form that the strength has left
Hard and curled and ready to snap.

   Half-past two,
The street-lamp said,
"Remark the cat which flattens itself in the gutter,
Slips out its tongue
And devours a morsel of rancid butter."
So the hand of the child, automatic,
Slipped out and pocketed a toy that was running along the quay.
I could see nothing behind that child's eye.   40
I have seen eyes in the street
Trying to peer through lighted shutters,
And a crab one afternoon in a pool,
An old crab with barnacles on his back,
Gripped the end of a stick which I held him.

Half-past three,
The lamp sputtered,
The lamp muttered in the dark.
The lamp hummed:
"Regard the moon,   50
La lune ne garde aucune rancune,[1]
She winks a feeble eye,
She smiles into corners.
She smooths the hair of the grass.
The moon has lost her memory.
A washed-out smallpox cracks her face,
Her hand twists a paper rose,
That smells of dust and eau de Cologne,
She is alone
With all the old nocturnal smells   60
That cross and cross across her brain."
The reminiscence comes
Of sunless dry geraniums
And dust in crevices,
Smells of chestnuts in the streets,
And female smells in shuttered rooms,
And cigarettes in corridors
And cocktail smells in bars.

The lamp said,
"Four o'clock,   70
Here is the number on the door.
Memory!
You have the key,
The little lamp spreads a ring on the stair.
Mount.
The bed is open; the tooth-brush hangs on the wall,
Put your shoes at the door, sleep, prepare for life."

The last twist of the knife.

DELMORE SCHWARTZ   *In the naked bed, in Plato's cave*

In the naked bed, in Plato's cave,
Reflected headlights slowly slid the wall,

---

[1] The moon holds no grudges.

Carpenters hammered under the shaded window,
Wind troubled the window curtains all night long,
A fleet of trucks strained uphill, grinding,
Their freights covered, as usual.
The ceiling lightened again, the slanting diagram
Slid slowly forth.
                Hearing the milkman's chop,
His striving up the stair, the bottle's chink,   10
I rose from bed, lit a cigarette,
And walked to the window. The stony street
Displayed the stillness in which buildings stand,
The street-lamp's vigil and the horse's patience.
The winter sky's pure capital
Turned me back to bed with exhausted eyes.

Strangeness grew in the motionless air. The loose
Film grayed. Shaking wagons, hooves' waterfalls,
Sounded far off, increasing, louder and nearer.
A car coughed, starting. Morning, softly   20
Melting the air, lifted the half-covered chair
From underseas, kindled the looking-glass,
Distinguished the dresses and the white wall.
The bird called tentatively, whistled, called,
Bubbled and whistled, so! Perplexed, still wet
With sleep, affectionate, hungry and cold. So, so,
O son of man, the ignorant night, the travail
Of early morning, the mystery of beginning
Again and again,
            while History is unforgiven.   30

JAMES DICKEY   *Cherrylog Road*

Off Highway 106
At Cherrylog Road I entered
The '34 Ford without wheels,
Smothered in kudzu,
With a seat pulled out to run
Corn whiskey down from the hills,

And then from the other side
Crept into an Essex
With a rumble seat of red leather

And then out again, aboard   10
A blue Chevrolet, releasing
The rust from its other color,

Reared up on three building blocks.
None had the same body heat;
I changed with them inward, toward
The weedy heart of the junkyard,
For I knew that Doris Holbrook
Would escape from her father at noon

And would come from the farm
To seek parts owned by the sun   20
Among the abandoned chassis,
Sitting in each in turn
As I did, leaning forward
As in a wild stock-car race

In the parking lot of the dead.
Time after time, I climbed in
And out the other side, like
An envoy or movie star
Met at the station by crickets.
A radiator cap raised its head,   30

Become a real toad or a kingsnake
As I neared the hub of the yard,
Passing through many states,
Many lives, to reach
Some grandmother's long Pierce-Arrow
Sending platters of blindness forth

From its nickel hubcaps
And spilling its tender upholstery
On sleepy roaches,
The glass panel in between   40
Lady and colored driver
Not all the way broken out,

The back-seat phone
Still on its hook.
I got in as though to exclaim,
"Let us go to the orphan asylum,
John; I have some old toys
For children who say their prayers."

I popped with sweat as I thought
I heard Doris Holbrook scrape 50
Like a mouse in the southern-state sun
That was eating the paint in blisters
From a hundred car tops and hoods.
She was tapping like code,

Loosening the screws,
Carrying off headlights,
Sparkplugs, bumpers,
Cracked mirrors and gear-knobs,
Getting ready, already,
To go back with something to show 60

Other than her lips' new trembling
I would hold to me soon, soon,
Where I sat in the ripped back seat
Talking over the interphone,
Praying for Doris Holbrook
To come from her father's farm

And to get back there
With no trace of me on her face
To be seen by her red-haired father
Who would change, in the squalling barn, 70
Her back's pale skin with a strop,
Then lay for me

In a bootlegger's roasting car
With a string-triggered 12-gauge shotgun
To blast the breath from the air.
Not cut by the jagged windshields,
Through the acres of wrecks she came
With a wrench in her hand,

Through dust where the blacksnake dies
Of boredom, and the beetle knows 80
The compost has no more life.
Someone outside would have seen
The oldest car's door inexplicably
Close from within:

I held her and held her and held her,
Convoyed at terrific speed
By the stalled, dreaming traffic around us,
So the blacksnake, stiff
With inaction, curved back
Into life, and hunted the mouse   90

With deadly overexcitement,
The beetles reclaimed their field
As we clung, glued together,
With the hooks of the seat springs
Working through to catch us red-handed
Amidst the gray breathless batting

That burst from the seat at our backs.
We left by separate doors
Into the changed, other bodies
Of cars, she down Cherrylog Road   100
And I to my motorcycle
Parked like the soul of the junkyard

Restored, a bicycle fleshed
With power, and tore off
Up Highway 106, continually
Drunk on the wind in my mouth,
Wringing the handlebar for speed,
Wild to be wreckage forever.

Gwendolyn Brooks   *The Blackstone Rangers*

I

As Seen by Disciplines

There they are.
Thirty at the corner.
Black, raw, ready.
Sores in the city
that do not want to heal.

II

The Leaders

Jeff. Gene. Geronimo. And Bop.
They cancel, cure and curry.

Hardly the dupes of the downtown thing
the cold bonbon,
the rhinestone thing. And hardly
in a hurry.
Hardly Belafonte, King,
Black Jesus, Stokely, Malcolm X or Rap.
Bungled trophies.
Their country is a Nation on no map.   10

Jeff, Gene, Geronimo and Bop
in the passionate noon,
in bewitching night
are the detailed men, the copious men.
They curry, cure,
they cancel, cancelled images whose Concerts
are not divine, vivacious; the different tins
are intense last entries; pagan argument;
translations of the night.

The Blackstone bitter bureaus   20
(bureaucracy is footloose) edit, fuse
unfashionable damnations and descent;
and exulting, monstrous hand on monstrous hand,
construct, strangely, a monstrous pearl or grace.

III

Gang Girls
A Rangerette

Gang Girls are sweet exotics.
Mary Ann
uses the nutrients of her orient,
but sometimes sighs for Cities of blue and jewel
beyond her Ranger rim of Cottage Grove.
(Bowery Boys, Disciples, Whip-Birds will
dissolve no margins, stop no savory sanctities.)
Mary is
a rose in a whiskey glass.

Mary's   10
Februaries shudder and are gone. Aprils
fret frankly, lilac hurries on.
Summer is a hard irregular ridge.

October looks away.
And that's the Year!
        Save for her bugle-love.
Save for the bleat of not-obese devotion.
Save for Somebody Terribly Dying, under
the philanthropy of robins. Save for her Ranger
bringing   20
an amount of rainbow in a string-drawn bag.
"Where did you get the diamond?" Do not ask:
but swallow, straight, the spirals of his flask
and assist him at your zipper; pet his lips
and help him clutch you.

Love's another departure.
Will there be any arrivals, confirmations?
Will there be gleaning?

Mary, the Shakedancer's child
from the rooming-flat, pants carefully, peers at   30
her laboring lover. . . .
        Mary! Mary Ann!
Settle for sandwiches! settle for stocking caps!
for sudden blood, aborted carnival,
the props and niceties of non-loneliness—
the rhymes of Leaning.

T. S. ELIOT   *Gerontion*

> *Thou hast nor youth nor age*
> *But as it were an after dinner sleep*
> *Dreaming of both.*

Here I am, an old man in a dry month,
Being read to by a boy, waiting for rain.
I was neither at the hot gates
Nor fought in the warm rain
Nor knee deep in the salt marsh, heaving a cutlass,
Bitten by flies, fought.
My house is a decayed house,
And the jew squats on the window sill, the owner,
Spawned in some estaminet of Antwerp,
Blistered in Brussels, patched and peeled in London.   10

The goat coughs at night in the field overhead;
Rocks, moss, stonecrop, iron, merds.
The woman keeps the kitchen, makes tea,
Sneezes at evening, poking the peevish gutter.
                  I an old man,
A dull head among windy spaces.

Signs are taken for wonders. "We would see a sign!"
The word within a word, unable to speak a word,
Swaddled with darkness. In the juvescence of the year
Came Christ the tiger   20

In depraved May, dogwood and chestnut, flowering judas,
To be eaten, to be divided, to be drunk
Among whispers; by Mr. Silvero
With caressing hands, at Limoges
Who walked all night in the next room;

By Hakagawa, bowing among the Titians;
By Madame de Tornquist, in the dark room
Shifting the candles; Fräulein von Kulp
Who turned in the hall, one hand on the door.
        Vacant shuttles   30
Weave the wind. I have no ghosts,
An old man in a draughty house
Under a windy knob.

After such knowledge, what forgiveness? Think now
History has many cunning passages, contrived corridors
And issues, deceives with whispering ambitions,
Guides us by vanities. Think now
She gives when our attention is distracted
And what she gives, gives with such supple confusions
That the giving famishes the craving. Gives too late   40
What's not believed in, or if still believed,
In memory only, reconsidered passion. Gives too soon
Into weak hands, what's thought can be dispensed with
Till the refusal propagates a fear. Think
Neither fear nor courage saves us. Unnatural vices
Are fathered by our heroism. Virtues
Are forced upon us by our impudent crimes.
These tears are shaken from the wrath-bearing tree.

The tiger springs in the new year. Us he devours. Think at last
We have not reached conclusion, when I   50
Stiffen in a rented house. Think at last
I have not made this show purposelessly
And it is not by any concitation
Of the backward devils.
I would meet you upon this honestly.
I that was near your heart was removed therefrom
To lose beauty in terror, terror in inquisition.
I have lost my passion: why should I need to keep it
Since what is kept must be adulterated?
I have lost my sight, smell, hearing, taste and touch: 60
How should I use them for your closer contact?

These with a thousand small deliberations
Protract the profit of their chilled delirium,
Excite the membrane, when the sense has cooled,
With pungent sauces, multiply variety
In a wilderness of mirrors. What will the spider do,
Suspend its operations, will the weevil
Delay? De Bailhache, Fresca, Mrs. Cammel, whirled
Beyond the circuit of the shuddering Bear
In fractured atoms. Gull against the wind, in the windy straits   70
Of Belle Isle, or running on the Horn,
White feathers in the snow, the Gulf claims,
And an old man driven by the Trades
To a sleepy corner.

Tenants of the house,
Thoughts of a dry brain in a dry season.

WILLIAM BUTLER YEATS   *Nineteen Hundred and Nineteen: I*

Many ingenious lovely things are gone
That seemed sheer miracle to the multitude,
Protected from the circle of the moon
That pitches common things about. There stood
Amid the ornamental bronze and stone
An ancient image made of olive wood—
And gone are Phidias' famous ivories
And all the golden grasshoppers and bees.

We too had many pretty toys when young:
A law indifferent to blame or praise,   10
To bribe or threat; habits that made old wrong
Melt down, as it were wax in the sun's rays;
Public opinion ripening for so long
We thought it would outlive all future days.
O what fine thought we had because we thought
That the worst rogues and rascals had died out.

All teeth were drawn, all ancient tricks unlearned,
And a great army but a showy thing;
What matter that no cannon had been turned
Into a ploughshare? Parliament and king   20
Thought that unless a little powder burned
The trumpeters might burst with trumpeting
And yet it lack all glory; and perchance
The guardsmen's drowsy chargers would not prance.

Now days are dragon-ridden, the nightmare
Rides upon sleep: a drunken soldiery
Can leave the mother, murdered at her door,
To crawl in her own blood, and go scot-free;
The night can sweat with terror as before
We pieced our thoughts into philosophy,   30
And planned to bring the world under a rule,
Who are but weasels fighting in a hole.

He who can read the signs nor sink unmanned
Into the half-deceit of some intoxicant
From shallow wits; who knows no work can stand,
Whether health, wealth or peace of mind were spent
On master-work of intellect or hand,
No honour leave its mighty monument,
Has but one comfort left: all triumph would
But break upon his ghostly solitude.   40

But is there any comfort to be found?
Man is in love and loves what vanishes,
What more is there to say? That country round
None dared admit, if such a thought were his,
Incendiary or bigot could be found
To burn that stump on the Acropolis,
Or break in bits the famous ivories
Or traffic in the grasshoppers or bees.

Chapter Nine

Poetic Integrity: Quest and Reconciliation

At the close of our book we return to the largest frame of reference of poetry—the extent of the poet's awareness of the discrepancies between what *is* and what *seems,* and between what *is* and what *ought to be.* All the resources of the great poet, all his powers of description, image-making, story-telling, dramatization, intellectual suppleness, and imaginative conception are put to the test in his ultimate effort to deal with these discrepancies. He needs both technical proficiency and tough integrity of character, and must not be satisfied with glib or easy solutions. He must recognize, as John Donne's *Third Satyre* has it, that truth "stands on a hugh hill," "craggy and steep,"

> . . . and he that will
> Reach her, about must, and about must go;
> And what the hill's suddenness resists, win so. . . .

Let us consider from this point of view Matthew Arnold's *Dover Beach,* a poem which, like many other poems of the later nineteenth century, sketches a bleak picture of the universe of modern man. Our universe, Arnold argues, is one in which the old faith in a life securely and eternally guided by a benevolent God has begun to disappear, leaving many people with the feeling that they have nothing to depend on but the affection of beloved individuals.

MATTHEW ARNOLD *Dover Beach*

> The sea is calm tonight.
> The tide is full, the moon lies fair
> Upon the straits;—on the French coast the light
> Gleams and is gone; the cliffs of England stand,
> Glimmering and vast, out in the tranquil bay.
> Come to the window, sweet is the night-air!

Only, from the long line of spray
Where the sea meets the moon-blanched land,
Listen! you hear the grating roar
Of pebbles which the waves draw back, and fling,   10
At their return, up the high strand,
Begin, and cease, and then again begin,
With tremulous cadence slow, and bring
The eternal note of sadness in.

Sophocles long ago
Heard it on the Ægæan, and it brought
Into his mind the turbid ebb and flow
Of human misery; we
Find also in the sound a thought,
Hearing it by this distant northern sea.   20

The Sea of Faith
Was once, too, at the full, and round earth's shore
Lay like the folds of a bright girdle furled.
But now I only hear
Its melancholy, long, withdrawing roar,
Retreating, to the breath
Of the night-wind, down the vast edges drear
And naked shingles of the world.

Ah, love, let us be true
To one another! for the world, which seems   30
To lie before us like a land of dreams,
So various, so beautiful, so new,
Hath really neither joy, nor love, nor light,
Nor certitude, nor peace, nor help for pain;
And we are here as on a darkling plain
Swept with confused alarms of struggle and flight,
Where ignorant armies clash by night.

In this poem the effect of calm beauty in the opening picture of Dover
Beach and the sea at night is soon submerged in the melancholy impression of the first stanza's closing lines. The sound of the waves reminds
the speaker of the "eternal" recurrence of this impression, for there have
always been men who lived near the sea and heard the same melancholy
note—the great Greek writer of tragedy, Sophocles, for example. Having
struck this philosophical note, the poem can then go on to the allegorical
third stanza, which is not about geographical places or historical personalities but about an abstraction—a state of mind that has changed the
meaning of life for most people. And finally there is the appeal to a

beloved woman that she and the speaker keep their faith in one another, since the calm, beautiful scene outside is mere deception, while in reality terror and confusion lurk everywhere.

Dover Beach is not "against" delight in the world's beauty and in religious faith. On the contrary, the images applied to them make it clear that they have a strong hold on the poet's affections. But he fears life, too, because of the challenge to old beliefs that has come from the new scientific developments of the nineteenth century; and between fear and loss of faith, much of the delight seems to have been spoiled for him.

Poetry often expresses ideas and emotions felt by all mankind to be true in the long run to the common experience of humanity. Such poetry is affirmative, traditional, and genuinely popular. It does not make its appeal by its originality or its unexpectedness, or even by its profundity (though it does not necessarily lack these qualities), but by its convincing rightness, by the *felt* truth with which it confirms people in what they have come to feel and believe without ever having been able to put it into memorable words. This is the idea of Pope's Horatian conception of poetry as "What oft was thought but ne'er so well expressed," and of Keats's psychological phrasing of the same idea:

> I think poetry should surprise by a fine excess, and not by singularity. It should strike the reader as a wording of his own highest thoughts, and appear almost a remembrance.[1]

Poems and images fitting these descriptions are immediately satisfying; they are accepted at once and never forgotten. Lines whose impressiveness are of this order are the easiest to call to mind:

> She walks in beauty like the night
> GEORGE GORDON, LORD BYRON

> The day is done and the darkness
> Falls from the wings of night
> As a feather is wafted downward
> From an eagle in his flight.
> HENRY WADSWORTH LONGFELLOW

> O my luve is like a red, red rose,
> That's newly sprung in June
> ROBERT BURNS

> The uncertain glory of an April day
> WILLIAM SHAKESPEARE

---

[1] Letter to John Taylor, February 27, 1818.

If we place alongside these beautiful images parallel ones of a more complex kind, we shall discover that the greater complexity is due to the distance between the arms of the comparison—between, for instance, the brightness of God and the depth of darkness in the first quotation below. The things compared or identified are not so easily seen to be alike. The effect is not so much to reassure us of what we already feel as to startle us awake, so that we experience something not experienced before:

> There is in God (some say)
> A deep but dazzling darkness.
> > HENRY VAUGHAN

> I should have been a pair of ragged claws
> Scuttling across the floors of silent seas.
> > T. S. ELIOT

> the fine, fine wind that takes its course through the chaos of the world
> Like a fine, an exquisite chisel, a wedge-blade inserted. . . .
> > D. H. LAWRENCE

> A serpent swam a vertex to the sun
> —On unpaced beaches leaned its tongue and drummed.
> What fountains did I hear? what icy speeches?
> > HART CRANE

> April is the cruelest month. . . .
> > T. S. ELIOT

The two types of images differ in a more fundamental way than in their relative complexity. The second type peers below the surface of life to its ever-present but often dark and confusing realities. It does not confirm what is established; it affirms new and sometimes terrifying perceptions. As the discoverer of "underground secrets" of the human consciousness, the poet is indeed often, as Louis MacNeice has said, an "informer"—and in the derogatory sense of the word. He "tells on" us, not caring what the telling may do to our self-esteem. There is, for example, another truth about the nature of life than that expressed by Burns in his intensely personal yet universal

> O my luve is like a red, red rose,
> That's newly sprung in June:
> O my luve is like the melodie
> That's sweetly played in tune.

What this truth is we can discern in some lines by Robert Bridges from his *Eros* (page 499). (Eros was the Greek god of love, to whom the poet addresses his thoughts.)

> Why hast thou nothing in thy face?
> Thou idol of the human race,
> Thou tyrant of the human heart. . . .
>
> Surely thy body is thy mind,
> For in thy face is nought to find,
> Only thy soft unchristen'd smile
> That shadows neither love nor guile,
> But shameless will and power immense,
> In secret sensuous innocence.

The paradoxical irony and seeming bitterness of these lines are conveyed particularly in certain double-edged words and phrases: "nothing," "idol," "soft unchristen'd smile," "shameless," "secret," "innocence." The attitude here is not, as in the Burns poem, that of a lover in the grip of the mindless ecstasy of Eros but that of a philosopher and critic who seeks to know rather than to feel; and the knowledge is the fruit of experience, not experience itself. In the truth it expresses, Bridges's poem is less happy, less pleasant to contemplate, and indeed, one is tempted to say, less respectable than Burns's. Yet both writers are telling the truth. The discrepancy between them lies in the different aspects from which the truth is viewed. Burns is joyously making love; Bridges is analyzing love with mixed feelings.

This is clear if we read a little further in *Eros*. The suggestion of paradox in the lines we have quoted is heightened and takes a sharp new turn in succeeding lines. So far, we have been shown the darker side of love, its instinctive mindless preoccupation with its prey; notice the faint but unmistakable air of moral disapproval in the second stanza: "unchristen'd," "shameless," "secret," Eros is called. But this darker side is not the main truth the poem is concerned with presenting. The much richer, more complete truth emerges finally—that the essential, characteristic, and defining quality of love is a luminosity coming not in spite of but because of its very mindlessness:

> O king of joy, what is thy thought?
> I dream thou knowest it is nought,
> And wouldst in darkness come, but thou
> Makest the light where'er thou go.
> Ah yet no victim of thy grace,
> None who e'er long'd for thy embrace,
> Hath cared to look upon thy face.

The concluding two lines have returned to the animality of love, which it is sometimes difficult for the idealist to accept, but the poet can hardly be said to reject the truth of love's luminosity because of this animality. He is not trying deliberately to be obscure or difficult; he is trying accurately to suggest the paradoxical nature of love in a manner that will be true to our actual experience.

Dover Beach and *Eros* both reveal the special quality of poetic integrity, which may take many forms but very often, like Bridges' god of love, makes a light of its own in the midst of the acknowledged darkness and complexity of life. Such an assertion of human values despite the knowledge of adversity is behind all ritual and art. The act of erecting a formal ceremony, design, or structural pattern for its own sake as well as for other purposes signifies a faith that human activity is more than worth the effort no matter what the world's condition may be.

This kind of affirmation can sometimes be made even more powerfully in works of pure imagination. Blake's strange poem *The Tyger* is a case in point. In this poem, the problem of evil—the existence of terrible, uncontrolled forces and their relation to the nature of God—is dynamically symbolized with naked directness.

WILLIAM BLAKE *The Tyger*

Tyger! Tyger! burning bright
In the forests of the night,
What immortal hand or eye
Could frame thy fearful symmetry?

In what distant deeps or skies
Burnt the fire of thine eyes?
On what wings dare he aspire?
What the hand dare seize the fire?

And what shoulder, and what art
Could twist the sinews of thy heart?   10
And when thy heart began to beat,
What dread hand? and what dread feet?

What the hammer? what the chain?
In what furnace was thy brain?
What the anvil? what dread grasp
Dare its deadly terrors clasp?

When the stars threw down their spears,
And water'd heaven with their tears,
Did he smile his work to see?
Did he who made the Lamb make thee?   20

> Tyger! Tyger! burning bright
> In the forests of the night,
> What immortal hand or eye,
> Dare frame thy fearful symmetry?

The very thought of the tiger, as he is presented in these six stanzas, excites the speaker here in a curious way. It is possible to look upon tigers as things in the zoo—fierce, striped animals that are worth staring at as they pace about inside their cages. And it is possible, with only slightly superior scientific knowledge, to see them as interesting examples of certain species. But the speaker in the poem can hardly be said to be *amused* by the tiger, nor does he seem to care much about the zoological facts as such. His reaction, rather, resembles the primordial terror of a child, an almost instinctive terror with which we can all sympathize, and he sees in the tiger a mysterious, sinister vision of supernatural power.

In this vision, the tiger looms as a freely moving force in the dark forests of, not Asia or Africa, but "the night." So we are led to think of him as ever-present, ever-dangerous, a "burning bright" symbol of the savagery in every human soul and in all existence; a satanic beast. As we follow the poem through its images of the strength, the dreadfulness, and the wonder of the tiger, we become more and more aware of the speaker's chilled sense of awe when he thinks of the inscrutable purposes and unimaginable power of the creator of such a being. This awe reaches a shocked climax in the fifth stanza, when the speaker, remembering the miraculous events on the night Christ was born, asks the natural but startling question, "Did he who made the Lamb make thee?" Without rationalizing away this frightening fact, that all we see as gentlest and all that we see as most violently and perilously dynamic proceed from the same vital, daring source, the speaker faces the double nature of the universe with a full awareness of its awful dangers and endless possibilities.

As the poem develops, we can see clearly how its form helps create and sustain the religious-emotional pitch of feeling. The first outcry, together with the simple rhyme, fixes a dynamic picture blazingly in our minds:

> Tyger! Tyger! burning bright
> In the forests of the night. . . .

Immediately afterwards we are drawn into a ceremonial dance of questions. Each question leads to the same answer as to the nature of the Creator, and each associates God with his untamable creation, so that the repeated questions beat their meaning at us like savage drums. God, we are being told, is not to be understood in human terms. There is something about him that matches the tiger: He is "dread"; he responds to the challenge of the "distant deeps or skies" whose dangerous fires he must seize to create this terrible symbol. The rhymes come very fast in an obsessive chant of fascinated horror at the concentrated vision that has seized upon the speaker.

At the end the tiger still ranges supreme in his own domain, and we feel that he is "real" in a sense not felt by the zoologist or the casual visitor to the zoo. He has the kind of reality that forces men to examine the meaning of their own lives because they have found a symbol with a truly compelling moral force. The profound questions raised in this poem, together with the stark pictures and the piled-up short phrases, may startle us into a kind of humility rare in our day. What we would ordinarily think of as evil has been shockingly related to what we think of as absolute good. We are sure of the compelling importance of the questions and of the image around which they are gathered. An emotional assertion of meaning has been made so vividly in these questions that it has brought into the open our sense of the terrible reality of evil.

This encompassing of evil without yielding to it, this fusing together of faith and candor, is one of the most significant characteristics of serious poetry of a high order.

In solving the moral and esthetic problem of how to tell the truth, the poet seems often to be hostile to the world around him. In truth, however bitter its savor, there is nevertheless always an implied affirmation of the essential value of honesty. One does not find a powerful poem of rejection without also finding a possibility implied of accepting life as a whole and in a better way. Though such poetry is often necessarily complex and ambiguous, it may also brilliantly simplify in order to strike to the heart of a situation and squeeze the real and the ideal as close together as possible. Blake's *London* is one of the brilliantly simple poems, presenting its criticism of life and its affirmations of value in the very same images.

William Blake *London*

> I wander thro' each charter'd street,
> Near where the charter'd Thames does flow,
> And mark in every face I meet
> Marks of weakness, marks of woe.
>
> In every cry of every Man,
> In every Infant's cry of fear,
> In every voice, in every ban,
> The mind-forg'd manacles I hear.

How the Chimney-sweeper's cry
Every blackening Church appalls;   10
And the hapless Soldier's sigh
Runs in blood down Palace walls.

But most, thro' midnight streets I hear
How the youthful Harlot's curse
Blasts the new-born Infant's tear,
And blights with plagues the Marriage hearse.

London, at first, seems an expression of outright rejection. Blake sees
not merely unrealized potentialities but deathly pain—"weakness" and
"woe"—everywhere. Each face, each voice, reminds him of the frustrations, lies, and cruelty of the city's life in the early years of the Industrial
Revolution. The pathetic little chimney-sweeps make religion and morality
seem arrant hypocrisy; the suffering of soldiers belies the benevolence of
governments and rulers; the cursing street-harlots force him to think of
the perversion of marital happiness that their existence means. (The final
lines compress references to illegitimate birth, syphilis, and the ugliness
that seems to the speaker to have blighted love in all its aspects; the
compression is achieved by a series of related outbursts of sound and
image, culminating in the paradoxical "Marriage hearse," which brings
the poem to its tragic close.)

Yet to feel so strongly on the subject of the "chartering"—the parceling
out for hire and profit—of the city while the potentialities for joy and
love are thwarted is to have a humane vision of the right relations between
man and man, man and woman, and man and God. The corruption of
society, the failure of Church and State, the perversion of love can
arouse savage condemnation only in someone with a blazing concern
for those right relations. Thus, *London*, in the very vehemence of its
description and its rejection of all that has blighted human life and
affection, gives us a pure affirmation of their intrinsic beauty. Blake
views evil and suffering in the light of his concept of *love* as the great
creative force. His *London* exemplifies the way in which many poems of
stature imply critical and affirmative attitudes at one and the same time.
The importance of such "opposite implication" must be recognized if
we are to understand the real functions of much of the paradoxical, ironic,
ambiguous, and mystical language of poetry. Blake's method here is to
give us images that paint the harsh truth as tragically and nakedly as
possible, and yet are also unmistakable emblems of what is valued most
(freedom, health, joy, enlightenment, the happiness of children, peace,
and innocent sexual love).

Walt Whitman's *Out of the cradle endlessly rocking* (pages 502–508) moves more explicitly from tragic observation to affirmation. It frames an attitude toward the fact of death through its opening evocation of the nostalgic, sense-laden memories of boyhood, its account of the two birds and the two songs of joy and of longing, and its colloquy between the boy and the sea. The opening chant, which summons up so freshly the mysterious sense of life and of an unbearable pain of experience, prepares us to accept death as essential to the most intense meanings of life and to the profound connection of elemental nature with man's highest thoughts and feelings. The poem is a major effort to recognize the fact of death for what it is and at the same time to redefine it mystically. We must remember that the mystical redefinition is less philosophical than emotional—part of the poet's memory of how he identified himself with the whole of nature:

> Demon or bird! (said the boy's soul,)
> Is it indeed toward your mate you sing? or is it mostly to me?

and later,

> O you singer solitary, singing by yourself—projecting me . . .

Here the poet helps make sure we do remember what he is doing—symbolically describing a subjective state by personifying bird, sea, and his own soul. He does not wish us to think these things literally happened, of course, but he does not wish us to think of them as mere make-believe either. If such things do not literally happen, their *meaning* is possible, it is devoutly to be desired, and its possibility alone makes all experience, even the most tragic, too rich to be diminished by fear or squeamishness. We are to face death and rejoice in it, not so much for consolation as for the realization that it is inseparable from all growth and love. It is the key to immersion in that strangely magnetic reality described in the first stanza and in the stanzas that follow the final song of the bird.

W. B. Yeats's *A Dialogue of Self and Soul* (pages 512–514) presents two opposed positions. The Soul speaks for a traditional Christian view: that concern for eternal life of the spirit after death must outweigh any mortal pleasures. The Self speaks for a secular and aesthetic view: that we can find no values greater than those given us by love, conflict, and beauty in this life.

The dialogue begins as the Soul recalls to the Self the limitations of human possibility unaided by spiritual grace: the "crumbling battlements" that are its poor mortal defences, the frivolity of fixing one's attention on emblems of love and war—of the gracious ceremony and brave meanings that are only man-made. The image of the star is valuable for suggesting its opposite: the light of the spirit that exists beyond death, which we must accept as true without questioning, and which we can arrive at only by detaching ourselves from the particular causes and desires and experiences that are the accidental markers of any life.

The Soul appears to win the argument, except that the Self takes a completely independent tack in the second part of the poem. Admitting the arguments against this life—it *is* ugly, painful, and unjust, and perhaps the Soul is right to castigate its frivolity and its "criminal" obsession with the cycle of reproduction and death—he nevertheless is willing to accept all this. And doing so, he is overwhelmed with a pure bliss of the sort felt by souls emerging from Purgatory and entering Paradise. He has detached himself, not from the specific love of material experience ugly or beautiful, but from the sense of guilt and "remorse." *Now* he is "saved," though his "salvation" is the exact opposite, theologically speaking, of what an orthodox Christian would mean by the word:

> When such as I cast out remorse
> So great a sweetness flows into the breast
> We must laugh and we must sing,
> We are blest by everything,
> Everything we look upon is blest.

The childlike ecstasy of these closing lines is very unlike the wise, sad, surging music of death-affirmation at the end of Whitman's poem. Yet considering the poem as a whole, it would be a rash reader who could say that the liberation of spirit expressed here is very different from that felt in the much freer and more loosely constructed *Out of the cradle endlessly rocking*. The reasons for the similarity are clear. Although both poems deal with Metaphysical and ultimately religious matters— life, death, love, and immortality—their rhetoric and structure is that of emotion rather than logic. They are poetry not philosophy. Both emerge into affirmation from the struggle to reconcile suffering with faith in the possibility of love and meaning, and both use essential methods of art. They evoke, they employ incantation and opposite implication, they set voices and modulations of tone against one another, and they move from one clearly set stage of insight or tension to the next and always toward the final moment of equilibrium or assertion.

As in most great poetry, the triumph in these poems is paradoxical— the affirmation of a condition of suffering in language that is exultant and that transcends a previous mood of despair. It is a triumph of the candid, passionate, and resurgent poetic imagination rather than of any particular creed or ideology. In fact, the very construction of an integrated and living poem is symbolically an affirmation of the value of human will and imagination.

Poems: The Moral Imagination

The poems with which we conclude are presented less for consideration of technique or form than for meditation on how the moral imagination works in them. They have to do with some of the abiding themes of man's everlasting quest for the meaning and significance of life. Such answers as the poet may find, or such guesses as he may hazard, are not stated in abstract terms as in philosophy or in dogmatic creeds. Rather, they are presented in concrete individualized atoms of experience, the sensuous materials of feeling and thought.

We begin with two songs of innocence, by William Blake and Theodore Roethke, dealing with the happy aspects of nature and animal life. Roethke's poem changes in tone, however, in its second part, and is followed by Wordsworth's deeply thoughtful and passionate treatment of nature as a maturing influence in the wonderful passage from *The Prelude*. This poem suggests what the poems by Blake, Bridges, Dickinson, Plath, and Yeats that follow it present more directly: the sense that a bitter and harsh necessity stands watch over man and his aspirations and that he cannot ignore it without falling into sentimentality, self-delusion, and futility. They demonstrate the bitter paradox that, as Crazy Jane in Yeats's poem has it, "Fair and foul are near of kin,/And fair needs foul." That good and evil, pleasure and pain, ecstatic joy and suicidal anguish are inextricably woven together is a constant realization of human and poetic wisdom. This realization is shown as clearly in the poems on death by Whitman, Lawrence, and Yeats as it is in the poems of passionate intensity that precede them. We conclude with three poems of spiritual affirmation, one Platonic, one humanistic, and one Christian, by Shakespeare, Muir, and Chaucer.

WILLIAM BLAKE   The Lamb

Little Lamb, who made thee?
　Dost thou know who made thee?
Gave thee life, & bid thee feed
By the stream & o'er the mead;
Gave thee clothing of delight,
Softest clothing, woolly, bright;
Gave thee such a tender voice,
Making all the vales rejoice?
　Little Lamb, who made thee?
　Dost thou know who made thee?

Little Lamb, I'll tell thee,
Little Lamb, I'll tell thee:

10

He is callèd by thy name,
For he calls himself a Lamb.
He is meek, & he is mild;
He became a little child.
I a child, & thou a lamb,
We are callèd by his name.
 Little Lamb, God bless thee!
 Little Lamb, God bless thee!   20

THEODORE ROETHKE   *The Meadow Mouse*

I

In a shoe box stuffed in an old nylon stocking
Sleeps the baby mouse I found in the meadow,
Where he trembled and shook beneath a stick
Till I caught him up by the tail and brought him in,
Cradled in my hand,
A little quaker, the whole body of him trembling,
His absurd whiskers sticking out like a cartoon-mouse,
His feet like small leaves,
Little lizard-feet,
Whitish and spread wide when he tried to struggle away, 10
Wriggling like a miniscule puppy.

Now he's eaten his three kinds of cheese and drunk from his
       bottle-cap watering-trough—
So much he just lies in one corner,
His tail curled under him, his belly big
As his head; his bat-like ears
Twitching, tilting toward the least sound.

Do I imagine he no longer trembles
When I come close to him?
He seems no longer to tremble.

II

But this morning the shoe-box house on the back porch is empty. 20
Where has he gone, my meadow mouse,
My thumb of a child that nuzzled in my palm?—
To run under the hawk's wing,
Under the eye of the great owl watching from the elm-tree,
To live by courtesy of the shrike, the snake, the tom-cat.

I think of the nestling fallen into the deep grass,
The turtle gasping in the dusty rubble of the highway,
The paralytic stunned in the tub, and the water rising,—
All things innocent, hapless, forsaken.

WILLIAM WORDSWORTH from *The Prelude, or, Growth of a Poet's Mind* (from Book I)

Fair seed-time had my soul, and I grew up
Fostered alike by beauty and by fear:
Much favoured in my birthplace, and no less
In that beloved Vale to which erelong
We were transplanted—there were we let loose
For sports of wider range. Ere I had told
Ten birth-days, when among the mountain-slopes
Frost, and the breath of frosty wind, had snapped
The last autumnal crocus, 'twas my joy
With store of springes o'er my shoulder hung   10
To range the open heights where woodcocks run
Among the smooth green turf. Through half the night,
Scudding away from snare to snare, I plied
That anxious visitation;—moon and stars
Were shining o'er my head. I was alone,
And seemed to be a trouble to the peace
That dwelt among them. Sometimes it befell
In these night wanderings, that a strong desire
O'erpowered my better reason, and the bird
Which was the captive of another's toil   20
Became my prey; and when the deed was done
I heard among the solitary hills
Low breathings coming after me, and sounds
Of undistinguishable motion, steps
Almost as silent as the turf they trod.

Nor less when spring had warmed the cultured Vale,
Roved we as plunderers where the mother-bird
Had in high places built her lodge; though mean
Our object and inglorious, yet the end
Was not ignoble. Oh! when I have hung   30
Above the raven's nest, by knots of grass
And half-inch fissures in the slippery rock
But ill sustained, and almost (so it seemed)

Suspended by the blast that blew amain,
Shouldering the naked crag, oh, at that time
While on the perilous ridge I hung alone,
With what strange utterance did the loud dry wind
Blow through my ear! the sky seemed not a sky
Of earth—and with what motion moved the clouds!

    Dust as we are, the immortal spirit grows   40
Like harmony in music; there is a dark
Inscrutable workmanship that reconciles
Discordant elements, makes them cling together
In one society. How strange that all
The terrors, pains, and early miseries,
Regrets, vexations, lassitudes interfused
Within my mind, should e'er have borne a part,
And that a needful part, in making up
The calm existence that is mine when I
Am worthy of myself! Praise to the end!   50
Thanks to the means which Nature deigned to employ;
Whether her fearless visitings, or those
That came with soft alarm, like hurtless light
Opening the peaceful clouds; or she may use
Severer interventions, ministry
More palpable, as best might suit her aim.

    One summer evening (led by her) I found
A little boat tied to a willow tree
Within a rocky cave, its usual home.
Straight I unloosed her chain, and stepping in   60
Pushed from the shore. It was an act of stealth
And troubled pleasure, nor without the voice
Of mountain-echoes did my boat move on;
Leaving behind her still, on either side
Small circles glittering idly in the moon,
Until they melted all into one track
Of sparkling light. But now, like one who rows,
Proud of his skill, to reach a chosen point
With an unswerving line, I fixed my view
Upon the summit of a craggy ridge,   70
The horizon's utmost boundary; for above
Was nothing but the stars and the grey sky.
She was an elfin pinnace; lustily
I dipped my oars into the silent lake,

And, as I rose upon the stroke, my boat
Went heaving through the water like a swan;
When, from behind that craggy steep till then
The horizon's bound, a huge peak, black and huge,
As if with voluntary power instinct
Upreared its head. I struck and struck again,   80
And growing still in stature the grim shape
Towered up between me and the stars, and still,
For so it seemed, with purpose of its own
And measured motion like a living thing,
Strode after me. With trembling oars I turned,
And through the silent water stole my way
Back to the covert of the willow tree;
There in her mooring-place I left my bark,—
And through the meadows homeward went, in grave
And serious mood; but after I had seen   90
That spectacle, for many days, my brain
Worked with a dim and undetermined sense
Of unknown modes of being; o'er my thoughts
There hung a darkness, call it solitude
Or blank desertion. No familiar shapes
Remained, no pleasant images of trees,
Of sea or sky, no colours of green fields;
But huge and mighty forms, that do not live
Like living men, moved slowly through the mind
By day, and were a trouble to my dreams.   100
   Wisdom and Spirit of the universe!
Thou Soul that art the eternity of thought,
That givest to forms and images a breath
And everlasting motion, not in vain
By day or star-light thus from my first dawn
Of childhood didst thou intertwine for me
The passions that build up our human soul;
Not with the mean and vulgar works of man,
But with high objects, with enduring things—
With life and nature—purifying thus   110
The elements of feeling and of thought,
And sanctifying, by such discipline,
Both pain and fear, until we recognise
A grandeur in the beatings of the heart.
Nor was this fellowship vouchsafed to me
With stinted kindness. In November days,

When vapours rolling down the valley made
A lonely scene more lonesome, among woods,
At noon and 'mid the calm of summer nights,
When, by the margin of the trembling lake,   120
Beneath the gloomy hills homeward I went
In solitude, such intercourse was mine;
Mine was it in the fields both day and night,
And by the waters, all the summer long.

    And in the frosty season, when the sun
Was set, and visible for many a mile
The cottage windows blazed through twilight gloom,
I heeded not their summons: happy time
It was indeed for all of us—for me
It was a time of rapture! Clear and loud   130
The village clock tolled six,—I wheeled about,
Proud and exulting like an untired horse
That cares not for his home. All shod with steel,
We hissed along the polished ice in games
Confederate, imitative of the chase
And woodland pleasures,—the resounding horn,
The pack loud chiming, and the hunted hare.
So through the darkness and the cold we flew,
And not a voice was idle; with the din
Smitten, the precipices rang aloud;   140
The leafless trees and every icy crag
Tinkled like iron; while far distant hills
Into the tumult sent an alien sound
Of melancholy not unnoticed, while the stars
Eastward were sparkling clear, and in the west
The orange sky of evening died away.
Not seldom from the uproar I retired
Into a silent bay, or sportively
Glanced sideway, leaving the tumultuous throng,
To cut across the reflex of a star   150
That fled, and, flying still before me, gleamed
Upon the glassy plain; and oftentimes,
When we had given our bodies to the wind,
And all the shadowy banks on either side
Came sweeping through the darkness, spinning still
The rapid line of motion, then at once
Have I, reclining back upon my heels,

Stopped short; yet still the solitary cliffs
Wheeled by me—even as if the earth had rolled
With visible motion her diurnal round!   160
Behind me did they stretch in solemn train,
Feebler and feebler, and I stood and watched
Till all was tranquil as a dreamless sleep.

WILLIAM BLAKE   *The Garden of Love*

I went to the Garden of Love,
And saw what I never had seen:
A Chapel was built in the midst,
Where I used to play on the green.

And the gates of this Chapel were shut,
And "Thou shalt not" writ over the door;
So I turn'd to the Garden of Love
That so many sweet flowers bore;

And I saw it was fillèd with graves,
And tomb-stones where flowers should be;   10
And Priests in black gowns were walking their rounds,
And binding with briars my joys & desires.

WILLIAM BLAKE   *Song: Never seek to tell thy love*

Never seek to tell thy love
Love that never told can be;
For the gentle wind does move
Silently, invisibly.

I told my love, I told my love,
I told her all my heart,
Trembling, cold, in ghastly fears—
Ah, she doth depart.

Soon as she was gone from me
A traveller came by   10
Silently, invisibly—
O, was no deny.

ROBERT BRIDGES Ἔρως (*Eros*)

Why hast thou nothing in thy face?
Thou idol of the human race,
Thou tyrant of the human heart,
The flower of lovely youth that art;
Yea, and that standest in thy youth
An image of eternal Truth,
With thy exuberant flesh so fair,
That only Pheidias might compare,
Ere from his chaste marmoreal form
Time had decayed the colours warm;   10
Like to his gods in thy proud dress,
Thy starry sheen of nakedness.

   Surely thy body is thy mind,
For in thy face is nought to find,
Only thy soft unchristen'd smile,
That shadows neither love nor guile,
But shameless will and power immense,
In secret sensuous innocence.

   O king of joy, what is thy thought?
I dream thou knowest it is nought,   20
And wouldst in darkness come, but thou
Makest the light where'er thou go.
Ah yet no victim of thy grace,
None who e'er long'd for thy embrace,
Hath cared to look upon thy face.

EMILY DICKINSON *'Twas like a Maelstrom, with a notch*

'Twas like a Maelstrom, with a notch,
That nearer, every Day,
Kept narrowing its boiling Wheel
Until the Agony

Toyed coolly with the final inch
Of your delirious Hem—
And you dropt, lost,
When something broke—
And let you from a Dream—

As if a Goblin with a Gauge—   10
Kept measuring the Hours—
Until you felt your Second
Weigh, helpless, in his Paws—

And not a Sinew—stirred—could help,
And sense was setting numb—
When God—remembered—and the Fiend
Let go, then, Overcome—

As if your Sentence stood—pronounced—
And you were frozen led
From Dungeon's luxury of Doubt   20
To Gibbets, and the Dead—

And when the Film had stitched your eyes
A Creature gasped "Reprieve"!
Which Anguish was the utterest—then—
To perish, or to live?

Sylvia Plath *Ariel*

Stasis in darkness.
Then the substanceless blue
Pour of tor and distances.

God's lioness,
How one we grow,
Pivot of heels and knees!—The furrow

Splits and passes, sister to
The brown arc
Of the neck I cannot catch,

Nigger-eye   10
Berries cast dark
Hooks—

Black sweet blood mouthfuls,
Shadows.
Something else

Hauls me through air—
Thighs, hair;
Flakes from my heels.

White
Godiva, I unpeel— 20
Dead hands, dead stringencies.

And now I
Foam to wheat, a glitter of seas.
The child's cry

Melts in the wall.
And I
Am the arrow,

The dew that flies
Suicidal, at one with the drive
Into the red 30

Eye, the cauldron of morning.

WILLIAM BUTLER YEATS   *Crazy Jane Talks with the Bishop*

I met the Bishop on the road
And much said he and I.
"Those breasts are flat and fallen now,
Those veins must soon be dry;
Live in a heavenly mansion,
Not in some foul sty."

"Fair and foul are near of kin,
And fair needs foul," I cried.
"My friends are gone, but that's a truth
Nor grave nor bed denied, 10
Learned in bodily lowliness
And in the heart's pride.

"A woman can be proud and stiff
When on love intent;
But Love has pitched his mansion in

The place of excrement;
For nothing can be sole or whole
That has not been rent."

WALT WHITMAN   *Out of the Cradle Endlessly Rocking* [1]

Out of the cradle endlessly rocking,
Out of the mocking-bird's throat, the musical shuttle,
Out of the Ninth-month [2] midnight,
Over the sterile sands, and the fields beyond, where the child,
    leaving his bed, wander'd alone, bareheaded, barefoot,
Down from the shower'd halo,
Up from the mystic play of shadows, twining and twisting as if
    they were alive,
Out from the patches of briers and blackberries,
From the memories of the bird that chanted to me,
From your memories, sad brother—from the fitful risings and
    fallings I heard,
From under that yellow half-moon, late-risen, and swollen as if
    with tears,   10
From those beginning notes of sickness and love, there in the
    transparent mist,
From the thousand responses of my heart, never to cease,
From the myriad thence-arous'd words,
From the word stronger and more delicious than any,
From such, as now they start, the scene revisiting,
As a flock, twittering, rising, or overhead passing,
Borne hither—ere all eludes me, hurriedly,
A man—yet by these tears a little boy again,
Throwing myself on the sand, confronting the waves,
I, chanter of pains and joys, uniter of here and hereafter,   20
Taking all hints to use them—but swiftly leaping beyond them,
A reminiscence sing.

Once, Paumanok,
When the snows had melted—when the lilac-scent was in the
    air, and the Fifth-month grass was growing,
Up this sea-shore, in some briers,

---

[1] This is a conflated (composite) text. See end of poem for an extended note.
[2] It is traditional Quaker usage to call the months by their numerical order.
Does this fact justify Whitman's doing so in this poem?

Two guests from Alabama—two together,
And their nest, and four light-green eggs, spotted with brown,
And every day the he-bird, to and fro, near at hand,
And every day the she-bird, crouch'd on her nest, silent, with
    bright eyes,
And every day I, a curious boy, never too close, never disturbing
    them,   30
Cautiously peering, absorbing, translating.

Shine! shine! shine!
Pour down your warmth, great Sun!
While we bask—we two together.

Two together!
Winds blow South, or winds blow North,
Day come white, or night come black,
Home, or rivers and mountains from home,
Singing all time, minding no time,
While we two keep together.   40

Till of a sudden
May-be kill'd, unknown to her mate,
One forenoon the she-bird crouch'd not on the nest,
Nor return'd that afternoon, nor the next,
Nor ever appear'd again.

And thenceforward, all summer, in the sound of the sea,
And at night, under the full of the moon, in calmer weather,
Over the hoarse surging of the sea,
Or flitting from brier to brier by day,
I saw, I heard at intervals, the remaining one, the he-bird,   50
The solitary guest from Alabama.

Blow! blow! blow!
Blow up, sea-winds, along Paumanok's shore!
I wait and I wait, till you blow my mate to me.

Yes, when the stars glisten'd,
All night long, on the prong of a moss-scallop'd stake,
Down, almost amid the slapping waves,
Sat the lone singer, wonderful, causing tears.

He call'd on his mate;
He pour'd forth the meanings which I, of all men, know.   60

Yes, my brother, I know;
The rest might not—but I have treasured every note;
For once, and more than once, dimly, down to the beach gliding,
Silent, avoiding the moonbeams, blending myself with the
    shadows,
Recalling now the obscure shapes, the echoes, the sounds and
    sights after their sorts,
The white arms out in the breakers tirelessly tossing,
I, with bare feet, a child, the wind wafting my hair,
Listen'd long and long.

Listen'd, to keep, to sing—now translating the notes,
Following you, my brother.   70

Soothe! soothe! soothe!
Close on its wave soothes the wave behind,
And again another behind, embracing and lapping, every one
    close,
But my love soothes not me, not me.

Low hangs the moon—it rose late;
O it is lagging—O I think it is heavy with love, with love.

O madly the sea pushes upon the land,
With love—with love.

O night! do I not see my love fluttering out there among the
    breakers?
What is that little black thing I see there in the white?   80

Loud! loud! loud!
Loud I call to you, my love!
High and clear I shoot my voice over the waves;
Surely you must know who is here, is here;
You must know who I am, my love.

Low-hanging moon!
What is that dusky spot in your brown yellow?
O it is the shape, the shape of my mate!
O moon, do not keep her from me any longer.

Land! land! O land!   90
Whichever way I turn, O I think you could give me my mate
    back again, if you only would;
For I am almost sure I see her dimly whichever way I look.

O rising stars!
Perhaps the one I want so much will rise, will rise with some
     of you.

O throat! O trembling throat!
Sound clearer through the atmosphere!
Pierce the woods, the earth;
Somewhere listening to catch you must be the one I want.

Shake out, carols!
Solitary here—the night's carols!   100
Carols of lonesome love! Death's carols!
Carols under that lagging, yellow, waning moon!
O, under that moon, where she droops almost down into the sea!
O reckless, despairing carols.

But soft! sink low;
Soft! let me just murmur;
And do you wait a moment, you husky-noised sea;
For somewhere I believe I heard my mate responding to me,
So faint—I must be still, be still to listen;
But not altogether still, for then she might not come immedi-
     ately to me.   110

Hither, my love!
Here I am! Here!
With this just-sustain'd note I announce myself to you;
This gentle call is for you, my love, for you.

Do not be decoy'd elsewhere!
That is the whistle of the wind—it is not my voice;
That is the fluttering, the fluttering of the spray;
Those are the shadows of leaves.

O darkness! O in vain!
O I am very sick and sorrowful.   120

O brown halo in the sky, near the moon, drooping upon the sea!
O troubled reflection in the sea!
O throat! O throbbing heart!
And I singing uselessly, uselessly all the night.

Murmur! Murmur on!
O murmurs—you yourselves make me continue to sing, I know
     not why.

O past! O life! O songs of joy!
In the air—in the woods—over fields;
Loved! loved! loved! loved! loved!
But my love no more, no more with me!   130
We two together no more.

The aria sinking;
All else continuing—the stars shining,
The winds blowing—the notes of the bird continuous echoing,
With angry moans the fierce old mother incessantly moaning,
On the sands of Paumanok's shore, grey and rustling;
The yellow half-moon enlarged, sagging down, drooping, the
    face of the sea almost touching;
The boy ecstatic—with his bare feet the waves, with his hair the
    atmosphere dallying,
The love in the heart long pent, now loose, now at last tumul-
    tuously bursting,
The aria's meaning, the ears, the Soul, swiftly depositing,   140
The strange tears down the cheeks coursing,
The colloquy there—the trio—each uttering,
The undertone—the savage old mother, incessantly crying,
To the boy's Soul's questions sullenly timing—some drown'd
    secret hissing,
To the outsetting bard of love.

Demon or bird! (said the boy's soul,)
Is it indeed toward your mate you sing? or is it mostly to me?
For I, that was a child, my tongue's use sleeping,
Now that I have heard you,
Now in a moment I know what I am for—I awake,   150
And already a thousand singers—a thousand songs, clearer,
    louder and more sorrowful than yours,
A thousand warbling echoes have started to life within me, never
    to die.

O you singer, solitary, singing by yourself—projecting me;
O solitary me, listening—never more shall I cease perpetuating
    you;
Never more shall I escape, never more the reverberations,
Never more the cries of unsatisfied love be absent from me,
Never again leave me to be the peaceful child I was before what
    there, in the night,
By the sea, under the yellow and sagging moon,
The messenger there aroused—the fire, the sweet hell within,
The unknown want, the destiny of me.   160

O give me some clew!
O if I am to have so much, let me have more!
O a word! O what is my destination? (I fear it is henceforth
  chaos;)
O how joys, dreads, convolutions, human shapes, and all shapes,
  spring as from graves around me!
O phantoms! you cover all the land and all the sea!
O I cannot see in the dimness whether you smile or frown upon
  me;
O vapour, a look, a word! O well-beloved!
O you dear women's and men's phantoms!

A word then, (for I will conquer it,)
The word final, superior to all, 170
Subtle, sent up—what is it?—I listen;
Are you whispering it, and have been all the time, you sea-waves?
Is that it from your liquid rims and wet sands?

Whereto answering, the sea,
Delaying not, hurrying not,
Whisper'd me through the night, and very plainly before day-
  break,
Lisp'd to me the low and delicious word Death;
And again Death—ever Death, Death, Death,
Hissing melodious, neither like the bird, nor like my arous'd
  child's heart,
But edging near, as privately for me, rustling at my feet, 180
Creeping thence steadily up to my ears, and laving me softly all
  over,
Death, Death, Death, Death, Death.
Which I do not forget,
But fuse the song of my dusky demon and brother,
That he sang to me in the moonlight on Paumanok's grey beach,
With the thousand responsive songs, at random,
My own songs, awaked from that hour;
And with them the key, the word up from the waves,
The word of the sweetest song, and all songs,
That strong and delicious word which, creeping to my feet, 190
The sea whisper'd me.

NOTE: This version of *Out of the Cradle Endlessly Rocking* is a conflated (composite)
text. The poem was first printed in 1859 as *A Child's Reminiscence.* A second version,
called *A Word Out of the Sea,* was included in the 1860 edition of Whitman's *Leaves
of Grass* and reprinted, with changes, in the 1867 edition. Other versions, with the
present title, appeared in the 1871 and 1881 editions.

Ordinarily, the 1881 text appears in anthologies. Many scholars and critics feel, however, that in certain respects Whitman's final version is inferior to one or more of the earlier ones, and that he was most freshly and richly involved with the poem during his forties (1859–1869). Some of the later changes may have improved it, but others may well have weakened its impact. Starting with 1860, no one version seems *absolutely* inferior to all others.

We have therefore thought it useful, for purposes of study, to present a conflated text combining what seems to us the best aspects of the several editions. Our aim is to suggest how open a process the making of a poem is, and how tentative is the poet's sense of its "final" form. The notes and questions that follow center on the major points of revision, though by no means all. They are intended not only to stimulate consideration of this one poem but also to indicate the kinds of questions students of literature must constantly face in thinking about successive versions of a text.

(1) *Which of the poem's successive titles, listed in the first paragraph of this note, seems to you the most appropriate?*

(2) The 1860 version begins with the following three lines instead of the two given in the foregoing text. They are:

Out of the rocked cradle,
Out of the mocking-bird's throat, the musical shuttle,
Out of the boy's mother's womb, and from the nipples of her breasts . . .

Are these lines as hypnotic in effect as those of the later version, in which we find the third line eliminated and the internal rhyme of "rocking" and "mocking" as well as the added word "endlessly"? Are there values in the harsh word "rocked" and in the details of female anatomy that might have been worth preserving?

(3) After the first stanza of the 1860 version, Whitman gave the rest of the poem the subtitle "Reminiscence." *Do the thought and language of the first stanza justify its being set off so sharply as introductory to the "reminiscence" of the main part of the poem? Was anything gained by dropping the division after 1860?*

(4) In lines 32, 52, 71, and 90, we find certain words repeated three times; in lines 74, 76, and 88, certain phrases are repeated twice. The same lines, before 1867, had one less word or phrase in each of these instances. Also, the 1867 version adds the phrase "and laving me softly all over" to the end of line 181. *How do these various changes enhance the poem's hypnotic sensuousness? How important is this effect to the overall meaning and structure?*

(5) The 1881 version omits lines 125–126 and 163–168 of the present text. It also changes line 161 to read: "O give me the clew! (it lurks in the night here somewhere)." It has been argued that in 1881 Whitman was speaking as a confident prophet rather than as the younger man he had once been who struggled for affirmation against depression and confusion. *Is this argument borne out at all by these changes? Do they make the poem more or less unified and effective?*

(6) In 1881, the following line was inserted just before the last line: "(Or like some old crone rocking the cradle, swathed in sweet garments bending aside)." Some critics have believed this a masterful touch. Others have called it sentimental and weak. *Comment on this disagreement.*

D. H. LAWRENCE *The Ship of Death*

1

Now it is autumn and the falling fruit
and the long journey towards oblivion.

The apples falling like great drops of dew
to bruise themselves an exit from themselves.

And it is time to go, to bid farewell
to one's own self, and find an exit
from the fallen self.

2

Have you built your ship of death, O have you?
O build your ship of death, for you will need it.

The grim frost is at hand, when the apples will fall   10
thick, almost thundrous, on the hardened earth.

And death is on the air like a smell of ashes!
Ah! can't you smell it?

And in the bruised body, the frightened soul
finds itself shrinking, wincing from the cold
that blows upon it through the orifices.

3

And can a man his own quietus make
with a bare bodkin?

With daggers, bodkins, bullets, man can make
a bruise or break of exit for his life;   20
but is that a quietus, O tell me, is it quietus?

Surely not so! for how could murder, even self-murder
ever a quietus make?

4

O let us talk of quiet that we know,
that we can know, the deep and lovely quiet
of a strong heart at peace!

How can we this, our own quietus, make?

5

Build then the ship of death, for you must take
the longest journey, to oblivion.

And die the death, the long and painful death   30
that lies between the old self and the new.

Already our bodies are fallen, bruised, badly bruised,
already our souls are oozing through the exit
of the cruel bruise.

Already the dark and endless ocean of the end
is washing in through the breaches of our wounds,
already the flood is upon us.

O build your ship of death, your little ark
and furnish it with food, with little cakes, and wine
for the dark flight down oblivion.   40

6

Piecemeal the body dies, and the timid soul
has her footing washed away, as the dark flood rises.

We are dying, we are dying, we are all of us dying
and nothing will stay the death-flood rising within us
and soon it will rise on the world, on the outside world.

We are dying, we are dying, piecemeal our bodies are dying
and our strength leaves us,
and our soul cowers naked in the dark rain over the flood,
cowering in the last branches of the tree of our life.

7

We are dying, we are dying, so all we can do   50
is now to be willing to die, and to build the ship
of death to carry the soul on the longest journey.

A little ship, with oars and food
and little dishes, and all accoutrements
fitting and ready for the departing soul.

Now launch the small ship, now as the body dies
and life departs, launch out, the fragile soul
in the fragile ship of courage, the ark of faith
with its store of food and little cooking pans
and change of clothes,   60

upon the flood's black waste
upon the waters of the end
upon the sea of death, where still we sail
darkly, for we cannot steer, and have no port.

There is no port, there is nowhere to go
only the deepening blackness darkening still
blacker upon the soundless, ungurgling flood
darkness at one with darkness, up and down
and sideways utterly dark, so there is no direction any more.
and the little ship is there; yet she is gone.   70
She is not seen, for there is nothing to see her by.
She is gone! gone! and yet
somewhere she is there.
Nowhere!

8

And everything is gone, the body is gone
completely under, gone, entirely gone.
The upper darkness is heavy as the lower,
between them the little ship
is gone
she is gone.   80

It is the end, it is oblivion.

9

And yet out of eternity a thread
separates itself on the blackness,
a horizontal thread
that fumes a little with pallor upon the dark.

Is it illusion? or does the pallor fume
a little higher?
Ah wait, wait, for there's the dawn,
the cruel dawn of coming back to life
out of oblivion.   90

Wait, wait, the little ship
drifting, beneath the deathly ashy grey
of a flood-dawn.

Wait, wait! even so, a flush of yellow
and strangely, O chilled wan soul, a flush of rose.

A flush of rose, and the whole thing starts again.

10

The flood subsides, and the body, like a worn sea-shell
emerges strange and lovely.
And the little ship wings home, faltering and lapsing
on the pink flood,   100
and the frail soul steps out, into her house again
filling the heart with peace.

Swings the heart renewed with peace
even of oblivion.

Oh build your ship of death. Oh build it!
for you will need it.
For the voyage of oblivion awaits you.

WILLIAM BUTLER YEATS   *A Dialogue of Self and Soul*

I

My Soul. I summon to the winding ancient stair;
   Set all your mind upon the steep ascent,
   Upon the broken, crumbling battlement,
   Upon the breathless starlit air,
   Upon the star that marks the hidden pole;
   Fix every wandering thought upon
   That quarter where all thought is done:
   Who can distinguish darkness from the soul?

My Self. The consecrated blade upon my knees
   Is Sato's ancient blade, still as it was,   10
   Still razor-keen, still like a looking-glass
   Unspotted by the centuries;
   That flowering, silken, old embroidery, torn
   From some court-lady's dress and round
   The wooden scabbard bound and wound,
   Can, tattered, still protect, faded adorn.

My Soul. Why should the imagination of a man
    Long past his prime remember things that are
    Emblematical of love and war?
    Think of ancestral night that can,   20
    If but imagination scorn the earth
    And intellect its wandering
    To this and that and t'other thing,
    Deliver from the crime of death and birth.

My Self. Montashigi, third of his family, fashioned it
    Five hundred years ago, about it lie
    Flowers from I know not what embroidery—
    Heart's purple—and all these I set
    For emblems of the day against the tower
    Emblematical of the night,   30
    And claim as by a soldier's right
    A charter to commit the crime once more.

My Soul. Such fullness in that quarter overflows
    And falls into the basin of the mind
    That man is stricken deaf and dumb and blind,
    For intellect no longer knows
    Is from the *Ought*, or *Knower* from the *Known*—
    That is to say, ascends to Heaven;
    Only the dead can be forgiven;
    But when I think of that my tongue's a stone.   40

II

My Self. A living man is blind and drinks his drop.
    What matter if the ditches are impure?
    What matter if I live it all once more?
    Endure that toil of growing up;
    The ignominy of boyhood; the distress
    Of boyhood changing into man;
    The unfinished man and his pain
    Brought face to face with his own clumsiness;

    The finished man among his enemies?—
    How in the name of Heaven can he escape   50
    That defiling and disfigured shape
    The mirror of malicious eyes
    Casts upon his eyes until at last

He thinks that shape must be his shape?
And what's the good of an escape
If honour find him in the wintry blast?

I am content to live it all again
And yet again, if it be life to pitch
Into the frog-spawn of a blind man's ditch,
A blind man battering blind men;   60
Or into that most fecund ditch of all,
The folly that man does
Or must suffer, if he woos
A proud woman not kindred of his soul.

I am content to follow to its source
Every event in action or in thought;
Measure the lot; forgive myself the lot!
When such as I cast out remorse
So great a sweetness flows into the breast
We must laugh and we must sing,   70
We are blest by everything,
Everything we look upon is blest.

WILLIAM SHAKESPEARE   *Sonnet CXLVI*

Poor soul, the center of my sinful earth,
Thrall to these rebel powers that thee array,
Why dost thou pine within and suffer dearth,
Painting thy outward walls so costly gay?
Why so large cost, having so short a lease,
Dost thou upon thy fading mansion spend?
Shall worms, inheritors of this excess,
Eat up thy charge? Is this thy body's end?
Then, soul, live thou upon thy servant's loss,
And let that pine to aggravate thy store;   10
Buy terms divine in selling hours of dross;
Within be fed, without be rich no more:
    So shalt thou feed on Death, that feeds on men,
    And Death once dead, there's no more dying then.

EDWIN MUIR   *The Horses*

Barely a twelvemonth after
The seven days war that put the world to sleep,

Late in the evening the strange horses came.
By then we had made our covenant with silence,
But in the first few days it was so still
We listened to our breathing and were afraid.
On the second day
The radios failed; we turned the knobs; no answer.
On the third day a warship passed us, heading north,
Dead bodies piled on the deck. On the sixth day   10
A plane plunged over us into the sea. Thereafter
Nothing. The radios dumb;
And still they stand in corners of our kitchens,
And stand, perhaps, turned on, in a million rooms
All over the world. But now if they should speak,
If on a sudden they should speak again,
If on the stroke of noon a voice should speak,
We would not listen, we would not let it bring
That old bad world that swallowed its children quick
At one great gulp. We would not have it again.   20
Sometimes we think of the nations lying asleep,
Curled blindly in impenetrable sorrow,
And then the thought confounds us with its strangeness.

The tractors lie about our fields; at evening
They look like dank sea-monsters couched and waiting.
We leave them where they are and let them rust:
"They'll moulder away and be like other loam."
We make our oxen drag our rusty ploughs,
Long laid aside. We have gone back
Far past our fathers' land.   30
                 And then, that evening
Late in the summer the strange horses came.
We heard a distant tapping on the road,
A deepening drumming; it stopped, went on again
And at the corner changed to hollow thunder.
We saw the heads
Like a wild wave charging and were afraid.
We had sold our horses in our fathers' time
To buy new tractors. Now they were strange to us
As fabulous steeds set on an ancient shield   40
Or illustrations in a book of knights.
We did not dare go near them. Yet they waited,
Stubborn and shy, as if they had been sent
By an old command to find our whereabouts
And that long-lost archaic companionship.

In the first moment we had never a thought
That they were creatures to be owned and used.
Among them were some half-a-dozen colts
Dropped in some wilderness of the broken world,
Yet new as if they had come from their own Eden.   50
Since then they have pulled our ploughs and borne our loads,
But that free servitude still can pierce our hearts.
Our life is changed; their coming our beginning.

GEOFFREY CHAUCER   *O yonge fresshe folkes*

(from *Troilus and Criseyde*, Book V)

O yonge fresshe folkes, he or she,
In whiche ay love up-groweth with your age,
Repeireth hom fro worldly vanité!
And of your herte up-casteth the visage
To th'ilke God that after his image
You made; and thinketh all n'is but a faire
This world, that passeth sone as floures faire!

And loveth Him, the whiche that right for love
Upon a cros, our soules for to beye,
First starf, and roos, and sit in hevene above;   10
For he n'il falsen no wight, dar I seye,
That wol his herte all hoolly on him leye!
And sin He best to love is, and most meke,
What nedeth feyned loves for to seke?

                    .   .   .   .

Thou oon, and two, and three, eterne onlive,
That regnest ay in three and two and oon,
Uncircumscript, and al mayst circumscrive,
Us from visible and invisible foon
Defende! And to thy mercy, everichoon,
So make us, Jesus, for thy mercy digne,   20
For love of mayde and moder thyn benigne!

Index of Authors, Titles, and First Lines

AUTHORS' names are in CAPITALS; titles of poems in *italics;* and first lines in Roman type. Poems analyzed, discussed, or commented on in the text are indicated by an asterisk (*). Where this critical material does not immediately precede or follow the poem its position is indicated by italicized page numbers. (See Index of Topics for further references to poets, passages, and poems in the expository text.)

Index of Topics